Forty-Seventh Star

12 SEPTEMBER 2012

To CHRIS —
    WITH BEST WISHES AND MAY
THIS BOOK FURTHER YOUR INTEREST
IN NEW MEXICO'S HISTORY.

        WARMEST REGARDS —

        David Holtby

New Mexico's Struggle for Statehood

Forty-Seventh Star

David V. Holtby

University of Oklahoma Press : Norman

Portions of chapter 5 and 9 were previously published in "Two Photographs and Their Stories of Statehood," *New Mexico Historical Review* 87, No. 1 (Winter 2012): 1–32. © 2012 by the University of New Mexico Board of Regents. All rights reserved. Reproduced by permission.

Title page illustration: Rose Cecil O'Neill, "The next candidate for statehood," *Puck,* 18 December 1901. Courtesy Library of Congress, Prints and Photographs Online, LC-DIG-ppmsca.

Library of Congress Cataloging-in-Publication Data

Holtby, David V., 1948–
Forty-seventh star : New Mexico's struggle for statehood / David V. Holtby.
   pages   cm
Includes bibliographical references and index.
ISBN 978-0-8061-4282-1 (hardcover : alk. paper)
1. New Mexico—Politics and government—1848–1950.
2. Statehood (American politics)—History—Case studies.
3. New Mexico—Race relations—History.
4. New Mexico—History—1848– I. Title.
F801.H67 2012
978.9'04—dc23

                    2012000251

The paper in this book meets the guidelines for permanence and durability of the Committee on Production Guidelines for Book Longevity of the Council on Library Resources, Inc. ∞

1 2 3 4 5 6 7 8 9 10

A recipient of

The Julian J. Rothbaum Prize

whose sponsor advocated
the highest standards of scholarship
in all disciplines

For two mentors

Joan Connelly Ullman,
Professor of Spanish History, University of Washington

Ferenc Morton Szasz,
Professor of American History, University of New Mexico

Contents

Illustrations

Figures

Map

Preface

I did not set out to write this book, which began as part of a longer account of a different subject. My change of direction parallels the trajectory of my career. Looking back on six years of graduate school and twenty-eight years in scholarly publishing, I can trace a route that brought me from a distant point, through many byways, to writing about New Mexico's path to statehood. The road taken after completing my dissertation made all the difference. My academic capstone—an award-winning study of the social origins of the Spanish Civil War between 1898 and 1936—led nowhere in a tight university teaching market. Fortunately, a background in Latin American history coupled with some editing assignments during four years in military intelligence opened a door in scholarly publishing.

I entered my editorial apprentice year in 1978–79 eager to learn a new career, but only much later did I understand I had also begun a long tutorial in the history of the West and Southwest. In hindsight I see a clear starting point for this book in my first editorial projects. My original tutors were authors of three of the initial six books I shepherded through the editorial process at the University of New Mexico Press: Marc Simmons, *People of the Sun: Some Out-of-Fashion Southwesterners*; Kenneth Balcomb, *A Boy's Albuquerque, 1898–1912*; and F. Chris Garcia, Paul Hain, and Harold Rhodes, *State and Local Government in New Mexico*. Each project introduced me to a perspective foundational for this study: from Marc Simmons's profiles, the bedrock provided by living aligned to long-standing traditions; from Balcomb's memoir, the changes in people's everyday lives during the dozen years prior to entering the Union; and from Garcia, Hain, and Rhodes's overview, the primacy of politics in understanding New Mexico.

Another mentor from those first years was Tony Hillerman, then a professor with whom I chatted occasionally as he passed my office in the Journalism Building. His third Joe Leaphorn mystery had just appeared when we met, and twenty-five years later, when I was about the age Tony had been in 1978, I drove to his house, delivered proofs of a foreword he had provided for one of the books I had edited, got his approval of some suggested revisions, and mentioned I would close the chapter on my publishing career in a year or so. I wanted to resume work as a historian. We had a long talk, and for a while thereafter I thought about his suggestion to investigate the political fallout from an unsolved murder outside Las Cruces in 1949. Tony had long been fascinated by the incident and included a summary of it in his 2001 memoir. But I never got interested in that project, and I dropped it when I learned another writer was on the same trail but far ahead of me. So I looked elsewhere in New Mexico's history for possible topics, ones documented in historical records. I quickly settled on a comparative account of government activities and people's expectations of its role in New Mexico between 1780 and 1940. Within that broad topic the statehood era held a special fascination.[1]

I wanted to unravel why it took New Mexico sixty-four years to gain entry to the Union. I began my research with a case study of delay—a fifteen-month fight over statehood in 1902–1903 capped by a three-month filibuster launched by Senator Albert J. Beveridge, an Indiana Republican and chair of the Senate Committee on Territories. But rather quickly I realized this incident obscured as much as it revealed. Soon I began developing two interconnected stories: one featured statehood's foes and the other examined the lesser-known activities of New Mexico's supporters. Statehood had many friends in the Congress, and they mustered a nearly unanimous House vote endorsing it in May 1902. This ground swell of support for New Mexico statehood is barely remembered today. What historians recall is how Senator Beveridge derailed the House's bill between June 1902 and March 1903, even though a majority of senators supported statehood, and national public opinion trended that way, too.[2]

Statehood's foes in the Congress were few but tenacious, and the *Atlanta Constitution*'s Washington correspondent, covering Beveridge's filibuster, explained their resistance to expanding the Union: "Nothing but the jealousy of the growing power of the west is responsible for the opposition to statehood in the United States Senate." After the Civil War the Republicans (the North) and the Democrats (the South) shifted their sectional strife to the West and vied for control as nine new states emerged between 1867 and 1896, which increased the number of U.S. Senators by 25 percent, from seventy-two to ninety. Statehood became entangled in Republican and Democratic politics, and both parties jostled for supremacy in New Mexico, Arizona, and Oklahoma by including statehood in their national party platforms in 1896 and 1900. But Republicans never reached a consensus on this plank, and intraparty fights between proponents and opponents fractured so-called debates over statehood for nearly fifteen years. In addition, the leading supporters of statehood included an array of New Mexico scoundrels. Their miscues, hoaxes, and frauds invariably surfaced at the most inopportune times, giving opponents ample evidence that the territory was unfit to enter the Union. This tug-of-war between foes and friends of statehood is my first theme. Every chapter traces how the push to add New Mexico's star to the flag oscillated with national political events, intraparty rivalries, and unsavory revelations in the Territory between 1894 and 1912.[3]

My second theme emerged from a question Tony and I speculated about in our meeting in 2004. How had a group of citizens impaneled as a grand jury in the 1949 murder we were discussing enlarged their powers, revolted against corruption, and called elected officials to account? Their bold action intrigued me and led to a question I wanted to examine. Where had the resolve to expand their sovereignty originated? The term *popular sovereignty* is usually defined as political power held by ordinary citizens who believe that government is of, for, and by the people. But it is actually far broader. Like the proverbial iceberg, what lies beneath is most important, particularly when the people exercise a greater measure of control than do those in positions of authority. The statehood era served as the seedbed for the grand jury's assertiveness at midcentury.[4]

Instances of popular sovereignty recur throughout this book, and a trace of it is even in the title. It was the spirit of "We the People" in the U.S. Constitution—the cornerstone of popular sovereignty—that inspired New Mexicans to sew or pin a new star on the U.S. flag two years before statehood, as soon as President William Howard Taft signed the Enabling Act authorizing the writing of a state constitution on 20 June 1910. They did so again on two other key dates—21 August 1911 (constitution fully accepted) and 6 January 1912 (statehood).[5]

To uncover people's ideas and attitudes, I researched two basic aspects of statehood. First I traced it as a political goal. What did the majority population in the territory, the native-born Nuevomexicanos, think of becoming full-fledged citizens of the United States? Then I tracked statehood as social and economic transformation. How did those residing in the territory react to statehood being contingent upon adding more people and more irrigated land? In time I merged these two themes into one issue: How did Euro-Americans, Nuevomexicanos, American Indians, African Americans, and Asians fare under territorial government? In answering this third question I set about uncovering long-forgotten stories of people striving to improve their lives. I found that most did so by bending before the winds of change.

Euro-Americans often affronted the dignity of peoples who had been in New Mexico for as few as several decades—Asians—to as many as several thousand years—the Ancestral Puebloan peoples and their successors the Pueblo Indians. However long they had been in the Territory, though, the non-Euro-Americans understood the difference between persisting and enduring. The distinction may seem slight to us, but in their lives it was fundamental. Persisting is empowering, while to endure merely means to last. What persists is a continuous legacy carried across time in culture and community and imprinted in people's minds, hearts, and souls in generation after generation. It is also present in relationships among peoples and with the land and water that sustains them, nowhere more than in the communal irrigation practices, or acequia culture, of many Nuevomexicano villages and in the rhythms of daily life among American Indians. Cultural persistence enabled Nuevomexicanos and American Indians to outlast those seeking to control them. Though conquered, these people relied on a strength centered in their traditions, habits, beliefs, and values. They used statehood to perpetuate what they most valued. Such continuity amid change is my third recurring theme.[6]

This book's nine chapters cluster into three subsets. In the first three chapters I describe the forces arrayed for and against statehood between the 1890s and 1907—and Nuevomexicano reactions to the setbacks. Chapter 1 is on Territorial Delegate Thomas B. Catron's political and judicial reverses during his one term (1895–97) and the separate campaign for statehood launched by his archenemy Governor Miguel A. Otero in 1901. Senator Albert J. Beveridge takes center stage in chapter 2, particularly his infamous November 1902 "investigation" in the Territory, his three-month filibuster to block a vote on statehood, and Nuevomexicano reactions to these developments. Chapter 3 looks at President Theodore Roosevelt to sort out the origins of his vacillating support for statehood during his first term (1901–1905). The next three chapters shift attention from Washington, D.C., to New Mexico. Chapter 4 is on political developments in the Territory that adversely impacted prospects for attaining statehood between 1903 and 1907. The discussions in chapters 5 and 6 center on how Nuevomexicanos and then American Indians, African Americans, and Asians in the Territory parried political and legal threats to their cultures and communities in the run-up to statehood. Two of the final three chapters put in relief maneuvering to become a state between 1907 and 1912, and the final chapter considers what statehood wrought. Discussed in chapter 7 are scandals in New Mexico that fueled new opposition to entering the Union from 1907 to 1909. Covered in chapter 8 are the decisive steps taken by President William Howard Taft to secure statehood, especially his political deals cut in 1910, and how New Mexicans prepared themselves to enter the Union in 1910 and 1911. The concluding chapter begins with a brief examination of two photographs taken at the White House on Saturday, 6 January 1912 to mark New Mexico's achievement of statehood and then expands the focus to consider what statehood changed, what remained the same, and the legacy we inherited.

The historian's duties are threefold: to write a coherent narrative; to advance understanding through interpretations; and to offer assessments. Overall my narrative approach is inductive—I focus on selected people or events and then build out from these to reach generalizations. In doing so I hope to engage readers and give them a reason to keep turning the pages. I also seek to hold readers' interest by offering interpretations based on the perspectives of all peoples present in New Mexico. As a result, this book is the first to fully incorporate Spanish-language sources on the statehood era, voices that have long needed to be heard. Finally, I hope my assessments and conclusions offer insights and spark discussions. I realize others can consider the same evidence and come to different points of view. History is always about the meaning we give it, which is why each generation interrogates the past anew.

December 2011

Acknowledgments

It is appropriate that the book's narrative is co-anchored in Washington, D.C., and New Mexico, because its first supporters were there, too. This volume grew out of a project suggested to me in the Capitol Hill office of David Pike, and across town Kristie Miller and her husband, T. L., offered encouragement and research tips over dinners. A few blocks from the Library of Congress Chuck McCutcheon and Liisa Ecola were congenial hosts for our own "Washington Week in Review" as we considered politics, publishing, and Polish recipes. Dr. Tobías Durán, director of the Center for Regional Studies at the University of New Mexico, immediately endorsed my interest and provided invaluable assistance throughout the twists and turns of completing and publishing my manuscript. Marina Cadena, unit administrator, likewise has been most supportive.

My archival research has been made possible by grants from the Center for Regional Studies, the Scholars Program of the New Mexico Office of the State Historian, the Guadalupe Institute, and the Ruth McCormick Tankersley Charitable Trust. At UNM, Dean Martha Bedard and her management team at the University Libraries have deftly maintained and extended research capabilities amid shrinking budgets. My work in Zimmerman Library was greatly assisted by Michael Kelly, Director, and staff of the Center for Southwest Research and by staff of the Interlibrary Loan office. Elsewhere in New Mexico I was ably assisted by staff at the Rio Grande Historical Collections at New Mexico State University in Las Cruces; and in Santa Fe at the New Mexico State Library, the State Records Center and Archives, and the Fray Angélico Chávez History Library. At national repositories I received assistance from capable staff at the following sites: the Library of Congress's Manuscript Reading Room, the Main Reading Room, the Microform Reading Room, and the Law Library; the National Archives and Records Administration in Washington, D.C., or NARA I. Particularly helpful on various occasions were staff at the Center for Legislative Archives located at NARA I and most especially Rodney A. Ross; the National Archives and Records Administration in College Park, Maryland, or NARA II; and the regional National Archives and Records Administration in Denver, Colorado, particularly Eric Bittner and David Miller. Research privileges were graciously extended by Wallace F. Dailey to use the Theodore Roosevelt Collection held in Widener Library at Harvard University.

My publishing career allowed me to work on more than seven hundred books, and many of their authors offered what amounted to tutorials in American, western, and New Mexico history and culture. While they are too numerous to mention individually, to these writers I owe much more than can be repaid with a hearty *¡mil gracias!* Not even the endnotes give full credit since a number of my author/mentors wrote about Latin American history, and among these none was more influential than Professor Lyman L. Johnson at the Charlotte campus of the University of North Carolina in modeling broad thinking and clear writing.

I had the honor to serve on two dissertation committees in the early 1990s, and both candidates revised and published their studies and became widely respected scholars. Nearly twenty years later they served as tough-minded guides in my foray into New Mexico history—Professor Durwood Ball of the University of New Mexico and Professor Jon Hunner at New Mexico State University. Each helped me enormously. Also consistently providing expertise and friendship were Dr. Calvin Roberts, Dr. Marc Simmons, Dr. Robert R. White, and emeritus professors Richard Etulain (UNM), Ray Sadler and Charles Harris (NMSU), and Howard R. Lamar (Yale University). During four fiscal years three different graduate students provided outstanding part-time research support: Natalie Heberling, Dr. Kari Schleher, and Brianna Stein. Each is a "digital native" who shielded this "digital alien" from electronic meltdowns.

Over its final eighteen months, this manuscript became an uninvited guest cordially welcomed in extended visits with Ron and Debbie Atkinson, John and Annette Schumacher, John and Margaret Discepolo, Bill Simpson and Nancy Augustus, and my mother-in-law, Jeannette Roberge, who was fascinated by the frequency of New Hampshire's appearances in my study.

It has been a special pleasure to work with former publishing peers at the University of Oklahoma Press, and especially a longtime friend Charles Rankin, the editor in chief. Beth Hadas, who hired me in 1978, again proved invaluable as the freelance copy editor. Applying her extraordinary talents on my behalf made all the difference. The professionalism of the staff at the University of Oklahoma Press—and in particular the work of the managing editor, Steven Baker, and the production manager, Emmy Ezzell—ensured good author relations.

My years in New Mexico have been immeasurably enriched by my wife, Jeanne, and our daughter, Michelle. Their unflinching support and love has been my anchor, and they are first among equals in my acknowledgments and gratitude. Tigger, too, left his paw prints in this manuscript—as he did with Michelle's two books. On evening walks, while Tigger closely inspected objects of interest, I rehearsed and mentally revised the opening paragraphs of each chapter.

I dedicate this book to two professors who deeply influenced my career and life. Professor Joan Connelly Ullman directed my senior-year seminars, which amounted to a boot camp in primary research and historical writing, and remains a dear friend. I enrolled in one of Professor Ferenc Morton Szasz's first graduate-level courses in 1969. I later published three of his books. He became an incomparable friend and consummate editor, offering critiques of early drafts prior to his death in June 2010.

Forty-Seventh Star

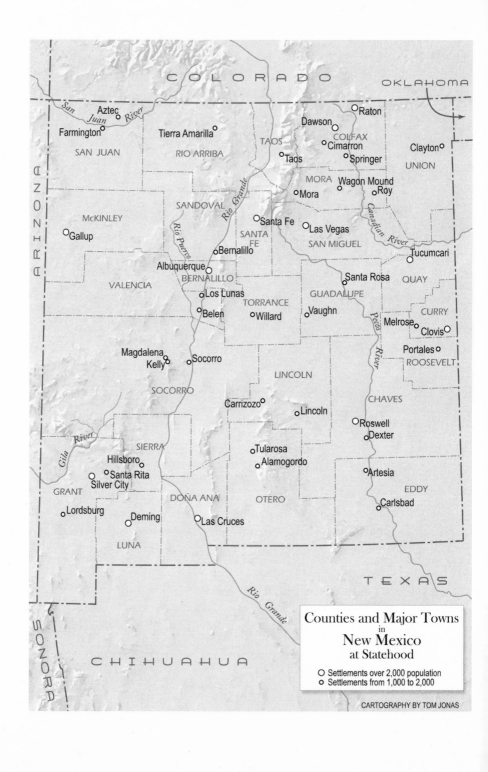

COLORADO

OKLAHOMA

ARIZONA

San Juan River

Aztec
Farmington

SAN JUAN

Tierra Amarilla

RIO ARRIBA

TAOS

Taos

Dawson

COLFAX
Cimarron

Springer

Raton

Clayton

UNION

Rio Grande

MORA   Wagon Mound

Mora   Roy

Canadian River

McKINLEY

Gallup

SANDOVAL

Rio Puerco

Santa Fe

SANTA
FE

Bernalillo

Las Vegas

SAN MIGUEL

Tucumcari

Albuquerque

BERNALILLO

Los Lunas

VALENCIA

Belen   Willard

TORRANCE

Santa Rosa

GUADALUPE

Vaughn

Pecos River

QUAY

CURRY

Melrose

Clovis

Magdalena

Kelly   Socorro

SOCORRO

Carrizozo

LINCOLN

Lincoln

CHAVES

Portales

ROOSEVELT

Roswell

Dexter

Gila River

SIERRA

Hillsboro

Santa Rita

Silver City

GRANT

Lordsburg

Deming

DOÑA ANA

Las Cruces

LUNA

Tularosa

Alamogordo

OTERO

Artesia

EDDY

Carlsbad

Rio Grande

TEXAS

SONORA

CHIHUAHUA

Counties and Major Towns
in
New Mexico
at Statehood

O Settlements over 2,000 population
o Settlements from 1,000 to 2,000

CARTOGRAPHY BY TOM JONAS

INTRODUCTION

"The Miracle-Breeding Imagination"

My goal in this book is to situate New Mexico's struggle to enter the
Union within the broad political, economic, and social currents
shaping the United States between 1848 and 1912. To understand the inter-
section of national events with statehood for New Mexico, it is useful to
refer to the work of two distinguished historians—James MacGregor Burns
and Elliott West. "The workshop of democracy" is how Burns described the
six decades preceding 1912, during which, in Walt Whitman's phrase, "not
merely a nation but a teeming Nation of nations" pulled itself together to
build an American state. One special project in that "workshop" was craft-
ing the Territory of New Mexico to fit into the American Republic. That
undertaking began with what West identified as the "Greater Reconstruc-
tion" of America between 1846 and 1877, an effort to consolidate the nation
in the wake of three quick expansions between 1845 and 1848 and the Civil
War.[1]

West reminds us that the admission of Texas as a state (1845), the acquisition of the Pacific Northwest from Great Britain (1846), and the addition
of 525,000 square miles in the American Southwest at the end of the Mexican War (1846–48) added more land than any of the nation's earlier expansions, including the Louisiana Purchase. Fundamental political questions
arose immediately after ratification of the Treaty of Guadalupe Hidalgo
in February 1848, enmeshing New Mexico in national conflict. Two long-
standing competing views on forced labor collided: Southern states insisted
on slavery in the new lands, but their northern opponents sought to block
spread of the "peculiar institution." New Mexico rejected slavery when its
legislature petitioned the Congress for statehood in 1848 and 1850, and

3

the rejection cost key support among southern states. The Compromise of 1850, struck to avert civil war over the unchecked flow of slavery into lands taken from Mexico, allowed California to bypass territorial status and immediately become a state barring slavery, while another provision established New Mexico and Utah as territories and empowered their citizens to decide whether to permit slavery. While the Compromise of 1850 temporarily averted secession by the South, it also fractured a nation divided by the issue of slavery well before the Civil War erupted in April 1861. In January and February of that fateful year, New Mexico figured in one last bid to keep the Republic together when members of Congress and president-elect Abraham Lincoln discussed allowing New Mexico to enter as a slave state to appease the South. But by the time Lincoln took his oath of office in March 1861, secession had moved too quickly for any further consideration of this proposal.[2]

"Expansion was double trouble," West reminds us. It not only pitted North against South, it also raised the specter of more non-Anglo-Americans becoming citizens. This prospect alarmed Senator Daniel Webster of Massachusetts, one of the most strident and influential foes of the war, the treaty, and adding new lands and people. In March 1848 he leveled charges against New Mexico that besmirched its reputation for more than sixty years. Webster condemned as a threat to the Republic the prospect of Nuevomexicanos exercising popular sovereignty. He asked, "Have they any notion of popular government? Not the slightest. . . . It is farcical to talk of such people making a constitution for themselves." He continued his attack by lodging in the public's mind mischaracterizations of the land and its people that foes of statehood employed for six decades. "Forty-nine fiftieths, at least, of the whole of New Mexico are a barren waste," he claimed, and labeled it "secluded, isolated, a place by itself" where "there would not be two hundred families of persons who would emigrate from the United States to New Mexico, for agricultural purposes, in fifty years." Webster went on to quote from an English writer who had recently spent a few months in New Mexico: "[Nuevomexicanos] are as deficient in energy of character and physical courage as they are in all the moral and intellectual qualities. In their social state but one degree removed from the veriest savages."[3]

Not until early March 1875 did momentum crest for allowing New Mexico (and Colorado) to become states. After two years' work, with the bill approved by the Senate, the delegates from these two territories—Stephen B. Elkins and Jerome B. Chaffee—awaited final concurrence by the House. Chaffee secured Colorado's statehood by a margin of six votes, while Elkins lost it for New Mexico by five votes. The difference in outcomes stemmed from an indiscretion by Elkins a few days before the vote. Just as a Michigan Republican wrapped up a blistering attack on southerners that rekindled hatreds from the Civil War, Elkins rushed to be among the first to congratulate him, causing influential southern Democrats once again to withdraw their support.[4]

Ten years of quiescence followed until interest in statehood resurfaced in the administrations of Democratic president Grover Cleveland (1885–89; 1893–97) and Republican president Benjamin Harrison (1889–1893). Harrison approved six new western states in the nine months between 2 November 1889 and 10 July 1890; Cleveland brought in Utah in January 1896. This spurt of support represented a new phase of sectional rivalries, with Democrats hopeful but Republicans wary. Between 1885 and 1895 a Democrat represented New Mexico as delegate in the Congress, and in the early 1890s farming and mining interests in the Territory briefly supported a third political party, the Populists, whose platform attacked Republican policies. In the 1896 elections New Mexicans briefly returned to the Democratic fold in their election of a delegate to the Congress. But this flirtation by the West—and the Territory—with Democrats in the 1890s was very costly. It led key Republicans to fear a shift in power, which they fought by obstructing statehood for nearly a decade.[5]

As America moved out of the horse-and-buggy era and into one where automobiles were common and even airplanes had been seen in New Mexico by 1912, Burns's notion of a "workshop of democracy" is a reminder that America in the early twentieth century remained very much a work in progress. Political cohesion had nominally been reestablished within a dozen years of the end of the Civil War, but just below the surface three fundamental rifts remained. Issues from the Republic's early years continued to be contested, and one was the tension between the states and the federal government, giving rise to two competing political formulae—states' rights versus federalism, or a strong central government. Each view had an articulate proponent among the nation's founders: Thomas Jefferson advocated states' rights and Alexander Hamilton pushed federalism. The Civil War ended slavery and put to rest a mainstay of the states' rights position, but its advocates had other cherished beliefs. Essentially they wanted government to provide them capital and land but otherwise to leave the states alone. This attitude resonated profoundly in New Mexico, but it collided head-on with federalism after 1901. President Theodore Roosevelt expanded the U.S. government's power in the Territory by adding to national forests millions of acres formerly designated as communal holdings within land grants. For their part, territorial officials ran afoul of Washington by asserting their autonomy and selling public lands they believed they controlled, and their land policies, shaped in part by their belief in states' rights, impeded entry into the Union.

A second basic division also involved the nation's political culture. In the Territory, as elsewhere across America, a tiny minority of powerful people manipulated government for their own ends throughout most of the final third of the nineteenth century. Infamously corrupt in New Mexico was the Santa Fe Ring, known for its acquisitiveness and greed, especially in taking over land grants. In reaction, a push for clean government gradually emerged in the 1880s and came to full fruition in the movement known as progressivism when Theodore Roosevelt entered the White House in 1901. Present to some extent in New Mexico, beginning with the governorship of Miguel A. Otero (1897–1906), it encountered pitched opposition and many self-inflicted setbacks, all of which protracted New Mexico's bid to become a state.

The third undertow was economic. Crosscurrents from three types of capitalism pulled at the nation in the late nineteenth century—mercantile capitalism, finance capitalism, and corporate capitalism, or government-subsidized private ventures. All three forms existed in New Mexico, but they were directed to different purposes. Mercantile capitalism had as its chief goal incorporation of the Nuevomexicanos into a cash economy and its associated consumerism. But finance and corporate capitalism often merged in New Mexico to become developmental capitalism directed toward large-scale projects—from railroad construction to irrigation and land reclamation. These enterprises used private and public investment, and the government became a willing partner because it controlled substantial amounts of capital and, more important, land—hundreds of thousands of square miles of public domain in the West.[6]

Beginning in the 1890s, a loose alliance of local business associations and small-scale entrepreneurs in the Territory coalesced around the common goal of promoting statehood by fostering economic growth, or developmental modernization, through that era's tried-and-true investments: railroads, irrigation, land, mining, and lumbering. The greatest of these were railroads, which first carried passengers into the Territory on 13 February 1879; within five years 1,255 miles of rail crisscrossed New Mexico. Its transformative, modernizing power was summarized in 1912: "The advent of the railroads in New Mexico was the beginning of the era of permanent prosperity for the people of the territory." Speaking of the "wonderful rapidity" with which railroads spread throughout the Territory, the writer found nothing "more marvelous than the astonishing awakening of the people to the fact that at last New Mexico was really in touch with the enlightened progress and modern methods of the people of the eastern states." Attaining habits comparable to those of easterners mattered a great deal to the Congress, and in a debate over Americanization in 1884 a congressman complained about people who "do not know to purchase any of the luxuries which tend to elevate and enlighten people." In New Mexico mercantile capitalism offered a solution through the creation of citizen-consumers, while developmental capitalism sought major economic and societal change.[7]

In the final decades of the quest for statehood, concerted efforts were made to show how Nuevomexicanos were an "elevate[d] and enlightened people." Modernity became a holy grail. The *Chicago Tribune* in mid-January 1894 lauded Territorial Delegate and native son Antonio Joseph for his success in business and politics and discussed other Nuevomexicanos in complimentary terms. Consider the profile of thirty-one-year-old "Don Felix Martinez of Las Vegas, a notable example of a patriotic Spanish-American citizen. . . . He is the editor of the *Voz del Pueblo* (Voice of the People), the most influential Spanish journal in New Mexico." In his interview Martínez said: "All our people are now anxious for Statehood. They know it means the influx of capital and Americans. This is what we want, for it will give more employment, business, and money to our people, who really want to progress."[8]

Three years later, in the spring of 1897, an editorial in the Albuquerque weekly *El Nuevo Mundo* (The New World) echoed the same desire for progress, but it also pointed to the considerable obstacles Nuevomexicanos faced: "But what has been the result of New Mexico's modernization? Unfortunately for our race it has brought no improvement. The railroads killed the traffic of our freight hauling; our agricultural products cannot compete with those that come in from Colorado and California; and our only resource today, our wool, cannot stay ahead of the competition of imports from Australia and Argentina." Modernization was proceeding unevenly. "The wonders of [Benjamin] Franklin, [Nicola] Tesla and [Thomas] Edison are today familiar to all who live in the major cities of New Mexico," but electricity did not benefit the majority of Nuevomexicanos. The newspaper feared that modernity would bypass those who did not adapt to the changing times: "Like the Indians of old who once held this land, the descendants of today's neomexicanos will also have to emigrate to another place." But *El Nuevo Mundo* offered Nuevomexicanos a remedy to overcome obstacles to progress—the newly created public school system. In placing their faith in education, they followed their contemporaries in the African American community in the South, such as George Washington Carver of Tuskegee Institute in Alabama, and advocated vocational and agricultural training in the expectation "that one day we can praise some of the measures that truly give Nuevomexicanos illustrious groups of artisans and practical experts, for only in this way is there salvation for our race, which now grows weaker day by day." Other voices in the Nuevomexicano community matter-of-factly prescribed a cultural transition deemed essential: "People who do not know how to speak English will not have much of a chance to be successful in their business life. The sooner our children learn English the better prepared they will be to win the battle and be successful in life."[9]

Success's siren song had long charmed the Territory. Early in his career Mark Twain had seen how a financial scheme in New Mexico affected someone: "The happy light in his eye, the abiding hope in his heart, the persuasive tongue, the miracle-breeding imagination . . . and before I could turn around he was polishing up his Aladdin's lamp and flashing the secret riches of the world before me." The man Twain referred to was a cousin on his mother's side, who described for him a "'small venture' he had begun in New Mexico 'only a little thing—a mere trifle.'" Half an hour later the "little thing" had grown into a grand venture, likely land speculation, worth "a couple of millions . . . possibly three, but not more, I think." Twain's relative became the model for Colonel Beriah Sellers in *The Gilded Age: A Tale of Today*, published in 1873. The novel's title is now used to describe the final third of the nineteenth century: the glittering veneer of money-making schemes hiding baseness. As if to underscore the shimmering mirage of the times, the book appeared at the start of a five-year economic depression. In situating his financial illusion in the Territory, Twain's relative typified the era's impulse to see New Mexico as ripe for the picking. Grandiose schemes by Euro-Americans abounded to build railroads, open mines, and bring water to parched land—projects promoted as essential to attracting immigrants. A few Nuevomexicanos, too, hoped to grab the Aladdin's lamp of riches, but most simply tried to touch it.[10]

A scholar writing in 1939 noted, "Throughout our history there have been Eastern leaders who opposed the growing influence of the West. . . . Fears that new states would add to the power of section or [a political] party have led forces in control of Congress to postpone the admission of many a territory." He continued his explanation: "There is nothing exceptionable [*sic*] about New Mexico having to struggle for statehood, except that her fight was the longest of any and probably the most dramatic." The length and drama arose largely from what Elliott West has called "the full racial crisis triggered by expansion." Specifically, a fundamental contradiction haunted political leaders and ordinary people alike for decades. America "had justified conquest by calling western natives [Mexicans and American Indians] cultural simpletons, political knuckle walkers[,] and violent drifters. . . . How then would they ever fit in once the West was made truly a part of the Republic?" By 1894 Euro-American elites in New Mexico, led by Thomas B. Catron, had settled on their answer: eventual numerical supremacy and exercise of *patrón*-like control over voting by Nuevomexicanos.[11]

Amid political, economic, and social turbulence, it is not surprising that New Mexico did not secure statehood on the merits of its case. Instead President William Howard Taft forged a compromise that used statehood as a bargaining chip to pass a railroad regulation bill. Indeed, on paper the case for becoming a state was not compelling, but Taft set aside evidence of the Territory's flaws, most notably its ingrained political corruption. He acted out of principled self-interest to forge a coalition of Democrats and Republicans to bring New Mexico into union with the American Republic. His exercise of presidential power made it the forty-seventh state.

This book has been labor of love. I have strived to make it "a personal encounter with the past," as Tony Hillerman said of Marc Simmons's *People of the Sun*, one "that evokes affection for our land and its people." May its readers take the occasion of the Centennial of Statehood to explore New

Mexico's past and reflect on statehood as a continuing legacy. The key questions of a hundred years ago persist in the twenty-first century—in issues of water and land, the role of government and its financing, problems of corruption, violence, and illegal immigration, and in challenges of balancing economic development with social and environmental justice.[12]

CHAPTER ONE

"Only a Licensed and Paid Beggar"

Thomas B. Catron had it all figured out. As New Mexico's delegate to Congress, he intended to put statehood back on track in mid-December 1896 by revising several parts of a bill rejected the previous summer. He told a confidant: "I had ascertained it from consultation with many of the Republicans that I would ask to amend the bill." Catron's optimism erased the indignity of two major setbacks suffered over the previous six months: in June, Congress had refused to act on his bill admitting New Mexico to the Union; in November, he had lost his reelection bid. But as December approached, he believed things were once again going his way. He expected all would soon turn out well for him and the Territory. Catron was as wily as he was portly, and his scheme comprised equal parts deceit and hubris. By the time he explained his plan to his New Mexican confidant, the other members of the House Committee on Territories had already refused to reconsider his revised bill. They also rejected his pleas for the committee to meet weekly on the matter. Instead they began a holiday recess and, upon returning in January, never took up his proposal in the remaining weeks of the Fifty-Fourth Congress. These reversals did not dent the self-assurance of a survivor and successful schemer.[1]

All his life Catron had been determined and forceful. At age twenty he joined the eight-thousand-member Missouri State Guard, quickly became a lieutenant, and served in the Confederate cause from June 1861 until May 1865. For more than half the war he fought under General Sterling Price, who after the Mexican War served briefly as military governor of New Mexico. Catron saw action in more than twenty battles, survived Vicksburg, but was captured and then freed in a prisoner exchange late in the summer of

1863. He returned to fight with artillery units and endured repeated defeats in engagements in Georgia, Tennessee, Louisiana, Alabama, and Mississippi. Just one in ten men from the Missouri State Guard survived the Civil War, Catron among them, and within a year he left Missouri for New Mexico. The "rigorous crucible of war" had a decisive impact on Catron and left him "never one to back away from a contest of wills or a marshaling of power to gain an objective."[2]

Over the next thirty years Catron's combativeness and ruthlessness became the brick and mortar with which he built his empire and his legal career. By the time he served as territorial delegate he had acquired several million acres in New Mexico and amassed an equal amount spread over five states, the Arizona Territory, and Mexico, making him "the largest individual landholder in the history of the United States." Catron allied himself with people similarly motivated to use law and politics to advance their ambition and self-interest, and he became a leading figure in the resulting enterprise—the infamous Santa Fe Ring, which operated across party lines and attracted men of cunning and greed. This "brilliant combination of able men . . . regarded land as their first medium of currency," and in the twenty years from 1866 to 1886 they acquired Spanish and Mexican land grants, manipulating territorial officials, the courts, and the Nuevomexicano owners of the lands in order either to purchase these lands or take them in lieu of payment for legal services. Catron owned or had an interest in at least thirty-four land grants and represented clients in sixty-three land-grant cases in New Mexico as well as several other suits in Arizona and Colorado. When extension of the railroad throughout New Mexico in the early 1880s changed the Territory's economy, and ranching expanded and mining boomed, the Santa Fe Ring soon dominated each of these areas, too. But few in the Ring acquired as much property as Catron. By the mid-1890s he had held interests in or owned outright at least fifteen mines and four large ranches.[3]

Beginning in the mid-1880s, though, a backlash developed nationally as well as in New Mexico against fraud and public corruption. Reform efforts emerged following the election of Democratic President Grover Cleveland, who appointed Edmund G. Ross as the Territory's governor. Ross immediately moved against the unchecked influence of the Santa Fe Ring by enlisting the U.S. attorney for New Mexico and the surveyor general in prosecuting land fraud. In challenging the legality of the ring's landholdings he sought to undermine its economic power. Ross's activities followed the lead of federal officials in the Department of the Interior who brought a reforming zeal to the General Land Office for much of the 1880s. But in New Mexico, these efforts yielded no convictions, although the pen of Surveyor General George W. Julian proved a potent weapon. His articles published locally and nationally drew much attention to land grant issues and supported calls for reform that eventually prompted the Congress to create the Court of Private Land Claims.[4]

In northern New Mexico, corruption rather than justice had often prevailed in land transactions, which led to hostility and resistance among Nuevomexicanos in San Miguel County, an area especially roiled over land-grant issues. For several years, beginning in the late 1880s, their discontent fueled direct action when a group of vigilantes in and around Las Vegas known as Las Gorras Blancas (the White Caps) began making night-riding raids to cut fences put up on the common lands within the Las Vegas Grant. But soon their attacks expanded to include torching stacks of railroad ties, threatening violence against any locals who collaborated with land-grabbers, and actually attacking some people and property at nearby ranches. This restiveness alarmed the Ring, whose members concluded that the territorial form of government had outlived its usefulness. After four years of chafing under a governor it did not control and seeing social and political tensions rise, the ring welcomed the return of a Republican president, Benjamin Harrison, and the prospect of tamping down seething resentments. The members of the ring decided "they wanted to make sure that never again could a hostile administration disturb the internal affairs of New Mexico. . . . To achieve this end they began a movement for statehood in the winter of 1888–89." Catron and the Santa Fe Ring sought statehood to protect their self-interest, perpetuate their money-making schemes, and reduce popular discontent.[5]

As head of the Territory's Republican Party, Catron led this statehood movement throughout the 1890s, motivated in large part by the expectation that it would produce a financial windfall. As he explained in an address delivered while a delegate, "In all the states when admitted into the Union property has had an extraordinary increase in value, so that in none has the same less than doubled in value in the first eighteen months and in many it has increased tenfold." In private correspondence Catron calculated the trade off between politics and profits from statehood, telling a close associate in

October 1894, "If I could get New Mexico as a State, be it Democratic or Republican, my property will be doubled in value. . . . I would gladly let the Democrats take and keep the State, if I can double the value of my property." Catron was willing to accept statehood at any political cost to solve his financial problems—ones that plagued him from the early 1880s until he died in 1921. His biographer succinctly stated Catron's financial predicament from 1890 onward: "he was harassed almost unbearably by financial problems that hit him from all quarters." In the early 1900s, for example, he was paying interest of more than sixty thousand dollars a year on outstanding loans totaling more than a million dollars. He was always overextended, a cash-strapped land baron dodging two pressing obligations: property taxes and loan repayments. He endlessly challenged tax assessments on both his vast land empire and even his personal property in Santa Fe. He also routinely refinanced loans with ever more complicated deals involving infusion of modest amounts of much-needed capital in exchange for shares in one of his extensive enterprises. Catron's indebtedness yoked him to statehood in the expectation that land prices would escalate. But he pursued an illusion. Statehood brought neither increased value nor eager buyers.[6]

Catron's precarious finances have long been overshadowed by his notoriously bad behavior. Allegations linger that he sanctioned strong-arm tactics and was even complicit in murder. Such charges dogged him because he stood at the center of two incidents of political violence in 1892. On 8 February Catron survived an attempted assassination, and on the night of 29 May gunmen killed Francisco Chávez, the most powerful Democrat in the Territory and former Santa Fe sheriff. It long has been alleged that Catron ordered Chávez shot in retaliation for the attempt on his life. The main evidence offered was Catron's vigorous defense of the four Nuevomexicanos accused of the murder. Court proceedings began in January 1894, but legal maneuverings delayed the trial until April 1895. Catron waged his 1894 political campaign under the shadow of Chávez's assassination.

Insinuations of Catron's complicity appeared in Democratic-leaning newspapers in the Territory, especially in Santa Fe and Albuquerque. A series of public accusations heaped calumny on him, but not even vigorous mudslinging in the weeks prior to the November election prevented him from being elected territorial delegate. His tenacity may even have aided him. His well-known capacity for getting things done appealed to many voters dissatisfied with Democratic incumbent Antonio Joseph's indecisiveness on the question of statehood during his ten years in the Congress. Catron also carefully attended to the details of precinct politics and continued his long-standing practice of paying the required poll tax in predominantly Nuevomexicano counties. When his archenemy the *Santa Fe New Mexican* sensed Catron's imminent victory, it consoled readers with this damning praise: "Why elect him to Congress? Because he can do less harm in Congress than he can do in New Mexico."[7]

After enduring blistering attacks in the campaign, Catron came under another cloud of suspicion before departing for Washington in late November 1895. His four clients' trial in April and May resulted in their convictions and death sentences. But Catron's legal tactics on their behalf led the district attorney for Santa Fe to initiate disbarment proceedings against him and his law partner, Charles A. Spiess, in August. Over the next two months the Territorial Supreme Court investigated charges of witness tampering and related improprieties before dismissing the complaint on 25 October. Three days later the Territory's bar association overwhelmingly elected Catron its president, further vindicating him.[8]

"A Cheap Political Game"

Catron no doubt welcomed the train ride east to take up his duties as a delegate in the Fifty-Fourth Congress. At the beginning of December, thirteen months after being elected and nine months following adjournment of the Fifty-Third Congress on 3 March 1895, Catron, his wife, and four sons arrived in D.C. and settled into a residential hotel, the Fredonia. This choice proved a harbinger of the first-term delegate's diminished status in Washington's hierarchy. The major political figures resided at either the Willard or the Shoreham. Catron had law-making experience from serving in several two-year sessions of the lower house of the Territory's legislature, but the Fifty-Fourth Congress was more than ten times that body's size. He was sworn in along with several other territorial delegates, 356 representatives and 88 senators (which grew to 357 and 90, respectively, when Utah became a state in early January). In that era the Congress convened for two extended periods divided by long recesses. Its first session ran from December to June, followed by a recess for the fall election, and then it reconvened between December and early March 1897 before adjourning, to be succeeded by the Fifty-Fifth Congress. Catron's brief tenure as the Territory's delegate to the House of Representatives required his presence for just ten months over two years, or barely two-fifths of that time. But he did other work in D.C., including serving the Republican National Committee and arguing several land-grant cases before the U.S. Supreme Court. In none of these roles—delegate, party leader, and lawyer—did he successfully advance the cause of statehood.

In 1896, at fifty-five years of age and after thirty years of expanding his power and imposing his will on New Mexico's political, legal, and economic landscape, Catron faced an unusual situation when he strode into the capitol. He was little heeded and not yielded to in pressing New Mexico's—or his—desire for statehood. In the Congress territorial delegates were second-class citizens, widely regarded as special pleaders for their single cause of statehood. Catron did not see himself as an ordinary delegate and refused to accept that he had limited personal or political clout. Despite Catron's self-confidence, his statehood bill went nowhere in the Congress. He fared no better within the Republican Party. He proved politically tone-deaf as a member of the Republican Party's Central Committee, and he found himself on the losing side in two key national issues. First, the Territory went Democratic in the 1896 presidential election, as national Republican leaders had predicted. The Territory's defection confirmed party leaders' hostility toward statehood. Second, Catron did not back candidate William McKinley in the Republican Party's convention. When McKinley won, Catron was unable to exert influence over presidential appointments or urge his support for statehood.[9]

But some among Catron's Nuevomexicano constituents, most notably Republican-leaning newspapers, did their best to steer him toward a constructive path. In mid-December 1895 the Las Vegas newspaper *El Independiente* offered sage advice in a thousand-word article discussing "the things most urgently sought by Delegate Thomas B. Catron's constituents." Speaking on behalf of the people, they put statehood at the top of the list. *El Independiente* hoped Catron's "characteristic energy and persistence" would deliver this goal. Twelve other expectations were set forth as well. They beseeched him "not to be asleep" when appropriations were made "for public works and other funds necessary for the government and to take care that New Mexico secures its fair share and, if possible, to double the current allocation." They also wanted "incompetent and tyrannical officials" removed, pensions secured for more of the Territory's sixty-two hundred Civil War veterans or their widows, and his vigilance to ensure the statehood bill contained nothing "injurious or prejudicial to the interest of the native citizens of New Mexico." They also expected him to provide jobs for his constituents, to revise upward the tariff on wool to protect against low-priced imports, and to "be the delegate of all the people and not just one political party" while at the same time ensuring that Republicans and their principles prevailed.[10]

Among these expectations, Catron vigorously pursued only three—statehood, the tariff issue, and pensions. He had long been a friend of wool growers, and in 1894 traveled to Washington with others from the Territory to press for higher tariffs. In January 1897 he again testified against the prevailing tariff schedule as part of a long parade of Republican opponents, but Democratic president Cleveland had no interest in their complaints. Change came only after McKinley became president and fulfilled his campaign pledge to revise rates upward to close the price gap between imports and domestic wool. Appeals for pensions dominated constituent mail, and Catron pursued claims through the Pension Bureau of the Department of the Interior. But he accomplished more, as commonly occurred, through special pension bills.[11]

El Independiente also urged Catron to "show that New Mexico has a delegate who possesses sufficient ability to participate in debates and discussions that are entered into there and do not engage in political intrigues or be an obedient servant of the powerful in pursuit of their ends, but have an ability to deal as an equal with all your colleagues and by doing so gain the respect and attention of the most prominent industrialists and businessmen." Catron ignored this advice. His first piece of successful legislation came in early February 1896 when he secured passage of a bill prohibiting boxing and all contests involving animals in the territories and the District of Columbia. His goal was to ban a prizefight set for 14 February near Las Cruces to determine the world champion. Within three days the bill had passed through committees and both chambers and President Cleveland signed it into law. This expedited legislation came about because Catron agreed to help Democrats in Texas and, in doing so, overrode the voice of the Territory's governor, who had often clashed with him. But Texas Governor Charles Allen Culberson had the ear of Catron, and when he got prizefighting outlawed in Texas he next turned to Catron to carry his cause and ensure the boxers were blocked from moving the venue north of El Paso. It is unclear whether Catron paid any attention to religious crusaders across the country thundering from their pulpits to whip up moral outrage against boxing's brutality—a campaign orchestrated locally by eighteen pastors of El Paso's Ministers' Union—but many in the House and Senate took notice of widespread religious opposition. Neither Catron nor New Mexico gained anything by being "an obedient servant of the powerful in pursuit of their ends." In fact the willing servitude of 1896 likely emboldened Culberson who, after being elected to the Senate in 1899, promptly continued a Texas tradition of coveting what New Mexico held. He accelerated legislative attempts to strip New Mexico of its claims to water in the Rio Grande in favor of reserving much of it for use by El Pasoans. Culberson may well have learned from dealing with Catron that New Mexico could be pushed into doing what he demanded of it.[12]

Another of *El Independiente*'s suggestions urged Catron to ally with U.S. Senator Stephen B. Elkins of West Virginia. They had been college roommates, and Elkins came to New Mexico after being discharged as a Union captain in late 1863. Both men practiced law in New Mexico and were partners for a few years in Santa Fe, and for the balance of their lives they remained associates in an oftentimes strained relationship. Elkins eventually relocated to West Virginia following two terms as delegate from New Mexico (1873–77). The Las Vegas newspaper predicted that Elkins's "powerful influence and ability" would be applied to secure statehood because of the "many reasons he has to support and boost" his former constituents. Their praise reflected a widespread sentiment that the newly elected Elkins would be influential in the Fifty-Fourth Congress and beyond.[13]

When the annual general bill for all appropriations came up in March, Catron did not follow the advice of *El Independiente* to secure more funds for the Territory. Instead, Catron and Elkins soon engaged in the very "political intrigues" *El Independiente* wanted eschewed. The House approved without discussion a paragraph Catron added to the legislative, executive, and judicial appropriation bill "changing the date of the beginning of the next session of the Territorial Legislature from December to May" and mandating that a late session be convened on odd-numbered years. The *New York Times* in a front-page account claimed Catron secured the insertion through masterful "political manipulation" and condemned his motives: "In the event of Republican success a Republican President might appoint

Territorial officers and thus take the control of legislation from the Democrats." No doubt few members of the House grasped that Catron's insertion targeted several influential Democratic appointees in New Mexico, including the secretary of the Territory who had recently ruled against Republican legislative candidates in contested elections. When the Senate took up the appropriation bill, Senator Elkins pushed for quick approval; however, some New Mexicans had alerted Democratic Senator David B. Hill of New York, who when the proposed change came up during the reading of the bill, immediately objected and demanded it be stricken.

Soon more than half a dozen senators from both sides were engaged in verbal jousting, with Senator Hill characterizing the attempted change as a "mean, small, contemptible trick." Within three minutes of Hill's objection, Delegate Catron rushed into the chamber and took a seat beside Senator Elkins. Quickly joining the fray and also coming to sit alongside Senator Elkins was Montana Senator Thomas H. Carter, the chairman of the Republican National Committee, a friend of both men, and an owner of a large expanse of land in New Mexico. For nearly two hours the Senate debated the matter, and positions hardened on each side. The Democrats claimed that the Senate was being "asked to indorse a cheap political game," while Republicans defended the insertion as necessary to ensure greater fairness in settling contested elections in the Territory. This explanation convinced no Democrats, and matters became so heated that the Democrats, joined by a few Republicans and Populists, threatened that "the [Appropriation] bill would be held up for an indefinite time." Catron and Elkins, newcomers to the Congress, had seriously breached congressional protocol by naively assuming the tactics they used in the Territory would succeed in Washington. At the end of the day's Senate session, the motion to strike the insertion passed. Catron "marched out of the chamber, wearing a look which showed that he was afflicted with a 'tired feeling.'"[14]

"Brazen and Unblushing Nepotism"

Beginning in the mid-1880s the seven territories that soon became states did so after years of lobbying the Congress and conducting national pro-statehood public-relations campaigns. But the New Mexico Territory had done neither. Instead, Catron applied his New Mexico–style freewheeling politics in Washington. His attempt to accomplish in one term what had eluded the Territory for nearly fifty years put him on a collision course with the Congress, a fact evident at the beginning of the first session and throughout its seven months. Within twenty-four hours of his arrival in the capitol, an influential midwestern newspaper reported on his plans to maneuver his statehood bill to a successful vote. Catron had already sized up "the composition of the committee on territories, and [he] believes he will get the bill favorably reported soon." He made his forecast without ever discussing statehood with the members of the House and Senate committees on territories, which had to approve the bill before their respective chambers voted on it. He also talked to the newspaper weeks prior to the public announcement of appointments to the House committee.[15]

His optimistic prediction drew a cautious reply from the *Albuquerque Morning Democrat*, which reported that "the opportunity [for approving statehood] is a rare one. The conditions are extraordinarily favorable for success" but also warned that Catron alone would "assume the responsibility of defeating statehood" should he continue "stubbornly maintaining his arbitrary, unjust and unreasonable" attitude. When the House Committee on Territories convened on 10 January, the paper was proved right. Five Republican members immediately signaled their opposition, and they succeeding in setting his bill aside. Catron's brashness in pushing the committee into rapid action irritated key members because he violated protocol by not consulting or being appropriately deferential.[16]

In February Catron, in league with Arizona's delegate, regrouped for another push on statehood. On 13 February Catron addressed the Senate Committee on Territories, but his arguments were met with substantial and principled opposition. As reported in the *New York Times*, "The committee has not yet taken up these statehood bills for serious discussion, but the expressions made in the committee room indicate that the majority of the committee is opposed to the admission of any State as this time." Later that week matters went even worse in the House Committee on Territories, which voted down statehood bills for New Mexico and Arizona. Barely two months into the Fifty-Fourth Congress, statehood seemed dead. But the next week Arizona's delegate, Nathan O. Murphy, urgently appealed to the House committee, and a face-saving procedural tactic was accepted. If two committee members "who were absent from the previous meeting asked for a reconsideration, it should be entered upon." But, as a correspondent covering the hearings observed, "It is intimated strongly that the reconsideration today was solely for the purpose of leaving the question at least open."

On 2 April the House Committee on Territories again discussed statehood for New Mexico and Arizona and, following a reportedly heated meeting, no vote was taken. By mid-April Delegate Murphy became so disgruntled with Catron that he planned henceforth to work independently for statehood rather than have to deal with Catron's off-putting methods, which were having the unfortunate effect of undermining Arizona's chances of securing sovereignty. But the capstone to Catron's audacious behavior came a few weeks later when it was revealed he had appointed two of his sons, John and Charles Christopher, to West Point and Annapolis, respectively. What really had people talking—and prompted sarcastic praise from the *Washington Post*—was "the happy inspiration that led him to double up his boys and make each the alternate for the other." The paper tipped its hat to him for superbly displaying "what he's here for"—to be "a very good provider." Democratic opponents in New Mexico excoriated him for an unparalleled abuse of a prerogative of his office and for embarrassing the Territory: "Mr. Catron has easily distanced all rivals in the line of brazen and unblushing nepotism." In December *El Independiente* had ended its article by asking Catron to step cautiously so that Republican officials did not retaliate against statehood with "acts of indifference and hostility." But in less than five months Delegate Catron's boorish behavior had alienated many in the Congress. And other dark clouds surrounded the issue of statehood in the spring of 1896.[17]

"An Object Lesson"

Perhaps most decisive in shaping congressional opposition in both House and Senate was a specter raised repeatedly between January and April. Foes claimed that admitting New Mexico and Arizona to the Union "would send silver senators to Washington," a fear that was particularly strong among members of the Senate Committee on Territories. So vocal and numerous were these opponents that by mid-March the *Albuquerque Morning Democrat* pronounced, "Statehood is as dead as a door-nail," a victim of "the anti-free silver forces, [who] whether justly or unjustly, have no intention of allowing us further representation in congress." The political leanings of new states became an issue early in 1896 because in the upcoming elections the West was seen as a center of populism with its credo of "free silver," which the Democrats fervently espoused and many Republicans regarded as an unparalleled evil.[18]

At issue was whether the government should make credit more accessible, and the debates revolved around how gold and silver should be used to underwrite the value of money. The quantity of gold stockpiled to back the currency had remained unchanged for nearly twenty years, which created a chronic undersupply of money and credit relative to demand. Against that background, political unrest over monetary policy spread, and silver emerged as a panacea. It was plentiful, and if the government accepted silver to back currency then small farmers and others could secure needed loans. The populists' silver "solution" was implemented when the Congress passed the Sherman Silver Act of 1890. But a run on gold held by the Treasury Department resulted when people redeemed their silver certificates for gold. The price of silver quickly plunged below the cost of mining it. Economic turmoil followed. While the Democrats won the White House in the 1892 election, incoming president Grover Cleveland staunchly defended the gold standard. Although he moved quickly to rescind silver purchases, it was too late: a national economic disaster known as the Panic of 1893 had begun. A four-year nationwide economic depression ensued, and monetary policy became a divisive national issue in both the 1896 and 1900 elections. The political tug-of-war between "goldbugs" and "silverites" became a contest between the East (pro-gold) and the West (pro-silver). The Democratic South, too, was pro-silver; hence the Republican resistance to adding new senators.

Delegate Catron's push for statehood occurred at a most inauspicious time. His efforts coincided with events he could not control, but just when all seemed doomed a powerful advocate stepped forth and put statehood back on track. Senator Matthew S. Quay of Pennsylvania, an influential Republican boss in the Tammany Hall tradition, struck a deal to dislodge the statehood bill from the House Committee on Territories. Quay's interest in statehood had almost nothing to do with the merits of New Mexico's case. It emerged in a backroom deal born of political expediency: it fit into his plans for the upcoming presidential election. Quay was a master of the quid pro quo in politics. In 1888 he had used his position as chairman of the Republican National Committee to engineer the election of the last Republican president, Benjamin Harrison. He intended to play a kingmaker role in 1896, too. In April, as Catron's bill floundered in committee, Quay offered his help in exchange for a favor from Catron, who was a member of the party's credentials committee and would hear challenges to delegates at the upcoming Republican convention in St. Louis in mid-June. Quay pledged to get the statehood bill out of committee and before the full House, and in exchange Catron was to work to seat delegates pledged to favorite-son candidates. Quay intended to kill the candidacy of two-term Ohio governor William McKinley by flooding the convention with delegates pledged to prominent leaders from a number of states, a maneuver common in the late nineteenth century as a way of preventing early momentum. Once multiple votes occurred and no clear leader emerged, Quay expected to assume a broker's role. Depending on how support aligned, he would either try for the nomination himself or swing the party to the candidate he and Catron backed, Speaker of the House Thomas B. Reed of Maine.[19]

Quay had no problem delivering on his promise to Catron. He convinced the chair of the House Committee on Territories, Pennsylvania Representative Joseph Scranton, to drop his opposition to Catron's bill, which ensured its move out of committee and into the full House for a vote. But Republican dissent accompanied the favorable report, and the objections voiced in a minority report became recurring themes in future battles over statehood. The report contended that Congress should continue to block an enabling bill because "it has never been made clear that New Mexico possessed all the requisites of statehood," and the "characteristics of the people rendered its admission as a state undesirable."[20]

Catron's bill arrived in the House one day before Congress recessed for the summer and fall break, which meant it received no attention. Catron knew substantial opposition existed, but introducing his bill at the eleventh hour served as a token gesture to fulfill a promise to seek statehood. It also provided him a starting point to resume the push for statehood when Congress reconvened in December. Opposition newspapers in the Territory chastised him severely for this half-hearted effort, one labeling it "a feeble bid for votes" in his upcoming reelection campaign.[21]

The Fifty-Fourth Congress wrapped up its first session on 10 June and its members headed to St. Louis and Chicago to pick their standard bearers in the upcoming presidential election. Catron went to work to fulfill his deal with Quay, but he had little success in seating Quay-backed delegates in the face of 160 separate challenges. Quay had waited too long to recruit supporters and had been outmaneuvered by Ohio industrialist Mark Hanna, who for more than a year had been building delegate support into an unstoppable groundswell for McKinley. It was all over on the first ballot when McKinley received 661.5 votes, Reed 84.5, Quay 60.5, and Levi Morton, a former vice-president and current New York governor, 58. Soon Quay made his peace with the party's nominee, swung into line, and delivered Pennsylvania to the Republicans.

New Mexico did not comport itself nearly so well. The six-member delegation stripped Catron of his position as the Territory's national committeeman, voted to support the silver plank—an anathema rejected by the national party and Catron—and continued to show its contrariness to the bitter end by giving its six votes for vice president to H. Clay Evans of Tennessee even though the convention had already overwhelmingly picked Garret A. Hobart of New Jersey. At the Democratic National Convention, the Territory's six delegates, who had been favorably impressed by William Jennings Bryan when he visited New Mexico in 1896 and spoke at most of the major towns, supported Bryan at the convention. In the fall election the only national official the citizens of the Territory could elect was their congressional delegate, and this contest became a bellwether for New Mexico's political leaning. The victory of Democrat Harvey B. Fergusson signaled the ascendancy of pro-silver sentiment within both parties in the Territory, a development that cost New Mexico support for statehood in a Republican-controlled Congress and White House.[22]

But in mid-June 1896 Catron had only begun his fight for statehood. He would make two more forays—one at the convention and another in the second session of Congress beginning in December. He submitted to the whole convention, sitting as the committee on resolutions, a plank on statehood. He proposed that "In the territories of Oklahoma, New Mexico and Arizona, said territories should be permitted, as a right inherent to them, to form for themselves constitutions and state government and be admitted into the union." The convention rejected Catron's resolution "by a large majority." But Senator Quay stepped in again to keep the issue alive by proposing as a formal party plank what had been merely a declaration in 1892: "Admission of territories when it should be made evident the conditions prevailing in territories are such as to entitle them to admission." This innocuously worded substitute passed. Likewise the Democrats meeting in Chicago pledged themselves to a plank supporting statehood.[23]

In Catron's fall 1896 reelection campaign, New Mexicans took little notice that each party had pledged to support statehood. This promise fell far short of what people wanted, and so Democrats—and some Republicans—called for a new delegate. But the election's dominant refrain became attacks on Catron. The Chávez murder case surfaced again early in the fall when Catron unsuccessfully appealed the death sentence to the Territory's Supreme Court. Then a second, unsuccessful attempt to disbar him occurred immediately prior to the election. These incidents were more than distractions—they reminded everyone of Catron's unsavory reputation. But his inability to deliver statehood contributed to his defeat, and Spanish-language newspapers were particularly pointed in criticizing him. *El Labrador* of Las Cruces in early September listed eleven ways Catron had not succeeded as a delegate, and the first was "he failed to have New Mexico admitted as a State." Seven weeks later, with the election a few days away, the same newspaper ran an eleven-hundred-word editorial on the urgent need for Nuevomexicanos to exercise popular sovereignty to protect themselves from Catron: "Neo-Mexicanos our interests are now in danger more than ever. . . . What has he done for us [in Washington]? We know of nothing. And in the Territory, who is Mr. Catron? . . . Someone who is only an insolent charlatan, a bulldozer of the first order, who with threats, intrigues, and frauds has obtained his millions of acres of land, property that he has usurped from thousands of poor, innocent families." In a close election, Albuquerque attorney Harvey B. Fergusson defeated Catron by 1,930 votes out of more than 36,000 cast.[24]

Undaunted by his defeat on 3 November, Catron returned to Washington in early December, this time residing amid the politically influential at the Willard Hotel. His failed reelection bid sharpened his interest in pursuing statehood, but it was also tied to his plan to attract potential buyers for his vast landholdings. He had long argued that one of the principal reasons to seek statehood was to be rid of restraints imposed by the Aliens Act of 1887, which barred foreigners from owning property or investing in the Territory. His final legislative attempts linked statehood and repeal of the 1887 law, and both were killed by nightfall on 10 December 1896. The day had begun inauspiciously with members of the House Committee on Territories "so obviously opposed to considering any of the statehood bills that the matter went over without discussion."[25]

The afternoon was even worse. Catron took to the House floor to introduce a bill allowing foreign investors to own real estate in the Territory and invest there for ten years. Both goals, he explained, would "enable the people of the Territories to get some of the benefits of foreign capital." Such an

infusion would unquestionably benefit the Territory and—not coinciden-
tally—bring well-to-do foreign investors to Catron's door. The bill, which
conformed to a Populist appeal for access to capital, promptly attracted the
attention of Iowa Republican Representative William P. Hepburn, a formidable figure widely regarded as the most skilled debater in the House.
Catron more than met his match in the ensuing exchanges. After forcing
Catron to acknowledge that "a combination of Populists and Democrats
had carried New Mexico" in the fall election, Hepburn delivered a knock-
out blow: "The people of New Mexico should have an object lesson. They
should be taught to understand that their Territory cannot grow under
Populist doctrines." Catron's bill went down to a resounding defeat, signaling Republican wariness over the West's political drift toward Populists,
Democrats, and Silver Republicans. But Hepburn and Republicans had
other lessons in mind, too. They were in no mood to hear more appeals
for statehood from a Territory so unreliable that its acknowledged political
boss, Catron, could not deliver a Republican majority. So, on a cold December day, the Fifty-Fourth Congress took Catron to the woodshed.[26]

In the Fifty-Fifth Congress Democratic delegate Harvey B. Fergusson introduced substantially the same statehood bill Catron had drafted,
but it never emerged from a House committee. But Speaker of the House
Reed, a scrupulously fair, civil, and incorruptible politician, recognized and
appreciated similar qualities in others—including members of the opposing
party. He came to accept that a land bill fervently sought by Fergusson represented genuinely public-spirited legislation that would materially aid the
Territory, contribute to its march toward statehood, and ensure a financial
legacy well into the future. The Fergusson Act passed into law with Speaker
Reed's backing in late June 1898. It set aside more than 3.6 million acres
of the public domain in New Mexico, and recurring lease revenue would
support educational institutions in perpetuity. When statehood arrived,
this permanent land fund increased. Fergusson's land bill has rightly been
called one of the most consequential pieces of legislation for New Mexico,
and its passage contrasts with Catron's dismal legislative record. In the election of 1898, Delegate Fergusson narrowly lost to Republican Pedro Perea,
also from Bernalillo County. Initially Catron believed Perea had an excel-
lent chance to gain support for statehood during the Fifty-Sixth Congress,
but following a trip to Washington Catron backed off from his prediction.

No movement on statehood occurred, and a new delegate, Republican Bernard S. Rodey, entered the Fifty-Seventh Congress.[27]

In his defense, Catron never had a chance of securing statehood given the nation's political divide over gold and silver in 1896. Among Republican U.S. Senators, any whiff of pro-silver sentiments led to great angst, and the winds out of New Mexico carried a strong odor indeed. While his plans faltered and eventually collapsed because of a hostile political climate in Washington, Catron's scheming also undermined his effectiveness. What Catron said and did in the Congress cast a shadow over him and the Territory, and influential people took his statements and actions as evidence of how New Mexico would behave if made a state. Judging the Territory based on Catron's behavior as a delegate became inescapable because he so thoroughly fused his political and personal interests and pursued both, as one Spanish-language Territorial newspaper remarked, "with his sophisms and lies" in the Congress, actions which "Democrats as well as Republicans condemned."

Such scathing appraisals were compounded by the damage visited on him by innuendo and suspicion during his legal problems in 1894 and 1895, prompting a Socorro newspaper to comment matter-of-factly in early June 1896, "Catron has made a record that would defeat any public man in any congressional district outside of New Mexico. In this territory, however, the Republican Party is under the control of one man, who allows no other to aspire—and that boss is Thomas Benton Catron, the 'gentleman with a job.'" But his once viselike grip on power was loosening, and Catron's reign as political boss began to crumble in the second half of 1896. Within the Territory, his abrasive and abusive behavior, the notoriety of the Chávez murder, and the subsequent attempts to disbar him undermined his power. But it was his pro-gold stance that finally led New Mexico's delegates—a majority of whom were silverites—to exact revenge in St. Louis by ousting Catron as national committeeman and to install Solomon Luna, who served in that capacity until his death on 30 August 1912. These reversals contributed to Catron's failure to win reelection to the Congress. Finally, many nationally prominent Republicans considered him unable to control the Territory's Republican Party. He had been appointed a national committeeman in 1892 in recognition of being undisputed "boss" in New Mexico. But that perception changed after he was stripped of his national committeeman's post, lost his reelection bid, and the Territory went Democratic, and so on 10 December Republican leaders in the House thoroughly rebuffed him. Catron never ran for delegate again, and as the years passed he spoke contemptuously of the position, even telling the chair of the Senate Committee on Territories that a delegate "is only a licensed and paid beggar." But when the opportunity arose in early 1912 to secure appointment by the new state's legislature as U.S. senator, he showed he still wielded influence, secured the position, and served until March 1917.[28]

"Unallotted Lands"

Catron's tenure in Washington has never been assessed in terms of his appearances before the Supreme Court between January 1896 and March 1897, but the three cases he argued violated *El Independiente*'s exhortations to do no harm to Nuevomexicanos. The court's rulings stripped Nuevomexicanos of more than 33 million acres, most of it communally held property awarded them in land grants. Property rights of Nuevomexicanos had been a contentious issue ever since the United States conquered New Mexico in 1846 and made it a territory in 1850. The Congress had final authority to confirm the more than 150 land grants made by Spain and Mexico, but by 1870 they had acted on only about 20 percent of them. Contested claims of ownership and allegations of improprieties in awarding titles created such controversy that the Congress discontinued approvals in the late 1870s. But the problem did not go away, and soon land takeovers by the railroad and new settlers made congressional inaction untenable. In response to repeated appeals, the Congress passed and President Benjamin Harrison signed an act establishing the Court of Private Land Claims on 3 March 1891, and later that year five judges set up their court in Santa Fe. They were given four years to adjudicate titles to land grants, but reauthorizations extended their work until 30 June 1904. Judicial rulings confirmed claims to 2.1 million acres, but claims to 33.4 million acres were rejected, and control of these passed to the federal government. These transfers of land have long been controversial. But not all the lands remained in federal hands. At statehood New Mexico received 5 million acres, while additional millions of acres of public domain lands were sold or opened to homesteaders.[29]

The procedures followed by the Court of Private Land Claims raised concerns about impartiality. Jury trials were not used. Instead the five judges, only one of whom came from a western state, heard cases and rendered decisions that, if appealed, went directly to the U.S. Supreme Court. In response to an early appeal, Delegate Catron stood before the Supreme Court in January 1896. He briefly set aside his congressional duties to defend his client, the City of Santa Fe, in a dispute with the U.S. attorney assigned to the Court of Private Land Claims, Matthew G. Reynolds. In *United States v. Santa Fe*, Catron argued in support of the Court of Private Land Claims ruling that the City of Santa Fe had title under Spanish law and customary practice to land the Crown granted it. U.S. Attorney Reynolds argued that the city had received no formal land grant and therefore had no title to the property it claimed, portions of which included federal buildings as well as Fort Marcy.[30]

The Supreme Court spent an uncharacteristic fourteen months deliberating before handing down a decision on 1 March 1897, just a few days before Catron's tenure as delegate ended. It is clear from the opinion that the justices steeped themselves in Spanish colonial-era law before siding with the government. They assiduously studied the lengthy and convoluted compilation of 6,447 Spanish laws published in 1681—the *Recopilación de Leyes de Los Reynos de Las Indias*—in addressing an issue of profound significance: what lands did the Spanish government confer in making land grants and which ones did it retain?

In the court's deliberations, though, Spanish law was only one of four legal currents informing the justices' views on land grants in New Mexico. Also exerting powerful influences were provisions of the 1848 Treaty of Guadalupe Hidalgo, a bias toward use of expropriation to expand the public domain in the West, and ideas of Thomas Jefferson and John Locke about land use and property rights. The Treaty of Guadalupe Hidalgo set forth a general obligation for the United States to respect the property rights of Mexican citizens in lands that nation ceded to the U.S. But President James K. Polk substantially undercut this concession when he opposed Article 10, which required the United States to recognize Spanish and Mexican land grants and accorded their owners the same legal protection they had under Mexican rule. The U.S. Senate acceded to President Polk's recommendation and removed Article 10 during the treaty's ratification. One legal scholar noted that this action left Nuevomexicanos (and all former Mexican citizens) vulnerable to "lose their property in the wake of the transfer of sovereign control over the region."[31]

The Supreme Court did not specifically target any one group in taking away land in the nineteenth century. Instead they went after everyone
under a judicial bent for expropriating property that lasted from the 1870s
into the 1910s. During these decades the court came to define the government as a jealous possessor of land. That is, government—whether Spain or
the United States—always set restrictions when it made land available, and
the court intended to protect their right to do so. The intellectual under-
pinning for the court's disposition had been created in rulings that favored
the government's power to control land defined as the public domain, even
when individuals already had made claims and improvements. In 1872 the
court rendered its initial decision in this vein, the Yosemite Valley Case or
Hutchins v. Low. The Court disallowed private land holdings in Yosemite
and restored them to the U.S. Government without any compensation,
although the legislature of the state of California soon paid the individuals
for their lost land. This ruling informed a trend in Supreme Court decisions
lasting for four decades, a period that has been called "the heyday of expropriation as an instrument of public policy."[32]

Nuevomexicanos came under the Court's scrutiny because of one zealous legal protagonist in the Court of Private Land Claims—U.S. Attorney
Matthew G. Reynolds. The Supreme Court did not single out Nuevomexicanos to suffer the largest losses in landholdings in that era. That act fell to
Reynolds. He repeatedly highlighted his triumphs in stripping away land
titles, and his annual report on Court of Private Land Claims proceedings
often featured assessments such as this one from 1894: "In New Mexico and
Arizona the total area claimed in the suits disposed of . . . was 4,784,651
acres; amount confirmed, 779,611 acres, amount rejected and not confirmed 4,005,040 acres. The result is very gratifying to me." No other official
in the territory's history inflicted so much damage on so many Nuevomexicanos.[33]

Reynolds's appeals to the U.S. Supreme Court were rooted in American
beliefs about property rights, combining ideas enunciated by Thomas Jefferson on land policy and John Locke on private property. The Jeffersonian
model of land tenure posited that the nation's future rested on a foundation
of yeoman farmers tilling their own small plots. To accomplish that end,
the government fostered homesteading after 1862 to promote settling the
West. Moreover, as territories became states, Congress and the president
transferred millions of acres from the public domain to promote and sus-

tain their growth. In this model the public domain served as a federal patrimony to be bestowed when granting statehood. Nine western states entered the Union between 1850 and 1896, and five of these states had a larger percentage of federal land than New Mexico. To secure a large public domain in New Mexico, the Supreme Court declared that communal lands passed to the U.S. government after 1848 in a line of succession from the Spanish crown to the Mexican government. The Supreme Court approved only titles for individual allotments. Doing so conformed to English legal traditions dating to John Locke's seventeenth-century ideas on private property, which in turn became a basic principle in American jurisprudence. That is, only individuals holding clear evidence of title to land had rights before the law.[34]

When the Court of Private Land Claims ruled in favor of a land-grant heir, as happened in the case that brought Reynolds and Catron before the Supreme Court in March 1897, Reynolds appealed on the basis that the land in question had not been properly conveyed to an individual. He alleged legal confusion existed regarding the amount of land actually ceded, and his argument advanced a theory that perfectly supported the Court's inclination to delimit the scope of land grants. Reynolds adopted a position first advanced by the U.S. government's surveyor general in New Mexico, George W. Julian, who in 1887 maintained that the Spanish and Mexican governments retained title to all communal lands when they made land grants and that therefore, after the United States took over the Southwest, the common lands belonged to the federal government. Reynolds forged a link between two trends that eroded the rights of property holders in New Mexico: expropriation and the government's superiority over private interests. Although modern legal scholars have repeatedly demonstrated the flaws in the Julian-Reynolds theory, in the 1890s no one convincingly challenged it, although Catron apparently tried to buttress his own arguments by traveling to Mexico City to do legal research in the summer of 1897. But the court had ruled against him three times, and another attorney told his client in mid-February 1895 that the "Supreme Court, with its new members, [was] a very uncertain tribunal in the adjudication of land grant questions. . . . [It] takes, at present, a very narrow view of these titles."[35]

In the first of their rulings against a Catron client, the City of Santa Fe, the Supreme Court maintained that the government of Spain never made a formal concession or allotment of land. Catron argued that destruction of records in the Pueblo Revolt precluded producing evidence of a grant, and that for the next two hundred years officials in Santa Fe believed and acted as if a grant had been made because the crown made grants when establishing new towns. The court rejected this claim as unsubstantiated, and also asserted that the crown exercised absolute control over all lands and that no claim such as Catron now made would have had standing in the king's eyes. This issue of what land the Spanish government granted, what it retained, and how the prerogatives of the crown were exercised received explicit attention in the case Catron argued before the Supreme Court on 8–9 March 1897. Contested was a decision of the Court of Private Land Claims handed down in April 1893 conferring full title to 325,000 acres of the San Miguel del Bado Land Grant, west of Las Vegas, to the heirs of a land grant made in 1794.

While it had taken the Supreme Court fourteen months to rule in the Santa Fe land-grant case, they took only two and half months to issue their decision in *United States v. [Julian] Sandoval* on 24 May 1897. Their promptness, and especially the scope of the ruling, resulted from the court using the legal research and decision in the Santa Fe case as precedent. This Supreme Court ruling marked the most significant decision in the history of land-grant litigation: "The general theory of the Spanish law on the subject indicates that, even after a formal designation, the control of the outlying lands, to which a town might have considered entitled, was in the King, as the source and fountain of title." With that sentence, the Supreme Court asserted that common lands within land grants did not belong to individuals but remained the possession of the crown. Once New Mexico was under American control, these lands become U.S. government property. As a consequence of the ruling, the heirs of the San Miguel del Bado grant received title to just 5,200 acres allotted as private property.[36]

The *Sandoval* ruling surely enraged Thomas Catron and his client, Levi P. Morton. Asserting their claim to ownership of these common lands, they had appealed the original decision of the Court of Private Land Claims. The Supreme Court merged their appeal with that of U.S. Attorney Reynolds, and while Reynolds prevailed in his argument, Catron did not. His client, Morton, was a prominent New York Republican, unsuccessful presidential candidate in the 1896 convention, wealthy banker, land speculator, former vice president of the United States under President Harrison, and most recently governor of New York (1895–97). The Court treated him just as it did Nuevomexicanos. It denied them title and stated "unallotted [or communal] lands were subject to the disposition of the [U.S.] government." Morton did not get his hands on the 310,000 acres of communal land, but the government did and added it to the public domain. With this ruling the Supreme Court replaced the Spanish conception of the social basis of property with English and American notions about private ownership of property. For all the time the justices spent reading the *Recopilación de Leyes de Los Reynos de Las Indias*, they failed to grasp a basic tenet of the crown's conception of its power. It governed over all the people and provided for them in ways that served both private and collective interests. The crown awarded lands to individual title holders, but a much larger portion was set aside for shared, or communal, use. The Supreme Court disregarded the crown's intent to protect communal interests.[37]

Catron's third loss at the Supreme Court in 1897 came on the same day as the *Sandoval* ruling when citizens of Abiquiú in the case *Rio Arriba Land and Cattle Company v. United States* lost their communal lands. The court cited itself from the *Sandoval* ruling to declare that nearly half a million acres of communal lands in a grant from 1806 were now public domain and not the private property of land grant heirs. The ruling presaged a further loss for Nuevomexicanos—and for Catron. The Court reiterated its rejection of the argument that codicils signed by Mexico and the United States while negotiating the Treaty of Guadalupe Hidalgo remained valid and therefore land grants were inviolable. This part of the decision opened up to review all remaining unsettled land-grant titles, not a few of which Catron claimed to own. Just 364 days later, on 23 May 1898, the U.S. Supreme Court handed down a decision in *Hayes v. United States* that confirmed Catron's worst fears. The case arose out of a Court of Private Land Claims ruling concerning a land grant in the Socorro-Sevilleta area made in the spring of 1825. On appeal, the U.S. Supreme Court affirmed a ruling by the Court of Private Land Claims that voided the authority of officials in New Mexico to make land grants during the Mexican period. As a consequence, any individual who subsequently bought such lands had no clear title to them. The Supreme Court said, "The lands covered by the grant being public lands of the nation, and not being subject to grant by the authorities of the territory of New Mexico, it follows that the title upon which the claimant relies vested no right in him."[38]

In surveying the Supreme Court's rulings on land grants at the turn of the twentieth century, one scholar recently concluded, "The Court opposed interpretations . . . that might hinder the growth of the American economy in the Southwest." The Supreme Court's ruling dispossessed Nuevomexicanos and displeased land speculators, but the Court's decision resonated well with most Euro-Americans in New Mexico, who resented that land grants tied up millions of acres for the exclusive use of a limited number of Nuevomexicanos engaged in subsistence farming and communal grazing. Territorial Delegate Bernard S. Rodey explained this viewpoint at a Senate hearing in June 1902: "The existence of these land grants is one thing that has kept the Territory back for many years. Now that the title is known, cattlemen and others are buying them with a view to using them for pasturage, for the timber, the iron, the coal, and one thing and another; and the result is a tremendous impetus to New Mexico."[39]

"Justice for New Mexico, Statehood!"

Friend and foe alike in Congress acknowledged that concern over granting Nuevomexicanos full voting privileges was one of the main reasons New Mexico had been repeatedly passed over while fifteen other states entered the Union between 1850 and 1900. Euro-American advocates of statehood such as Catron advanced a counterargument to allay such fears. They pledged that only responsible New Mexicans—Euro-Americans and a few wealthy Nuevomexicanos—would hold the upper hand under statehood. Typical of such discussions was correspondence between a business associate of Catron's from Minnesota and that state's Republican U.S. Senator C. K. Davis, a member of the Senate Committee on Territories. As Catron's business associate saw it, "the average Mexican scarcely contains sufficient material out of which to manufacture good loyal American citizens. Yet I am still inclined to think, that with proper restrictions and limitations in the act admitting the Territory there is but little danger from that element." Senator Davis was not as supportive or optimistic, noting, "The large Mexican population of that Territory is a mighty undesirable element out of which to form a state." Catron always believed that reservations such as expressed by Senator Davis would be resolved quickly because "the voting population of the two races is about even." He confidently expected that "immigration wil[l] be stimulated," eventually yielding a Euro-American majority in population and at the ballot box.[40]

It was precisely to create these "proper restrictions and limitations" that Catron sought a constitutional convention under his control in his December 1896 plan to revive statehood. This was not his first try at forging a constitution. He had been a driving force behind a convention in 1889, but Nuevomexicano voters rejected the document and Catron's high-handed role in its creation. By the late 1890s it was clear Catron no longer held the Republican Party under his thumb, and a formidable rival emerged in the person of thirty-seven-year-old Miguel A. Otero, the territorial governor appointed by President McKinley in 1897. Once in office Otero, a one-time confidant of Catron, quickly asserted his independence by gathering to himself a younger generation of Euro-Americans and elite Nuevomexicanos—and Democrats from both groups—to forge a new Republican faction. Doing so was a clear repudiation of the old politics of schemes, fraud, and public scandals. Instead Otero projected a new image and aligned himself with an emerging force in the Republican Party nationwide—reformers gathered under the banner of progressivism, whose young leaders at the turn of the twentieth century were men such as Albert J. Beveridge in Indiana and Theodore Roosevelt in New York. Catron became an avowed enemy and told Otero he would fight him "to the bitter end and by any means."[41]

In his calculation for reviving statehood, Otero eschewed Catron's conclave of elites; instead, he created a public event. He placed the meeting at the large Reynolds Building in Albuquerque, and convened the two-day statehood convention on 15 and 16 October, dates coinciding with the Twenty-First Annual Territorial Fair in Albuquerque. Large crowds and people from all parts of the territory came to the fair, and Otero drew upon that attendance to ensure broad-based popular representation: "All citizens of the Territory who may be present upon the occasion are also delegates to said convention." This open invitation supplemented the call for each county and major cities to select and send delegates as well. Chaired by J. Francisco Chaves of Valencia County, a former territorial delegate to Congress and longtime Republican Party leader and government official, the convention welcomed hundreds of delegates and nearly as many visitors watching the deliberations.[42]

The tone of the document they sent to Washington showed that the will of the people had prevailed. Popular sovereignty now reigned. The preamble to the four pages of resolutions echoed the Declaration of Independence: "That when in the course of human events it becomes necessary for the people of a Territory to make an effort peacefully and legally to dissolve the temporary and inadequate political bonds which have connected them with the nation, and to assume among the sovereign states of the Union, the separate, independent and equal station, to which our destiny and inherent rights as well as the laws of nature and of nature's God entitle us, . . . we should set forth the causes which impel us to the action." Continuing this theme of colonial restiveness, W. B. Childers, outgoing president of the Territory's bar association, told the Congress in February 1903: "The answer of the [Senate] committee to the demands of New Mexico [for statehood] does not differ in principle or logic from the answer of Lord North and [King] George the Third to Massachusetts and Virginia when they refused to submit to taxation without representation."[43]

But rather than break the bonds that tied them to the rest of the Union, New Mexicans sought to become at one with the nation in 1901: "We declare that we have been kept entirely too long in a subordinate condition, and that we are now thoroughly fitted to assume and support a higher form of government [statehood]." They set forth seventeen deficiencies of their status as a territory along with nineteen reasons why they were entitled to join the Union. Their first grievance summed up their argument in favor of statehood: "A territorial form of government is intolerable to a free people; it is an incongruity under American institutions, and should be maintained only so long as is absolutely necessary to prepare its people for the higher form." They beseeched "Congress and the nation" to heed them, and they echoed the famous phrases of natural rights' sovereignty used by President Abraham Lincoln in his Gettysburg Address: "That it will not permit a government of our people, for our people and by our people to perish from our hopes, but that Under God it will grant us a new lease of Freedom by granting us—STATEHOOD."[44]

Talk of statehood excited New Mexicans in 1901, and their resolution affirmed their readiness to enter the Union. Even President Theodore Roosevelt "expressed the greatest interest and the strongest friendship for the cause." A palpable sense of enthusiasm propelled delegates into the Statehood Convention in Albuquerque in mid-October with a messianic fervor captured by one journalist: "Their voices will resound in clarion tones for the cause of New Mexico until in the halls of Congress, over the heads of members, the words 'Justice for New Mexico, Statehood!' will echo from wall to wall along the corridors and swell the hearts of our lawmakers to the end that success will be attained."[45]

An emerging ally in the Senate was the chair of the Committee on Territories, George L. Shoup of Idaho. He visited New Mexico in 1899 and Governor Otero courted his support, but Shoup was not reappointed and stepped down from the Senate in early March 1901. That fall, nearly coinciding with the Albuquerque convention, Senator Albert J. Beveridge, a first-term Indiana Republican who had entered the Fifty-Sixth Congress in December 1899, learned he had been tapped to head the Senate Committee on Territories.[46]

CHAPTER TWO

"A Strong Case against the Admission"

A n autopsy is needed. A statehood bill overwhelmingly approved by the House of Representatives in May 1902 died in the Senate upon adjournment of the Fifty-Seventh Congress on 4 March 1903. Political historian Lewis L. Gould explained its demise: "Led by a coalition of Republicans and Democrats, an attempt to obtain the admission of the territories of Arizona and New Mexico ran into the determined opposition of Senator [Nelson] Aldrich [R-R.I.] and the Republican leadership." What was so objectionable about statehood that key Republicans killed a bipartisan move to pass it? The short answer is that Senate Republican leaders feared that new western states would usher in a debilitating shift in power—away from the East, away from their party, and away from four decades of Republican dominance of the White House and the Congress. Historical forensics reveal the tools employed in the killing.[1]

Although Article IV of the Constitution vested in the Congress the authority to create new states, New Mexico's fate rested in the hands of two senators: Nelson Aldrich and Albert J. Beveridge. Senator Aldrich's name should be associated with his role in creating the Federal Reserve System, but if he is remembered, it likely is for his namesake and grandson, Nelson Aldrich Rockefeller, the forty-first vice president of the United States. Yet during the presidency of Theodore Roosevelt (1901–1909) Senator Aldrich controlled the Senate. The position of Senate majority leader did not then exist, but Aldrich exercised an equivalent power. Appointed to his fourth term in 1898, he settled in as the new chair of the Senate Finance Committee. He also controlled committee assignments, which permitted him to act as gatekeeper to legislation winding its way through hearings.

Aldrich's opposition to statehood was related to his loss of power under Democratic president Grover Cleveland's second administration (1893–97). In Aldrich's view, the Democrats had seized political control because six new western states had entered the Union several years prior to the 1892 presidential election. Voters in these new states overwhelmingly supported Cleveland, and as Aldrich's biographer noted, "he had burnt his fingers once admitting States that proved a danger to his party, and he did not propose to do it again." So deep was Aldrich's opposition to statehood that he maneuvered to kill the Omnibus Bill of 1902 when it actually had sufficient votes to pass. Aldrich did so by manipulating the Senate's handling of the bill passed by the House of Representatives. His chief agent of obstruction was Senator Albert J. Beveridge (R-Ind.), who enjoyed Aldrich's full backing to use any means necessary to keep New Mexico and Arizona as Territories.[2]

"Empire of Our Principles"

Senator Albert J. Beveridge enjoyed verbal jousting. He found much to amuse himself on the last full day of the first session of the Fifty-Seventh Congress—Monday, 30 June 1902. Senator Joseph W. Bailey (D-Tex.) had just said he could "fathom the intelligence of every man in the Senate Chamber except that of the Senator from Indiana." Beveridge retorted, "I am very glad to find the Senator beyond his depth." Laughter rocked the Senate gallery. Beveridge enjoyed the moment and did not notice the visible anger sweeping over the physically imposing Texan. Bailey grabbed Beveridge by the neck, lifted him off the floor, and choked him until pulled away by fellow senators. The attack marked the second time that day Senator Beveridge's comments affronted others. In hearings that morning he had riled half-a-dozen New Mexicans. Beveridge chaired the Senate Committee on Territories, on which Senator Bailey also sat, and his persistent questioning had besmirched the good name of the territory's citizens. Beveridge claimed they were not a literate, law-abiding, industrious people.[3]

These conflicts culminated several months of increasingly hostile and emotionally charged arguments that had their epicenter half a world away— in the Philippines. America's presence there led to impassioned wrangling over the country's colonial intentions. In the Committee on the Philippines, on which Senator Beveridge also sat, as well on the Senate floor, anger turned white-hot over allegations of U.S. Army atrocities. Pro-imperialist Republicans squared off against anti-imperialists, most of them Democrats, plus a few Republicans. The supercharged atmosphere was close to an explosion, and Beveridge's goading of Bailey provided the spark during a dispute about an unrelated issue. While both Democrats and Republicans rebuked Senator Bailey, he got more sympathy in a letter to the editor of the *New York Times* that reminded everyone of Beveridge's culpability and suggested, "A few more precedents, commenced by Senator Bailey, ought to be established."[4]

U.S. imperialism in the Philippines became entwined in the politics of statehood because Senator Beveridge planted himself in the very center of both issues. His views on the Philippines and New Mexico mixed righteous certitude with petulance. For Beveridge, promoting colonialism in the Philippines and postponing statehood for New Mexico and Arizona grew out of the same principle: hold each in a dependent status until the United States could uplift the peoples living there. These beliefs launched his political career.

Late in the summer of 1898, Beveridge was thirty-five years old, a successful lawyer in Indianapolis, and politically ambitious. He gained national attention following a speech in Boston in April 1897 calling for military action against Spain to place its colonies under American control. The following year President William McKinley (1897–1901) declared war in April, and the United States crushed Spain in Cuba, Puerto Rico, and the Philippines between May and July. A decisive moment in Beveridge's political ascendancy came when veterans of a Civil War contingent marched to his home and escorted him to the state's Republican Party Convention in mid-September 1898. There his keynote speech electrified the several thousand attendees. The symbolism of a Civil War honor guard escorting Beveridge coupled with the delegates' enthusiastic response to his speech shows the extent of military and civilian support for Beveridge's imperialistic message. Thunderous applause greeted him in Indianapolis when he asked, "Would not the people of the Philippines prefer the just, humane, civilizing government of this Republic to the savage, bloody rule of pillage and extortion from which we have rescued them? . . . Will you remember that we do but what our fathers did . . . we only continue the march of the flag?"[5]

In what became known as his "March of the Flag" speech, Beveridge repeatedly reminded his audience of the country's slow recovery from the financial ruin associated with the Democratic Party in the Panic of 1893. He subscribed to the prevailing view that American prosperity required new markets, asking rhetorically, "And shall we reap the reward that waits on our discharge of our high duty; shall we occupy new markets for what our farmers raise, our factories make, our merchants sell—aye, and please God, new markets for what our ships shall carry?" In the popular mind, Spain's imperial motives in the sixteenth century represented a quest for God, gold, and glory. At the turn of the twentieth century Beveridge recast this triad, arguing for an American empire in terms of Providence, profits, and politics.[6]

But Beveridge's imperialism went beyond the economic imperative. "March of the Flag" posited a fundamental principle that underlay his political ideals, including how he looked upon Nuevomexicanos. He told the audience in Indianapolis that no current U.S. territory was capable of self-rule. With regard to New Mexico, he reminded the convention it "had a savage and alien population." Beveridge believed New Mexico incapable of home rule, which necessitated that "we govern our territories without their consent." Moreover, because "American energy is greater than Spanish sloth," he said, Spain's former colonial areas would improve only when "the empire of our principles is established." Divine will guided and consecrated this mission: "It is a glorious history our God has bestowed upon His chosen people. . . . We cannot retreat from any soil where Providence has unfurled our banner; it is ours to save that soil for liberty and civilization."[7]

Beveridge's embrace of empire building was part of a century-long process of undermining Spain's status as a colonial power in North America and the Caribbean, a process capped by the recent American victory in the Spanish-American War. That victory thrust America onto the world stage, and Beveridge believed the nation to be destined to rule over weaker, so-called unfit peoples. He whipped up these imperialist impulses during his relentless campaigning for the Republican Party throughout the fall of 1898, passing out several hundred thousand copies of his Indianapolis speech. In early November the state's Republican candidates won election and took control of the legislature, and one of their first acts involved naming a new United States senator to succeed the incumbent Democrat whose term expired in early March 1899. (Not until ratification of the Seventeenth Amendment in 1913 were all U.S. senators required to be elected by a state's voters.) The legislators convened in January, waded through seven rounds of balloting, and finally Albert J. Beveridge emerged victorious from the field of eight aspirants. Ironically, the leading contender had been former New Mexico Territorial Governor Lew Wallace (1878–80), who had bowed out the previous spring, thus opening the field to Beveridge.

The new senator had a trim, muscular body—five foot eight inches, 158 pounds—which barely contained his seemingly limitless energy. Few men anywhere could equal his oratory, which, coupled with his intellect, tenacity, and single-mindedness, quickly set him on a fast track in Washington. He savored the attention lavished on him by such newspapers as the *Los Angeles Times*: "Senators will find in the young giant from Indiana a new power among them." Such national recognition stoked his already considerable ambition. He began to look ahead and to compare himself to another favorite son of Indiana—Benjamin Harrison. They lived only three blocks apart, and Harrison, too, had been a lawyer from Indianapolis, and had—a decade earlier—gone from his first term in the U.S. Senate to being twenty-third president of the United States (1889–93). Beveridge saw the U.S. Senate as a stepping stone and believed his opportunity would come upon completion of President McKinley's second term.[8]

Although selected early in 1899, Beveridge was not sworn in until 10 December when the first session of the Fifty-Sixth Congress convened. This gave him time to travel to the Philippines as well into the Far East and Russia before he went to Washington. By the time he took his oath as senator, he had emerged as a rising star. He solidified his stature within a month of taking his seat. On 9 January he delivered his maiden address in the Senate, devoted to urging the Senate to support a full conquest of the Philippines. Speaking to a packed Senate floor and gallery in an hour-plus oration praised by the *New York Times* as "replete with striking sentences and well-arranged information [and] spoken with all the earnestness, vigor and eloquence of a fine orator," Beveridge resurrected themes from his "March of the Flag" speech. He began by telling his colleagues the "natives are ignorant," which meant they were "incapable of self-rule," and therefore God ordained the United States to take over the Philippines to carry out "our saving, regenerating, uplifting work." In the "March of the Flag" speech he had asserted that "the rule of liberty that all just government derives its authority from the consent of the governed applies only to those who are capable of self-government." He reiterated this position: "How dare any man prostitute this expression of the very elect of self-governing peoples to a race of Malay children of barbarism, schooled in Spanish methods and ideas." He explained that America was predestined to rule in the Philippines: "God has not been preparing the English-speaking and Teutonic peoples for a thousand years for nothing. . . . No. He had made us master organizers of the world to establish system where chaos reigns. He has made us adept in government that we may administer government among savage and senile peoples."[9]

Beveridge's addresses in Indianapolis and at the capitol espoused two powerful pathological strains in American thought at the turn of the twentieth century—colonialism and racism. The classic assessment of his prejudice offered more than fifty years ago by Richard Hofstadter situated Beveridge's ideas within intellectual currents and rationalizations coursing through America: "The idea of inevitable Anglo-Saxon destiny figured in the outlook of Senators Albert Beveridge and Henry Cabot Lodge and of John Jay, Theodore Roosevelt's Secretary of State, as well as of the President himself." Beveridge and others of a like mind were as dismissive of immigrants as they were of foreign peoples recently brought under American control. To improve and uplift both groups required Americanization, to be undertaken by three institutions: schools teaching English and inculcating citizenship; courts administering laws that sprang from and sustained America's enduring values and principles; and elected officials responsibly conducting the public's business. By such efforts would the millions of immigrants arriving in America become upright, productive, and law-abiding.[10]

But what did Americanization mean for Nuevomexicanos, who had recently been incorporated into the United States and found themselves aliens in their native land? Beveridge thought an infusion of American settlers would be the best hope for the Southwest. To him, Americanization meant improving New Mexico and Arizona through extinguishing their cultural heritage: "You have the so-called Mexican population overwhelmed by the American population, ideally located for the purpose of Americanizing within a few years the last vestige of the blood of Spain." In his stump speeches delivered during the fall 1902 political campaign, he described the nation's responsibility to Americanize New Mexico and the other territories: "American soldiers, American teachers, American administrators all are instruments of the Nation in discharging the Nation's high duty to the ancient and yet infant people which circumstance has placed in our keeping." Beveridge's embrace of U.S. imperialism in the Philippines is inseparable from his contempt for Spain, and by extension, New Mexico. "An Anglo-American supremacist," one historian wrote, "[Beveridge] identified New Mexico with the Philippines." Both were backward places, burdened by the legacy of Spain's deficiencies, and much effort would be needed "to save that soil for liberty and civilization."[11]

"Packing the Senate from Unpopulated Regions"

By 1901 Senator Nelson Aldrich recognized Beveridge's debating skills, mastery of parliamentary tactics, and facility in gaining expertise on any topic he set his mind to. Aldrich also heard in Beveridge's speeches a thread of disdain extending from the Philippines into New Mexico, which made him the ideal person to carry out Aldrich's scheme to obstruct statehood. In December Aldrich engineered the appointment of the junior senator from Indiana to chair the Senate Committee on Territories. Beveridge immediately transferred his contempt for Spain and his prescriptions for Americanizing the Philippines to his role as gatekeeper of the Union. Under Aldrich's tutelage he worked to waylay the statehood movement—even when it meant going up against other Senate Republicans and the president.[12]

Within weeks of being selected Indiana's U.S. Senator, Beveridge wrote to an influential New York editor and public intellectual, Albert Shaw. He sent him copies of "March of the Flag" and other speeches, and a friendship blossomed. Each man cultivated the other for his own ends. Beveridge craved publicity. Shaw, who had a national forum in his political magazine *Review of Reviews*, sought access to power. When Beveridge took over as chair of the Senate's Committee on Territories in December 1901, Shaw immediately wrote to him stating his opposition to New Mexico and Arizona: "The union of Oklahoma and the Indian Territory might give us a promising State which could be admitted in the course of the next year or two. I do not at all believe that New Mexico or Arizona ought to be admitted. The territorial system gives them all the home rule they need for local purposes." Shaw continued by asking Beveridge to "consider the question in its large national bearings. Too often the admission of new States has turned upon immediate party exigencies." The term "party exigencies" referred to the practice of "packing the Senate from unpopulated regions which were admitted to the Union fifteen or twenty years too soon."[13]

Shaw thought the Senate had expanded too quickly with the addition of fourteen new members since 1888, and their sectional loyalty particularly galled him. In the presidential elections of 1896, six of the seven new states voted for the Democratic candidate, William Jennings Bryan, who lost to William McKinley. Although only two of the new states went for Bryan when he again ran against McKinley (and lost) in 1900, a disturbing trend became apparent in the Senate. Among the Senators from these seven states in the Fifty-Sixth Congress (1899–1901) were two Populists (Idaho and South Dakota), two Democrats (Utah and Montana), and a Silver Republican (Washington). In the Fifty-Seventh Congress (1901–1903) the opposition made a net gain of one seat: a second Silver Republican (Washington). The Silver Republicans proved especially repugnant because they illustrated what Shaw, and Beveridge, most resented. These senators gave primary allegiance to narrow regional interests to the detriment of eastern priorities.[14]

Shaw predicted continued sectional partisanship if New Mexico and Arizona entered the Union, and such a prospect hardened his opposition. Beveridge replied promptly to Shaw and concurred in his concerns that statehood posed a threat to Republican majorities: "I tell you in the strictest confidence: my present tendency is in favor of Oklahoma and Indian Territory as a single state and the rejection of the application of New Mexico and Arizona. My reasons for this are along the lines indicated by you. The whole subject will require a careful and not a hurried study by me." Such an approach fit Beveridge's temperament, as a newspaper recognized in 1899: "He is not content with an investigation of a subject unless it is exhaustive." Throughout 1902 Beveridge applied himself to learning about New Mexico. He drew on four sources to map the territory's political and social landscape: confirmation hearings to reappoint Miguel Otero as the Territory's governor in January; testimony before his Committee on Territories in late June; data from the 1900 census (published in 1901); and hearings that he and three members of his committee held in the Territory in November. From these sources Beveridge built his case against New Mexico and Arizona's bid to become states.[15]

The same week in January that he and Shaw discussed delaying statehood, Beveridge opened hearings on President Theodore Roosevelt's reappointment of Miguel A. Otero as territorial governor. The previous summer the Interior Department and the White House reviewed, discussed, and secured Otero's written replies to allegations of malfeasance, creating a dossier reportedly of thousands of pages. President McKinley announced plans to renew Otero's appointment (and that of all other territorial federal appointees), but an assassin's bullet felled him before the process could be completed. No sooner had Theodore Roosevelt been sworn in than opponents of Otero began lobbying the president to remove the governor. Roosevelt personally liked Otero and remained indebted to him for his aid in securing volunteers for his Rough Riders in 1898. The president quickly set aside all complaints and concurred in the four-year reappointment—pending approval by the Senate's Committee on Territories.[16]

Senator Beveridge witnessed New Mexico's factionalism when the two titans of the Territory's Republican Party—Thomas B. Catron and Governor Miguel Otero—laid out vituperative charges and countercharges in formal testimony between 7 and 16 January. Catron submitted a list of thirty-one grievances to Senator Beveridge, and also to President Roosevelt, to support his allegation that Otero's administration "has been extravagant, impure, oppressive, tyrannical, partial, and has been run by rings and cliques." Otero rebutted these assertions as "1 per cent truth and 99 per cent political chicanery." Thus did the mud fly for more than a week. Finally Otero prevailed and secured committee and full Senate approval for a second term.[17]

Between June and December, Beveridge used his position as chair of the Committee on Territories to undermine support for statehood. In doing so, he cut against the grain in both the Republican and Democratic parties and turned back a nearly unanimous House of Representatives, which had approved an Omnibus Statehood Bill (House Bill 12543) in May calling for "the people of Oklahoma, Arizona, and New Mexico to form constitutions and state governments and be admitted into the Union." A historically favorable disposition toward statehood prevailed in the House, and Representative William S. Knox (R-Mass.), chair of the House Committee on Territories, introduced a statehood bill to his committee on 14 March. It received overwhelming committee support and moved to the full House on 1 April. Knox's accompanying report implored quick action: "There is neither justice nor reason in longer denying statehood to the Territories which are here through their representatives petitioning as they have again and again in the past." Anticipating arguments over the so-called fitness issue, Knox reminded his colleagues of the territory's accomplishments: "Cities and towns, with all that modern civilization demands, homes of culture and refinement, schools and higher institutions of learning, public and private charitable institutions, everywhere the free church and free press. These are not the monuments of the Indian nor the Mexican, the idle nor the vicious." Knox concluded his appeal by endorsing New Mexicans as "a patriotic people," vowed they were worthy of "enjoying the benefits of American citizenship," and brushed aside all remaining objections by averring, "If education, integrity, and devotion to American institutions make the bulwark that insures recognition, then Congress, in our judgment, should by legal enactment admit her to the sisterhood of States."[18]

Knox used purposeful rhetoric in his unqualified endorsement of New Mexico's loyalty to "American institutions." He explicitly affirmed they met all the goals and values prerequisite to joining the Union. His report convinced most of his colleagues, and the Omnibus Statehood Bill passed the House with overwhelming bipartisan support on 9 May. Next it went to the Senate's Committee on Territories, where Chairman Beveridge gave it a hostile reception.

"The Forty-Sixth [Bill] New Mexico Has Had before Congress"

Beveridge had not intended to hold hearings on the House bill until the end of the year. But on 23 June the Senate learned of his planned delay, and a floor fight ensued to remove the bill from Beveridge's hands and place it before the full body. This challenge prompted him to relent and schedule hearings on the final days of the session. Beveridge's decision to convene hearings pleased fellow Republican Bernard S. Rodey, New Mexico's new delegate to Congress. As he prepared to testify, he felt confident of statehood's prospects, even telling newspaper reporters beforehand that the committee would soon approve the bill. Optimism came naturally to Rodey, as did a quick smile to his pleasant face. Born fifty-six years earlier in County Mayo, Ireland, Delegate Rodey distinguished himself by tirelessly promoting his adopted homeland. Dubbed "Mr. Statehood" for his boosterism, he delivered countless impassioned addresses, and whenever anyone of influence spoke favorably about New Mexico, Rodey immediately sent a personal note thanking him.[19]

The Senate committee's Saturday morning session on 28 June opened with Rodey explaining why New Mexico merited statehood. He mentioned all the gains the Territory had made in the twenty years he had lived there, including how legislation he sponsored—and the Territory's legislature approved—expanded public education over the past dozen years. He described the contributions new settlers made to the Territory by helping towns to grow and businesses to open. He also praised the homesteaders in the eastern half of the Territory for creating ranches and farms. But the morning had its disappointments, too. The first came when Senator Beveridge, the person Rodey most needed to impress, excused himself and turned the gavel over to Senator Knute Nelson (R-Minn.).

No doubt Rodey felt more at ease when the session resumed at 2:30 P.M. and Senator Beveridge settled in. But the tenor of the hearings quickly turned to confrontation as Beveridge directed his full and critical attention to Delegate Rodey and his companion Major William H. H. Llewellyn, a fifty-one-year-old attorney from Las Cruces and former officer in the Rough Riders. Senator Beveridge thumbed through the stenographer's transcript of the morning's testimony and began firing questions as his eyes landed on remarks that displeased him. One particularly irritating comment involved Rodey's assertions about "carpetbaggers"—that too many government officials sent to New Mexico were outsiders lacking an understanding of the Territory (an ironic complaint coming from an Irish immigrant). Beveridge, a skilled trial attorney, launched into a blistering cross-examination of Rodey and Llewellyn intent on discrediting the notion the Territory suffered under its appointed officials.[20]

Beveridge reminded them that Governor Miguel A. Otero was not a carpetbagger. His reference to Governor Otero made a point, but it completely missed the larger significance, which was that complaints about the undue influence of outsiders referred to the power struggle for control of the Territory's Republican Party. During Otero's first term as governor, influential Euro-American and Nuevomexicano leaders had built a splinter Republican Party to challenge the leadership of Thomas B. Catron and his wing of the party. But they lacked the money Catron and his cronies marshaled. In particular, Catron had the full support of the major railroad in the Territory, the Atchison, Topeka, and Santa Fe Railway (AT&SF). Moreover, backing that corporation's New Mexico projects was Wall Street investor Levi P. Morton, a powerful Republican who headed one of the largest banks in the United States and was a former vice president of the United States (1889–93).

To go up against such formidable interests, Otero and Llewellyn needed powerful allies. In 1901 they traveled to Pennsylvania and met with financiers in Pittsburgh and Philadelphia as well as with the state's two influential Republican U.S. Senators—Matthew Quay and Boies Penrose. Out of their contacts emerged a new business, the Pennsylvania Development Company, which invested in New Mexico in support of Otero and Llewellyn's plans. Their emissary was William H. "Bull" Andrews, and his company, the Santa Fe Central Railroad, became a principal financial conduit for Pennsylvania money. Beveridge appropriated the discussion of carpetbaggers to attack Andrews's financial interests in the Territory and thereby derail statehood.

Andrews was an easy target, in part because Llewellyn seemed not to have realized the trap Beveridge led him into during his interrogation. Llewellyn spoke enthusiastically about the importance of expanding railroads and mentioned that Andrews and a group of Pennsylvania investors had agreed to build a new line in the Territory. No doubt Llewellyn naively thought it helped to drop the name of nationally prominent Republicans who supported New Mexico's economic advancement. Beveridge was not impressed and stopped him. He wanted to know more about Andrews's role in the company and about the proposed railroad. Washington insiders knew all about Andrews, a former head of the Republican Party in Pennsylvania and a protégé of Senator Matthew Quay, the political boss of Philadelphia who had recently been acquitted in a corruption case. Quay also had led the attempt the previous week to remove statehood from Beveridge's control.[21]

Beveridge despised men like Quay and Andrews who he believed abused their positions and skirted justice. Nothing angered Beveridge more than money-making schemes floated by railroad interests. Seemingly oblivious to his irritation, the New Mexicans repeatedly praised Andrews for guiding railroad expansion in their territory. But from Beveridge's perspective as a progressive reformer, "Bull" Andrews was aligned with Otero's political machine while in the background lurked an arch political foe, Senator Quay. Rumors abounded that Quay was a major investor in Andrews's railroad and that he intended to ensure Andrews became a senator upon statehood. A biographer of Beveridge summarized the senator's conclusion that the quest for statehood was being used for personal gain: "Federal law limited the amount of Territorial indebtedness. Statehood would remove that stumbling block—and Quay was not the man to begrudge a friend a favor."[22]

Andrews, sixty years old when he came to southern New Mexico in 1899, had been in the territory less than three years and already his presence complicated the prospects for becoming a state. But Rodey's testimony also created problems for statehood, most notably when he complained about mistakes in the official census of 1900, which he denounced as "absolutely wrong and worthless." He sought to rebut the "general impression [held] all over the country that New Mexico is somewhat of a crude place." He ticked off the errors: illiteracy was much lower than the 40 percent reported; "about three-fifths of our population are people from the States, who have come in since [1848] and their descendants"; the total population is closer to 300,000 than the 195,310 reported in the census; and "a very large majority [of Nuevomexicanos] speak English as well as Spanish." An impassioned Rodey informed Beveridge that House Bill 12543 was "the forty-sixth New Mexico has had before Congress for admission to the Union." He reminded Beveridge that a quarter-century earlier the Congress "said that because our people were so illiterate and so ignorant they would not let us in." Conditions were now different. "The citizens of this country whose minds were filled with ideas with reference to conditions twenty [-five] years ago have now a wholly inadequate idea of her condition [today]." [23]

"We Are Not Ready to Support Statehood"

Rodey's assertions about census errors coupled with his claim that New Mexico was ready for statehood played directly into Beveridge's plans to expose the territory's unfitness to enter the Union. Rodey presented him a charge to investigate—errors in the federal census—and a group of vulnerable witnesses—census workers, known as enumerators. Approximately four hundred New Mexico men and a few women were part of a vast army of 59,373 temporary federal employees nationwide serving as enumerators and field supervisors for the 1900 census. In New Mexico, the census takers had just thirty days to cover the entire Territory. Walking or riding mule, horse, buggy, or train, they traveled to complete their count. San Miguel County had the largest population and dispatched seventy-eight census workers, almost all of whom were Nuevomexicanos. One census worker reportedly "traveled 1000 miles on horseback to collect 600 names." They asked questions in twenty-eight categories of all people the government considered "white," or Euro-Americans and Nuevomexicanos, as well of those labeled "colored—Negro, Chinese, Japanese." American Indians fell into a separate category of "colored," and they were asked only ten questions. The dual tasks of completing the count and ensuring its thoroughness sometimes proved mutually exclusive. Even Governor Miguel A. Otero acknowledged that "No doubt many [residents] were overlooked as the cost to an enumerator [to travel to remote areas] was frequently much more than he was paid."[24]

Beveridge headed a four-member Senate investigative subcommittee that traveled west in mid-November, after the fall elections. The three Republicans and one Populist on the subcommittee spent most of their time in New Mexico, where they grilled eighty-five witnesses and collected 120 pages of testimony during stops at Las Vegas, Santa Fe, Albuquerque, Las Cruces, El Paso, and Carlsbad. But Beveridge had decided what he would report before ever calling a witness. Shortly after Congress recessed at the end of June, Beveridge wrote Minnesota Senator Knute Nelson seeking advice on how to derail the Omnibus Statehood Bill when the Senate resumed deliberations in early December. They agreed "that Oklahoma and Indian Territory ought to be admitted as one state," but they would oppose statehood for New Mexico and Arizona because "neither is fit to become states, and our investigation should be largely confined to those two territories."[25]

A comparison between the Territory of New Mexico and his home state of Indiana gave Beveridge ample reason to oppose statehood. The census reported the following breakdown for the 195,310 people living in the Territory: about 13,200 were American Indians; 135,000 Nuevomexicanos (69.1 percent); 31,000 Euro-Americans, who had emigrated from the United States; 14,000 foreign-born whites, of whom 6,800 were from Mexico; 1,600 blacks; and 340 Chinese. In Indiana, out of a total population of 2,516,462, the number of whites totaled 2,459,000 (97.7 percent), and the remainder were 57,500 blacks, 243 American Indians, and 207 Chinese. Other comparisons from the 1900 census reinforce just how different the Territory of New Mexico was from Indiana: population density per square mile, 70 in Indiana and 1.6 in New Mexico; literacy, 95.4 percent in Indiana and 66.8 percent in New Mexico (but greatly improved from the Territory's 35 percent in the 1880 census). The most damning statistic involved the number of Nuevomexicanos who spoke only Spanish. Census officials were only responsible for tallying the number of "white persons of foreign parentage" who spoke no English, and in New Mexico this included 8,272 individuals, of whom more than 7,000 were from Mexico. But the enumerators in New Mexico actually collected data on native-born residents who did not speak or understand English. "Such persons number 53,931 and constitute 51.1 per cent of all native white persons of native parentage 10 years [old] and upward." Before he ever set foot in New Mexico, Beveridge read the census data as proof Nuevomexicanos were unfit for statehood.[26]

Beveridge's subcommittee called numerous witnesses to gauge the success of three key agents of Americanization—public schools, courts, and public officials. A school principal in Las Vegas spoke English haltingly, and when Beveridge asked the superintendent of schools in Bernalillo County to identify Christopher Columbus, he replied, "I no know him." A court official in Santa Fe had scant familiarity with the U.S. Constitution and had only read an excerpt in Spanish. Moreover, some officials sang the praises of "Bull" Andrews and pleaded for more government help in building railroads in the Territory. But the census enumerators were the most numerous witnesses interrogated. The subcommittee's questions put them on the defensive, and all admitted that they had not counted everyone in their assigned areas. Beveridge's motive quickly became evident to reporters in Santa Fe, the second stop: "There was a general impression that the committee is following a line of investigation that is really the strongest against statehood."[27]

Beveridge's investigation was only half of his plan. He needed a publicity hook that encapsulated the many problems he found. He did not get quite what he hoped for from the only Nuevomexicano witness who volunteered to testify against statehood—sixty-four-year-old Martínez Amador from Las Cruces. Amador said his generation of Nuevomexicanos were "ignorant," and "we are not ready to support statehood yet for about ten years, until our children grow up" and are educated in American schools. The incident that did become the publicity coup was the Bernalillo County school superintendent's unfamiliarity with Christopher Columbus. Beveridge relished the irony that the man who planted Spain's flag in the New World should be unknown in New Mexico, and similarly pundits and journalists in Washington, D.C., seized on it to lampoon Nuevomexicanos. Soon the exchange over Columbus took on a life of its own. Reportedly Beveridge recast the story in Senate cloakrooms so that the question became, "When did Christopher Columbus die?" The superintendent's reply, "What! Is Cristoforo dead?" elicited much guffawing among Beveridge's colleagues. By

1905 a long piece in the *New York Times* retold it as an exchange in which the school superintendent, when asked about Columbus, was quoted as saying, "Sí, Señor, very well I know him. He lives over there—down street."[28]

"Unlike Us in Race, Language, and Social Customs"

In addition to exaggerating stories, Beveridge also trolled for nationally known witnesses to deliver testimony critical of New Mexico when his committee reconvened in early December. Beveridge understood that his effort to stymie statehood could succeed only if he rallied public and official opinion to his position, so he launched a quiet opposition with the help of Albert Shaw. Calling this effort a "matter of patriotic duty," Beveridge enlisted Shaw to find experts to tell "the *truth* [emphasis in original] concerning the soil, its aridity, the impossibility of further population till irrigation shall have done its work and the character of the present population." He also entreated Shaw to recruit "any authors like Owen Wooster [sic], Fred Remington and that crowd [who] can help me in this seriously important work." Wister had no firsthand knowledge of New Mexico, whereas Remington had repeatedly visited the Territory, most recently while sketching in October and November 1900. Both men declined to become involved.[29]

Shaw succeeded in enlisting his close friend Nicholas Murray Butler to help Beveridge. Butler, the nation's foremost authority on education, had headed Columbia's Teachers College prior to being named president of the university in 1902 (a position he held until 1945). Butler adamantly opposed statehood for New Mexico largely because of the deficiencies in its schools. In an essay written in 1900 he summed up turn-of-the-century educational beliefs: "The future of democracy is bound up with the future of education." But illiteracy posed a major obstacle to such accomplishments, and in his essay he lamented that among all states and territories west of the Mississippi only in New Mexico was illiteracy "as scandalously high as the rate found among negroes in the American South" (approaching 60 percent). He approvingly quoted Daniel Webster's famous endorsement, made in 1820, about public schooling as an agent of socialization and stability, goals achieved by "inspiring a salutary and conservative principle of virtue and of knowledge in an early age." But New Mexico's schools—with their high illiteracy and reliance on Spanish—had not yet imparted the requisite "good and virtuous sentiments" Butler identified as essential to forming new citizens. Beveridge's inquiry into the Territory's school system led him to conclude "New Mexico is in much worse condition educationally" than anyone had suspected. "The popular view in the east is that we are a rude, illiterate set out here," stated a territorial newspaper in December 1903.[30]

Albert Shaw eagerly abetted Beveridge's anti-statehood campaign. He believed, "There is hardly any question we have to deal with more serious than the admission of new States," and he planned to write about Beveridge's tour of the Southwest in the December issue of his *Review of Reviews*. Just prior to departing, Beveridge passed along negative information about New Mexico gleaned from the June hearing and urged Shaw to follow several lines of attack:

"If you say anything about it the truth ought to be told that a Democratic minority stands as a unit knowing that these territories will after the first Senators consistently send Democratic Senators to Congress and that that is their only reason [for supporting statehood]. It already appears in the [*Congressional*] *Record* that Mr. Quay's interest in the admission is due to Pennsylvania capital building a railroad under the direction of Mr. Andrews. . . ; and that Senator [Boies] Penrose's [R-Penna.] brother is a miner in Arizona." When Shaw's glowing article on Beveridge's investigation appeared, it endorsed his opposition to statehood: "We think the admission of those Territories [New Mexico and Arizona] at the present time is without justification from the larger point of view of the welfare of the United States." But whereas Beveridge leveled specific allegations of self-interest, Shaw used broad generalities, arguing that "Such issues [as statehood] should be decided upon their true merits, and quite apart from private scheming, political log-rolling, and party exigencies."[31]

Other journalists, though, pursued details Beveridge mentioned. Early in December writers for the *Chicago Tribune* exposed the self-interest pursued by advocates of statehood, and likely they had Beveridge to thank for their leads. Prior to departing, Beveridge had pledged to Senator Nelson Aldrich that his tour of the Southwest would uncover facts that "will make an unfavorable impression on the people and investors, which will set the territories back for many years." When the investigation ended, Beveridge and his entourage went to Chicago to recuperate from working nonstop for nearly two weeks. While there, Beveridge likely made good on his plan to dampen the interest of "people and investors" by relaying to journalists information he had unearthed about financial deals involving key supporters of New

Mexico becoming a state. His focus became William H. Andrews and his railroad schemes. Just prior to heading west, Beveridge noted that "If the territories are admitted the bond of the [rail]road can be sold for several points higher," and upon his return he wrote Shaw that statehood was a ploy to get Andrews "a seat in the United States Senate and also to help him to sell his bonds for his new railroad down there." Over the next three months, Beveridge consistently received editorial support from such pro-reform, clean-government newspapers as the *Chicago Tribune* and the *Chicago Inter-Ocean*, and also from the *New York Times* and the *Washington Star*. The *Washington Post* backed Quay and proponents of statehood.[32]

Whereas Shaw shied away from taking on Andrews directly, the *Chicago Tribune* seemed to relish doing so and also targeted Pennsylvania's two senators—Quay and Penrose. On 4 December 1902 the paper claimed that "a squad of Pennsylvania capitalists," made up of "close friends of the two senators, to say the least, have been behind the statehood movement for Arizona and New Mexico." The paper quoted New Mexico's and Arizona's delegates to Congress to buttress the charge that investors and their corporate backers "wanted statehood for the express purpose of securing a decided advantage in the stock market"—higher interest paid to buyers of bonds. Investors also preferred statehood because it reduced uncertainty. So long as New Mexico remained a territory, the U.S. Congress and the Supreme Court could unilaterally nullify any legislation or court decision, as each did from time to time, which chased off investors seeking a safe and stable environment in which to do business.[33]

To Quay, Penrose, and Andrews, the territories represented an economic tabula rasa onto which they expected to write a bright story of success. Between 1901 and 1906 Pennsylvania investors pumped millions of dollars into New Mexico through the Pennsylvania Development Company and its subsidiaries: the New Mexico Central Railroad, headed by William H. Andrews; the New Mexico Fuel and Iron Company, whose president Francis J. Torrance had substantial political influence nationally and access to significant sums of capital, including a "large amount of Pittsburg[h] capital invested there [New Mexico]"; the Aztec Land and Cattle Company; and the American Lumber Company. Collectively these investments generated a boom in railroads, mining, and lumber, confirming that there was money to be made in New Mexico. The "squad of Pennsylvania capitalists" expected even greater profits after statehood.[34]

Beveridge marshaled and rehearsed his arguments against statehood before returning to Washington. All his recent efforts had pointed him toward the meeting he and Senator Knute Nelson would have with the one person who carried the most weight in this matter—President Theodore Roosevelt. Beveridge already enjoyed the president's trust and respect, and he joined him in frequent lunches at the White House with two of Roosevelt's closest advisors from his years as governor—Albert Shaw and Nicholas Murray Butler. In early December Beveridge met with Roosevelt and shared the results of his investigation into New Mexico's fitness for statehood. He highlighted these in a long-winded statement provided the Senate: "On the whole the committee feels that in the course of time, when education, now only practically beginning, shall have accomplished its work; when the mass of the people, or even a majority of them, shall, in the usages and employment of their daily life, have become identical in language and customs with the great body of the American people; when the immigration of English-speaking people who have been citizens of other states does its modifying work with the 'Mexican' element—when all these things have come to pass, the committee hopes and believes that this mass of people, unlike us in race, language, and social customs, will finally come to form a creditable portion of American citizenship."[35]

President Roosevelt had been mulling over statehood for some time, as will be discussed in the next chapter, but on 2 December 1902 he signaled a major shift in position by omitting any reference to the Territories in his annual message to Congress. The omission disturbed those who, like Pennsylvania Senator Matthew Quay, had counted on the president's support in the upcoming fight to pass the Omnibus Statehood Bill.

"This Homogeneousness We Must Adhere to and Maintain"

President Theodore Roosevelt likely felt conflicted as he dictated a letter in early December explaining himself to Senator Quay. He owed much to the aging Pennsylvania senator, including his decisive support in the summer of 1900 at the Republican convention in Quay's hometown of Philadelphia which helped Roosevelt garner the nomination for the vice presidency. Now Roosevelt wrote to share his reservations about a matter the senator eagerly sought—statehood for New Mexico and Arizona: "I have been talking with Senator Beveridge as well as with Senator Nelson about the territories which are to be admitted as States, and I am very seriously concerned by the facts presented to me in reference to New Mexico and Arizona. I should like to have a chance of talking the matter over with you, for the facts as laid before me do certainly make a strong case against the admission of these 2 territories. I am anxious to see you." Senator Quay did not take this news well, but he also realized his real foe was Beveridge. The two sat on the eleven-member Committee on Territories, which was split six to five, with Quay and four Democrats supporting statehood.[36]

Rather quickly the political calculations of both sides in the statehood debate became high drama. Beveridge had expected to take on influential Republicans and seemed to welcome a fight. Just before leaving for New Mexico in November he cautioned Senator Aldrich about likely Republican defections over a statehood vote. He especially worried about "Quay, Penrose, Wellington, and the Nevada Senators," and he unsuccessfully beseeched Aldrich to enforce party discipline and solidarity by making the vote on the territories a caucus matter. As predicted, Quay and Penrose fought tenaciously, which made for fascinating political journalism as newspapers had a field day describing the Republican infighting. The *Chicago Tribune* trumpeted the intraparty melee with the headlines "STATEHOOD BILL STARTS SCANDAL" and "QUAY BOLTS TO DEMOCRATS." The paper reported Quay expected to carry all the Democrats in the Senate and "by picking up a few republicans here and there could pass the omnibus statehood bill over the head and in spite of the protest of every recognized republican leader in the senate."[37]

A consummate vote counter, Quay tallied at least eight fellow Republicans among his supporters. These men swung in line behind him for a variety of reasons: some had personal loyalty such as Maryland and New York senators George L. Wellington and Thomas C. Platt, respectively; others—including Nevada's two Republicans—showed regional loyalty by supporting another western state. Still others had economic and personal links to New Mexico, including Joseph Foraker (Ohio), whose brother was appointed U.S. marshal in the territory in 1897 and served for over a decade; Stephen Elkins (W.Va.), a former resident and delegate to Congress from New Mexico who remained close to his former law partner Thomas Catron; Addison Foster (Wash.) whose state's timber interests sold "lots of lumber down in Arizona and New Mexico," and John Mitchell (Ore.), from whom Quay called in a past favor to secure his vote. The thirty-five Democratic senators eagerly sought more western states in the expectation voters there would quickly shift electoral support to their party.[38]

As Quay prepared to fight his fellow Republicans, he had a slight tactical advantage. He had ensured at the end of June 1902 that the Senate would take up the bill as "unfinished business to continue from day to day until disposed of." Beveridge would be forced to filibuster, but doing so meant holding hostage all legislation until the statehood bill had come to a vote. The brewing intraparty rivalry worried President Roosevelt. Statehood had always been a second-tier issue in the president's legislative queue behind such key domestic priorities as regulation of trusts and revision of tariffs or in foreign affairs securing trade reciprocity with Cuba and pursuing a canal across Panama. Feuding within his party threatened to devour the limited time remaining and therefore possibly derail final approval of his legislative priorities.

Consequently the Senate agreed to sit as a committee of the whole when it formally took up the Omnibus Statehood Bill on 10 December 1902, and further agreed to divide the time each day to consider other legislation until two in the afternoon and then devote the balance of the day, generally between two to four hours, to the statehood bill. But these arrangements meant Beveridge had the formidable task of lining up speakers to "debate" the bill until daily adjournment. Any break in his orchestrated debate, even if only for a few seconds, and Quay would pounce and call for a final vote. For the first six weeks or so, a fairly predictable process unfolded. It began with Republican members of the subcommittee speaking at considerable length, beginning with Senators Nelson and Beveridge during the second week of December. They read into the record the entire report of their trip and some related documents from experts familiar with the territories. The next week subcommittee member William P. Dillingham (R-Vt.) spoke for two days.[39]

Following the holiday recess, debate resumed in early January. The afternoon of Wednesday, 7 January is representative of the tactics and tone adopted by opponents for the next two weeks. Beveridge immediately lodged a procedural challenge claiming the Committee of the Whole lacked a quorum and therefore the bill could not be taken up that day. A roll call ensued, and after some time forty-six senators out of ninety were counted present and debate commenced. Beveridge requested a reading into the record of a resolution passed the previous day in which Oklahoma citizens endorsed statehood in union with the Indian Territory. For the next hour Beveridge parried with Senator Quay and several Southern Democrats over what weight to attach to resolutions from some Oklahoma tribes protesting incorporation with the rest of the Territory. In these exchanges Beveridge alternated between being polite, succinct, and matter-of-fact and then turning, sarcastic, verbose, and bombastic.

Repeatedly throughout the hour-plus Beveridge devoted to these petitions, he trotted out the disclaimer that "I did not expect, Mr. President, to utter more than three or four sentences when I rose." He coyly blamed the supporters of statehood for needlessly extending the day's discussion. A clearly exasperated Senator Quay retorted, "I do not wish to induce the Senator to continue his remarks. I give notice of that. I desire to reach a vote on this bill." Instead of quickening the pace, Beveridge slowed it even more through protracted exchanges over a host of questions relating to the Indians of Oklahoma; by the time he finished describing them he concluded "a very large number are pure white men, so far as blood is concerned, quite as white as we are." Beveridge deftly dismissed any race-based objections to Oklahoma's bid for statehood by asserting that nearly half a million whites lived in the Territory and only 10 percent of the eighty-seven thousand Indians there were "full-blood." He omitted entirely any mention of the cultural heritage of Native peoples in Oklahoma and instead stressed how much Oklahoma and its Indian Territory resembled the rest of America.[40]

When attention finally turned to New Mexico a wholly different tone emerged. Senator Nelson rose and began discussing the course of Americanization in the Territory, contending that New Mexico was "more of a Spanish country than an American country." In closely argued remarks he drew extensively on data collected for the 1900 census and testimony gathered over the previous half-year. His conclusions repeated a familiar refrain regarding New Mexico's unfitness for statehood. "In respect to language, in respect to education, in respect to intelligence, and all that goes to make up the leading and prominent characteristics of a self-governing American citizen," Nelson intoned, "the people of that Territory were to a large extent deficient." He further claimed the people of the Territory "are still, Mr. President, to a large extent un-American," by which he meant they lacked "homogeneousness in language and in fitness for self-government [which] is one of the fundamental elements and essentials of the American Union. . . . This homogeneousness we must adhere to and maintain under all circumstances." Its clear absence in New Mexico, Nelson argued, would long persist because the people's "education and training are far from complete" and therefore "New Mexico should for some years to come remain in preparation, training, and development for statehood."

Much irony exists in Senator Nelson's attack on Nuevomexicanos because no one in the Senate more exemplified the contradictions inherent in Americanization. Born in Norway, Nelson came to the United States at about age ten, and for the rest of his life he spoke heavily accented English. He had a double standard when it came to use of a foreign language in school. Although he railed against students using Spanish in New Mexico, Nelson had successfully sponsored legislation early in his career allowing Norwegian to be taught and spoken in Minnesota classrooms. His biographer characterized his attacks on Nuevomexicanos and other minorities as "elitist, Anglocentric, undemocratic, [and] culturally condescending."[41]

Nelson not only lambasted the people of New Mexico, he criticized everything about where they lived—the land, water, agriculture, and mining—claiming that "the country will be in a dormant and comatose condition" for a very long time. Irrigation offered a potential solution, and in June 1902 the president had signed a bill committing the government, through the Bureau of Reclamation, to such an endeavor in the arid West and Southwest. But Nelson told his fellow senators to be wary of such undertakings for two reasons: "Irrigation is a work that will take years," and it will be accompanied by unbridled opportunism "through the schemes and plans of promoters, stockjobbers, and schemers who will come with specious plans for irrigation and will want bonds issued for their schemes."[42]

And so it went day after day over the next two weeks. The opponents bludgeoned the Territory, endlessly arguing that "the character of the industrial and material and intellectual development which has taken place, the whole history of the past, and the present conditions all go to show that New Mexico is deficient in all those essential conditions so vital to the success of the American Union." The arguments changed no senator's mind since both sides had drawn their conclusions well in advance. Yet Beveridge droned on, and as one senator commented to colleagues after looking in on the Senate proceedings from a cloakroom door, "'The [Indiana] Wabash [River] is still overflowing its banks.'"[43]

While Beveridge's words rolled on and on, a majority of senators soon signaled their intention to allow New Mexico to enter the Union. Senator

Quay's tally of support held up on the first key procedural vote in the debate held on Wednesday, 21 January. Although only two-thirds of the Senate's members attended the day's session, the pro-statehood side secured thirty-six votes, while a rump of twenty-seven Republicans opposed it. Quay and everyone else knew he had the votes to prevail, and immediately Senator Beveridge shifted tactics from a protracted debate to a series of delaying actions aimed at killing it by running out the clock on the Fifty-Seventh Congress. He launched new and truly desperate maneuvers to stymie a final vote; no tactic was too odious to be employed. Beveridge reduced the time allotted to statehood debates by diverting discussion to a matter very much on the minds of Southern Democrats—President Roosevelt's nomination of African Americans to government positions. Beveridge, ever the opportunist, used their ire to his advantage, an approach that drew comment by the *New York Times*: "The Southern Senators cannot refrain from talking *ad libitum* [without restraint] on the President's policy in making appointments of colored persons, and the longer they debate the matter the more they aid the opposition to the Statehood measure. It is believed the Republican leaders will encourage the race debate for a week or more, unless Senator Quay should succeed in getting an agreement for a vote on the Statehood bill." Because Southern Democrats provided the majority of votes in favor of statehood, Quay did not risk alienating them by pressing for an end to their attacks on Roosevelt's alleged favoritism toward blacks. The Southern Democrats diluted the time allotted to debate statehood, and soon securing a quorum introduced further delay.[44]

Still, by early February it seemed probable the Omnibus Statehood Bill would come up for a vote. It nearly happened one afternoon when Senator Quay came within seconds of successfully forcing a final vote before a frantic Beveridge outwitted him. New York Senator Chauncey M. Depew, an infamous reactionary on the subject of foreigners in America, was winding up his remarks, and Beveridge realized he had no one ready to speak. He immediately rushed a note to Depew. "'You must not conclude. You must hold the floor at all hazards until adjournment, no matter how long that is.' Senator Depew got that note just as he was uttering these words: 'In conclusion, Mr. President'—Glancing at the note he resumed: 'I was saying, Mr. President, in conclusion *upon this branch* of the question'" [emphasis in original]. Beveridge knew Depew understood almost nothing about either statehood or New Mexico, but he admired his friend's resourcefulness. What Depew engineered earned him Beveridge's lasting gratitude: "He attacked the supporters of the bill with such fierceness that in fifteen minutes he had three senators on their feet angrily interrupting him. This was just what he had designed to do—a design formed upon the instant and executed as soon as it was formed." That afternoon Depew carried on for more than four hours and resumed speaking for several hours the next afternoon. Twenty years later Depew offhandedly mentioned in his memoir that "unlimited discussion defeated no good measure, but talked many bad ones to death."[45]

Just when it seemed Beveridge might be unable to hold off Quay and proponents of statehood, he employed the ultimate trick. He disappeared for more than a week. In doing so he abused a Senate privilege that required the presence of a bill's Senate committee chair to be present when taking the final floor vote. Beveridge preemptively foiled any such attempt by hiding first in a secret third-story room at the Washington home of another opponent of statehood, Gifford Pinchot, who believed forest conservation efforts were best pursued by the federal government and not states. Pressure mounted to investigate Beveridge's unexplained absence, and not wanting to compromise his friendship with Pinchot, Beveridge stole out of town one night and took a train to Atlantic City. When he finally returned to the Senate, he threw himself and everyone he could enlist into a final flurry of parliamentary maneuvers. For seven days in late February he feigned party loyalty and even negotiated a compromise measure in a stamina-draining marathon lasting nearly seventy-two continuous hours, only to have Democrats reject it, as Beveridge must surely have known they would. During the final two weeks of February other Republicans tried to find different legislative solutions to ensure statehood, including an amendment by Senator William E. Mason (R-Ill.) added in committee to the Post Office appropriation bill providing for statehood for Oklahoma, Arizona, and New Mexico. This amendment, like all the other last-ditch efforts, failed. At noon on Wednesday, 4 March the Fifty-Seventh Congress adjourned. A biographer of Beveridge offered a succinct scorecard: "The session ended without action [on statehood]. Quay had the votes, but the parliamentary tactics of Beveridge had robbed him of a triumph."[46]

"Talking Away the Time"

In New Mexico, criticism of Beveridge and his subcommittee had been gaining momentum since his November investigation. A brief review of coverage from English- and Spanish-language newspapers in Las Cruces encapsulates how New Mexicans reacted to events as they unfolded in Washington. At the end of November, a Las Cruces newspaper summarized the gloomy mood: "Many of the territorial papers are freely saying that an adverse report by the committee is a foregone conclusion and that there is little hope for statehood. . . . It is entirely possible that the committee regarded the question to be, not how good we are, but, how bad are we?" Spanish-language newspapers offered a mixed message on the prospects for statehood throughout December and into January. At the end of the first week in December, *El Tiempo* observed that "Senator Beveridge as always opposes [statehood], but the territories' friends stand firm, and in Washington they say that those in favor will prevail in spite of Senator Beveridge and his supporters." As debate wrapped up in advance of the holiday recess, *El Labrador* pointed out a seeming lapse in logic in the Beveridge report, which had also been noted by at least one Eastern newspaper: "It is difficult to understand . . . how the Senate's Committee on Territories has decided that the Indians of the Indian Territory [in Oklahoma] deserve to be citizens of a sovereign state but deny this privilege to the inhabitants of New Mexico and Arizona because they are not sufficiently Americanized." By the middle of January, though, *El Tiempo* began to wonder about Beveridge's strategy in proposing joint statehood for the Indian Territory within Oklahoma. Beveridge and a few cohorts were expected to take a week presenting their side, after which "Other Republican Senators have agreed to speak in opposition to the proposed joint statehood, and it is assumed there will be no less than fifteen speeches by this side." Following these a few Republicans, including Senator Foraker, were to speak in favor of joint statehood, all of which will "take up much [valuable] time." Full-scale delaying tactics were in place.[47]

During February *El Tiempo* and *El Labrador* turned increasingly distrustful of Beveridge. Early in the month both newspapers stridently condemned one of his desperate measures. They reported that Beveridge received a "large number" of anonymous letters threatening assassination and he read "some of them in the Senate," claiming they came from

New Mexico and Arizona. *El Tiempo* retorted, "No . . . these are his ruses, done to bring him the Senate's sympathy and to gain votes." *El Labrador* acknowledged the possibility that such letters might exist, but they were surely sent as a joke, and they categorically stated "there do not exist in New Mexico anarchists who can carry out such misdeeds." By mid-month *El Tiempo* fully grasped Beveridge's intent: "The enemies of statehood are making it possible to kill the proposal by talking away the time," and Beveridge did exactly that. Sarcasm overcame *El Labrador*. In noting that an American humorist once called burros "Arizona mockingbirds," the paper announced, "We will write the Honorable Albert J. Beveridge asking him if he is kin of the long-eared western songbird." Their comment turned on the word burro. It suggested that Beveridge was stubborn and brayed like a donkey and that he was, in the colloquial metaphor, a stupid jackass.[48]

Prior to the statehood debate the *Las Cruces Progress* noted that an adverse report by the Senate's subcommittee would "show themselves to be the basest of base political tricksters." Forty-four years later a historian of Beveridge's home state concurred: "[Beveridge] believed almost nothing very deeply, and nearly everything he did believe deeply was false or base." This assessment has echoes of William Gladstone's comment upon learning of the death of his archrival Benjamin Disraeli in 1881: "All display, without reality or genuineness." Beveridge was fighting a rearguard action against the tide of opinion in the Congress and in the public in favor of adding new states, which is why he turned to desperate measures between June 1902 and March 1903 to defeat the statehood bill.[49]

Among New Mexico's politicians, the demise of the Omnibus Statehood Bill brought differing responses. Delegate Rodey tried to be upbeat in a letter printed in *El Labrador* in mid-March. "We feel that this is a delay and not a defeat." Rodey also attempted to add comments to the *Congressional Record* that "answered many of the allegations made against New Mexico by certain senators during the debate on statehood." Senator Beveridge objected and Rodey's rebuttal was omitted. Governor Otero blamed President Roosevelt. Otero believed that Roosevelt should never have yielded this issue to Senator Beveridge. Instead he ought to have stuck by his pledge made at the first reunion of the Rough Riders in Las Vegas in late June 1899: "If New Mexico wants to be a state, you can count me in, and I will go to Washington to speak for you or do anything you wish." Otero concluded Roosevelt had broken his word: "Time was to show, however, that his enthusiasm vanished when [Roosevelt] found himself in a key position where he could have carried out his pledge if he had wished." Otero also subscribed to a view touted by some opponents—that Roosevelt "never favored statehood" and would have vetoed it had it passed. The president had disappointed many New Mexicans, who by the end of 1903 felt increasingly that "the rights of the territories to admission" did not count.[50]

CHAPTER THREE

"Politically Realistic Alternatives"

Vice President Theodore Roosevelt delivered a speech at Colorado Springs in early August 1901 entitled "Manhood and Statehood" to commemorate the twenty-fifth anniversary of Colorado's entry into the Union. Among the several thousand in the audience were New Mexicans celebrating the third reunion of the Rough Riders; three of the four incoming officers were from the Territory. Roosevelt had honed his speech's twin themes over the previous fifteen years, having first linked manhood and statehood in a Fourth of July address in the Dakota Territory in 1886. His four-volume *Winning of the West* (1889–96), which told of the young nation's growth from 1769 to 1807, expanded on the themes. He never turned loose of them, revisiting them in an address delivered at the Sorbonne in Paris in 1910. Found in these three speeches between 1886 and 1910—but especially in 1901—are Roosevelt's ideas about how statehood should be pursued and what qualities were expected in those seeking to enter the Union.[1]

Colorado Springs was a perfect setting to talk about America's recent conquest of the West. The Rockies dominated the background, a visible reminder of nature's power. Roosevelt's speech was a creation story in which manhood begat statehood. He described how authentic men—Euro-Americans all—remade the West, conquering both people and places, efforts that culminated in statehood. "Save only the preservation of the Union itself," Roosevelt told his audience, "no other task has been so important as the conquest and settlement of the West. This conquest and settlement has been the stupendous feat of our race for the century just closed." His comments articulated a point of view espoused by many Americans in the final decades of the nineteenth century—that Euro-American men fulfilled the country's destiny to take control of the continent from the Mississippi River to the Pacific Ocean. Roosevelt had looked forward to this conquest in his 1886 address: "We have been told that in the end we are to fall heir to most of the continent. Well, I think so myself." In 1901 he celebrated that accomplishment.[2]

Roosevelt had remade himself from a fragile, asthmatic child into a vigorous, take-charge man in large part by going west in 1884, and he believed his transformation was being writ large in American history. Men yearning to prove themselves became masters in new domains secured by their physical prowess. Heralding a new century, Roosevelt in Colorado celebrated the triumphal progress of "our race" in "the way in which our people have filled a vacant continent with self-governing commonwealths, knit into one nation." Warming to his theme of Euro-American conquest forging civilization, he told the crowd, "And of all this marvelous history, perhaps the most wonderful portion is that which deals with the way in which the Pacific Coast and the Rocky Mountains were settled." Roosevelt proclaimed, "The winning of the West was the greatest epic feat in the history of our race" because it produced "victory after victory in the ceaseless strife waged against wild men and wild nature." The territories began as military outposts to subdue Indians, expanded as new settlers arrived, and gradually evolved under civilian takeover until eventually new states emerged.[3]

Conquest of "wild men and wild nature" reshaped people and landscape, according to Roosevelt, "because the conditions of development in the West have steadily tended to accentuate the peculiarly American characteristic of its people." In predicting this inevitable triumph Roosevelt embraced Americanization, or the planting of American institutions and values in conquered lands. He saw this vitally important process at work in New Mexico, and heralded it in a letter to the head of the four-hundred-member Republican Club of Las Vegas in September 1900. "I do not have to argue for expansion to you in New Mexico for you are yourselves the best possible example of it. You or your fathers have expanded into the waste places of the great Southwest exactly as America is now expanding. You have red blood in your veins, and are not of the kind to tolerate a nation shirking its work."[4]

Roosevelt's phrases "waste places" and "shirking its work" are reworkings of his ideas on statehood and manhood. Growth and prosperity, in his view, could be gained only through the benefits of late-nineteenth-century modernization. Developmental capitalism in the form of railroad expansion and new settlements by Euro-Americans would accomplish economic and political transformations that Roosevelt believed were beyond the capacity of American Indians and Nuevomexicanos. Moreover, just as men who "have red blood in their veins" were carrying civilization to other lands, principally the Philippines, so, too, could Euro-American men in the Southwest replicate the nation's colonial project, but with a key difference. Their territorial status was temporary, a necessary phase preparatory to statehood. But the transition hinged on right living, personal responsibility, character, obligation, fortitude, and liberty. The single word encompassing all of these was "righteousness," and its advocacy became his lifelong obsession. Upon Roosevelt's death a devoted friend remembered him as "a preacher of righteousness . . . he made right living seem the natural thing." New Mexicans listening to Roosevelt in Colorado Springs understood what was expected of them. They must prove themselves worthy, fulfill their destiny, and claim their prize—sovereignty. Thus were territories transformed into states.[5]

In late April 1910 Roosevelt spoke at the Sorbonne. He started in a familiar vein: "The pioneer days pass; the stump-dotted clearings expand into vast stretches of fertile farm land; the stockade clusters of log cabins change into towns." But quickly he took a different tone, one focusing on what happened after manhood begat statehood. In essence, travail followed triumph. "To the hard materialism of the frontier days succeeds the hard materialism of an industrialism." Gone was Roosevelt's unrestrained embrace of conquest. In its place was a critique of the excesses of modernity in industrialization—and the monopolistic, big-business trusts directing it, which were "far more conscious of [their] rights than of [their] duties." But Roosevelt believed a new stage of civilization was emerging, one defined by a rejection of the excesses of capital concentrated into corporate conglomerates: "As the country grows, its people, who have won success in so many lines, turn back to try to recover the possessions of the mind and the spirit, which perforce their fathers threw aside in order better to wage the first rough battles for the continent their children inherit." Roosevelt lauded the "first rough battles" in Colorado Springs, but in Paris he offered a more contemplative assessment of nation building, one that took into account widespread changes associated with the transition from a nineteenth-century agrarian economy to twentieth-century industrialization.[6]

During his presidency Roosevelt's view of modern life evolved, and by 1910 its unsettling complexities had led him to a nostalgic yearning for a simpler time, for the manhood he experienced and admired in the frontier West. Hence his call to "turn back to try to recover the possessions of the mind and the spirit" lost in the pell-mell rush toward modernity. Roosevelt was profoundly shaped by nineteenth-century western experiences, but these proved ever more at odds with twentieth-century practices, especially the reality of corporations—"industrialism"—crushing individuals through monopolies. But the winds of change in early twentieth-century America never blew Roosevelt off the course he set for statehood. He remained steadfastly tied to late-nineteenth-century ideas, which had profound consequences for New Mexico.

Roosevelt and Beveridge, born four years apart, were products of the same intellectual milieu. In embracing imperialism, each promoted manhood in terms familiar to late-nineteenth-century audiences—strength of character and Euro-American superiority. Their imperialist views also coincided in regarding Spain as decadent and needing to be overthrown in the Caribbean and the Philippines. Moreover, they shared a disdain common among Euro-Americans, who "perceived Nuevomexicano peasants as practically another Indian tribe—wild, savage, superstitious, and ignorant." Both were also reformers committed at the turn of the century to bringing about good government by channeling their paternalism into progressivism. But they parted ways over a fundamental definition of statehood. Beveridge in "March of the Flag" branded the New Mexico Territory as hapless and incapable of self-government. Roosevelt saw the Territory in conventional nineteenth-century political terms—as an incubator of home rule.[7]

Roosevelt's ideas on statehood were part of a political problem that had concerned him since his student days at Harvard in the late 1870s—how best to promote participatory democracy in a republic as heterogeneous as the United States. When he spoke in Colorado in 1901, he recognized that within that issue was a political imperative peculiar to the territories: to keep "our race" advancing until they secured sovereignty. To achieve this progress, he set an ethical standard. A Euro-American man must always "demand liberty for himself, and as a matter of pride he will see to it that others receive the liberty which he thus claims as his own." Nothing more fundamentally separated Roosevelt and Beveridge than their views of who merited liberty and therefore who benefited from statehood. According to Beveridge, the Territory's Nuevomexicano majority were unfit to govern themselves and must remain as colonists. Roosevelt saw Euro-Americans as agents of a new order who had "expanded into the waste places of the great Southwest" and were transforming it. Neither American Indians nor Nuevomexicanos had roles in Roosevelt's view of statehood. It was solely a Euro-American project. He told the Colorado Springs audience that whenever sufficient numbers of Euro-Americans "have taken possession of some great tract of empty wilderness, they should be permitted to enter the Union as a state."[8]

His use of "should" is significant. A true man always welcomed an opportunity to prove himself and, as Roosevelt explained, he had "to persevere through the long days of slow progress or of seeming failure which always come before any final triumph." The admonition to remain steadfast against all setbacks figured prominently in his Sorbonne address, too. Adversity both built and tested character—this was his experience and he generalized it for his audience in 1901 and reiterated it in 1910. In Colorado he offered a prophetic coda: "It is not given to us all to succeed, but it is given to us all to strive manfully to deserve success." In Paris he would say, "The credit belongs to the man who is actually in the arena, whose face is marred by dust and sweat and blood; who strives valiantly; . . . and who at the worst, if he fails, at least fails while daring greatly."[9]

In Roosevelt's view, the privileges of democracy were earned by those who tirelessly sought its benefits. The pursuit of statehood validated one's worthiness to aspire to attain it. Manhood for Roosevelt meant steadfast striving, and statehood became a protracted test. All Roosevelt ever really promised New Mexicans was that he would do what he could to aid their cause, but it was up to them to prove their worth and outlast all opposition. Beveridge, on the other hand, cared little about extending liberty, participatory democracy, or home rule to New Mexico. Righteousness inspired Roosevelt, but realpolitik guided Beveridge.

President Theodore Roosevelt, it has been observed, "was an intelligent and forceful person, well able to form his own conclusions or at least to select the politically realistic alternatives from the abundance of advice he was offered." His "conclusions" and the "politically realistic alternatives" he pursued between 1901 and 1909 largely overrode his personal beliefs about how manhood begat statehood. Indeed, Roosevelt's actions toward New Mexico were mainly shaped by four late-nineteenth-century developments: the statehood policy he inherited from President McKinley; his Rough Rider days; the limits of his power as president; and his shallow understanding of the land and people of the Territory.[10]

"More Water and People"

President William McKinley's trip to Buffalo, New York, in early September 1901 came exactly six months into his second term. While attending a public reception on Friday afternoon, 6 September, McKinley was shot twice at close range by Leon Czolgosz, an avowed anarchist. He succumbed to his wounds eight days later, and Theodore Roosevelt became the third vice president since 1865 to be thrust into the presidency following an assassination. A shocked nation rallied to its new leader, and New Mexicans immediately pledged their fealty and reaffirmed their deep personal affection for the former Rough Rider commander. They also honored the memory and service of President McKinley and grieved his death.[11]

During the six months of McKinley's second term New Mexicans had four encounters with him. The first—and most substantive—occurred when the president visited the Territory. His train stopped at Deming on Monday, 6 May 1901. There he spoke for about ten minutes, telling those assembled, in the words of a journalist covering the trip, "they would have to wait for statehood—that what we needed here are more water and people." The previous afternoon McKinley had conferred privately for about an hour with some New Mexicans promoting statehood. He listened respectfully, but "he had no promise to make." He did, though, acknowledge the legislature's naming of a new county after him two years earlier. He also surely heard a report on the activities of the Territory's Bureau of Immigration, which since its creation in 1880 mimicked the projects of its counterparts throughout the South and promoted the virtues of settling in New Mexico through pamphlets, advertisements, and similar booster activities.[12]

In August the Republican press enthusiastically greeted announcement of the renomination of all federal officials in New Mexico, seeing in this decision evidence that McKinley approved of the conduct of the Territory's affairs, and especially of their governor, Miguel A. Otero. On Friday, 9 August an Albuquerque rabbi, Piser Jacobs, was perhaps the last New Mexican to encounter the president. Rabbi Jacobs visited Canton, Ohio, and on impulse decided to take a ride to see President McKinley's private residence, where the president had just begun his summer vacation. To Jacobs's surprise, McKinley was outside and alone. The visitor stopped, approached the president, and presented his card, "adding at the same time that he was from New Mexico, and immediately his face lit up with interest, and smiling he extended his right hand and shook mine firmly. . . . Knowing that I was from New Mexico, his first thought was of the people and their status." After a short conversation Jacobs took his leave. The rabbi included this recollection in his eulogy on the day of national mourning, illustrating what a biographer described as McKinley's "kindly nature and innate courtesy" that disposed him to treat those he met with "dignity and politeness." McKinley never wanted to have security guards, but following his death the Secret Service added presidential protection to its duties.[13]

The fourth encounter takes us back to the assassination. Sometime toward the end of July or in early August, a young, slightly built Italian musician working in Santa Rita in Grant County reportedly told a few acquaintances that President McKinley would be killed before the first of October. Immediately following the assassination, Territorial officials arrested Antonio Maggio and brought him to Albuquerque. He was charged with conspiring to kill the president, and bond was set at ten thousand dollars. Fluent in Spanish, Maggio admitted to being an anarchist in an interview with the editor of the town's Spanish-language newspaper, *La Bandera Americana*. He claimed his goal was to overthrow monarchs and denied ever predicting McKinley's death or being involved in any plot to kill him. The paper claimed "he knows more than he is telling." The actual murderer, Leon Czolgosz, was quickly tried, convicted, and executed at the end of October 1901. Maggio was indicted by a grand jury in Las Cruces in mid-October and a trial date set for the following April, but the case against him fell apart.[14]

McKinley's death prompted Roosevelt to take decisive steps to reassure a shaken nation. He immediately pledged to carry out McKinley's policies and retained all eight of his cabinet secretaries as well as his private secretary, George B. Cortelyou, who became Roosevelt's choice to be Secretary of Commerce and Labor when Congress created that ninth cabinet department in 1903. Among the ongoing issues Roosevelt inherited was statehood for New Mexico, Arizona, Oklahoma, and the Indian Territory.

On McKinley's May trip he met with Otero in Deming and took a cautious approach. No doubt Otero briefed the president on the statehood conventions planned for the fall in Arizona and New Mexico. McKinley acknowledged the arguments of the opponents but also said he would endorse home rule "when the matter came before congress again."[15]

Both McKinley and Roosevelt believed that statehood had to be negotiated between Congress and the Territory, and that the Territory had to prove its worthiness. They shared a belief that good government required honest men, and the political facts of life in New Mexico did not look like good government. In the minds of many influential people in Washington, New Mexico's politics at the end of the nineteenth century soiled the Territory's reputation. McKinley—and likewise Roosevelt—sought to remove these stains. The cleanup began when McKinley appointed Miguel Otero as governor. The two had become acquainted a decade earlier through work on a national Republican committee, and after McKinley's election Otero sought to be the Territory's U.S. marshal. But the president had other plans. Otero's selection as governor angered Thomas B. Catron as it quickly became apparent that Otero's chief qualification was his opposition to Catron and his cronies. Roosevelt likewise supported Otero, who had been instrumental in recruiting Rough Riders, and concurred in Otero's reappointment for a second term as governor (1902–1906). The president also summarily dismissed Catron's vigorous objections to Otero and ended his access to the White House. Roosevelt's good-government ethic accounted for his contempt of Catron.

Both McKinley and Roosevelt judged human behavior in absolute moral terms, which meant they held all public officials to high standards of conduct. Each made unequivocal statements about public service as a sacred trust in 1901. In his second inaugural address, McKinley stated, "Honesty, capacity, and industry are nowhere more indispensable than in public employment. These should be fundamental requisites to original appointment and the surest guaranties against removal." Roosevelt summarized his clean government views in an essay published in 1901: "Honesty is not so much a credit as an absolute prerequisite to efficient service to the public." He staked out an uncompromising position: "We need absolute honesty in public life." These statements expressed bedrock convictions of his progressivism and were backed up by his record as police commissioner in New York City and as governor. As we will see, moral transgressions by prominent New Mexicans in the fall of 1902 disposed President Roosevelt to align with Senator Beveridge's anti-statehood position in the Fifty-Seventh Congress.[16]

Roosevelt also continued McKinley's policy of placing statehood in the second tier of legislative priorities. While both parties' platforms endorsed statehood for the territories in 1896 and 1900, Democrats repeatedly criticized Republicans in the 1900 election for failing to carry out their pledge. Democrats pointedly argued that "liberty, as well as the Constitution, follows the flag," a phrase that simultaneously tweaked Senator Beveridge's militaristic "March of the Flag" and underscored the territories' lack of basic freedoms. But throughout McKinley's first administration, domestic legislation was edged aside by foreign policy—principally the Spanish-American War of 1898 and the subsequent insurrection in the Philippines, which prompted an ongoing military presence. On the home front McKinley pressed the Congress on protective tariffs, trusts and their regulation, and monetary issues, with statehood well down on his list of priorities. He omitted mention of it in his annual report to Congress in early December 1900 and in his second inaugural address on 4 March 1901.[17]

But McKinley miscalculated one key political issue—he misread the depth of hostility to statehood. He thought the nation's parochial divisions had been consigned to the dustbin of history and claimed in his second inaugural address, "We are reunited. Sectionalism has disappeared. Division on public questions can no longer be traced by the war maps of 1861. Those old differences less and less disturb the judgment." He believed that "existing problems demand the thought and quicken the conscience of the [whole] country" and said responsibility "for their righteous settlement rests upon us all—no more upon me than upon you." In fact, though, New Mexico's bid to become a state spawned sectional rivalries. Political leaders in New England, the East, and Midwest aligned against a growing western influence in the Congress. They were not disposed to a "righteous settlement" that would alter the status quo.[18]

Upon entering the White House, Roosevelt continued McKinley's cautious, moralistic approach to the question of the Territories' future. Unlike McKinley, however, he had no illusion that admitting new states threatened the political balance of power in the Congress. Moreover, Roosevelt made a major change in his handling of statehood—he injected into the issue his affection for New Mexico.

"The Strongest Friendship for the Cause"

New Mexico had a special place in Theodore Roosevelt's heart. Throughout his life he fondly repeated a boast he first uttered early in 1899: "New Mexico raised half the Rough Riders." Actually the four hundred or so New Mexicans who accompanied him to Cuba in June 1898 formed three of the eight companies within the First United States Volunteer Cavalry, known as the Rough Riders. Fully ninety percent of New Mexico's volunteers were Euro-Americans, with the politically connected serving as officers while mostly cowboys filled the enlisted ranks. Led by U.S. Army Colonel Leonard Wood with Lt. Colonel Roosevelt as second-in-command, the New Mexican volunteers acquitted themselves valiantly and repeatedly in combat. Their courage under fire inspired Roosevelt's lifelong fondness for New Mexicans.[19]

The initial reunion of the Rough Riders, in Las Vegas, New Mexico, in late June 1899, occurred on the first anniversary of their initial battle. Roosevelt, then governor of New York, addressed several hundred of his former soldiers and pledged, "If New Mexico wants to be a state, you can count me in, and I will go to Washington to speak for you or do anything you wish." Uttered in the enthusiasm of the moment, his pledge was typical of his rhetorical flourish; to those assembled, however, and soon to all New Mexicans, it was a political promise, one they repeatedly asked him to honor. Another fateful seed in his future relationship with New Mexico was also planted at that first reunion in Las Vegas. His two most important invited guests epitomized his position between competing loyalties. On the one hand his commanding officer, Leonard Wood, personified the glory of their recent military service with the Rough Riders. But also invited was his longtime closest personal friend, Henry Cabot Lodge, Republican senator from Massachusetts. Lodge was an implacable foe of statehood and aligned with Senator Aldrich in opposing it as a threat to their—and New England's—political clout.[20]

Lodge did not make the trip, but immediately upon his return Roosevelt wrote "Dear Cabot" about his trip. At each of the train stops in eight states, "I was greeted by dense throngs exactly as if I had been a presidential candidate." This outpouring of support set Roosevelt to thinking about moving on from Albany to a national political office. He speculated on the possibly of becoming either vice president or a U.S. senator, but the posi-

tion that most interested him was secretary of war. Roosevelt's rumina-
tions, though, never got the better of his judgment: "I am not taken in by
the crowds in the west or by anything else in the way of vociferous enthusiasm for the moment. It would be five years before it would materialize and
I have never yet known a hurrah to endure five years." In the event, it was
not a "hurrah" but a "good riddance" that propelled him forward. McKinley's vice president, Garret A. Hobart, died of heart failure at age fifty-five
on 21 November 1899, and no successor was named. In New York, Roosevelt's progressivism and reform agenda increasingly angered entrenched
interests, and early in 1900 New York politicians looked ahead to the summer's Republican National Convention as a way to get Roosevelt out of the
way. They began lobbying for him to become vice president. The convention picked him, McKinley won reelection, and six months after the March
inauguration Roosevelt became president. Many in New Mexico assumed
he would soon bring them into the Union.[21]

Just a month after being sworn in, President Roosevelt cabled a statehood convention in Albuquerque to acknowledge their invitation and, with
carefully chosen words, expressed his regrets at being unable to attend. An
equally tepid response came from the leaders of the several hundred convention delegates, who noted, "That in the successor to President McKinley,
we recognize one who will with all his great ability and experience carry
out the policies so wisely begun by him." The delegates could scarcely have
grasped the import of linking Roosevelt to McKinley's policies, but very
soon they would see how Roosevelt continued the late president's moral
absolutism. Early in Roosevelt's career a journalist irritated by his sermon-
izing and moral zealousness observed, "There is an increasing suspicion
that Mr. Roosevelt keeps a pulpit concealed on his person." Once in the
White House, Roosevelt used his office as a "bully [wonderful] pulpit," and
political conditions in New Mexico frequently prompted his moralizing.[22]

"Tied to a Cow's Tail"

Roosevelt set expectations high and held people accountable, and even
amid all the demands on him he always paid close attention to the Territory
and its problems. When disquieting revelations came to light, he responded
with sharp rebukes and even removed officials whose conduct he believed
violated a civic duty to be honest and competent. Two such instances of

his wrath occurred while the Omnibus Statehood Bill was winding its way through Congress. The first involved Roosevelt's reaction to what he considered William H. Andrews's repeated deceit in raising campaign money for Senator Quay. Twice Andrews ignored laws barring mailing letters of solicitation to civil service employees. The president deemed Andrews's activity "irritating and purposeful folly," and following the second fund-raising letter he turned him over to the U.S. Attorney General to investigate after Andrews made no reply within three days to Roosevelt's telegram telling him to withdraw the solicitation. Roosevelt knew that Andrews expected to become a senator from New Mexico, and he took a dim view of Andrews's disregard for the law and disrespect of his office.[23]

The second incident casting a pall over the Territory's quest to enter the Union also involved the Department of Justice. Beginning in the fall of 1902, department attorneys conducted several investigations over more than six months into the activities of New Mexico Supreme Court Judge Daniel H. McMillan. Their inquiry pursued accusations of immoral conduct lodged against him for an alleged tryst, a transgression that deeply offended the president. The damage was more than a reputation soiled. It led Roosevelt to question how New Mexico would deal with misconduct by judges should it become a state. As he angrily told Governor Otero at a White House meeting in late 1902, "With statehood you will be burdened with dishonest judges and be forced to keep them, while as a territory they can be removed and their places filled by the President."[24]

Otero instantly realized Roosevelt's call for presidential checks against judicial impropriety jeopardized statehood. He vigorously protested to Roosevelt but could not dissuade him. The McMillan contretemps raised questions about the Territory's worthiness to be released from the president's paternalistic control. Roosevelt's White House meeting with Otero occurred precisely when a debate between pro- and anti-statehood advocates brought much of the business of the Senate to a standstill. In this supercharged atmosphere the alleged tryst and its investigations added doubt in the president's mind about New Mexico's fitness to become a state. Roosevelt eventually removed the fifty-four-year-old McMillan, a prominent attorney from New York, but not before telling Otero what he really thought ought to happen to him: "A corrupt judge ought to be taken out to the corral, tied to a cow's tail, and sh— to death."[25]

"A Happy Compromise"

Upon entering the White House, Roosevelt continued McKinley's dual agenda for New Mexico—clean up its political culture and work on getting Congress to take up an enabling bill for the Territories. The two were entwined, of course, but the latter task proved especially difficult because Roosevelt could not exercise with Congress the same overarching authority he had in New Mexico. Two factors diminished his influence—the accidental nature of his presidency and the prevailing distribution of power in Washington. Each of these tilted control toward the Congress and away from him.

Roosevelt's unexpected ascension to the presidency left him without his own national political organization or strong allegiances in Republican-dominated states, including his native New York. He had to build support while he served as president, and during 1902 and 1903 Roosevelt moved to consolidate his power. In doing so, he worked with forceful congressional leaders such as Senators Nelson Aldrich and Albert Beveridge, who opposed statehood for New Mexico, as well as Pennsylvania's Senators Matthew Quay and Boies Penrose, who sought it. But his main concern was to outflank his chief rival, Republican Senator Mark Hanna of Ohio. Within weeks of Roosevelt's coming to the White House, he knew Senator Hanna was angling to gain the upper hand among Republican Party loyalists in advance of the 1904 convention. Hanna's presidential ambition was well grounded: he had been President McKinley's chief lieutenant, was a favorite of party stalwarts, and sat in the U.S. Senate. He soon began to carve out a legislative agenda that would draw support away from Roosevelt. Statehood for the territories became one such issue, and he sought a tactical resolution. Hanna revived a proposal from the late nineteenth century—joint statehood—a position that advanced statehood, which the Republican Party had pledged to do, but also minimized the threat posed to Senate power brokers in the East and Midwest by cutting in half the number of new states—and senators—from the Southwest. It is also possible he decided to dabble in statehood to retaliate against Senator Matthew Quay, who had outwitted and outmaneuvered him at the 1900 Republican Convention and forced him to retract his opposition to Roosevelt as vice president.[26]

Joint statehood had currency at the beginning of the twentieth century, especially the plan to unite Oklahoma and the Indian Territory into one state. That idea had been proposed and defeated in the House in early May 1902, as had a similar joint statehood bill for New Mexico and Arizona. Senator Hanna, though, quietly built congressional interest in joint statehood throughout 1902 but did not go public with his position. Roosevelt, too, kept his intentions under wraps in both his 1901 and 1902 annual messages to the Congress. By omitting mention of statehood, he bought time to map a political path to follow with the Congress. For advice on how to proceed, the president turned to Albert Shaw and Nicolas Murray Butler, key figures in his "Tennis Cabinet," as well as Senator Albert Beveridge. Among these three, a consensus emerged favoring joint statehood but limiting it to Oklahoma and the Indian Territory.[27]

But President Roosevelt had other ideas. Writing in 1906, Beveridge recalled events unfolding as follows in 1902: "It was, in the beginning, the policy of Senator Hanna to do with New Mexico and Arizona what I proposed, under your [Albert Shaw's] suggestion, to do for Oklahoma and Indian Territory. I resisted this at first, but later I consented to it. . . . President Roosevelt thought the thing over for more than a year and came to the unalterable position that joint statehood was the only possible thing to do." But before finally committing to this solution, Roosevelt went back and forth, and in December 1902 Beveridge told Shaw, "The President has come around finally again to the original position in which he was when you last saw him." But Roosevelt did more than merely accept Hanna's proposal. He co-opted it, and by doing so he cut off Hanna's attempt to create division within Republican ranks and thus drain support from the president.[28]

Also in December, newspapers began circulating stories about joint statehood for New Mexico and Arizona, and on 18 December Charles A. Spiess, a confidant of Governor Otero, met with the Secretary of the Interior and promptly wrote to Otero that he needed to come to Washington immediately and that joint statehood seemed inevitable. In early January 1903 the president informed Otero he had endorsed it. In describing Roosevelt's decision, Otero made a perspicacious assessment: "President Roosevelt favored it as a happy compromise which might satisfy the territories without running the risk of disturbing the balance of power in the Senate." The president's tactical choice, the "politically realistic alternative," distressed Otero.[29]

Joint statehood was but one of many issues that would influence state delegations at the 1904 Republican national convention. Delegate counting began in earnest early in 1903, and Roosevelt boarded his train at the beginning of April and embarked on a sixty-six-day, fourteen-thousand-mile cross-country trip, spending most of his time in the West. Already he had 286 committed delegates of 498 needed to wrap up the nomination, and he wanted to see and be seen by Republicans, especially convention delegates, but also by the public. The trip soon was called the Great Loop because his circuitous route looked like a lasso tossed around states in the upper Midwest, the Southwest, and the Pacific Northwest. At each stop Roosevelt made a speech defending his policies and pitching conservation. His quest for the nomination soon took a most favorable turn. Senator Joseph B. Foraker, Ohio's senior Republican senator and a statehood advocate whose brother was U.S. marshal in New Mexico, maneuvered his state's delegation to endorse Roosevelt in May. In putting Senator Hanna's home state in his camp, Roosevelt eliminated a potential opponent to his renomination.[30]

"Out of the Way"

As president, Roosevelt opted to work incrementally on behalf of statehood. In taking this course, he had to bend to the prevailing distribution of power in Washington. In 1900 there was no "imperial presidency" as that term came to be understood by the end of the twentieth century. Indeed, so circumscribed was the president's influence that no one objected when Senator George F. Hoar, the powerful senior Republican senator from Massachusetts, publicly rebuked Roosevelt in January 1903 for "unofficial interference" and "meddling with legislation" during the debate over the Omnibus Statehood Bill. Hoar reminded the president that unless he provided the entire Senate a formal communication stating his legislative recommendation, no White House lobbying would be tolerated. "The time for the president to make up his mind about statutes is after we have passed them and not before," thundered Hoar.[31]

Theodore Roosevelt's plan to secure statehood for the territories must be understood in the context of contested power. Roosevelt dared not ignore Senate prerogatives, nor did he want to challenge such powerful senior Republican senators as George Hoar and Nelson Aldrich. He had to abide by congressional protocols, which were easily manipulated to obstruct and stall action on statehood. Roosevelt knew that the road to statehood narrowed and got quite steep on Capitol Hill. He chafed under that political reality, which clearly curbed his power as president, but he largely acceded to the Congress on domestic legislation.

But on matters that fell outside the purview of the Senate, Roosevelt's energy and impatience left their mark in his first administration. He had begun to change forever the scope of the presidency by asserting a new political principle—augmented presidential authority exercised through managing, regulating, and administering agencies of the executive branch. The emergence of the conservation movement was a prototype of this expanded authority emanating from the White House and carried out by the cabinet departments.

The slowly expanding arc of presidential power inevitably pitted the White House against the Congress, particularly the Senate, in certain foreign policy issues, most notably over the Philippines and the Panama Canal. On questions of imperial expansion, Roosevelt crossed swords with key members of his own party—as had McKinley. But when Roosevelt calculated which fights he would wage against opponents in the Congress, he decided that on statehood he would let Senators Beveridge and Aldrich have their way in the short term. He knew the Republican senators arrayed for and against statehood held much sway over their state's convention delegates, and he did not want to antagonize them and thus complicate lining up convention support for his reelection bid. Consequently he took a cautious approach and remained largely on the sidelines during Beveridge's filibuster of the Omnibus Statehood bill. That decision, though, had its own political cost. As one newspaper noted in late February, Republicans wearied of the standoff between Senators Beveridge and Quay and complained that it "has occupied most of the time of the present session, interfering seriously with far more important legislation." Democrats and some Republicans roundly criticized Roosevelt for having to call a special session immediately upon adjournment of the Fifty-Seventh Congress to take up bills pushed aside by the protracted debate over statehood. The special session soon wrapped up the important legislation, including the Panama Canal agreement negotiated in the Hay-Herrán Treaty.[32]

The special session demonstrated that President Roosevelt could generally count on the Republican majority in the House and Senate to pass and send him legislation he sought. But on the issue of statehood, and particularly in the Beveridge-Quay standoff, Roosevelt had to navigate a potentially divisive intraparty conflict. Late in the Fifty-Seventh Congress, however, the Republican proponents warmed to the idea of joint statehood. As one newspaper explained Quay's position, "The commercial advantages of Statehood with the improvement of credit, the security of bond issues, and the invitation of capital for the purpose of developing the natural resources of the region would all follow just as surely with one big state made up of the two as with two States."[33]

When the Fifty-Seventh Congress adjourned on 4 March, the Omnibus Statehood bill died. In December the Fifty-Eighth Congress convened, and statehood gained some attention, though in a new form. During the fall, the president and Senator Quay met and discussed joint statehood, among other topics, but Quay soon returned to his original position in favor of separate states. Also over the summer the president met with Senator Beveridge to assign joint statehood a place on the president's legislative agenda. At the beginning of July, Beveridge informed Senator Aldrich of the "long talks" he was having with President Roosevelt. The two men wrapped up their agreement in early September, with Roosevelt reportedly wanting the "subject dropped" until after the 1904 election, although he agreed, if it must go forward, to support joint statehood, with the four territories becoming two states. But the clear preference of both the president and Beveridge was to put aside this divisive issue for a year. They agreed to focus "on other matters in the current session" and avoid engaging Republican leaders over a secondary, contentious issue. Beveridge made a prescient observation to Aldrich: "The chief promoters of the Statehood proposition in the last session are out of the way in the coming session." He no doubt meant that Senator Quay had, for the moment, joined with Hanna and the president and favored joint statehood; however, within the year these two key figures died—Hanna in February and Quay in May 1904.[34]

"New Mexico's Star of Progress Has Risen"

Roosevelt's western trip in the spring of 1903 gave him an opportunity to mend fences within New Mexico, principally with Governor Otero, following the president's embrace of joint statehood. Roosevelt also sought to reassure the Territory's citizens following the dashing of their aspirations by the Senate. As one Albuquerque journalist wrote, the "visit was planned as a means of uniting the people in demanding their right to rule themselves." The president wanted New Mexicans to believe in themselves and know that sovereignty would eventually arrive, but until then he needed them to be patient, add more citizens, and irrigate more land.[35]

Coming into New Mexico from Colorado on a clear morning the first Tuesday in May, the president's train stopped first in Santa Fe for a busy three-hour-and-twenty-minute visit, which began with Roosevelt addressing a crowd estimated at ten thousand in front of the Capitol building for twenty minutes. To encourage attendance, specially discounted train tickets permitted people from throughout New Mexico to travel to either Santa Fe or Albuquerque. In his remarks, Roosevelt never mentioned joint statehood, but instead told his audience, "I think that your progress has been astonishing. I congratulate you on all that has been done and I am certain that the future will far more than make good the past." Reportedly Roosevelt's "ringing address stir[red] the hearts of the people deeply," which was exactly the impact he sought to counter the bitterness left from Beveridge's tour and his delaying tactics in the Senate. Before leaving Santa Fe, Roosevelt attended a lunch reception in the governor's residence. The social visit likely became unintentionally strained when Mrs. Otero and a few other prominent women joined the president for conversation. One was the wife of the philandering federal judge whose behavior had long outraged President Roosevelt. Three weeks after his trip ended the president sacked Judge Daniel McMillan on a morals charge.[36]

Roosevelt arrived in Albuquerque in midafternoon on 5 May, greeted by a crowd estimated by one local newspaper at fifteen thousand, gathered in front of the recently opened Alvarado Hotel. Territorial Delegate Rodey formally welcomed the president and launched into a patriotic tribute noting the people's "respect for and devotion to our flag and our country" and pledging "our patriotism is as deep and as true as that of any people in the nation." Rodey acknowledged recent adversities and seized the opportunity "afforded us to demonstrate as best we may how unjust were the slanders cast upon us by a recent report of men in very high place." He ended by praising both New Mexico and President Roosevelt and expressed the hope that "the great man we welcome here today will be the executive whose signature will adorn New Mexico's enabling act."[37]

The platform across which the president strode to the podium overlooked a large elevated tableau about 150 feet in front on him "containing a prodigious map of the United States." On it stood young girls carrying banners representing each of the forty-five states, and "just outside a low railing in front stood a little girl with extended hands appealing for admission to Uncle Sam." The president paused to survey the tableau and then spoke, pointing out the importance of irrigation and observing that "when New Mexico had a little more irrigation" the young girl before him would surely be welcomed into the union of states. Most of his five-minute address described good citizenship in terms frequently used by the president—duty, diligence, and democratic freedom. At a private reception at the Commercial Club hosted by Rodey, Roosevelt continued to speak vaguely about statehood, confining his remarks to platitudes and lofty generalities. He assured Rodey, "New Mexico's star of progress has risen. Statehood will be its sun that will cover the Territory with the liberty of the light of day."[38]

Given the scale and proximity of the tableau, the president could not but help comment on it; however, not everyone in New Mexico thought it necessary to be "flaunting statehood in the president's face." Prior to the visit, the *Las Cruces Progress* cautioned, "We need not force our claim upon his attention. . . . He will see the stability and progress of our people, the enterprise of our businessmen, and the beauty and fertility of our valleys and will be impressed far more favorably than should we overshadow our welcome with demands of statehood." The newspaper would have been greatly disappointed by what Roosevelt wrote about New Mexico as his train carried him west out of Albuquerque toward the Grand Canyon. He stared out the window at "the waterless desert country of New Mexico, a desolate land but always attractive with its strange coloring and outline." Absent was any recognition of "the beauty and fertility of our valleys" as the president observed the harsh frontier landscape on all sides.[39]

What most shaped Roosevelt's knowledge of New Mexico was his three months serving with the Territory's Rough Riders. It is difficult to square this narrow, in some ways superficial, experience with his considerable intellectual curiosity and voracious appetite for information. Roosevelt had a keen appreciation for foreign languages and knew four, but in later years when Nuevomexicanos needed translators to understand him he reportedly became angry that English speakers were not more common in the populace. He could talk in great detail and for hours on matters in the sciences, literature, politics, and world affairs, yet what he knew about New Mexico was based largely on memories of the Rough Riders' courage. But even his daily encounters with his fellow Rough Riders showed that he was less a student of their experiences than he was their tutor on matters of interest to him. For example, on the trip from San Antonio, Texas, to Tampa, Florida, he stopped the train to lecture the Rough Riders about a book he was reading on the journey, the French sociologist Edmond Demoulins' *Supériorité des Anglo-Saxons* (1897), which went through ten editions in France in two years. Roosevelt wholeheartedly embraced Demoulins' explanation of the superiority of Anglo-Saxons: Darwin's natural selection applied to people along with all other living beings, which led to Social Darwinism in which only the fittest cultures survived. He ended his lecture by arguing that Americans were superior to the Spaniards in Cuba.[40]

We don't know what New Mexican Rough Riders thought of Roosevelt's impromptu discourse, but his mixing of jingoism, militarism, and racism was more than merely a commanding officer's exhortation to prepare his troops for battle. It was characteristic of his understanding of New Mexico. In May 1903 Roosevelt not only failed to grasp basic facts about the Territory, he continued to believe that Euro-American migrants were the best hope for New Mexico's future. The president regarded New Mexico as a blank slate on which Euro-Americans would write a record of accomplishment by bringing in more settlers and irrigation to prepare the way for statehood. His general approach was simply a variation on Albert Beveridge's report. Both men were captives of their mind-set, and neither sought to know the complexity of New Mexico or its people.

New Mexicans who greeted the president on his tour of Santa Fe and Albuquerque got caught up in their boosterism, with Albuquerque's statehood tableau being an over-the-top example. Each city he visited proudly feted him at their Commercial Club where speakers gave glowing reports of the new construction by railroads throughout the Territory. Because the taxes paid by railroads funded much of the cost of local county government, businessmen sought to assure the president that when statehood arrived a tax base existed to support it. But railroads also powerfully influenced patterns of growth of the Territory, a fact nowhere more in evidence than in Las Vegas. Throughout much of the nineteenth century, that community had enjoyed a commercial boom, first with the Santa Fe Trail and then after 1879 with the railroad. But at the turn of the century Las Vegas was beginning to lose its economic advantages, something Roosevelt completely missed when he had attended the inaugural Rough Rider reunion. Just before boarding a train to depart after his first-ever visit to the Territory, Roosevelt remarked to a companion: "Say, isn't this a hell of a country? It beats anything I have ever imagined; it's the country of the future."[41]

In fact Las Vegas's days of economic dominance were rapidly fading. One poignant example came in Roosevelt's 1903 visit to the Territory. Las Vegas did not merit a stop; the several hundred locals who came out to the train station at 4:15 A.M. did not even glimpse the president. Feeling snubbed, the town's Spanish-language newspaper vented its Democratic Party sympathies and criticized Roosevelt for backing away from his earlier pledge to support statehood, noting that whereas in 1899 he had said the Territory was "ready for statehood," just four years later he was saying "it is not yet ready—needing more irrigation and agriculture."[42]

The president's special train passing through town before dawn was an emblem of the waning of Las Vegas's economic influence. In 1901 the recent loss of business owing to the growth of other railroads alarmed the town's Board of Trade: "Since the year 1887 we have seen the encroachment on Las Vegas trading Territory by the building of the Fort Worth and Denver railroad up through the Panhandle of Texas and consequent loss of business to our merchants. This was followed by the construction of the Pecos Valley Railroad up to Carlsbad and on to Roswell, which cut off the remunerative trade of all that section from Las Vegas." The newspaper went on to cite two other railroads sapping the town's economic vitality before concluding that "during all these years of gradual diminution nothing had been done to replace the loss." The Board of Trade proposed an eighty-five-mile railroad to Taos but admitted that townspeople were lukewarm to the ambitious capital campaign needed to underwrite the venture. Worse, some residents candidly expressed their misgivings to the eastern investors recruited by the Board of Trade. The proposed railroad never got built, and Las Vegas's status as the largest, most commercially active city in the Territory continued to decline. Concurrently, the surrounding San Miguel County, the Territory's most populous throughout the second half of the nineteenth century, also declined, and the center of growth shifted into the Rio Grande Valley.[43]

Las Vegas's reversals contrasted with Albuquerque's fortunes, which were on the uptick when Roosevelt visited in 1903. Besides the new Alvarado Hotel, built in 1902, two new manufacturing businesses had opened the previous year: the American Lumber Company, allied with William H. Andrews's railroad venture, operated a sawmill and box factory; the Rio

Grande Woolen Mills, where "home-grown wool is made into home-spun cloth," also started up. Together, these two firms employed hundreds of workers, and *La Bandera Americana* announced that "more than half are Nuevomexicanos." Much earlier, in the 1880s, the Atchison Topeka and Santa Fe Railway opened its machine shop and roundhouse in Barelas, which drew many local Nuevomexicanos to its jobs and away from small-scale farming.[44]

Few local industries existed in New Mexico in 1900. The real engine of the economy was the railroad with its freight-hauling and passenger services. Almost all of the Territory's twenty-one towns depended on the railroad for their survival. Just seven towns had more than 2,500 residents in 1900, with Albuquerque and its Old Town the largest at 8,848 citizens. Of the remaining fourteen towns in the Territory, Roswell had 2,049 residents and five others had populations between 1,000 and 2,000. Another eight communities had fewer than 975 occupants, the largest being Carlsbad with 963 residents. In the vast expanse of New Mexico's 121,365 square miles, these twenty-one towns had only 47,417 residents or 24 percent of the Territory's population. Just over three-fourths of all New Mexicans lived on farms or ranches, or in small villages of fewer than 100 people. New Mexico remained a sparsely settled frontier, and its vast expanses of semiarid lands supported limited ranching and even less intensive farming.[45]

It is not surprising that President Roosevelt thought New Mexico "desolate" as his train carried him west from Albuquerque to Arizona. His native New York in 1900 had 7,268,894 residents and a population density of 152.6 persons per square mile, whereas New Mexico had 195,310 residents and 1.6 persons per square mile. Moreover for a president who was surely the greatest naturalist since Thomas Jefferson to occupy the White House, the train trip across west-central New Mexico contrasted dramatically with the landscape around Sagamore Hill, his home on Long Island. The red rock country he described as having "strange coloring and outline" could not have been more different from the verdant landscape, bay, and expanse of water his home overlooked. While all presidents take the measure of the men around them, Roosevelt also took careful account of natural surroundings. And no doubt Roosevelt greatly missed the flowers that began blooming around Sagamore Hill in April. He had a special kinship with a "hillside near us which glows like a tender flame with the white of the bloodroot." No such seasonal reminders of his beloved flora caught the president's eye as he rode west through arid New Mexico.[46]

The train did not take him through the upper Río Puerco Valley, recently settled by Nuevomexicanos. Some twenty-five miles northwest of Albuquerque, this land and its settlers might have piqued Roosevelt's interest because they represented unexpected variations on his themes of migration and irrigation. Nuevomexicano homesteaders from central New Mexico began settling the Puerco Valley in the 1890s, when the area became safe from Indian raiding. These settlers fused past and present: they employed acequia irrigation on government-granted homesteads. Acequias had been the basis of communal, self-sustaining agriculture for three centuries, and the network of irrigation ditches brought water from a small community-built dam (*atarque*) to fields and gardens around more than a half-dozen settlements in the Río Puerco Valley. The farmers' harvest included cash crops sold to buyers in Bernalillo and Albuquerque.

This farm-to-market trade would have challenged Roosevelt's prescription for New Mexico: the homesteaders were Nuevomexicanos, not Euro-Americans, and their irrigation followed traditional practices. Moreover, the money they earned proved that modernity and its attendant change brought unintended consequences. In 1903 Bersabé Márez and Antonia García posed for a photograph in their tiny Río Puerco community of Casa Salazar. They wore fashionable late Victorian-era dresses accentuating their tiny waists in the curving hourglass style. The design was quite familiar to Roosevelt, but their hats, prominently decorated with bird feathers, would have horrified him. One of Roosevelt's first conservation crusades as governor of New York occurred when he secured legislation attacking the large millinery factories in New York City. Annually a veritable slaughter of wild birds, especially in Florida, provided materials for hat makers churning out ever more ornately designed headwear. In 1900 Roosevelt in New York and President McKinley in Washington signed, respectively, state and federal legislation establishing nongame birds' rights that effectively outlawed the use of their feathers in the millinery industry. Enforcement proved lax, and stores—even in New Mexico—continued to cater to demand.[47]

In the recesses of Territorial New Mexico, irrigation and migration were

uniquely complex. Consider the implications of Márez and García keeping
in step with national fashion trends. Their dresses and hats had surely been
paid for with money earned by selling produce from their irrigated gardens
or farms. As recent homesteaders in the Río Puerco Valley, they had followed the prescription for statehood—"more water and people"—and they
also embraced modernity in their attire. But their ethnicity and their irrigation practices inverted the president's and the Congress's requirements
for statehood. Some other New Mexicans, too, began to note contradictions
in government irrigation projects in the Territory, especially on the Navajo
Reservation in west-central New Mexico along the route of the president's
departing train. The *Santa Fe New Mexican* reported in January 1905 on
government-built small-water impoundments and canals so successful that
one Navajo sold fifteen thousand pounds of wheat from his recent harvest.
Such success contrasted with the noticeable lack of support for irrigation
among Euro-Americans in the eastern portion of the Territory.[48]

The small-scale Nuevomexicano cash economy blending traditional
practices with modern consumer tastes in the Río Puerco Valley was not
what either Roosevelt or Beveridge had in mind as the forerunner of statehood. Yet the presence of these homesteaders—and of the many thousands more living and farming in small communities throughout central
and northern New Mexico—provided a model of irrigation and a scale
of agriculture ideally suited to the available land and water. The president
and Nuevomexicanos were on parallel but opposite courses. While Roosevelt looked to large-scale water projects to support intensive agriculture
by Euro-Americans, the Nuevomexicanos adapted their long-held acequia
practices to survive as small-scale farmers in an emerging cash economy.[49]

"If Senator Beveridge's Report . . . Was Justified"

President Roosevelt had an imperfect understanding of New Mexico and its
people, but he did know one thing quite well—he wanted the Territory to
remain solidly Republican. The Democratic Party, though, intended to put
up a fight. Four months after Roosevelt completed his western tour, a Democratic presidential hopeful came through New Mexico—U.S. Representative William Randolph Hearst of New York, heir to a chain of newspapers.
Hearst, ever the opportunist, wanted to court possible delegates, and each
of the territories had six up for grabs. His preconvention strategy included

garnering all the Territories' delegates, southern Democrats, and the party faithful in strong Republican states. But he needed a pretext for a visit to the Southwest, so he cast the trip as an inquiry into the territories' suitability for statehood.[50]

When Hearst's special train pulled out of Chicago on the evening of 12 October it carried thirty-five guests, including two senators, seventeen of his fellow representatives, journalists from his newspapers, and some wives of the guests. During their eleven-day excursion, dubbed a "voyage of investigation" by one writer, they sought to "see if Senator Beveridge's report of the conditions in those territories was justified." At stops in major towns in New Mexico, Arizona, and Oklahoma, they met with citizen and business groups and toured the communities to learn firsthand the answer to their question.[51]

At trip's end, Hearst pronounced that all participating "were much impressed by the character of the citizenship of these Territories and by their mineral and agricultural resources," and all would support statehood. Although the House of Representatives approved a joint statehood bill that created two states out of four territories on 19 April 1904, it went nowhere until after the fall elections. In the Senate, joint statehood had no support among Democrats. It cut in half the number of potential new senators, and Democrats wanted the opportunity to compete for as many as eight new Senate seats. On the Republican side, Quay reintroduced the Omnibus Statehood bill in late January 1904; later that day he departed for Florida for health reasons, never to return to the Congress, and the bill stalled upon his death in late May.[52]

The most immediate, tangible result of Hearst's trip came when the *Atlanta Constitution* endorsed him. But New Mexico gained little from the Hearst and Roosevelt visits of 1903 beyond some favorable publicity. Each man had his sights on the 1904 elections, and trips to the Territory were maneuvers to secure their party's nomination. Democrats in New Mexico rewarded Hearst at their party's national convention when they joined with Arizona and the states of Nevada, Idaho, Montana, and half of the Colorado delegation to support his candidacy. One scholar has suggested that Democrats continued to reap dividends from Hearst's trip when Woodrow Wilson carried the Southwest and Rocky Mountain region in both his presidential campaigns.[53]

As residents of a territory, New Mexicans could only watch Theodore

Roosevelt handily defeat his Democratic challenger, Judge Alton B. Parker of New York. As Roosevelt embarked on his own full term, he made joint statehood a legislative priority. But in the Territory intra-Republican rivalries led to bitterness, divisiveness, and chaotic factionalism, all of which caused President Roosevelt much gnashing of teeth.

Solomon Luna. For sixteen years, from June 1896 until his death in August 1912, he served as the Territory's national committeeman for the Republican Party. During his tenure he preferred to exert influence behind the scenes, and he had a role in every major political event in the Territory's struggle to gain statehood. (Courtesy Center for Southwest Research, Pictorial Collections, University Libraries, University of New Mexico, #000-021-0107; hereafter, CSWR, PC, UL, UNM)

Thomas B. Catron. Long a controversial figure for his prominence in the Santa Fe Ring and the Republican Party in the Territory, he served as delegate to the Congress (1895–97), a delegate to the Constitutional Convention of 1910, and as U.S. senator (1912–17). He sought statehood in the expectation it would increase the value of his multi-million-acre land holdings. (Courtesy CSWR, PC, UL, UNM, #000-742-0039)

Miguel A. Otero. As territorial governor for nine years (1897–1906), he served two presidents—William McKinley and Theodore Roosevelt. But he lost his grip on the Territory's Republican Party and vigorously opposed Roosevelt on joint statehood, lapses that cost him his job. His stand against joint statehood was applauded by an influential politician from northern New Mexico, T. D. Burns, who sent this photograph of Otero as a holiday greeting in late December 1904. (Courtesy CSWR, PC, UL, UNM, #000-021-0006)

Matthew S. Quay. His national stature in the Republican Party as a U.S. senator, coupled with his wiliness as Pennsylvania's political boss, helped him secure a plank in the Republican Party platform endorsing statehood in 1896 and 1900. His protégé William H. ("Bull") Andrews convinced the legislature to name a county after him in 1903. (Courtesy Library of Congress, Prints and Photographs Online, LC-USZ62-46420; hereafter, LC, PP)

Albert J. Beveridge. He chaired the Senate Committee on Territories from December 1901 to March 1911 and blocked statehood throughout the presidency of his good friend Theodore Roosevelt. A Republican senator from Indiana, he obstructed statehood at the request of key colleagues from New England. (Courtesy LC, PP, LC-USZ62-61460)

Nelson W. Aldrich. A five-term Republican senator from Rhode Island and the most powerful man in the U.S. Senate between the 1890s and 1911, he appointed Senator Beveridge to chair the Committee on Territories and instructed him to keep New Mexico and Arizona out of the Union. He sought to limit the number of senators to avoid diluting his power. (Courtesy LC, PP, LC-DIG-hec-16628)

Bernard S. Rodey. The Territory's Republican delegate to the Congress for two terms (1901–1905) and known as "Mr. Statehood" for his incessant advocacy, he supported President Roosevelt's push for joint statehood, which prompted Governor Otero to oust him in favor of William H. Andrews. In 1910 he joined an attempt to rename New Mexico as Acoma, the last of seven alternative names—Jefferson, Lincoln, Salado, Sierra, Arizona, Montezuma, and Acoma—advanced over the years. (Courtesy CSWR, PC, UL, UNM, #000-119-0220)

William H. "Bull" Andrews. After arriving in New Mexico from Pennsylvania in 1899, he quickly parlayed his role as a railroad magnate into prominence in the Territory's Republican Party. Between 1905 and 1912 he served as delegate to the Congress, where his ties to key eastern politicians enabled him to wield influence to pass statehood legislation in 1910 and 1911. (Courtesy CSWR, PC, UL, UNM, #000-742-0256)

The Court of Private Land Claims. From 1 July 1891 to 30 June 1904, Chief Justice Joseph R. Reed of Iowa (seated, center) presided over the congressionally mandated adjudication of disputes over titles to land grants. The court's rulings often favored Nuevomexicanos, but the U.S. Supreme Court routinely reversed the findings. (Twitchell, *The Leading Facts of New Mexican History*, vol. 2: facing p. 472; hereinafter Twitchell, *Leading Facts*)

Theodore Roosevelt. The Spanish-American War of 1898 brought Roosevelt to national attention for his successes as the second-in-command to Colonel Leonard Wood in leading the volunteer cavalry known as the Rough Riders against Cuban fighters between June and August. (Twitchell, *Leading Facts*, facing p. 496)

SAGAMORE HILL. Nov 12th 1911

My dear Col. Twitchell,

Half the officers and men of my regiment came from New Mexico; and no Colonel ever commanded a finer fighting regiment. Moreover they were just as good on the march and in camp as in battle, these men of the plains and mountains, bold riders and skilled riflemen, who faced danger unflinchingly and endured hardship uncomplainingly. I regard the fact that I was one of them as well-nigh the most precious heritage I can leave my children.
Sincerely yours
Theodore Roosevelt
erstwhile Colonel 1st U.S.V. cavalry

Roosevelt's letter about New Mexicans serving as Rough Riders. The former president's nostalgia and pride were evident in 1911 when he wrote, "I regard the fact that I was one of them as well-nigh the most precious heritage I can leave my children." (Twitchell, *Leading Facts*, facing p. 528)

Irrigation ditch. In May 1901 President McKinley told New Mexicans they needed "more water and people" before they would become a state. Six months later McKinley was assassinated, but his successor Theodore Roosevelt followed the same prescription. Irrigation projects to support new farms in arid lands became a federal priority after passage of the National Reclamation Act of 1902. (Courtesy CSWR, PC, UL, UNM, #000-119-532)

(Facing page, top) Elephant Butte Dam under construction. Construction of the largest irrigation project in territorial New Mexico began in 1907 and was completed in 1915 at a cost of over twelve million dollars. It irrigated more than 100,000 acres, and in 1923 the harvested crops sold for over nine million dollars. (Courtesy CSWR, PC, UL, UNM, #991-031-0021)

(Facing page, bottom) Pecos River Valley aqueduct near Carlsbad. When a former Rough Rider officer, who lived in Carlsbad, made a personal appeal at the White House, President Roosevelt himself intervened to direct the Reclamation Service to fund irrigation projects to aid southeastern New Mexico. (Courtesy LC, PP, LC-DIG-ppmsca-17316)

Medallion from the Sixteenth International Irrigation Congress, Albuquerque, 1908. This organization consistently passed resolutions endorsing statehood. Their support followed a renewed call for statehood in the Republican Party platform in 1908 and came amid widespread public acceptance for New Mexico and Arizona to enter the Union. The Democratic Party's platform included a statehood plank in each election from 1896 through 1908. (Courtesy Paul A. Ryan)

First automobile in Albuquerque. By the time this car arrived in town in 1900, modernity had been relentlessly advancing in New Mexico since the arrival of passengers on a train in February 1879. In the 1890s, three new technologies began transforming daily life in the Territory—electricity, telephones, and movies. The three African Americans (right) were 1 percent of Albuquerque's black population. (Courtesy CSWR, PC, UL, UNM, #000-119-0747)

Pueblo Indians selling pottery. Albuquerque's Alvarado Hotel opened in 1902 as both a railroad depot and a tourist attraction. Several buildings were devoted to Native American arts, and to spur tourist interest samples were displayed track-side. Native American pottery became a salable commodity featured in railroad promotional literature, and tourism was both a cause and an effect of the economic change wrought by modernization. (Courtesy CSWR, PC, UL, UNM, #000-282)

Two Nuevomexicana friends in Casa Salazar, Rio Puerco Valley. When Bersabé Márez (left) and Antonia García posed in 1903, they wore the latest in fashion and were in step with women's wear in the East. Their clothes were a marker of modernization in that people shifted to wage labor to earn the money for new consumer items. (Bersabé Márez [?] and Antonia García, 1903. Courtesy Teodorita García-Ruelas. Permission to publish photograph granted by Nasario García)

Mrs. Sallie L. Robert. A homestead she filed on in 1890 became valuable real estate in the town of Artesia, especially after she drilled the first artesian well in the area to irrigate her land. Seizing a new opportunity, she purchased property in and around Artesia and by 1907 was successfully selling city lots and farm sites, the latter priced at $125 an acre. (Anderson, *A History of New Mexico: Its Resources and People*, vol. 2: facing p. 775)

CHAPTER FOUR

"Full Knowledge of Its Fraudulent Character"

Word of J. Francisco Chaves's shooting reached Governor Miguel A. Otero early Sunday morning, 27 November 1904. The murder had been carefully staged. A lone gunman crept to an isolated ranch house in Torrance County, peered through a window into a room where Chaves was eating dinner at a friend's home, shot him through the head, and escaped on horseback. A shocked Otero mourned the death of his longtime friend and political ally. During Otero's tenure Chaves chaired the October 1901 Statehood Convention, served as superintendent of public instruction, and earlier in the month had been reelected to the Territory's legislature, where he had served continuously since 1875. He had also been the Territory's delegate to Congress for three terms beginning in 1865. Known as the father of the Territory's Republican party and its elder statesman, the seventy-one-year-old Chaves wielded power in ways that inevitably earned him enemies. An arrest occurred, but the trial resulted in an acquittal, and the unsolved killing marked another violent and mysterious ending to a New Mexican's life.[1]

Chaves's murder made the front pages of both the *New York Times* and the *Washington Post* on 28 November. The *Times* characterized it as "another incident in a feud of long standing, in which there have been a number of murders, arson, and other criminal act," while the *Post* attributed it to the "work of a political enemy." Such publicity reinforced the popular view of the Territory as a violent frontier, an impression given recent play in newspapers nationwide reporting the brutal kidnapping of the founder of the Bank of Portales in August 1904.[2]

Violence in New Mexico had been stamped into America's consciousness first as fact—notably in Indian wars during the 1850s and 1860s and in the Colfax County War (1876–77) and the Lincoln Country War (1878–81)— and then as fiction in dime novels. It also figured prominently in the novels and stories of Emerson Hough. Having been an attorney in the central New Mexico mining town of White Oaks, where he witnessed numerous harrowing incidents of frontier violence, Hough relocated to Chicago in the 1880s and published twenty-two books on the West. Violence in the Territory remained a problem. Nuevomexicanos cited it as an obstacle to their advancement, and the 1900 census reported that, per capita, Arizona and New Mexico had the highest homicide rates in the United States. Newspapers continued to portray violence as the norm in the two territories and described them as the "most lawless" places in America.[3]

Such accounts impeded statehood because they belied the "claim that peaceable and settled conditions prevail there." Statehood became hostage to the perception of frontier lawlessness. Alarmed by such notoriety, the territorial legislature created a new law enforcement unit in 1905, the mounted patrol, a forerunner of the state police, to impose order and improve chances for statehood. The mood of the nation was transitioning away from the embarrassing abuses and corruption of the Gilded Age and toward the reformist agenda of the Progressives. Against this background, New Mexico's prospects for statehood rose and fell on how well it managed its affairs, and between 1904 and 1906 the Territory had a dismal record.[4]

Both President Roosevelt and Senator Beveridge championed honest, clean government, and in New Mexico they saw too much evidence of an incomplete transition to modernity. Believing that New Mexico remained mired in the corrupting practices of an earlier era, following his re-election in November 1904 Roosevelt intended to reform the Territory's politics, which at the turn of the twentieth century have been aptly labeled "chaotic factionalism." Engaging in a "type of disruptive, confused, intensely combative, and highly personal form of politics," the Territory's leaders manipulated public affairs in pursuit of power and perquisites—and used any means to achieve their ends. Roosevelt and Beveridge had been exposed to this bitter infighting during the reappointment of Otero as governor in 1901, and that experience left both men wary of Thomas B. Catron and watchful of Miguel A. Otero.[5]

The president's plans to end "chaotic factionalism" collided head on with entrenched interests in the Territory. But Roosevelt relentlessly forged ahead with three modernization projects: backing joint statehood; rooting out fraud and corruption in the Territory's Republican Party; and attracting more settlers by expanding irrigation. His reforms met with stiff resistance that slowed their pace, and even his promotion of irrigation became highly contentious. The overarching goal was to foster honest government, and in its pursuit the president's temperament and political philosophy stand out. Here was the union of his crusading, hard-charging approach to leadership and his principled call to end corrupt practices and dismiss dishonest politicians. He began at the top and removed two of his appointed governors between November 1905 and April 1907. He was determined to end corruption before contempt for the current order soured the prospects of Republicans to dominate when statehood arrived.[6]

"Black Treachery [and] Shameless Treason"

For seven months prior to his death, J. Francisco Chaves was caught up in escalating conflicts that culminated in a very public display of "chaotic factionalism" in September 1904. In February, as a part of his duties for the Territory's Republican Party central committee, he issued routine calls for counties to hold precinct meetings to select representatives to attend county conventions. These meetings sent delegates to the Territory's party convention in Las Vegas on 19 March, where six primary and six alternate delegates were picked to go to Chicago on 21 June for the national convention. Chaves believed these grass-roots meetings would "help to grow the great Republican Party, which during our lifetime has brought happiness and prosperity to the country."[7]

But in Chicago the party betrayed Chaves's faith. Rather than delivering "happiness and prosperity," the convention acted on the long-standing private agreement between President Roosevelt and Senator Beveridge and ignored statehood for the territories when writing their platform. In charge of that document was Senator Henry Cabot Lodge, the president's closest friend, and, as one newspaper reported, all mention of sovereignty got dropped "under the censorship of Senator Lodge and a select coterie of New England members of the Congress who have always looked with dread and fear upon the prospect" of statehood for New Mexico and Arizona. Although Governor Otero received the obligatory honor to represent the Territory on the committee that traveled to the president's home on Long

Island to inform him of his nomination, the governor soon began to speak out against the president by attacking his support for joint statehood as a senseless step backward from their division into two Territories in 1863.[8]

The public rift between the governor and the president mirrored a political division in New Mexico in 1904. This drama marked the opening act in a new series of bitter feuds that plagued the quest for statehood over the next seven years. Throughout the first eight months of 1904 Delegate Bernard Rodey believed he had his party's unified support in seeking his third re-election—even though he had sided with Roosevelt in support of joint statehood. Unbeknownst to him, however, Otero had been working against Rodey behind his back even while continuing publicly to endorse him. At the mid-September convention in Albuquerque, when the moment came to place Rodey's name in nomination, the delegate assigned to do so rose and promptly announced for William H. "Bull" Andrews, a foe of joint statehood. Thus did Otero oust Rodey.[9]

Immediately recriminations abounded. For his part, Otero claimed Rodey had double-crossed him by not fulfilling a pledge to dismiss Frank Hubbell, a Republican official from Bernalillo County long despised by the governor. Pro-Rodey sentiment echoed comments from *La Voz del Pueblo*, which had long been hostile to Otero. They labeled Rodey's dismissal as "black treachery" and "shameless treason," "the result of a pact between Andrews and the governor, where Andrews promised to assist Otero's candidacy for a third term as governor, if Roosevelt were elected, in exchange for Otero supporting Andrews for Delegate." In the weeks prior to the election, Chaves took control of the new county of Torrance to ensure William H. Andrews prevailed, an act resented by many locals.[10]

The fall election was a four-way race. Andrews had lived in the Territory about five years but exercised considerable influence in business and politics because of his prior political experience in Pennsylvania. He introduced himself to Spanish-speaking voters in mid-September in a letter accepting his party's nomination. The first sentence of his platform signaled his support for Otero: "I will work with great care to secure the adoption of an enabling bill for admitting New Mexico as a State with its own name and its current borders." He easily defeated the Democrat George Money by more than five thousand votes. Rodey ran as an Independent Republican, but he and a fourth minor candidate trailed far behind, with Rodey needing his supporters "to scratch the head of your ticket [i.e., Andrew's name] and substitute mine" to vote for him. The Las Vegas newspaper accused Andrews of stealing the election through intimidation and vote buying, securing "victories obtained by the force of money" in the key counties of Valencia, Sandoval, and Rio Arriba. *La Voz del Pueblo* noted that "Mexicans" predominated in those three counties and implied that they behaved as peones doing whatever their patrón commanded. After the election *La Voz del Pueblo* alleged that Andrews "spent fifty thousand dollars in this Territory [buying votes] to be elected delegate to Congress. The position pays him $5,000 a year."[11]

"Andrews Has Worked My Ruin"

Catron's political chicanery in the Congress was soon outdone by Andrews, who within a year of his election became the Territory's most notorious delegate. While in Pennsylvania, Andrews had been well schooled in skulduggery and party intrigue, and he honed those skills as a henchman and machine politician for Senator Quay. His longtime association with Pennsylvania's Republican boss inspired him to cap his career by becoming a U.S. Senator. In 1899, when he was in his mid-fifties, he relocated to New Mexico. The Territory also offered economic opportunities in which Andrews enlisted Quay and others to invest in the expectation that statehood would follow quickly and bring with it windfall profits.[12]

Once in New Mexico, Andrews realized that advancing his political future required an arrangement with Governor Otero. The deal they struck in 1901 brought them each some immediate gain. For his part, Otero needed major financial backing to take on the Catron faction, which drew on money supplied by the Atchison, Topeka, and Santa Fe Railway. Andrews could help him secure similar backers. Vouched for by Pennsylvania's Senators Matthew Quay and Boies Penrose, Andrews lined up wealthy industrialists tied to railroad and steel interests in the state and channeled millions of dollars into the Territory through a network of enterprises he controlled under the umbrella of the Pennsylvania Development Company. The principal enterprise was the Santa Fe Central Railroad and its 117 miles of track between Santa Fe and Torrance, which made money in various underhanded ways from the timber, coal, and salt along its route.[13]

Late in the morning of Monday, 4 December 1905 newly elected Delegate William H. Andrews trudged up the steps of the main entrance to the Capitol. It was a cold day—the temperature reached only 32 degrees at noon—with overcast skies and streets still wet from the previous evening's rain. Inside he joined the 386 members of the House elected to the Fifty-Ninth Congress, 81 of them newly elected. But none of the representatives had such a dark cloud surrounding him as Andrews. Just seven weeks earlier a scandal in Pennsylvania engulfed him. In the immediate aftermath, the *New York Times* and the *Washington Post* openly questioned whether New Mexico merited statehood with men such as Andrews elected to represent it. The *Post* wrote, "Congress on the one hand, and New Mexico on the other will be strangely obtuse if they fail to perceive the bearing upon the Statehood question of five words in the pathetic note left by Cashier T. Lee Clark, of the wrecked Enterprise National Bank, of Allegheny, Pa., just before he committed suicide. 'Andrews has worked my ruin,' wrote the cashier to his wife."[14]

When Senator Quay died, statehood lost its most forceful advocate, but his absence also put in jeopardy the capitalization of Andrews's railroad and other investments. Pennsylvania money had been bet in anticipation of a quick gain from two financial advantages conferred with statehood: it removed Congress as the sole authority to approve bond requests, and it raised the ceiling on the amount of indebtedness and the interest paid investors. These changes made state- and municipal-issued bonds more attractive. But Quay's death in May 1904 put on hold all such expectations.[15]

Delay soon pressed upon Andrews, and he needed much more money than income from operations provided. He turned for additional capital to the Enterprise National Bank in Allegheny, Pennsylvania. Its chief cashier, T. Lee Clark, became the railroad's treasurer and helped secure $2.5 million in loans, the money coming from Pennsylvania tax receipts and other state funds placed on deposit at the bank. The loaning of state tax money to influential politicians had very nearly ruined Senator Quay in 1899, but a Philadelphia jury acquitted him of manipulating state deposits for private use. A few years later, Andrews followed Quay's financing model and likewise ended up in trouble. His scheme began to unravel when a first installment repayment of $700,000 came due in the fall of 1905. It could not be covered. Working late into the night on 17 October Clark tried to obscure a paper trail connecting the loan default to the collapse of the bank. Then Clark went home. He could have stepped out of Edwin Arlington Robinson's 1897 poem "Richard Cory." He lived in a $300,000 home with his wife and four children and was an elder in the Presbyterian Church. Early the next morning Clark walked out into a crisp autumn morning on his expansive porch and, humming a tune, shot himself.[16]

Delegate Andrews arrived in Washington just a month after a *New York Times* article appeared under the headline "BANK WRECK MAY DASH HOPES OF TERRITORIES." More pointed and damning was the article's subheading: "Case of Andrews Increases Distrust as to Quality of Possible Colleagues from New States." The article reported that "opponents [of statehood] put Andrews and the Enterprise Bank forward as their main argument, not in the Senate, but in the real debates which actually settle the fate of bills and are held in the cloak rooms and committee rooms." In late March 1906 five men were arrested, including the failed scheme's alleged ringleader, Forest R. Nichols, described as "private secretary and confidential clerk to W. H. (Bull) Andrews, . . . [who] is and has been for years the expert financial man of Representative [sic] 'Bull' Andrews in all of his moves." Two years of legal proceedings ensued, but three of those implicated avoided conviction—including Nichols. Only the bank's bookkeeper and a collateral guarantor were found guilty. Andrews avoided any criminal prosecution because the loan documents did not directly link him to the transactions.[17]

"Evil Days for the Commonwealth"

Andrews's notoriety was not alone in damaging the cause of statehood. Governor Miguel Otero's actions in 1905 likewise undercut the cause, especially his official conduct. Immediately following his engineering of Delegate Rodey's ouster, Otero faced a barrage of vituperative attacks, especially in the influential *La Voz del Pueblo,* which alleged his complicity in corruption, incompetence, and nepotism. As serious as these accusations were, the worst offense seemed to be that Otero had turned his back on Nuevomexicanos. The paper's masthead proclaimed it to be "Dedicated to the Interests and Progress of the Hispano-Americano People," but in their view Otero too often ignored his fellow Nuevomexicanos. In an editorial entitled "The Sell Out of Hispano-Americanos by Otero," the paper complained about his lack of allegiance to and solidarity with Nuevomexicanos: "The Hispano-Americanos in this territory provide three-quarters of the vote that has put the Republican Party in power. . . . In view of this, we say once again: Is there any reason in the world that the native sons of New Mexico cannot have more representation in the administration of public affairs?" While Otero had put his brother and father-in-law on the payroll, his inner circle included only a couple of Nuevomexicanos.[18]

The call for "more representation" formed part of an ongoing campaign for clean government waged for years by *La Voz del Pueblo*. They were frank in admitting the challenges: "We do not deny that among our people are found conditions of ignorance, weakness, and baseness, and no one knows better than we do that we have had to fight these in our struggle for the peoples' rights." Electoral fraud, especially buying votes, had long been practiced by both parties, but after the turn of the twentieth century its critics spoke out. About all *La Voz del Pueblo* could do, though, was rail against the practice and admonish eligible voters to be honest, which meant turning down offers of money to support a candidate.[19]

The erosion of Otero's authority accelerated each month in 1905. In March a disgruntled former employee's allegations of financial and personnel improprieties led to rumors that the president would soon sack him, which brought denials from officials in Washington. Throughout the summer a drama played out in revelations of three failed attempts to kidnap his son. By September the maelstrom engulfing Otero included threats— and at least one attempt—to kill him. This descent into violence prompted fortification of the governor's residence so that it was described as "almost literally an arsenal." By late September a *Los Angeles Times* correspondent concluded the governor was caught in a veritable "political war." But it was not just his public life that brought Otero grief. His private life had also taken a turn unacceptable to the president. On 1 February Otero left his wife, Caroline, with the divorce agreement citing abandonment due to "irreconcilable differences." Divorce deeply offended Roosevelt, who felt so strongly about the sanctity of marriage that in 1906 he proposed Congress make divorce much more difficult, arguing, "When home ties are loosened, . . . then evil days for the Commonwealth are at hand."[20]

By the fall of 1905 Governor Otero had become a political liability. Since presidents looked to territorial governors to develop a strong party system that would preserve their political advantage in the Congress and in national elections following statehood, the disarray in New Mexico's Republican Party caused much consternation in Washington. In late November Roosevelt announced that Otero would not be reappointed upon completion of his second term on 22 January 1906. The nine years he served as Territorial Governor (1897–1906) placed him in an elite group: of 160 territorial governors in the United States between 1787 and 1912, only 9 served for eight or more years—and only 5 served longer than Otero. Given Otero's unusually long time in office, his dismissal surprised no one, and Roosevelt never publicly explained his decision. Speculation, though, centered on a political calculation: in the upcoming push for statehood, the president did not want the distraction of Otero's actions, which had increasingly suggested incompetence and insubordination.[21]

"A Blaze of Political Pyrotechnics"

Roosevelt tapped Herbert J. Hagerman to become governor, relying principally on the recommendation of Secretary of the Interior Ethan Allen Hitchcock, who as ambassador to Russia had been ably served by Hagerman, secretary of the legation from the late 1890s to 1904. Also in Hagerman's favor were his lack of involvement in the Territory's political factionalism and his father's prominent role promoting agriculture and settlement in the Pecos River Valley. Governor Hagerman turned thirty-four less than a month before assuming his duties in January 1906, and it is tempting to speculate that he believed that observing the contentious, volatile social and political scene in Tsar Nicholas's Russia had somehow prepared him to handle a deeply unsettled Territory. He received a clear mandate from the president: dismiss all "unsatisfactory and improper government officials."[22]

Hagerman's appointment coincided with Roosevelt's initiating a concerted attempt to get a statehood bill through Congress, and the success of the initiative was entwined with the clean-government campaign prompting Hagerman's appointment. The president invested himself deeply in the issue of honesty in government as part of his larger project of progressivism—reforming the American political order. At the 1904 Republican National Convention, Senator Albert J. Beveridge delivered a speech seconding the president's re-nomination and reminded his fellow delegates that "while he is President no wrongdoer in the service of the government will go unwhipped of justice. Americans demand honesty and honor." In a second term, Beveridge promised, Roosevelt would be "vigilant and fearless" in their pursuit. Within New Mexico, he would attack factionalism and official fraud and corruption. Evidence of the latter had been accumulating over the past year, and its potential to derail statehood had to be forcefully countered by the president.[23]

Roosevelt did not mention his plans to pull New Mexico out of its quagmire of inept administration and brewing scandals when he delivered his annual message to Congress on 5 December 1905. But he did endorse joint statehood publicly for the first time in several years, calling for merging Oklahoma and the Indian Territory into one state as well as uniting New Mexico and Arizona into a single state to be called Arizona. His proposal had strong support in the House and Senate Committees on Territories, but in the previous Congress—the Fifty-Eighth (1903–1905)—a vocal opponent to joint statehood had emerged. Senator Joseph Benson Foraker, an Ohio Republican whose brother, Creighton M. Foraker, ranched in the Territory and had served as its U.S. marshal since 1897, spoke out repeatedly against the unprecedented move to force two Territories to unite when they did not wish to do so. Senator Foraker renewed his attack in the Fifty-Ninth Congress. He worked to amend the statehood bill by requiring voters in New Mexico and Arizona to approve separately the constitution for the new, unified state. Such a requirement was widely seen as a way to defeat joint statehood and was also regarded as picking "a fight with the President."[24]

While his initial amendment did not pass, it served as a warning shot. Conflict between Foraker and advocates of joint statehood intensified in the next several months, culminating in a bold political showdown when Foraker administered a two-part defeat to the president in early March. By a vote of 42 to 29, the Senate approved removing an enabling act for Arizona and New Mexico from the omnibus statehood bill, leaving Oklahoma and the Indian Territory to be merged. Having shown its resolve to act independently on statehood, the Senate promptly broke with Roosevelt. By a one vote margin, 36 to 35, it disapproved joint statehood for New Mexico and Arizona.[25]

The battle was joined: Senator Foraker and colleagues opposed to joint statehood squared off against the president. Moreover, neither side could be sure of support from the House, where members were at odds with Speaker Joe Cannon, who was blocking legislation in a clumsy show of his authority. Over the next three months intense political jockeying occurred until finally a compromise emerged. Separate joint statehood bills would go forward, but for New Mexico and Arizona a new Foraker Amendment required a referendum in each Territory to approve or reject joint statehood. Then in "a blaze of political pyrotechnics, the long-drawn-out State-hood fight was brought to a close in the Senate" in mid-June. Oklahoma and the Indian Territory would enter as one state in 1907, while the For-aker Amendment's referendum would be part of the fall election. President Roosevelt signed the final bill on 16 June, ending seven months of political brinkmanship, but intra- and interterritorial wrangling continued.[26]

"Many Years before the Chance Again Offers Itself"

New Mexicans had been thinking about joint statehood for several years. When talk of it first emerged in the Congress early in 1903, legislators in Santa Fe seemed resigned to accept it. Nine representatives from both parties and all quadrants of the Territory told a Spanish-language news-paper they believed it offered the most likely route for entering the Union. A McKinley County legislator had a special reason for favoring it—Gal-lup could be the capital because "it will be the most central point in the new state." A Carlsbad newspaper conducted an informal opinion survey in mid-September 1903 by asking forty-six Eddy County residents "of all political faiths and of every station in life 'What They Think of State-hood,'" the opinions solicited "in general conversation, none of those inter-viewed knowing that their views were to be published." Four declined to give an opinion, and of the remainder only one was a Nuevomexicano, a local sheep raiser. He opposed uniting with Arizona, and his preference for single statehood resonated with twenty-one others (52 percent), while fif-teen (36 percent) favored joint statehood, and five (12 percent) opposed any form of statehood, citing the problem of corruption in the Territory. Sev-eral hundred miles north of Carlsbad in predominantly Nuevomexicano Mora County, the Spanish-language newspaper in Wagon Mound noted in December 1903 that "we believe that the number of those who desire union [with Arizona] would not reach ten percent." The paper favored statehood, but if the only option was to merge with Arizona, then "we prefer to remain in our current [Territorial] position."[27]

Throughout 1904 and 1905 opinion vacillated on whether to support joint statehood. Territorial politicians continued to lobby in Washington for separate statehood, and as late as December 1905 they pressed their case by explaining that Rodey's loss in the 1904 election stemmed from his pro-joint-statehood position. Governor Otero remained an implacable foe, and such Republican newspapers as the *Albuquerque Morning Journal* echoed Otero's outspoken opposition. But in one of Otero's first public statements against joint statehood early in 1903, he made a prescient statement: "I believe that eventually public opinion would be reconciled to and would accept whatever arrangement ensures equal rights for our people." Following Otero's dismissal from office in January 1906, public opinion began to shift toward joint statehood.[28]

The same week the Congress approved the enabling act, Roosevelt issued an open letter to the residents of Arizona that circulated widely in New Mexico, too. The president appealed to those opposing jointure to give it "their sober second thought." He pointedly reminded Arizonans that should they refuse this offer, "they condemn themselves to an indefinite continuance of a condition of tutelage." He also explained a political reality: resistance would gain them nothing. He would not change his mind about joint statehood if they rejected it. "It is my belief," Roosevelt wrote, "that if the people of Arizona let this chance go by they will have to wait very many years before the chance again offers itself, and even then it will very probably be only upon the present terms—that is upon the condition of being joined with New Mexico."[29]

New Mexicans attached much weight to the president's claim that joint statehood represented their best option, and various key officials echoed his advice. A week after the president's letter circulated, W. E. Martin addressed himself to Nuevomexicanos. He reminded them that he was "an Anglo-Saxon native of New Mexico" who headed the Territory's Bureau of Immigration and was "a friend to the native people of New Mexico. . . . Their language was the first I began to utter." He supported joint statehood and called "upon every native son of New Mexico to walk to the polls in solid phalanx and cast his vote in favor of it." In mid-August, former Territorial Delegate Rodey, then a federal judge in Puerto Rico, told readers of *La Voz del Pueblo*, "I am of the opinion that no good reason exists to oppose joint statehood." In late September five members from the central committees of both the Republican and Democratic parties issued a statement citing six reasons to approve joint statehood for the sake of "the children of the state, representation in congress and full rights of American citizens for all our people." Delegate Andrews also threw his support behind joint statehood, reversing his 1904 campaign pledge. He did so as part of a calculated move to keep on the good side of the president: "By supporting the proposal as a Party measure New Mexico might possibly gain much needed favor from the [Roosevelt] administration."[30]

In his memoir Senator Foraker depicted his referendum as a major, though unacknowledged, benefit: "I have confidence that what I did in this respect will sometime be appreciated as an important public service to the people of those States and the whole country." But not only did New Mexicans never formally express gratitude to Senator Foraker for his fight on their behalf, they did not even avail themselves of the chance to reject the forced union. The ballot put the question simply: "Serán Arizona y Nuevo México Unidos para Formar un Estado. Will Arizona and New Mexico Be United to Form a State." When New Mexicans went to the polls on 6 November they approved President Roosevelt's plan by a resounding 11,460 vote margin, 26,195 in favor and 14,735 opposed. Arizona's electorate overwhelmingly rejected the proposed union—3,141 voting in favor and 16,265 opposed, which killed the measure.[31]

The vote surprised no one. Although public-opinion polling for elections did not exist in 1906, the outcome had been widely predicted in advance given that Arizona's opposition had long been known. Having gained separate Territorial status when severed from New Mexico during the Civil War, Arizonans had no intention of being reunited, or "Siamesed." The *New York Times* noted early in 1905, "The revolt of Arizona against being unequally yoked together with New Mexico in the bonds of Statehood seems to be sincere and general." Arizonans objected that two-thirds of the legislative representation went to New Mexico, the new capital was Santa Fe, and government jobs and patronage would be lost. Moreover, use of Spanish in business and politics was unacceptable to them.[32]

"Given Away Their Consciences to Be Governed by a 'Gang'"

Voters separated their decision on joint statehood from that of retaining Andrews as their congressional delegate in the election. Early returns showed Andrews trailing Octaviano A. Larrazolo, a Democrat and forty-seven-year-old Las Vegas lawyer, by several hundred votes. Three days after the election the Territory's leading Republican newspaper, the *Albuquerque Morning Journal*, ran a headline announcing the "LATEST RETURNS INDICATE VICTORY FOR LARRAZOLO" by a slim margin of 274 votes. But final tallies had not come in, and the newspaper noted that the count from the north seemed unusually slow. The next morning the paper's readers awoke to this headline: "ANDREWS GOES TO CONGRESS; MAJORITY SMALL." Andrews's win, first reported at 283 votes, eventually shrank to an officially certified margin of 266.[33]

The Andrews victory received much critical attention from *La Voz del Pueblo*. On Saturday, 10 November its readers learned that Larrazolo had outpolled his opponent by 995 votes and would be their new delegate. But the paper also ominously said that some people "are making efforts to falsify the returns of certain counties in order to steal the election from Larrazolo." To support that claim, *La Voz del Pueblo* documented specific instances of voting irregularities in three counties. Included in these charges were allegations that hundreds of immigrant miners, all ineligible to vote, were paid to do so in Colfax County. A reported campaign fund of $6,000 enabled the Republicans to finance such activities, a tactic also successfully employed by large mining companies in Colorado in the same election (and subsequent ones). The following Saturday, *La Voz del Pueblo* featured translated articles from Republican newspapers in Springer, Estancia, and Albuquerque offering accounts of election fraud. Republican-led violence, including physical assaults on voters, occurred in northeast New Mexico, according to the newspaper in Springer. In Democratic-leaning Abo, according to the *Estancia News*, the local post office received notices on 30 October assigning voters to one of two polling locations, but these were not delivered until election-day afternoon. The *Albuquerque Morning Journal* printed a letter from a Socorro resident claiming his county's election officials were operatives of "the Bursum gang" who routinely undercounted Democratic ballots. Holm O. Bursum, from Socorro County, headed the Territory's Republican Party and also directed Andrews's campaign in 1906.[34]

Irregularities marred the 1906 election for delegate, but results for all other offices showed strong voter independence. Incumbent Republicans won handily by large margins, usually at least a thousand votes. But the delegate race was the closest in the Territory's history and, according to the *Albuquerque Morning Journal*, that was due "not so much to the kind of campaign made by Mr. Larrazolo and his committee, but to the kind of club furnished him by the Republican party." The Democrats, the paper said, capitalized on Andrews's notorious association with the collapse of the Enterprise Bank and its link to his role in the Pennsylvania Development Company. Voters were reminded of the tragic events of a year earlier in stump speeches and newspaper articles, turning questions about the candidate's character and reputation into major issues. In an article on "other very strong reasons [Andrews] ought to be defeated," *La Voz del Pueblo* attacked his conduct as akin to an "eel" to suggest his chameleon or shape-shifting behaviors. Moreover, at least five Republican papers—in Las Vegas, Clayton, Roswell, Alamogordo, and Estancia—endorsed Larrazolo, and Republicans in Torrance County asked themselves if "they had given away their consciences to be governed by a 'gang.'"[35]

The charge that the Nuevomexicano vote was controlled by a gang or a boss had been leveled in early June by a Republican newspaper, the *Carlsbad Current*. A vigorous denial by *La Voz del Pueblo* followed, and the exchange of charges and countercharges reveals prejudices and social attitudes just below the surface of politics that could be easily stirred up by a few provocative words. All that remains today from the two papers' dispute is *La Voz del Pueblo*'s translation of the offending editorial and their rejection of it as "a cowardly campaign of defamation against the native people of New Mexico."[36]

The *Carlsbad Current*'s attack on Nuevomexicanos vented racial resentments and fears. The *Current* questioned whether Nuevomexicanos would be loyal to a country whose language they did not know and argued against allowing them to vote on joint statehood. Employing racial stereotypes common in that era, the Carlsbad newspaper derided Nuevomexicanos "as a mixture of the descendants of Castilians, Aztecs, Sioux, and Ethiopians." To make a more graphic case, the *Current* took its readers on a tour of "the village of San José on the outskirts of Carlsbad. The living conditions present among this gathering of Mexican aborigines would bring shame to other savage peoples."[37]

These racist views challenged voting rights: "The *Current* desires to make its position so clear, so evident that there will be no misunderstanding of it. . . . [The *Current*] says it emphatically would remove the privilege of voting from anyone . . . whose moral nature is so low, whose intellectual capacity is so limited that it cannot exercise this privilege with intelligence, virtue, and honesty, but instead falls under the whip of the [political] party and of a partisan lackey." The *Current* maintained that "there is but one race on the earth qualified by its nature to manage and govern man's destiny—the pure Anglo-Saxon." Anglos alone, said the Carlsbad paper, should decide New Mexico's fate in elections. The Las Vegas newspaper realized that turning back attempts at disfranchisement required more than editorial rebuttal. Accordingly, they promised that at the next session of the Territorial Legislature "we will demand [of the representatives] that they give their views on the position of the *Current* toward the people of New Mexico." By pledging to ask the Territorial Legislature to rebuff the *Current*'s posturing about barring Nuevomexicanos from voting, *La Voz del Pueblo* reminded everyone that the votes of native New Mexicans decided all elections.[38]

The newspapers' exchange over who should be permitted to vote on statehood brought into the open the racist fears of some Euro-Americans. Similar hostilities were sometimes expressed far from the earshot of Nuevomexicanos. For example, Albuquerque businessman and rancher J. G. Dargen visited Washington in June 1905 and told a reporter, "Statehood for New Mexico simply means that the white people of the Territory will be put under the domination of the Mexicans, who greatly outnumber us. The white element in this nation has never yet submitted to the rule of an inferior race, and in order to avoid trouble it will be far better not to bring about such a situation. In course of time we shall be ready for Statehood." Several months later a *New York Times* correspondent visiting Las Cruces reported, "I met not a single American of substance or standing who spoke in favor of Statehood. . . . [They] wish to postpone admission to the Union until an American, and not a Mexican, population dominates the Territory." While racism adversely affected local attitudes toward entering the Union, at the national level it is unlikely that it was "the major obstruction to the territory's statehood aspirations," as one historian claimed. Instead, after 1900 political manipulation by Senators Aldrich and Beveridge coupled with President Roosevelt's unwillingness to challenge them over their opposition meant that a few senators could block statehood until 1910.[39]

The racial animosity expressed in the dispute between the *Carlsbad Current* and *La Voz del Pueblo* was replayed in postelection accusations between Octaviano A. Larrazolo and William H. Andrews. Whereas the *Current* had charged that a Democratic machine influenced all Nuevomexicanos, in fact it was Republican bosses who ensured Andrews's return to Washington. But Larrazolo and the Democrats did not accept their defeat without a final fight. In late February 1907 the House of Representatives formally investigated their allegations of voter fraud, intimidation, and rigged counts. All the charges leveled in newspaper accounts in the weeks following the election found their way into the depositions. For more than seven weeks attorneys for each side collected a total of 1,012 pages of testimony from 260 witnesses in New Mexico—203 on behalf of Andrews and 57 backing Larrazolo. The Democrats documented fifty-two instances of alleged voter fraud in four counties—Colfax, Torrance, Socorro, and Valencia. Their charges centered on illegal registrations prior to the election, voter intimidation on election day, and irregularities in postelection vote counting. When Larrazolo testified, he focused on improprieties in Colfax County, alleging that more than 300 immigrant miners ineligible to vote had cast ballots for his opponent. But these miners could not be subpoenaed because all had left the Territory. Larrazolo also implied that Colfax County Coal and Coke Company and the Nevada Construction Company colluded with Republican leaders in arranging for these miners to vote and then disappear. There was no attempt to investigate his allegation.[40]

Delegate Andrews denied and rebutted all the charges alleged in Larrazolo's petition and countered by claiming eighteen new irregularities on the part of Larrozolo. He went through each county's canvassing of votes to challenge decisions to award Larrazolo ballots where the choice for delegate was unclear. He also contended that "false, fraudulent, and illegal ballots" were both cast and counted for Larrazolo. Yet in spite of such widespread improprieties, he claimed he had prevailed and therefore "was legally elected." The Republican-controlled House concurred, and the incumbent William H. Andrews returned to the Sixtieth Congress, where he remained as delegate until statehood.[41]

"You Have Been an Unsatisfactory Governor"

Voter fraud was not the only impropriety in New Mexico investigated by the House of Representatives, which probed fraudulent land schemes in the Territory in the spring of 1906—just one more in a long series of questionable land transactions that had become an acute embarrassment to Roosevelt, challenging his credibility as a clean government reformer. Fraudulent land deals had plagued the West for decades, but beginning in 1901 and continuing for the remainder of Roosevelt's tenure, corrupt practices in land sales were exposed in three western states—Oregon, Washington, and California—as well as in Arizona and New Mexico. These transactions were so complicated and extensive that they overwhelmed the legal and audit units of the Department of the Interior and the Department of Justice.

In response President Roosevelt yielded to a request by his attorney general to set up a new office of special investigators in July 1908, the forerunner of the Federal Bureau of Investigation.[42]

On the same day in March 1905 that a story entitled "trying to oust Gov. Otero" appeared in the *Washington Post*, a land sale quietly transpired in Santa Fe whose repercussions would contribute to Otero's removal and ultimately also bring about the dismissal of his successor, Herbert J. Hagerman. The federal commissioner in charge of public lands in New Mexico, Alpheus A. Keen, described by a contemporary as a "life-long friend of [the] governor," had received his appointment from Otero in March 1899. On 11 March 1905 he signed an agreement with Las Cruces attorney and Republican state legislator Herbert B. Holt for the sale of more than 9,900 acres of homestead land in the Mesilla Valley. Holt presented more than sixty separate bids, each for the 160 acres allowed any individual buyer of public domain land, and each bid was for $1.50 an acre. In the spring of 1906 the U.S. Justice Department would allege to the Congress that Holt and Keen conspired to defraud the federal government through "attempted evasion of the provisions of the act of June 21, 1898, which directs that 'not more than one-quarter section of land [160 acres] shall be sold to any one person.'"[43]

This report began a series of Justice Department probes in New Mexico between 1906 and 1908 that alleged land fraud identical to the Keen-Holt arrangement—one person presenting multiple bids from numerous individuals on contiguous 160-acre allotments and all offering the identical amount as the bid price. Keen, in turn, presented the purchase offers to the other two members of the land board—Governor Otero and the secretary of the Territory. Beginning in 1901 this board had routinely given its approval to nearly two dozen sales of large tracts of the public domain, all similar in form and scale to that of Holt's offer. Public outcry over alleged land fraud by Keen and his board became so loud that, in the spring of 1907, it precipitated an investigative committee in the New Mexico Legislature. Its report excoriated Governor Hagerman, and to a lesser degree ex-Governor Otero. Shortly after the legislature's investigation, President Roosevelt removed Territorial Governor Herbert J. Hagerman in mid-April 1907, but the land-fraud charges dogged him as late as 1931–32 in a congressional investigation.

In their 1906 report to the House, investigators presented twenty instances of suspicious land sales in New Mexico that began in 1901 and continued for nearly five years. And who was Keen's first petitioner in a bogus land sale and the principal behind most of the land-sale legerdemain? It was the Pennsylvania Development Company, whose president was William H. Andrews, New Mexico's delegate to the Congress. President Roosevelt had been suspicious of Andrews for a few years, and the House of Representatives had gone on record in May 1906 opposing land transactions pushed by the Pennsylvania Development Company. But Hagerman went ahead and signed deeds for lands bought by that company, sealing his own fate.[44]

As a contemporary observer noted, "It was the general belief that Governor Hagerman had been appointed with the purpose of correcting abuses in the matter of the disposal of public lands." But the abuses had not been corrected, and soon the president retaliated against both Secretary of the Interior Hitchcock and Governor Hagerman. For four months beginning in the summer of 1906 Hitchcock publicly criticized the president for tolerating abuses in land sales. By November Roosevelt had heard enough; he dismissed Hitchcock and appointed James R. Garfield secretary of the interior in December 1906. Garfield, a well-known reformer and an attorney, had helped to enact a corrupt practices act in Ohio. He had also proven his mettle to the president over the previous three years in addressing excesses by corporations. The urgency Roosevelt attached to cleaning up allegations of land fraud was evident in the promptness with which he conferred with his new secretary of the interior. He brought Garfield to the White House on Saturday, 5 January 1907 for lunch and to go over "Public Land matters." Garfield returned to the White House that evening "further considering the question" from 9:30 to 11:00.[45]

Roosevelt shared with Garfield confidential correspondence totaling more than sixty-five pages he had received between mid-September and early December 1906 from Governor Hagerman, William H. H. Llewellyn, the U.S. attorney in New Mexico and a former Rough Rider officer, and William Moody, the U.S. attorney general. The central issue was Hagerman's active part in approving the sale of more than 10,000 acres of public lands in the Manzano Mountains, much of it with timber, to William H. Andrews and associates in the Pennsylvania Development Company. Llewellyn characterized Hagerman's actions as a cavalier disregard for legal requirements, and Moody urged a thorough investigation.[46]

At the end of March Roosevelt forwarded to Garfield a confidential report from Solomon Luna, the Republican Party's national committeeman from New Mexico, substantiating allegations of Hagerman's complicity in fraudulently transferring public lands to the Andrews group. This confidential report referred to the findings of a five-member committee of the New Mexico Legislature released in mid-March. Appended to the twenty-one-page document were more than one hundred pages of testimony and exhibits substantiating allegations of fraud in eight land transactions between the Territory and the Pennsylvania Development Company. The headline from the Republican *Santa Fe New Mexican* summarized the findings: "GOVERNOR'S ACTION ILLEGAL AND IMPROPER." Hagerman denied all charges and made the counterclaim that his vigorous pursuit of corruption had led the Legislature to retaliate through a biased inquiry engineered by his archfoe Holm O. Bursum. Hagerman had dismissed Bursum shortly after taking office, alleging malfeasance as head of the penitentiary, a charge a district court rejected.[47]

In mid-February 1907 the president instructed Garfield to clean up the fraudulent land transactions in New Mexico and remove Hagerman, who resigned rather than be fired. But the matter did not end there, and Hagerman did not go quietly. He pleaded for his job, but Roosevelt rebuffed him, noting that his appeal rendered it necessary "for me to write you very plainly. . . . I think you have been an unsatisfactory governor and that your removal from the position is imperatively demanded." Roosevelt vented his disgust over the governor's conduct: "It was impossible in my judgment to retain you in office unless I am content to abandon all idea of holding public officers in New Mexico, or indeed elsewhere, to any proper standard of conduct." The president also repeated the conclusion of a Department of Justice investigator that Hagerman approved sale of public lands to the Pennsylvania Development Company "with the full knowledge of its fraudulent character." Hagerman then went to the court of public opinion and released their correspondence to refute being, in the words of the *New York Times*, "scathingly arraigned for the part he took in the Pennsylvania Development Company land transaction." He also self-published a booklet he believed would exonerate him.[48]

"To Vest the Power . . . in the National Government"

In early December 1902 Theodore Roosevelt delivered his second Message of the President and praised the Congress for "inauguration of the system of nationally aided irrigation for the arid regions of the far West". He called for "liberal appropriations" to ensure the success of his "policy of irrigation" on public lands, including those of New Mexico. In spite of the president's obvious pride in passage of the Reclamation, or Newlands, Act of 1902, unintended consequences would eventually surface. Roosevelt, who personally negotiated the final terms of the bill, explicitly identified its chief beneficiaries as "the home builder, the settler who lives on the land, and . . . no one else."[49]

In siding with the homesteader and against speculators, Roosevelt endowed the federal government with an enlarged, activist mission and the legislation (albeit rudimentary) to pursue it. This expansion of government's role came to be known as federalism, and it abetted his modernization project. But Roosevelt not only expanded government's responsibilities, he also placed obligations on the citizens who benefited. Once the government built dams and created reservoirs to irrigate arid public lands claimed by homesteaders, these water rights had to be bought by the settlers and managed collectively through a water users' association.[50]

On paper it looked straightforward, but it created winners and losers because the government injected itself into matters that speculators wanted to control. An immediate casualty in New Mexico was Nathan E. Boyd, M.D., who would claim that the government's action usurped his right to develop a large-scale private irrigation project to bring water to land he planned to sell. A basic question divided the government and Dr. Boyd: Who could best manage the waters of the Rio Grande in southern New Mexico? The U.S. government's newly created public policy—the Reclamation/Newlands Act—aided homesteaders in arid regions by financing construction of sizable public works projects. But Boyd, who had incorporated the Rio Grande Dam and Irrigation Company in 1893, regarded the government's action as little more than claim jumping. The two parties fought continuously in the courts from the 1890s to 1923, first over who controlled the waters in the Rio Grande and then, after the government began building Elephant Butte Dam in 1907 (it opened in 1915), over whether Boyd should be paid seventeen million dollars he insisted was owed him for lost revenue.

In broadening the government's role and tying it to promoting the nation's well-being, Roosevelt sought out and empowered competent, take-charge administrators who, in the words of one observer, exhibited "efficiency, self-sacrifice, and an absolute devotion to their country's interests." Four such men—all cabinet secretaries—played key parts in battling Boyd. Their goal was establishing federal control over building the largest irrigation dam in the world in the early twentieth century—Elephant Butte Dam on the Rio Grande to irrigate 100,000 acres stretching south below Socorro, past Las Cruces, to the border. To them, New Mexico's irrigation needs were a national priority.[51]

Their actions inevitably conflicted with Boyd's scheme. He began his venture in 1893 with high expectations of building a reservoir some 125 miles north of El Paso and near Elephant Butte. All went relatively well for four years. Boyd, an American citizen who had spent some time abroad, recruited English investors to capitalize his project and also incorporated his company in England. He secured a permit for his project from the secretary of the interior in 1895. But within three years, the four cabinet secretaries voiced major objections to his plan, and after 1901 they relentlessly foiled his every move. Secretary of State John Hay (1898–1905) opposed Boyd's plan because it would reduce, if not at times virtually cut off, the flow of the Rio Grande along the border with Mexico from El Paso to Brownsville, Texas. The Rio Grande ran dry part of the summer below El Paso in the mid-1890s, prompting Mexican complaints that the United States owed it water. Secretary of the Interior Hitchcock (1899–1905) moved to void Boyd's license after listening to farmers in the Mesilla Valley and residents in El Paso predict dire results if Boyd were allowed to control water vital to their livelihood. Secretary of War Elihu Root (1899–1904) joined in the dispute out of concern for how much water flowed in the river. He insisted on retaining the river as a navigable waterway for defensive purposes along the border with Mexico. He pursued his military goal by declaring the Rio Grande in the Territory of New Mexico to be wholly under federal control as a way to ensure water flowed downstream. To enforce his order, he turned to Attorneys General J. W. Griggs (1897–99) and P. C. Knox (1899–1904) to initiate legal proceedings against Boyd. Collectively these government actions prompted six lawsuits between 1898 and 1909, three of which went to the U.S. Supreme Court. In the end, the government prevailed against Boyd.[52]

Throughout the administration of President Roosevelt, Boyd never ceased to press his company's claims. He repeatedly told Governor Otero to push for statehood because it would free New Mexico (and, not coincidently, Boyd's company) from onerous federal control of its waters. In March 1901 he told Otero that he was afraid the federal government would conclude a treaty with Mexico as "a means of prohibiting the impounding of the flood waters of the Rio Grande above Elephant Butte and possibly at Elephant Butte." Boyd completely misrepresented plans for ensuring adequate water flowed past El Paso, and the U.S. government negotiated a binational agreement by which sixty thousand acre-feet of water from the Rio Grande were to be delivered to Mexico annually. Boyd charged that such a quantity impaired New Mexico's water rights. Disagreeing with Boyd, the Territorial engineer in 1907 estimated (accurately) the reservoir's storage capacity to be two million acre-feet.[53]

With his opinions disregarded and his legal arguments rejected, Boyd clung tenaciously to states' right claims, which posited superiority of the states over the federal government except as constitutionally delimited. He found a kindred spirit in Colorado's Democratic Senator Henry M. Teller, and widely distributed his speech "The State's Control over Its Waters," delivered in the Senate on 31 March and 2 April 1908. Teller lambasted Secretary of State (and former Secretary of War) Elihu Root, who had succeeded John Hay in 1905 but continued the government's legal pressure on Boyd. Teller expressed exactly what Boyd felt about Root: he was a dangerous person who advocated what the senator and Boyd regarded to be a radical departure in the "general theory of government." Root had claimed in 1906 "that sooner or later construction of the Constitution will be found to vest the power [to act on behalf of the people] where it will be exercised, in the National Government." Teller argued passionately that the government's control over reclamation amounted to an unwarranted expansion of power, which intruded and impinged upon states' rights. Teller and Boyd's hostility to the federal government exemplifies the contrast between an older, nineteenth-century view of government in which states' rights predominated and the modernization endorsed by Roosevelt and carried out by means of reclamation and irrigation—part of an expanded and active role by the U.S. government.[54]

The government's preliminary decision in 1904 to build a dam at Elephant Butte coincided with the push to allow New Mexico into the Union as a combined state with Arizona. Political calculations as much as engineers' reports influenced the selection of Elephant Butte rather than El Paso as the dam's site. New Mexico had two entwined political advantages. First, New Mexico was a stronghold for Republicans, the majority party controlling the federal government, whereas Texas was solidly Democratic. Second, New Mexicans resented an attempt by Texas to build the new dam at El Paso, which was coupled with a ban on New Mexico using additional water from the Rio Grande for irrigation. This ill-conceived, growth-choking bill, introduced by Texas Senator Charles A. Culberson and Representative John H. Stephens, permanently limited irrigation in New Mexico to the volume of water used in 1900, thus giving Texas all future appropriations of surplus water flowing in the Rio Grande. Such an action would render moot the precondition for statehood—"more water and people."

New Mexicans mounted a successful campaign against the Culberson-Stephens bill in congressional hearings during 1902. In 1903 the Reclamation Service weighed in with a report recommending Elephant Butte as the sole dam on the Rio Grande, but several miles distant from where Boyd proposed his impoundment. The Reclamation Service's report came to be seen as the answer to the diplomatic, domestic, and technical questions that had vexed government officials for nearly a decade. It was also widely recognized that the multi-million-dollar project would benefit New Mexico by providing several thousand new jobs and drawing people to a sparsely settled area.

By the fall of 1904 representatives from New Mexico, Texas, and Mexico had set the basic terms for allocating water from the Rio Grande. The U.S. Senate formally approved the treaty in late June 1906, the same week that the Congress also authorized the Territory's residents to vote on joint statehood. President Roosevelt signed both bills, pleased that two crucial pieces of his modernization plan for New Mexico were moving forward. Planning by Interior's Reclamation Service began promptly, and over the next nine years construction of Elephant Butte Dam would cost more than ten million dollars and employ three thousand workers. It became the first large-scale federal public works project in New Mexico, but in the decade before statehood it was only one of several undertaken in the Territory by the Reclamation Service.[55]

New Mexico's aridity made it a prime candidate for irrigation projects. The Reclamation Service's chief, Frederick Newell, visited the Territory in October 1902 to look at the Pecos River Valley between Roswell and Carlsbad, where irrigation projects had been proposed since the late 1860s. But the most intensive interest dated from 1888–89 following formation of the Pecos Irrigation and Improvement Company by Charles Eddy and investors he recruited. But by 1902 the company had run out of money, and Eddy and residents of Carlsbad were eager to convince Newell to buy out their company, take over repairs, and begin new construction. The Reclamation Act barred such a transaction, yet within six years it had been carried out under intense political pressure.

Aid to Carlsbad followed assistance to Roswell, which had its own history of speculators promoting irrigation, principally James Hagerman beginning in the 1890s. Newell's 1902 visit prompted study of a long-discussed reservoir at Hondo, seventeen miles southwest of Roswell which the government approved in June 1904. Carlsbad immediately protested the decision, claiming it reduced their volume of irrigation water. A heated three-day hearing ensued in September, but matters changed completely on Sunday, 2 October 1904 when heavy rains turned the Pecos River into a force of destruction from above Roswell to below Carlsbad, wiping out fifteen years of privately financed irrigation infrastructure, including channels and dams. By December the reservoir at Hondo was under way, as was a study to assess needed repairs to the entire area's irrigation network.

The Reclamation Service did not want to be stuck fixing the Pecos Irrigation and Improvement Company's extensive system because a government report from five years earlier had documented shoddy work in its construction. Soon, though, politics would trump their reservations. The company appealed to two of its key financiers in New Bedford, Massachusetts. They sent no additional money; instead, they contacted Massachusetts congressman William S. Greene "to lobby for the Reclamation Service to buy the property." Greene, in turn, enlisted Massachusetts Senator Henry Cabot Lodge, the president's closest friend. By early in 1905 various delegations had pitched their case at Interior and on Capitol Hill, but only one group—"a committee of interested [Carlsbad] farmers and irrigators"—met with President Roosevelt. Among these men was Charles L. Ballard, who had served as a lieutenant in the Rough Riders. At the White House meeting "his influence helped induce Roosevelt to pressure the Interior Department and Reclamation to adopt Carlsbad as one of its initial projects." Between 1904 and 1908 the Reclamation Service would spend nearly a million dollars to take over irrigation projects from private investors and try to make successes out of their failures. The Hondo Reservoir proved a disaster because it failed to hold water. The Carlsbad area's project fared slightly better, but only by becoming a steady supplicant, prompting one foe in 1922 to characterize "the Carlsbad people [as] eternally after extending this project and spending more [federal] money."[56]

President McKinley's call for "more water" in May 1901 made irrigation a continual selling point in the push to secure statehood. When William H. Andrews appealed for Nuevomexicanos' support in the 1904 election he promised, "I will also work diligently to secure for New Mexico the assistance of the Reclamation Service in all ways possible to build irrigation reservoirs." In fact, though, Andrews had no clout in such matters. The only person in Washington who could influence the Reclamation Service was the president. But in applying pressure to gain action he sought, Theodore Roosevelt became part of the Territory's twin dilemmas: factions and favoritism continued to plague New Mexico's politics, placing the Territory's well-being in the eye of the beholder.[57]

CHAPTER FIVE

"People Who Are to the Manor Born"

A "curious result" concluded the ladies' vocal competition in the three-day territorial musical contest held at Las Vegas in September 1895: a tie occurred. "Senora Hernandez and Mrs. R. C. Rankin both received an average of thirty-six out of a possible fifty. . . . Mr. [A. J.] Goodrich hesitated in making the award, but finally decided to give the first prize to Senora Hernandez (a Spanish lady educated in Madrid) on account of greater cultivation." Why did Goodrich, an "eminent musical author" from Chicago, hesitate in awarding the twenty-five-dollar first prize? Did he pause to consider that bestowing the award on a Nuevomexicana might seem a slight to Mrs. Rankin? In contrast to his criticism of other performers, Goodrich seemed solicitous toward her, remarking that "his individual preference was for the beautiful voice and artless style of Mrs. Rankin."[1]

As Goodrich departed, he told a local reporter that "the effects of the contest would be far-reaching and beneficial." The territorial music competition was held in one of Las Vegas's two opera houses. Such venues dotted the West in the late nineteenth century; an opera house was found in almost every town between Raton and Socorro. The level of cultural interest along the Gallinas River would have delighted those who wanted evidence that the East's influence had taken root in the Southwest. Here was culture of their culture, a transplanting of values and institutions.[2]

For New Mexicans the nineteenth century ended as it had begun. They were appendages of a distant capital, ruled by Spain up to 1821, Mexico until 1846, and the United States thereafter. Each government imposed its priorities upon a diverse and growing population. In 1785 there were about

16,000 Nuevomexicanos. Their number nearly quadrupled to about 61,000 by 1850 and had increased nearly 125 percent to about 135,000 when the 1900 census tallied 195,310 residents in the Territory. The balance of about 60,310 comprised some 31,000 Euro-American emigrants, 14,000 foreign-born immigrant whites, and about 15,140 nonwhites (reported as 13,200 American Indians, 1,600 black persons, and 340 Chinese). In the censuses of 1890 and 1900 the Territory's population increase had exceeded the average throughout the United States, and in 1900 it was also younger than the country on average—39 percent of the population was under fifteen years old, and another 24 percent fell between the ages of fifteen and twenty-nine.[3]

This population mix meant New Mexico was in flux throughout the nineteenth century as people adapted to one another and to changes in the prevailing political order. During that period three flags flew over New Mexico, with each of the countries aligning the local economy and government to their respective national interests. Unquestionably this outside control was the most consequential force shaping everyday life, and the impact on Nuevomexicanos of the last of these regimes—the American Territorial Period—is examined in this chapter. The next chapter takes up how American Indians, African Americans, and Asians fared. Each chapter focuses on what Euro-Americans imposed and how people responded between 1880 and 1912.

American rule began with military conquest and government between August 1846 and March 1851, which yielded to presidential control through appointed officials for the next sixty-one years. But the shift to civilian control was an exceedingly complicated process, perhaps best understood by visualizing it as an inverted pyramid. That is, the president's first agents were a few officials—governor, U.S. marshal, U.S. attorney, and Indian Affairs superintendent—but each passing decade brought more federal activities and appointees—including U.S. surveyor and district judges in the 1850s, Indian agents and U.S. post office officials during the 1860s and 1870s, and inspectors to investigate conflicts over water and land in the 1880s.

But between the 1850s and 1890s the expansion of American power came less through the arrival of appointees than in government policies to develop the West in the 1860s and 1870s, especially its economy. This kind of change exemplifies the workings of corporate capitalism, or the marshaling of public policy to benefit private enterprise. Favorable federal legislation began in the 1860s when railroads received land to spur transcontinental construction. Then in the 1870s new laws fostered mining (1872) and encouraged logging (1878). Such legislation affected the economy first but spread quickly to the political and social order. Railroads as well as large-scale coal and copper mining benefited most residents of the Territory. Also during these decades the U.S. Congress passed bills to promote social change, none more significant than the Homestead Act of 1862 and its supplements, which brought more than 100,000 settlers to New Mexico by 1910.[4]

Beginning in the 1890s Euro-Americans renewed a push for statehood. But what did entering the Union mean to Nuevomexicanos? We can answer this question by examining how federal activities after 1880 impacted them; how Nuevomexicanos melded change with continuity; and how they took control of their future. By 1910 Nuevomexicanos had redefined their place in the Euro-American order, exhibiting three qualities invaluable to their quest for statehood—adaptability, self-reliance, and a commitment to popular sovereignty.

"It Was Our Duty to Do Justice"

By the time James S. Calhoun assumed office as the Territory's first civilian governor in 1851, Nuevomexicanos had resigned themselves to American domination. Most of the elite participated in what one scholar has called a "peace structure," acceding to Euro-American control in exchange for undiminished influence. This arrangement emerged in the first decade of the American conquest and lasted through statehood. Another tier of Nuevomexicano politicians, likely numbering fewer than twelve hundred, existed below the elite, and for four decades they exercised power in villages, precincts, and counties as well as serving as delegates in both houses of the legislature. But after 1890 their influence waned, diminished by the twin assaults of a burgeoning Euro-American population and the corresponding addition of new precincts and counties.[5]

But the majority of Nuevomexicanos largely fended for themselves when faced with American domination. For example, beginning in the 1880s, "with increasing frequency, water cases were litigated in territorial district courts instead of county probate courts, which brought a diminution of local control." By 1897 district courts had taken over all water (and land) disputes, which shifted decisions away from "pragmatic solutions in keeping with community values" rendered by "members of the Hispano elite." Instead Euro-American attorneys argued abstract legal principles before district judges, who "were almost always federal appointees from outside the territory, with limited knowledge of water administration in New Mexico." At the same time, Nuevomexicano land grant heirs were the victims of collusion between unscrupulous attorneys and corrupt government officials—with both parties often active in the Santa Fe Ring—resulting in a massive transfer of land grant titles.[6]

While legal assaults eroded water use and landholdings, an equally consequential change had gradually swept through Nuevomexicanos' daily lives beginning in 1821, when wagon trains on the Santa Fe Trail began to bring an unprecedented volume and variety of goods into the Territory. That trade started to turn Nuevomexicanos into consumers and began to institute a new ethic: materialism. These changes were important preconditions for mercantile capitalism, or merchants selling consumer items, because they drew people into the new economic rhythm of wanting, buying, using, and discarding, in endless repetition. After the U.S.–Mexican War, mercantile and corporate capitalism had thoroughly subverted preindustrial agrarian self-sufficiency. Collectively these forces of modernization unleashed change pell-mell upon Nuevomexicanos, most of whom lived in small villages in the upper Rio Grande region (*río arriba*). They quickly became conscripts in the march of mercantile capitalism that followed the railroad's arrival in 1879. Merchants significantly expanded their wares. Consumers bought stoves and sewing machines, clothes and cosmetics, canned goods, jewelry, and tools. This consumption necessitated earning money and thus created a cash economy among the villagers. Within another ten years, taxes intensified the move toward cash transactions.[7]

Wage labor transformed New Mexico following American occupation. By the late 1850s, for example, large numbers of Nuevomexicanos in the Las Vegas area filled service jobs at nearby Fort Union. Twenty years later, the railroad created more seasonal wage labor, another step away from self-sustaining farm and livestock work. Soon travel to find employment became necessary, and by 1900 ten percent of the Territory's Nuevomexicano population worked in Colorado (10,222) and Arizona (3,351). Their numbers continued to rise in the decade before statehood as Colorado needed more

Nuevomexicanos for its fields, mines, and railroads. A Colorado sugar beet producer imported a hundred Nuevomexicanos from Las Vegas in 1903, and six years later nearly one-quarter of Colorado's more than 10,000 sugar beet workers were Nuevomexicanos. Migration soon became institutionalized, and by 1929 "about one member of every village family was leaving home each year to find work."[8]

While modernization forced long-term adaptations such as seasonal migrations, economic events specific to the 1890s brought much immediate misfortune and forced people to relocate. Agriculture had been suffering since 1887, and when the nation lapsed into a four-and-a-half-year economic depression known as the Panic of 1893, banks failed and falling prices further drove down wages and earnings. While this depression's effects in New Mexico have not been systematically investigated, it is clear that the slump had profound consequences for Nuevomexicanos.[9]

The Panic of '93 visited two specific economic adversities upon Nuevomexicanos during the 1890s: counties became much more assertive about collecting property taxes, and they stepped up foreclosures against those unable to pay. A parallel process occurred in Texas, and the impact on its Hispano citizens, the Tejanos, has been studied in an intensive, courthouse-by-courthouse investigation, revealing that a massive, unprecedented dispossession of land occurred in the 1890s. A similar pattern emerges from fragmentary evidence for northern New Mexico, but people resisted, especially in fending off tax collectors. For example, J. B. Watrous, a leading rancher and businessman in the Las Vegas area, related, "That depression lasted eight years, or rather ten, from the beginning and got worse and worse and caused innumerable failures." He did what he could to help those in distress: "In 1899 I was Chairman of [the] County Commissioners [of] Mora County. Many [Nuevomexicano] citizens begged me to save their property from being sold for taxes and . . . some . . . had not paid because the assessors made grave mistakes in assessments and could not get the Boards to look into it and make corrections. . . . I convinced my companions . . . it was our duty to do justice to those parties and our county. . . . I helped to save those parties." Watrous even paid back taxes to forestall evictions of local residents. Other, less altruistic, tactics emerged as well to shield Nuevomexicanos from tax delinquency. The *Santa Fe New Mexican* complained bitterly that between 1898 and 1901 almost no surveys had occurred on land grants, which allowed those landholders to "escape the payment of all territorial, county, school, and city taxes." The newspaper hinted at collusion: "One is almost tempted to suspect that the surveyor general and the [land] grant owners know how to stand in for each other [in evading taxes]."[10]

"At the Mercy of the Government Officials"

In spite of these examples of adaptive resistance, though, many Nuevomexicanos relocated within the Territory in response to hard times. Some homesteaders left one rural area for another, and some communities resettled to form new towns, as in the Río Puerco Valley. These patterns are not well documented, but scattered sources suggest some trends. The counties of Guadalupe, Mora, and San Miguel, which already had the highest number of Nuevomexicanos, also attracted the most Nuevomexicano homesteaders in the decade preceding statehood. They led all counties with a combined 32,878 filings in 1903–1904. The ten other counties reporting on homesteading collectively had a total of 26,073 filings. Some generalizations about Nuevomexicano homesteading emerge from a sampling from 1,500 Government Land Office records filed by Nuevomexicanos between 1900 and 1935. Entries for 1900–1912 reveal that just over 40 percent of all Nuevomexicano homesteaders were in San Miguel and Mora counties. The remaining Nuevomexicano homesteads were in seven other counties, with three of these contiguous to either San Miguel or Mora: Rio Arriba, Torrance, and Guadalupe, each of which had long-established Nuevomexicano populations. Of these three counties, the population growth in Guadalupe County between 1900 and 1910 was the most dramatic, rising from 5,429 to 10,827, a 99.4 percent increase.[11]

In comparing these Nuevomexicano homesteading data with a sampling from 2,000 Government Land Office homestead entries made by Euro-Americans between 1900 and 1912, some distinct differences emerge. None of the Euro-American entries were from San Miguel and Mora counties; indeed, these homesteaders went into only two counties frequented by Nuevomexicano homesteaders—Guadalupe and Torrance, both comparatively new creations. The preferred destinations for Euro-American homesteaders were the three counties created after 1900, in which Euro-Americans predominated: Roosevelt, Curry, and Quay (in order of frequency), which collectively drew 46 percent of the

Euro-American homesteaders, and had a total population of 37,819 in 1910.[12]

Of those filing homestead claims, 40 percent were Nuevomexicana, whereas just 18 percent of Euro-American homesteaders were women. While the latter percentage is consistent with data on women homesteaders in Colorado (and elsewhere), the large number of Nuevomexicana homesteaders invites closer attention. Within the population of rural New Mexico in 1900, it has been estimated that Nuevomexicanas amounted to 88 percent of all women in the Territory (68,640 out of 78,000). Nationally, 60 percent of all women lived in the countryside, which meant that Nuevomexicanas were more predominantly rural than the national average and perhaps more inclined to seek to own property.[13]

In addition, two related developments contributed to this higher than expected rate of homesteading by Nuevomexicanas—one legal and one social. Homesteading reversed discriminatory ownership practices imposed when U.S. law took effect in the nineteenth century. The rule known as coverture gave all property rights in marriage to the male, which meant that Nuevomexicanas lost the separate ownership of land provided under Spanish law. Contrary to the letter of the homesteading law, either husbands or wives, or single males or females, filed in New Mexico, and this practice allowed Nuevomexicanas to recover a right they had lost to coverture. The social milieu likewise proved hospitable to Nuevomexicanas seeking to own land. With more than 13,000 Nuevomexicanos migrating seasonally to Colorado and Arizona, a general loosening of long-standing family ties and roles occurred, breaking down the traditional bonds characteristic of the tight, insular communities of northern New Mexico. Personal opportunities increased as a result, especially for young Nuevomexicanas. That they claimed homesteads at a rate more than twice that found among Euro-American women shows both their desire to own property in their own name and their willingness to enter into new settings and roles.[14]

Few case studies document the actual homesteading experiences of Nuevomexicanos and Nuevomexicanas between the 1890s and 1912, but some trends are apparent in the experiences of settlers in the Río Puerco Valley south of Cuba (mentioned in chapter 3). Additional details emerge from a systematic study of homesteading in areas southwest and southeast of Las Vegas. When the Supreme Court's 1897 ruling in *United States v. [Julian] Sandoval* stripped 310,000 acres from a nearby land grant, it took a dozen years for the government to sort out titles to the remaining private lands. But while they waited, the residents of Cerrito, one of the villages within the land grant, began to file on homesteads within the boundaries of the grant as well as about fifty miles to the east in Variadero. The contrasting fortunes of these two sets of homesteading claims—the former for farming and the latter for grazing livestock—was not evident until after statehood when holdings in Cerrito began to fail in the 1920s while those at Variadero underwent downturns and consolidation—but ultimately survived. Whereas in 1889 and 1890 armed resistance protested the loss of nearby common land, in the early twentieth century the residents of Cerritos decided to reinvent themselves as best they could. They also benefited from congressional legislation doubling the size of homesteads from 160 acres to 320 in 1909, and seven years later the Congress further increased grazing prospects by approving homesteads of 640 acres, or a square mile. The residents of Cerrito homesteading in Variadero took full advantage of these changes, especially by having women file on lots adjacent to a family's existing homestead to maximize acreage, a practice that allowed Nuevomexicano families to lock up 95 percent of all homesteads on 108 square miles of land.[15]

Along with allowing larger homesteads, the government also sought to redress widespread grievances lodged following expropriation of land for national forests, which had forced people to relocate. Between 1901 and 1909, Nuevomexicanos and other landowners throughout the West lost their holdings when President Theodore Roosevelt placed over 234 million acres under federal control to be protected for posterity. Roosevelt's action significantly advanced the conservation movement, but it also displaced people across the West. Senators from western states began to resist and forced the Roosevelt administration to help displaced land owners. In 1906 the Congress approved and Roosevelt signed the Forest Homestead Act, which permitted homestead claims of 160 acres or less in national forests, along with grazing and private-use timber rights, thus restoring arable public lands to individuals. Moreover, priority went to anyone who had recently or currently occupied lands within a national forest, allowing Nuevomexicanos to file homestead claims on the common lands they had used prior to federal takeover.[16]

Assigned to carry out this act in New Mexico and Arizona between 1908 and 1916 was forester Arthur C. Ringland. The difficulty of his task was succinctly stated in a letter from New Mexico's new lieutenant governor, Ezéquiel C. de Baca, to his congressman, Harvey B. Fergusson, in 1913. He relayed complaints by his friends and neighbors, residents of a former land grant west of Las Vegas, about how government policies trampled customary use, reminding Fergusson that the grant "was ceded to the community by the Spanish government, among other reasons, to enable them to have grazing privileges as well as wood for their hearths." The 1897 *Sandoval* ruling reduced the 315,000 acre land grant to just over 5,200 acres of personal property, transferring the rest to the federal government, which placed much of it within the Pecos National Forest. C. de Baca spelled out the impact of the Forest Service's actions: "[Government regulation] deprives the people of free pasture and free wood in those lands in places rather thickly populated for centuries." He further claimed that "the department or officials [of the U.S. Forest Service] are taking undue advantage of these people. They have their holdings inside of the [forest] reserve and are, therefore, at the mercy of the government officials." No doubt also irksome was that five million acres of public domain ceded to New Mexico at statehood included some former land grant acreage.[17]

Ringland would spend much time addressing the "holdings inside of the reserve," and indeed he had been sent to New Mexico in 1908 because of his recent experience handling that problem in the state of Washington. In New Mexico implementation of the Forest Homestead Act began slowly. The Carson National Forest in late 1910 listed as open for homesteading a total of 1,598 acres available in four areas of the forest. The Pecos National Forest similarly returned thousands of acres to residents of the former San Miguel del Vado Grant near Las Vegas. Soon, though, thousands of homestead entries were filed for lands in the National Forests throughout New Mexico, and for the fifteen months between March 1913 and June 1914, a total of 200,528 acres in national forests in New Mexico were "restored as homesteads entries," with Nuevomexicanos regaining much of the acreage. Occasionally a Nuevomexicano sought a homestead in a national forest intending to either resell it or harvest the timber, but when uncovered these "speculative claims" were disallowed. Overall, while the Forest Homestead Act was a laudable attempt to aid the dispossessed, it returned but a miniscule percent of the millions of acres expropriated.[18]

Homesteading was the government's plan for settling the West, and it succeeded. More than 100,000 new residents came to New Mexico, but where they put down roots generally reinforced the separation of Euro-Americans from Nuevomexicanos. Like immigrants everywhere, people tended to settle among those sharing language, custom, and national identity. As a consequence, homesteading reinforced a racial divide that perpetuated suspicions and prejudices, allowing foes of statehood to sow seeds of hate, as in the 1906 dispute between the Carlsbad newspaper and *La Voz del Pueblo*.

The categories economists often use to describe why people migrate—push and pull factors—are applicable to Nuevomexicanos. Aside from eviction from land grants, either by coercion or legal proceedings, two other factors pushed people to leave their homelands. First, Nuevomexicano private holdings were a dwindling patrimony. Throughout the nineteenth century, population increase led to ever smaller plots being divided among siblings in each successive generation. A second downward spiral existed in many villages, too. Continuous cultivation and grazing leached the soil of its nutrients and reduced the amount of vegetation—all of which increased erosion. Some Nuevomexicanos, dismayed by their current meager prospects, looked beyond subsistence agriculture and small-scale ranching. In such circumstances wage labor and homesteading offered ways to earn a living and support families and communities, especially on the lower slopes of the Sangre de Cristo Mountains, and to ease pressure on a depleted land base. Greater economic opportunity also pulled Nuevomexicanos to new settings, and Albuquerque proved particularly attractive. Beginning in the early 1880s, the Atchison Topeka and Santa Fe opened its machine shop and roundhouse in Barelas. It employed hundreds of Nuevomexicanos and created a new community of workers east of Barelas in the parish of San José. In both locales Nuevomexicanos abandoned small-scale or subsistence farming for jobs with the railroad, and the same pattern repeated itself in Las Vegas, Socorro, San Marcial, and Tucumcari. Moreover, lumber, box manufacturing, and woolen mill jobs in Albuquerque beginning in 1902 employed hundreds of Nuevomexicanos for over a decade. Nuevomexicanos moving south in about 1900 worked at carpentry in Albuquerque, the railroad in Tucumcari, merchandising in San Marcial, and construction at Elephant Butte.[19]

Nuevomexicanas also found employment in towns, some as poorly paid domestics, others in commercial laundries, but a few in better paid jobs, including as post office employees earning between sixty and seventy-five dollars a month in the decade before statehood. In rapidly growing Guadalupe County, for example, between 1891 and 1912 all the postmistresses were Nuevomexicanas, and they held 20 percent of all appointments. Nuevomexicanos filled 60 percent of the postmaster positions, and Euro-Americans the remaining 20 percent. The Territory had 634 post offices in 1912, and women, including Nuevomexicanas, were routinely appointed.[20]

"Mired in [Debt] Obligations"

Mercantile capitalism spread rapidly across the Territory with demand outpacing the available supply of currency, which worked to benefit merchants in two distinct ways. First, stores issued their own scrip, paid it to Nuevomexicanos in exchange for produce or livestock, and took it back when selling them goods. By buying low, overcharging for what they sold, and carrying creditors at 10 percent interest, merchants made a tidy profit. This arrangement bound Nuevomexicanos to the store, but the stores also fostered dependency through a form of indentured servitude tied to sheepherding in which Nuevomexicanos (and some Euro-Americans) became *partidarios*. The terms of these labor contracts varied depending on whether the store or the partidario provided some or all of three necessities: the sheep, the land on which they grazed, and the rams. Over time, though, the stores almost always provided the latter two, and in exchange the partidarios returned a quantity of wool and a number of lambs to fulfill "rental" obligations. Partidarios faced great risks to fulfill their contracts—the elements, predators, sick animals, and mounting debt. Few Nuevomexicanos could long hold out against reversals. "It was not unusual for a partidario to become so mired in [debt] obligations to the sheep dealer that he could not expect—and was not expected—ever to extricate himself." But when the Congress enacted the Bankruptcy Act of 1898, only Euro-American partidarios availed themselves of it in Las Vegas's Fourth Judicial District.[21]

A few Nuevomexicano sheep ranchers did profit handsomely from the new economic order in the second half of the nineteenth century. Not surprisingly these were the already well-to-do, almost all of whom lived in the lower Rio Grande Valley (*río abajo*), and they added substantial acreage to support larger and larger numbers of sheep. These Nuevomexicanos, the most prominent of whom was Solomon Luna, soon expanded their influence by becoming members of the first business lobbying group in the United States—the National Wool-Growers' Association founded just after the Civil War. In early December 1895, for example, the Territory's delegation of ten attendees at the national meeting in Washington, D.C. was divided equally between Nuevomexicanos and Euro-Americans. All were of one mind, though, in wanting tariff reform to improve their revenue. "The importance of the protection of the wool industry, to Las Vegas and her merchants, can be realized when it is understood that any law or measure which would add five cents per pound to the price of wool, would put $250,000 more in circulation here annually." Following the election of President McKinley, the wool tariff was revised upward, an example of public policy abetting corporate capitalism at the expense of consumers, who had to pay the resulting higher prices. The New Mexico Wool-Growers' Association exercised considerable power as a special interest group for decades before and after statehood.[22]

Another group of prosperous Nuevomexicanos looked out for their own interests by turning their backs on their neighbors. In doing so they precipitated intraethnic strife on the eastern slopes of the Sangre de Cristo Mountains and particularly around Las Vegas. Antedating federal expropriation of this forest was the railroad's encroachment on common lands, often abetted by land-grant heirs eager to reap a profit. On the Las Vegas grant, for example, the locally powerful brothers Eugenio and Margarito Romero profited handsomely for more than two decades by cutting timber from the grant's common lands and selling it to the railroad. Indeed, Las Gorras Blancas (the White Caps) took particular aim against the wealthy Romeros. They repeatedly destroyed Eugenio Romero's property and even attempted to murder him in his home while he slept. The Romeros were hardly alone among grant holders in profiting from logging. Ezéquiel C. de Baca, an heir to the Las Vegas Grant, complained bitterly about the grant's board of officers and their favoritism in awarding contracts for "cutting ties and timber on the grant" in 1912. "No bids were asked for," he reported, "nor were any notices given of the fact that the board was going to let the contract." The board awarded two contracts—one to the "son of one of the members" and the other "to a friend of the brother of another member of the board." Moreover, he pointed out, the contracted price "was ridiculously low."[23]

"*Against the Peace and Dignity of the United States*"

Nuevomexicanos in the late nineteenth century faced broad challenges to the traditions that shaped both their economy and their society. Their communal orientation, reinforced by religious practices, was suddenly attacked not only by secular impulses but also by the hierarchy of the Catholic Church. During the early nineteenth century, Nuevomexicanos had initiated religious practices that filled a void created by the absence of regular and ordinary clergy. But these pious activities by an isolated people did not meet with the Church's approval. Concurrently, secular trends confronted a hitherto closed value system and reoriented personal morality. These twin challenges, of course, were not unique to the lives of the faithful in New Mexico. They paralleled a major shift in the late nineteenth and early twentieth century, a time when religion was gradually rendered less and less powerful by modernity. The general processes of this transition, and its inevitability, have recently been summarized in a broad study of secularization: "The modernization process reduces the threats to survival that are common in developing societies, especially among the poorest strata; and this enhanced sense of security lessens the need for the reassurance religion provides." In positing that faith is akin to a safety net, sociologists of religion often point to the pivotal role a younger generation plays in moving beyond religious values and finding fulfillment in heightened economic and political activity. As Nuevomexicanos advanced toward statehood, secularization cut a broad swath in their lives.[24]

Between 1879 and 1912, all these changes in daily life for Nuevomexicanos—the arrival of the railroad, consumerism, seasonal migration for wage labor, Euro-American settlements, modernization, and secularization—put enormous pressure on families and altered the traditional patterns long sustained by clearly defined gender roles, static social hierarchy, and religious proscriptions. Many prevailing familial practices broke down as a result. For example, marriages between Nuevomexicanas and Euro-Americans accounted for about ten percent of all unions in Albuquerque at the turn of the century. An acute sense of what was lost is evident in the following four stories.[25]

The Denver and Rio Grande Railroad pushed south from Colorado to reach Santa Fe in the late 1880s. Along its route it hired Nuevomexicanos to work in a commercial lumber industry where none had previously existed.

But it also brought in Euro-Americans, and some of these men discovered mica and formed a company to mine it near Petaca (eleven miles southeast of Tres Piedras). By about 1900 the old social order had been turned upside down. "This [mining] company hired many single men from the Eastern states, and in a short time they started to take our women and began to live with them without being married. So the people of Petaca complained to the authorities in Santa Fe. They were brought to court." The judge ordered the men to either get married or go to jail. They all promptly went before a justice of the peace, who performed a large wedding ceremony. This account, suggestive of so many dramatic tensions—cross-cultural sexual contact outside marriage; affronts to parental and community standards of morality; civil rather than ecclesiastical mandates to marry; and a civil union rather than a wedding in the Catholic Church—shows how quickly the social fabric became stretched, if not actually torn apart, by powerful secular currents.[26]

A second account is by Cleofas Martínez, born in 1878 into a well-to-do family in the village of Arroyo Hondo, near Taos. In about 1895 she caught the eye of a young man about six years her senior, Venceslao Jaramillo, and immediately he was smitten. But Cleofas had another year at Santa Fe's Loretto Academy, and then she "even wanted a year at one of those fine colleges I saw advertised in my *[Ladies']* Home Journal magazine." Between the late nineteenth century and the 1920s, mass-circulation journals for women opened vistas onto new choices in life, and for awhile Cleofas was more interested in these than in Venceslao. Her courtship became a contested terrain: the Jaramillo family adhered to the traditions of an arranged marriage, which collided with Cleofas's ambition and her ambivalence about marrying. Her independent behavior, and most especially her resistance to family wishes, caused much angst. Eventually she yielded to Venceslao's entreaties, and they married. His rising political career gave her a life far beyond anything she had imagined from reading magazines—beginning with attending the second inauguration of President McKinley in March 1901, and over the next fifteen years "traveling half the time, visiting cities, fairs, and other amusement places."[27]

Of fifteen children born to Martín and Refugio Amador between the early 1860s and the late 1880s, eight survived infancy—five girls and three boys. As children of a well-to-do father, the daughters' lives in Las Cruces afforded them the privileges available to elites in the Victorian and progressive eras—they attended Catholic girls' schools, traveled widely, formed opinions by drawing on a deep religiosity, were devoted to their parents, and participated in social relief and even some educational philanthropy likely animated by the sense of duty common to the upper class. By the time statehood arrived, though, each had experienced sufficient hardship to prompt financial independence "in managing their inherited properties and generating income." As a result, and although married, "they paid their own taxes and negotiated leases in their own names." While exhibiting their father's knack for business and making money, they also remained deeply linked to their culture and its enduring values.[28]

The fourth story is a collective experience—Nuevomexicanas and Nuevomexicanos confronting adultery. The Congress on 3 March 1887 added adultery as a criminal act to the nation's Revised Statutes, declaring infidelity a crime "against the peace and dignity of the United States." News of the law spread fast, and within a year New Mexico's Territorial courts began hearing adultery cases, which for over a decade overwhelmingly involved Nuevomexicanos and Nuevomexicanas. Of eighty-four cases filed in the First Judicial District (Santa Fe) and the Fifth Judicial District (Roswell) between 1888 and 1897, nine contained allegations of a Euro-American husband or wife committing adultery, one Euro-American women brought suit against a man other than her husband for an affair with another Euro-American woman, and two cited Euro-American males consorting with Nuevomexicanas. But the remaining seventy-two liaisons were distributed as follows: in forty-one suits a Nuevomexicano accused his wife of an affair with another Nuevomexicano; thirty-one times a Nuevomexicana alleged a tryst between her husband and another Nuevomexicana.[29]

In spite of the absence of court testimony, some trends are clear. Promiscuity as it is understood today seemed rare: only one Euro-American named two males involved with his wife and just one Nuevomexicano named multiple partners in his suit against his wife—two Nuevomexicanos and two Euro-Americans. The data are fragmentary on the question of when adultery occurred, but it is clear that some Nuevomexicanos believed their absences for seasonal work contributed to infidelity. The courts were especially attentive when witnesses supported—or refuted—accusations, and dismissals soon became common in the absence of a reliable witness. While convictions were not readily attained, when guilt was established the punishment could be either a fine of several hundred dollars or time in jail, although the latter sentence was seldom imposed. Courts seemed uneasy with the criminalization of adultery, as did the Congress, and in 1902 they revised the 1887 statute and made infidelity a civil matter for states.[30]

The disparity in the number of allegations by native New Mexicans versus Euro-Americans is consistent with a racial divide between the two in sex crimes in the Territorial Period, whereby criminal proceedings fell disproportionately on minorities. But the disparity might also arise from differing cultural views of the law. Nuevomexicanos resorted to criminal proceedings when they felt societal norms were violated—that occurred in Petaca, but it had been evident early in the Territorial Period. In 1853 the U.S. Attorney for the Territory ordered dismissal of a witchcraft case "because there was [sic] no such offenses under our laws." Nuevo-mexicanos might have made more allegations because they were accustomed to Spanish law setting normative standards of behavior. Adultery and its relation to divorce needs to be better understood, too. Given the frequency of divorce in the West in the late nineteenth century—a rate more than triple that found in the states of the North Atlantic and South Atlantic regions—it seems probable that in a certain number of instances Nuevomexicanas engaged in adultery as a way to leave their husbands. That being so, adultery could have been used by either party: by a male as a way to cast shame or to obfuscate having been abandoned, and by a female to nullify a marriage or to retaliate for behaviors that forced her to leave.[31]

"Those Who Steal Our Lives, Honor and Property"

Cleofas Jaramillo's comfortable world fell apart when her husband died about 1916, but she soon reinvented herself as a businesswoman. Yet she also solidified her identity as a Nuevomexicana by becoming a leading activist in the preservation of the cultural traditions of her upbringing. She was not alone in anchoring herself to her heritage. Between the 1850s and the early years of statehood, religious beliefs were one pillar of traditional values among Nuevomexicanos, but folk practices were more important to them than institutional obligations. Such social disruptions as adultery were formidable problems for Catholicism, but the Church's hierarchy did not comfort their congregations—instead they pushed them away. The gulf dividing the hierarchy from their Nuevomexicano faithful replicated a split that roiled Catholicism from the late eighteenth century until the Second Vatican Council of the 1960s: how to effectively minister to the laity. The approach of New Mexico's first bishop of the American era, Jean-Baptiste Lamy, was simply to repress popular religious tendencies. His ecclesiastical training inculcated "traditionalism, [manifested in] reactionary and authoritarian" views, and he applied these harsh principles in reshaping the Church in New Mexico. During his nearly thirty-five years as bishop (1851–85), Lamy tried to root out all vestiges of local influence, including removing Nuevomexicano priests and replacing them with clergy from France and Italy. He likewise attacked popular religious expressions that had sprung up in New Mexico over the previous half century, suppressing locally made santos, or religious figures, and sacred dramas performed on important feast days.[32]

In Lamy's mind Nuevomexicanos' religious practices deviated from Church-centered faith and veered toward extremes of self-centered religiosity. One of his consistent targets was a lay Catholic brotherhood active in New Mexico since about 1800—*La Fraternidad Piadosa de Nuestro Padre Jesús de Nazareno* (the Pious Fraternity of Our Father Jesus of Nazareth), known familiarly as the Penitentes (penitent ones). They had drawn condemnation from Lamy's Mexican predecessor beginning in the 1830s, and Lamy continued the attack. He banned public displays of personal penance rituals, specifically whipping oneself and carrying a wooden cross on one's back, rituals central to the Holy Week activities of the Penitentes. Lamy's successor, Bishop Jean-Baptiste Salpointe, reaffirmed these bans in 1889 in an open letter read at all masses in the weeks prior to Easter. He explained his ban in terms of the Church's teaching about errors of faith. He believed the Penitentes' displays of piety led to practices that "did not serve to edify," or leaven the spirit, and instead "could lead to false devotion and excesses." He reminded his listeners that "those who had a true spirit of contrition and penance choose other more appropriate and private [expressions] following the counsel and guidance of their confessors."[33]

A month after Bishop Salpointe's decree, the newspaper *La Demócrata de Mora* reported that many among the Penitentes "had faithfully obeyed the decree of their Pastor and Guide." But the newspaper went on to note that many more might heed his admonition except that it seemed "to threaten the existence of the *Santa Hermandad* [the Holy Brotherhood] as a political organization." The article concluded with a pointed reminder: "The votes of the hermanos [the Penitente brothers] are needed." One observer noted in 1881 that "the Penitentes dominate in the control of their own village church," and their political clout, already considerable in the 1880s, would increase in the following decades. When proto-folklorist Charles F. Lummis observed Penitente practices in communities around Mount Taylor in the late 1880s, he disapproved of a young, well-to-do Nuevomexicano from San Mateo being initiated in exchange for the brotherhood's support of his candidacy for local office. One scholar has noted that "a large percentage of Hispanic males in New Mexico and southern Colorado retained Penitente ties" throughout the years 1850 to 1900. Recently a leader of the Catholic Church in New Mexico claimed that in the early twentieth century "virtually every male member of the village became a member of the morada, [and] the penitentes were the only comprehensive organizing unit for communal life."[34]

By 1900 the Penitentes had endured nearly seventy years of official condemnation, but these repeated denunciations testify to the Church's ineffectiveness in moving against them. Having been stripped of their role in administering some sacraments when priests were unavailable, Penitentes retreated into secrecy to practice their banned rituals annually on Good Friday. During the rest of the year these men took care of widows and orphans, helped the young and elderly, and practiced good works among their neighbors. They also supplied a cadre of voters for the local patrón during elections. The actual votes cast by Penitentes, though, were competed for vigorously by Democratic and Republican leaders and candidates. This competition for a Catholic vote contrasted markedly with political activities elsewhere in the nation, especially among the millions of Irish Catholics who voted overwhelmingly Democratic well into the twentieth century.[35]

While Church officials and Penitentes were divided on many issues, they did occasionally unite when threatened by outside forces—as when Thomas B. Catron tried to ram through a constitution in 1889–90. The boycott of the convention by Nuevomexicanos presaged their overwhelming rejection of the constitution at the ballot box. Also in 1889 the territorial legislature passed a public education law making it mandatory to pay taxes in support of local, secular schools. The Catholic Church in New Mexico regarded this move as an attack and mobilized their faithful, including the Penitentes, in protest. New Mexico in the early 1890s became a late battleground of church-state conflict over compulsory secularization of public schools, a fight that had been going on in Catholic countries for much of the nineteenth century. But the tide of change flowed against the Church in the Territory, and data reported in a Catholic publication in 1910 summarized the rapid, wholesale shift in control over education after 1890. About a thousand public schools enrolled nearly 50,000 students, of whom 20,000 were Spanish-speaking and 100 were African American. The U.S. government provided twenty-five schools for 1,933 American Indian pupils. The Catholics and Presbyterians each had twenty-five schools, three other denominations ran a total of twenty-two schools, and the collective enrollment for all five denominations was less than 5,000. In addition eighteen private schools educated 288 pupils.[36]

The Church had not picked many of its battles wisely, but it did everything right in supporting devotion to Our Lady of Guadalupe, to whom Nuevomexicanos had given reverence for nearly two hundred years. Twenty chapels were devoted to her throughout the Territory by 1888 when church officials, "moved by the complete devotion of their faithful [Nuevomexicanos]," petitioned Rome to permit the celebration of her feast day on 12 December. The legislature sought to lessen tensions over religion and created a new county in her honor in 1891, and three years later Pope Leo XIII authorized New Mexico's Archbishop Placide Louis Chapelle to celebrate her feast day. The Church's embrace of Marian devotion did not so much signal a new respect for the spirituality of Nuevomexicanos, and especially Nuevomexicanas, as it continued a trend toward "a feminization of [Catholic] religion [that] took place in the nineteenth century." The piety of Catholic women in a number of countries made them indispensable allies of the Church, and in many instances its hierarchy took steps "to prevent the flight of women from its ranks." When Lamy died in 1888 the Church had yet to advance replacements for all that he had suppressed in New Mexico, which had the effect of allowing his successor to ally with Nuevomexicanas. Acknowledging and accepting Nuevomexicana religious devotion to Our Lady of Guadalupe became expedient in the struggle against secularism.[37]

Communal religious practices at the core of Penitente observances and Marian devotion are also evident in the growth of the mutualista movement, a broad-based Nuevomexicano response that revived traditional patterns of collective action. For several centuries villages had organized around their acequias, or local irrigation networks. But after 1880 the acequia associations took on new purposes in northern New Mexico—to counter threats to their *querencia*, their beloved homeland, the place that represented true peace. In direct reaction to Euro-American encroachment in the 1880s, northern New Mexicans created community-based protective associations to defend their fields, their irrigation water, and the mountain pastures supporting their livestock. They did so by transforming traditional acequia associations into legal corporations with formal constitutions dedicated to "the united defense and mutual protection of its associates in their homes, property rights and domain." The mutualistas also embraced the Church as their protector in these struggles.[38]

A new mutualista movement emerged in 1900. A former resident of Santa Fe who had recently returned to his home across the border in Antonito, Colorado, organized La Sociedad Protección de Trabajadores Unidos (Society for the Mutual Protection of United Workers). This movement quickly took hold among Nuevomexicanos through the creation of *concilios locales*, local councils, in New Mexico and at seasonal work sites in Colorado and eventually in Utah. The migrating workers supplied muscle for mining, logging, building and maintaining railroads, ranching, and picking crops. But in these jobs Nuevomexicanos endured exploitation, low wages, and discrimination. By banding together in La Sociedad, they took a decisive first step in the formation of both ethnic and class consciousness. In addition, they provided welfare services not available from employers or the government, including financial assistance to injured, sick, or disabled workers or their families, as well as funeral benefits. They formally incorporated in 1910, and their 1911 constitution required members to pledge loyalty to the flag of the United States but also "to protect each other against the injustices of tyrants and despots, the usurpers of law and justice, and those who steal our lives, honor and property." Their forceful proto-civil-rights stance anticipated by nearly twenty years the founding of the League of United Latin American Citizens (LULAC) in 1929.[39]

Throughout the Territorial Period New Mexico remained overwhelming Catholic, and it is often assumed that anti-Catholic sentiment, which ran high for much of that time, contributed to the political prejudice against statehood. This argument has validity from 1848 into the 1890s, but by the turn of the twentieth century religious bigotry faded as a pretext for keeping New Mexico from entering the Union. Several factors coalesced to diminish anti-Catholic bias in the political arena. When the Congress allowed Utah and its Mormon population to become the forty-fifth state in 1896, it signaled an end to overtly religion-based arguments. Moreover by 1900 Catholics—especially Irish Catholics—were so numerous in so many parts of the country that blatant anti-Catholicism could have potential electoral consequences. Finally, Senator Albert J. Beveridge in all his bluster against New Mexico did not single out their religion as he did their language and ethnicity. Perhaps this was because in Indiana Catholics ran a close second in membership to the Methodist Church, Beveridge's religious affiliation.[40]

But within the Territory, religious hostility occasionally erupted. An incident in Taos typifies the passions generated by denominational rivalries. Protestant preacher Lauriano Vargas condemned Catholic funeral rituals in November 1896: "[T]he only outcome of this whole tragedy consists of profit to the store owners from whom you buy coffee, rice, sugar, chile for making tamales, and all the other things you prepare to stuff people with on the night you hold your vigil. The bartenders also get their share of your saints' miracle during the vigils because of the whiskey you purchase to give the men who lead the *alabados* [hymns of praise]." Whereas the Protestant pastor saw materialism corrupting reverence, others might look at the same activities and see sacred and profane intermingled. This difference in viewpoints is important. The minister's judgmental tone surely arises as much from the frustration of a preacher struggling to gain followers as from anger over perceived sacrilegious behavior. But if the food and beverage are not viewed as transgressions but instead as part of a popular religious practice, then the focus shifts from people sinning to people sharing. Their actions become an extension of who they are, of what they understand about themselves, and of how they brought these forth in their daily lives. Seen this way, the Nuevomexicanos' religious celebration is profoundly their own creation, dedicated to a sacred connection one to another, a fact the preacher recognized in calling it "your vigil." As with so much of their religious experience after 1850, these Nuevomexicanos exhibited self-reliance and assertiveness—qualities carried into the struggle to attain statehood.[41]

"The Dignity of Our Forebears and Descendants"

In the summer of 1883 Walt Whitman was unable to visit Santa Fe, where he had been invited to read a poem as part of a celebration of the city's founding. Instead he sent an essay of nearly seven hundred words entitled "The Spanish Element in Our Nationality," which praised New Mexico as a pluralistic society and paid homage to the citizens' heritage: "To that composite American identity of the future, Spanish character will supply some of the most needed parts. No stock shows a grander historic retrospect— grander in religiousness and loyalty, or for patriotism, courage, decorum, gravity and honor."

Whitman's tribute to Nuevomexicanos flowed easily from his life's work. Beginning with his first self-published edition of *Leaves of Grass* in 1855 until his death in 1892, by which time he enjoyed international acclaim, Whitman celebrated ordinary people and their vitality. For him, diversity was an asset, and the Territory's Hispanic heritage enriched the nation. He told Santa Feans, "We Americans have yet to really learn our own antecedents, and sort them, to unify them. They will be found ampler than has been supposed, and in widely different sources."[42]

Nuevomexicanos were one of Whitman's "widely different sources" essential to understanding of "our own antecedents." Throughout his life Whitman affirmed that the common people carried the nation forward, and "By Blue Ontario's Shore" (1871) included a ringing endorsement of their power:

> What we are we are, nativity is answer enough to objections,
> We wield ourselves as a weapon is wielded,
> We are powerful and tremendous in ourselves,
> We are executives in ourselves, we are sufficient to the variety of
>   ourselves.

The strength conferred by one's identity, the potential for good inherent in people, the affirmation of a redeeming future—these themes find echoes in Whitman's letter of 1883.

A decade earlier the First Spanish Republic had inspired Whitman's "Spain, 1873–74," and that biennium of popular government "arising out of the feudal wrecks and heap'd-up skeletons of kings" likely remained in the back of Whitman's mind as he thought about the indomitable spirit Spain bequeathed to New Mexico. Although a restored monarchy soon reclaimed power in Spain, even in this setback, where "the clouds close again around thee," Whitman found hope:

> Thou hast given us a sure proof, the glimpse of thyself,
> Thou waitest there as everywhere thy time.[43]

Whitman's—and Nuevomexicanos'—coda on statehood might well have been, "Thou waitest there as everywhere thy time." Whitman extended "the most cordial, heartfelt congratulations of your American fellow-country-men," and offered as words of encouragement that "you have more friends in the Northern and Atlantic regions than you suppose." We can read Whitman's letter as an example of what one scholar has called his "double-ness," or attempting to find his footing on the shifting ground of opposing, even polarizing political tendencies. "Whitman's doubleness is also in many ways America's doubleness, as the nation has always struggled to reconcile its ambitious ideals with the ugly realities that seem to belie it."[44]

The pursuit of statehood juxtaposed "ambitious ideals" held by Nuevo-mexicanos for gaining full political sovereignty "with the ugly realities" of repeated delays, setbacks, and frustrated expectations. But against all odds, Nuevomexicanos steadfastly pressed to fulfill their political aspira-tions—behaving exactly as Whitman had written, "We are powerful and tremendous in ourselves." In 1890 the newly formed El Partido del Pueblo Unido, United People's Party, emerged out of and replaced the vigilantism of Las Gorras Blancas. Among planks unanimously adopted in the party's convention in early September were several calls for the U.S. Congress and territorial officials to settle land-grant titles. Their demand for justice epito-mized popular political mobilization. That is, the Nuevomexicanos asserted the essence of America's formative political credo, the Declaration of Inde-pendence: that government derived its power only through the consent of the people and therefore it had to be responsive to the petitions of its citi-zens. Two months later the candidates from the Partido del Pueblo Unido triumphed. Territorial leaders and members of Congress took notice of the electoral success of this people's movement and decided to act on some of their demands. In 1891 the Congress approved the Court of Private Land Claims and dispatched five federal judges to New Mexico. But the Partido del Pueblo Unido's cohesion frayed amid internal dissent and its members drifted into the Territory's Democratic Party.[45]

Active support for both Las Gorras Blancas and El Partido del Pueblo Unido came from the Las Vegas Spanish-language newspaper *La Voz del Pueblo*. Las Vegas was the largest city in the Territory in the 1880s and 1890s, but the arrival of the railroad bisected it, creating a predominantly Nuevomexicano West Las Vegas and a Euro-American East Las Vegas. Soon there were also separate post offices and two newspapers: *La Voz del Pueblo* and *The Optic*. Against this background of division and recent conflict, *La Voz del Pueblo*'s very name signaled its intent to speak out on behalf of Nuevomexicanos. Interestingly its offices were always in East Las Vegas, perhaps the better to be heard by its Euro-American neighbors.

Popular resistance to oppression animated Las Gorras Blancas and El Partido del Pueblo Unido, and as these movements waned, *La Voz del Pueblo* picked up their drooping flag. The newspaper positioned itself as a driving force in the community as early as mid-November 1891 in an editorial trumpeting the paper's role: "So we hope that the long-suffering neomexicano community will collect its thoughts and work with deliberation on public matters. . . . recognize[ing] that the newspapers and literature in general are the surest way toward science and prosperity." *La Voz del Pueblo* tirelessly defended Nuevomexicanos over the next several decades by exposing "Anglo-American encroachment on the communal land base, anti-Mexicano bias in the legal system, a dual wage system for Anglos and Mexicanos, and the unequal living standards between an Anglo East Las Vegas and Mexicano West Las Vegas."[46]

They were not a lone voice, though, and just a month after exhorting its readers to "awaken from the[ir] lethargy," *La Voz del Pueblo* convened a meeting in Las Vegas in December attended by a number of *periodiqueros*, or New Mexico Spanish-language journalists. These writers represented papers from across the Territory, and they agreed to create their own newspaper association, La Prensa Asociada Hispano-Americana. The major towns of Las Vegas, Santa Fe, Albuquerque, and Las Cruces each had more than one Spanish-language newspaper, while many small communities had at least one. These Spanish-language weeklies circulated broadly, were widely read, and consistently defended the social, political, and economic interests of Nuevomexicanos. Over the next four decades journalists from these publications dedicated themselves to "contesting social and historical erasure."[47]

When La Prensa Asociada Hispano-Americana formed, its charter set an adversarial tone. It criticized the United States for betraying promises of full citizenship made in the Constitution: "Inasmuch as the prevailing credo of society and businesses in the United States of America has not proven able to date to protect the full rights we are guaranteed by the American constitution, it is incumbent upon us to form associations so that our capacities increase in equal measure to those of the rest of our fellow citizens with the goal that the dignity of our forebears and descendants be justly respected." Editorials in member newspapers consistently argued that Nuevomexicanos should enjoy full political participation via statehood. While Ezéquiel C. de Baca as coeditor of the Democratic *La Voz del Pueblo* often disagreed with his Albuquerque counterpart Nestor Montoya of the Republican *La Bandera Americana* (The American Flag), they shared the desire to enter the Union.[48]

One of the crucial early successes in the pursuit of statehood occurred when Nestor Montoya, an original member of La Prensa Asociada Hispano-Americana, convened a meeting of more than thirty territorial politicians from both parties as well as fellow journalists at the offices of *La Bandera Americana* in late September 1901. He wanted to ensure Nuevomexicanos' voices were heard and heeded in the upcoming Territorial statehood convention. He reminded those assembled that delegates were "specifically instructed to represent at the statehood convention the views of the different counties regarding our admission as a state." This pointed comment alerted everyone that from twenty-two counties, the six with large Nuevomexicano majorities intended to be vocal. Montoya also believed that "the suggestions, propositions, and exchange of ideas" begun in his office would carry over into the mid-October convention, where they "will be of considerable value and lead to securing our sovereignty as one of the states of the Union." Montoya envisaged representative democracy: delegates freely exchanging views and melding these into a consensus. Like Governor Otero, he sought citizen-driven, grass-roots participation, which derived its authority from the will of the people and not a contrived process such as Thomas B. Catron had long tried to engineer. Transparency was lauded by one of the member newspapers in La Prensa Asociada, which predicted the event would be "nothing less than the public's convention."[49]

Where did this faith in the people as a repository of political wisdom originate? It had a long and distinguished genealogy. One strand drew directly from the experience of Nuevomexicanos throughout the Territorial Period. They had proven their mettle in countless individual and collective acts of self-assertion vis-à-vis the new American order. In their economic decisions, in daily behaviors whether shaped by religion or secularism, and in their political solidarity, Nuevomexicanos and Nuevomexicanas stood on their own and looked out for themselves. They practiced what Whitman had first preached in 1855: "the genius of the United States is not best or most in its executives or legislatures, . . . but always most in the common people. Their manners speech dress friendships . . . the terrible significance of their elections—the President's taking off his hat to them not they to him."[50]

Popular sovereignty, of course, was a major tenet of American political philosophy. A surge of popular will inspired the U.S. Constitution to declare "We the People" to be the government in 1787. It was reaffirmed by President Abraham Lincoln in his Gettysburg Address in 1863 when he proclaimed in a cadence at once arresting and awe-inspiring "that this nation, under God, shall have a new birth of freedom—and that government of the people, by the people, and for the people, shall not perish from the earth." These legacies informed Walt Whitman's faith in the power of the people, including Nuevomexicanos. By mid-October 1901 they were full participants in the statehood convention chaired by J. Francisco Chaves.[51]

The territorial thrust toward popular sovereignty was also connected to the yearning of people around the world to govern themselves rather than be controlled by a colonial power. This impulse, known as decolonization, manifested itself at the end of the nineteenth century in four popular, or mass-based, political uprisings: the Cuban Revolution (1895–98); the Philippine Insurrection (1898–1906); the Boxer Rebellion in China (1898–1901); and the Boer-Anglo Wars (1899–1902). In each instance long-suffering peoples asserted the desire to exercise sovereignty by ridding themselves of colonial, Western powers. Brutal repression followed, and news of these clashes appeared regularly in both the English- and Spanish-language newspapers in New Mexico.[52]

Anti-imperialist sentiment ran hot in the territories. In the run-up to the mid-October convention, the *Albuquerque Morning Democrat* printed a letter urging statehood as necessary to break the grip of oppressive colonialism in New Mexico: "Talk about imperialism! No need to go to the far-away Philippines to find it. It is here in Arizona, in New Mexico, and in Oklahoma. It is rank and smells to heaven. Worse, a thousand times than it could by any possibility be in those far-off island possessions. For here you are applying this vile despotism and usurpation to people who are to the manor born, who are bred up to the idea and in the enjoyment of liberty of American citizens." Calling himself a "subject" and not a "citizen," the letter's author exhorted New Mexicans (and residents in other Territories) to arm themselves with words and not weapons.[53]

Nuevomexicanos worked within the political system to gain statehood. As a gauge of their political culture following the statehood convention in 1901, consider the activities of Republican delegates from eighteen precincts gathered at the Taos County courthouse on 17 February 1904 to pick eight delegates to attend the Territorial Republican Convention a month later in Las Vegas. An audience estimated at three hundred watched while about fifty delegates conducted the county party's business, but they also witnessed a contest for control of local patronage and its distribution among supporters. Two factions clashed in Taos—Malaquias Martínez, the dominant patrón, with twenty-nine delegates, and Pedro Sánchez with an unspecified, but lesser, number. The showdown came when Sánchez tried to open the floor to resolutions presented by anyone attending, arguing the people "have as much right to vote in this convention as any delegate." Much excited discussion followed but presently "all protested and said they did not favor setting aside parliamentary rules and that the convention comprised intelligent men." Order was restored, but a populist fervor prevailed. They declared "emphatically that we are in favor of statehood with the present boundaries." Opposition to joint statehood was coupled with an affirmation of their political maturity: "We are able to manage our own affairs and are entitled to have an equal position among our fellow states in this great American Republic." The delegates also approved a Sánchez-backed resolution praising Roosevelt as "the right man in the right place. He is a man of the people and for the people." Then the meeting closed amid three cheers for the "Glorious Republican Party." The Taos County convention validated that Nuevomexicanos had survived conquest and entered the first decade of the twentieth century ready to claim full citizenship through statehood.[54]

In about 1880 a few Nuevomexicanos added a new santo to their pantheon—Santo Jo' (Saint Job). That the Old Testament story of a righteous man whose faith is tested by great suffering inspired the creation of a santo has been interpreted by a historian of late colonial New Mexico as a metaphor for how Nuevomexicanos viewed themselves at the close of the Spanish era. After surviving decades of Indian raids, privations, and reversals, they no longer saw themselves as settlers on a frontier but as citizens of a new locale—New Mexico. Santo Jo' has significance for the Territorial Period as well. Under U.S. rule, and particularly after the arrival of the railroad in 1879, Nuevomexicanos again faced Job-like tribulations, but also like Job their resilience sustained them. They never lost sight of political redemption through statehood.[55]

CHAPTER SIX

"Steady, Persistent, Unrelaxing Determination"

Governor George Curry was welcomed "in the name of the common people of the territory" at his inauguration in August 1907. "When I say the common people," the Territory's attorney general, Albert B. Fall, explained, "I mean the next president, the miner and the sheep herder—we are all common American people, whether the blood of Spain flows in our veins, or whether we speak in the coarser tongue of Anglo-Saxon ancestors, we are all common people." Walt Whitman would have applauded Fall's linking "the next president, the miner and the sheep herder" and acknowledging Nuevomexicanos and Euro-Americans as equals. But Whitman's egalitarian spirit did not stir Albert Fall. His seemingly enlightened definition of "the common man" stemmed from political calculation. He understood that both groups were cocreators of the Territory's political future. New Mexico was in the midst of an unprecedented growth spurt, and statehood would not be postponed much longer. When it arrived, Fall intended to draw support from both groups and indeed both parties. He had switched from being a Democrat to a Republican about four years earlier to better position himself to become a U.S. senator, and the several hundred Nuevomexicanos at Curry's inauguration were undoubtedly reassured that Fall valued their contributions to the Territory's development and future, particularly because their numerical majority was rapidly slipping away.[1]

The Territory's 195,310 residents in 1900 grew to 327,301 a decade later, a population increase of 68 percent. But a considerable disparity existed in growth rates—the Nuevomexicano population increased only 15 percent, to 155,155, whereas the number of Euro-Americans exploded 382 percent to 149,439. When Presidents McKinley and Roosevelt prescribed more people as a precondition of statehood, they really had in mind only more Euro-Americans. Attracting new residents was a given, but Fall understood the continued importance of Nuevomexicanos to New Mexico's political and economic future. The influence they exercised was self-evident to most politicians of that period and reflected in fluency in Spanish among ambitious Euro-Americans like Fall and Thomas B. Catron.[2]

Among the hundreds at the inauguration inside the capitol, few, if any, would have objected to a definition of the "common people" that omitted Indians, blacks, and Asians. Collectively they accounted for only 7 percent of the Territory's population in 1910—20,573 American Indians, 1,628 African Americans, 248 Chinese, and 258 Japanese. But they were ignored for reasons other than their limited numbers. The 1910 census identified them as nonwhites. Even though blacks could vote, all three groups were considered inferior to whites. Like all the states, the Territory had a hierarchy of race, class, gender, and age that favored Euro-American and Nuevomexicano men. Moreover, U.S. law set sanctions against nonwhites.[3]

For four centuries in the New World, law—in the form of decrees, legislation, and court rulings—was a key instrument of social control, allowing those in power to make the rules and exercise their authority. During the territorial period, notions of justice and right versus wrong had far less sway in law than did carrying out the dictates of the American government. Federal legislation and jurisprudence were tools of domination applied to whites and nonwhites alike during the territorial period. But whites had at least the expectation of relief through statehood. Nonwhites had little hope for betterment, and reacted with either resignation or resistance. Thus during New Mexico's sixty-two years as a territory, the law as an instrument of conquest permeated policies and left a legacy passed along with statehood. For Euro-Americans the most objectionable policy was written into the act creating the Territory—nullification. This meant that all acts of their legislature and rulings by local courts were subject to review and rescission by either the Congress or the Supreme Court. While nullification was rarely invoked, the very possibility reminded New Mexicans that so long as they were a territory they were under federal domination. White residents who chafed at being subjects vented their feelings in decolonization sentiments and channeled their efforts toward statehood. In addition, Nuevomexicanos focused their discontent on the courts, hoping for eventual reversals of or relief from the adverse actions of district courts handling water cases and the Supreme Court's decisions of 1897 stripping land grants of their communal holdings.[4]

The legal history of nonwhites in the Territory, though, is a record of their status as second-class citizens. For them the prospect of statehood offered little chance of lifting oppressive laws and policies. Indeed, joining the Union would produce mostly adverse consequences for them, with American Indians faring best among nonwhites. Although the forces of Americanization tried to fit them into an imposed model of citizenship, they also benefited from having a few well-placed white advocates at crucial moments in the statehood movement. African Americans in New Mexico and elsewhere had no choice but to bow before the power of Jim Crow laws endorsed by the U.S. Supreme Court in *Plessy v. Ferguson* (1896), which shaped the racism under which they lived before and after statehood. Finally, there were the Asians, the illegal immigrants of that era. For them the push for statehood brought a vigorous campaign of expulsion pursued in President Roosevelt's second term. In general, congressional legislation and the rulings of the federal judiciary had an unmistakable aura of coercion when applied to nonwhites, especially blacks and Asians, and these did not change with statehood.

"Must Not Be Attributed to a Thirst for Knowledge"

James A. Carroll, a Bureau of Indian Affairs (BIA) superintendent assigned to oversee the 540 Apaches on the Mescalero reservation in south-central New Mexico, reported to his superiors on the government's Americanization policies in 1902–1903. In gathering statistics on twenty-two indices of assimilation, he reported on economic activities as well as social conditions, noting the number of adult Mescalero Apache who wore "[American] citizen's dress wholly" (100 percent), spoke and understood "English enough for ordinary intercourse" (42 percent), and were literate (33 percent). No missionaries worked among them. The economic data showed a similar mix of acculturation and traditional lifeways: only 8 percent of their subsistence was from government handouts; they produced all their own wheat (4,000 bushels), corn (200 bushels), and beans (10,000 bushels). The tribe earned $2,878.40 from two cash crops: 50,000 pounds of oats sold from the 8,000 bushels grown (c. 353,520 pounds total) and 15,100 pounds of wool from 6,405 sheep. But the largest portion of their revenue—$8,856.36—

came from the government selling the reservation's timber and authorizing non-Indians to graze livestock. Carroll unilaterally decided to reinvest
just over $5,200 of these proceeds to "purchase thoroughbred rams, wag-
ons, harness, plows, disks, seed drills, and wheat, onion sets, potatoes, and
beans for planting."[5]

The numbers the superintendent reported revealed efforts to remake the
Indians. His data were presented as a progress report on assimilation, and
his predictions were explicit. Within two years he expected "to build a comfortable frame house for each family, with outhouse for wagon and team."
Sixty-two such dwellings had already been constructed, but equipment
breakdowns at their sawmill slowed construction. Also ongoing were efforts
to introduce new economic values and integrate the Mescalero Apaches
into a market economy. Doing so involved new approaches to farming and
livestock. Carroll had for the first time put aside 35,000 pounds of oats as
seed to be planted the following year. The Mescalero strenuously objected,
but with obvious pride the superintendent showed them a basic principle
of the marketplace. They sold their oats for between $1.25 and $1.50 per
hundredweight, but when it came time to purchase seed they had to pay
between $2.00 and $2.10. By holding back some oats, he solved a recurring
problem that had previously disrupted farming: "Frequently many of them
had neither money nor credit; hence no oats were planted."[6]

But his lesson on saving and planning was merely part of an even more
fundamental BIA objective, which stemmed from a congressional mandate
in the Dawes Act of 1887—ending meager pastoral and subsistence practices by making Indians into yeoman farmers tending individual plots. Carroll wrote: "The purpose of this office is to reapportion the farming lands
on the basis of a given per capita acreage; . . . induce the Indians to sell their
numerous worthless ponies, investing the proceeds in cows and encourage
them to plant a variety of garden truck [crops] in addition to their oat and
wheat." To that end 2,700 acres had been fenced in the previous year. The
goal was to shift the Mescalero Apaches from common pastures to individual farms: "Only a few of this tribe, possibly five, have made any success [with sheep], and these will eventually control the industry." Carroll
believed that all the others needed to become self-sufficient farmers.[7]

Superintendent Carroll's report tells us much about the government's view of the Mescalero Apaches—their perceived inferiority to
Euro-Americans across a host of activities. But on closer examination,

the report also reveals much about tribal life. Gleaning that perspective from government documents is consistent with recent suggestions by several American Indian scholars arguing for a new approach to studying Indian history. They seek to learn how Native experiences are stories of adaptation and survival based on choice, on what amounted to informed consent or at least an understanding of what they were doing. As one indigenous scholar noted, "Some Indian people—more than we've been led to believe—leapt quickly into modernity and not necessarily because they adopted political and legal tools from whites or because they were acculturated into the educational, political, and economic order of twentieth-century America. They leapt, I think, because it became painfully clear that they were not distinct from the history that was even then being made. Whether they liked it or not, other people were building a world around, on top of, and through Native American people."[8]

Abundant evidence exists in Carroll's report that the Mescalero Apaches recognized "they were not distinct from the history that was even then being made." More than BIA coercion was evident in their acceptance of new clothes, houses, farming practices, and other aspects of modernity. They coped with change by actively participating in shaping their lives under a government that had conquered them. They elected to survive in a new order, but on their own terms. It is significant that no missionaries worked among them, although a priest said mass regularly in Carroll's home. Their spirituality, though, was an inviolable essence. But in many other matters they made a choice to accept change. Their Native identity was altered but not erased by government policies.[9]

Both Carroll and his wards understood their accommodation as a calculated decision. As the superintendent reported, "The Mescalero School still enjoys the unique distinction of showing an attendance exceeding100 percent of the scholastic population. Runaways and expulsions are unknown. This must not be attributed to a thirst for knowledge, but rather to a longing for something to eat and wear. The Indians have been on a starvation basis for years. . . . Many of them have suffered from hunger and cold and have been more than willing to see their children provided with the necessities of life." Tribal members understood a universal life lesson: you cannot do the same things in the same ways and expect to get different results. They recognized that their old agricultural ways had proved inadequate to feed their children, so they chose to use the reservation school to fulfill their needs. Dire circumstances brought them across this threshold, but a clear-eyed understanding that they had to make a new life under the tutelage of Euro-American Indian agents prompted endless negotiation along a line separating their essence from their existence, of who they were from what they did to survive.[10]

At times, though, BIA officials forced some American Indians to yield against their will. The Superintendent of the Navajo, G. W. Hayzlett, thought himself a capable administrator when he matter-of-factly reported in 1902: "Since the order of the Honorable Commissioner requiring the Indians to have their hair cut they are complying with the order quite readily, fully 300 have already complied with the order. So far I have had to punish but one who showed resistance to the matter. He claimed the government had no control over him. It required but a short time in the guardhouse to bring him to realize the fact that the Government did have some control." Yet only three hundred complied out of several thousand Navajo men under Hayzlett's purview. Many Navajos did not openly challenge him but simply went about their old practices. Some continued "using paint on their faces," and Hayzlett thought "the change in adopting citizen's dress is wonderful. I am safe in saying that over one-half of the tribe now wear citizens' clothing in whole or in part." He praised this wholly imperfect result as having "been almost magic" and took credit for those Navajo who elected to conform to government dictates, all the while ignoring the thousands who defied him, so long as they did it without challenging his authority.[11]

But there are limits to reading Indian agents' reports as evidence of a negotiation over identity and an accommodation to modernity. Genuine losses did occur. Euro-American policy makers of the late nineteenth century considered themselves superior to everyone else. This attitude bred arrogance and intolerance and manifested itself in campaigns to Americanize American Indians. One way to assess the impact of such coercion is to examine whether it disrupted lifeways. American Indian gender roles are an example of equilibrium suddenly assaulted, while the persistence of traditional religious practices attests to survival skills honed during three centuries of attempts to disrupt their spirituality.

Government officials systematically redefined and undermined American Indian women's accustomed roles. These Euro-Americans did not recognize the traditions that gave American Indian women the primary position in organizing social and familial life in a tribe or pueblo, and their actions forced these women out of their customary place in a matrilineal society. Having negated women's power and identity, government teachers on reservations and in pueblos imposed a turn-of-the-century American model of domesticity. The Euro-American woman heading the eighteen Pueblo day schools reported for the 1902–1903 school year: "By contact with intelligent, sympathetic women, associating with them on lines of work common to women the world over, the Indian woman finds that . . . doors are opened for the elevation of the home life, through which civilization must enter if it is to come at all. . . . Our best teachers realize that the day school exists, most of all, for the Pueblo girls, in whose hands rest the molding of all the character of the next generation of children, and that their training in home making is the most important work the teacher has." This official expected Native women to embrace Americanization and thereby improve their homemaking and child-rearing practices and their family's future.[12]

Did any, some, or all of these imposed changes occur? Based on the experiences of the Mescalero and the Navajo, the answer is "a little of each." Yet some American Indian women experienced great disruption. A Laguna Pueblo woman recently observed, "The coming of the white man created chaos in all the old systems, which were for the most part superbly healthy, simultaneously cooperative and autonomous, peace-centered, and ritual oriented." Whereas a Pueblo woman saw traditional practices as strengths and virtues, BIA policy makers took the opposite view and tried to foster social development based on Euro-American gender roles.[13]

While Euro-Americans believed in the superiority of their institutions and thus expected them to prevail easily when introduced into American Indian societies, the actual process of remaking Indians proved a good deal more difficult than officials in Washington calculated. Creating a new people involved continuous contact, which in turn opened opportunities for American Indians to disrupt and block what they most opposed in government policies. In this process Americanization among the Native peoples of New Mexico exhibited one of the hallmarks of imperialism in its decline. It transformed both sides through grinding, countless daily exchanges, wearing down the arrogance and confidence of the powerful, which was watched and then seized upon and exploited by those considered the wards. This redistribution of power, mostly a trickle between 1900 and 1912, created irreversible precedents for independent action that had profound importance for American Indians, particularly Pueblo Indians, who within fifteen years of statehood asserted themselves against the government in no uncertain terms.

It is impossible to say when government authority began to crack and splinter, but early instances occurred with the Jicarilla Apaches. In 1886, following more than fifteen years of the government breaking its promises to create a reservation, the Jicarilla Apaches learned of a new government plan, the General Allotment Act, or the Dawes Act, approved by the Congress and signed by the president in early February 1887. Concurrent with the legislation moving through the Congress, several hundred Jicarilla Apaches walked away from temporary placement on the Mescalero Apaches' reservation and returned to a small portion of their traditional homeland in north-central New Mexico. There they took up homesteads rather than continue to seek a tribal reservation. Their action was consistent with provisions of the Dawes Act, which mandated a transition in the trust responsibility from guardianship to full citizenship. This meant forcing American Indians to assimilate into the American mainstream by ending tribal allegiances over the next twenty-five years. A first step involved dividing communal holdings to create individual farms. Out of this transfer of land the government planned to create a new Indian cum American citizen. Private ownership of land, the law postulated, bred good work habits and a thrifty, self-reliant farmer. Capitalism, in short, would mold the Indians into American citizens. The General Allotment Act became the basis of all Indian policy in early February 1887, and at exactly the same time the Jicarilla Apaches petitioned the government to open a portion of their ancestral lands under the terms of the new law. They were the only American Indians subjected to the Dawes Act in New Mexico, and they subverted it.[14]

The twenty-five-year timetable the Congress set for the Dawes Act envisaged full assimilation by 1912. Statehood arrived, but the Dawes Act had not achieved its desired results, so the legislation was extended for another two decades before being scrapped in 1934. From 1887 until 1909, the government tried unsuccessfully to assign the individual Jicarilla Apache acreage as prescribed by the Dawes Act, and delay mounted on delay, exacerbated by the government's inability to legally identify intended recipients. An exasperated agent explained the difficulty to his superiors in 1903: "The [774] members of the tribe have not been compelled to retain the names by which they were allotted but were either enrolled by a 'nick name' or given an arbitrary name." Finally in 1909, following additions of land in 1907 and 1908 that nearly doubled the size of their new homeland—granted to compensate the Jicarilla Apaches for encroachment by non-Natives—all tribal members received allotments of 160 acres for agriculture and 640 acres for grazing. The valuable timber on their mountains remained held in common, and proceeds from sales went into a tribal account controlled by the U.S. Department of the Treasury. These funds were to be spent to benefit the entire tribe by buying sheep and cattle and providing for social services. Substantial sums were involved. In the early spring of 1912, for example, the tribe earned $178,500 from timber sales. But instead of disbursing it as intended, the government simply held the money in a non-interest-bearing trust account on the assumption that Indians lacked competence to manage their affairs. The funds remained locked away until 1925. When the money was finally released, a substantial amount went to reimburse the government for prior expenses and to pay the salaries of Indian agents. When the federal government scrapped the Dawes Act in 1934, the Jicarilla Apaches received their lands as a tribal reservation.[15]

The slow unraveling of the Dawes Act is an important object lesson. Plans devised elsewhere did not necessarily unfold as expected in New Mexico. The mandated assimilation of the Jicarilla Apaches had not been attained after twenty-five years, and instead traditional ways persisted amid a selective embracing of modernity. Drought, unreliable irrigation, and limited arable lands continually plagued the tribe's farmers, so it is not surprising they accepted new agricultural practices to better their lives. Young Jicarilla Apaches learned improved techniques for planting and harvesting in arid lands while at boarding school, and "the returned students spread among the people ideas and methods acquired." But agents expressed dismay when, "on their return, however, they [students] drop their civilized dress and go back to the blanket and moccasin." Both the Mescalero and Jicarilla Apaches incorporated what benefited them and shed what did not.[16]

Sacred practices were nonnegotiable, a fact the Euro-Americans generally accepted. Government officials accommodated religious practices even when they did not like them, realizing they had no alternative. An agent at the Jicarilla Apache Reservation in 1898, for example, capitulated to prevailing custom during a four-day healing ceremony. He assisted in countless ways, including supplying much of the food, after realizing they would not

be deterred. Other officials likewise proved flexible in the face of Indian traditions when it became clear they had no choice but to go along. For example, Pueblo school officials, in realizing their powerlessness, accommodated
the religious calendar of "conservative villages" such as Acomita when "the
Indians return to old Acoma in the winter [December and January] for religious feasts and dances, taking their children with them." When in April
1905 three members of Jemez Pueblo stopped Antonio Maestas from driving his mail stage into the pueblo during a religious festival, a confrontation
landed both parties in court. The judge dismissed the charges at trial, but
before releasing the defendants, he offered them some advice: "Almost anyone if courteously requested would refrain from intruding on their ceremo-
nials." Euro-American officials in New Mexico seemed to have learned one
of the lessons of the Pueblo Revolt of 1680—do not threaten the Pueblos'
traditional religious practices. Unfortunately overly zealous Washington
officials ignored these precedents in the early 1920s.[17]

Euro-American commercial interests also understood that Indian art had
the potential to create interest in New Mexico and found ways to use it for
such purposes. By 1900 descriptions of new landscapes and unparalleled vistas had become a staple of railroad promotional literature that lured tourists to the Pacific Northwest, and presently similar publicity began for New
Mexico—but featuring American Indians and their pottery, rugs, and jewelry. "In 1902 the Fred Harvey Company generated excitement by announcing the establishment of a large-scale museum to be housed at the site of
the Alvarado Hotel [being built] in Albuquerque." A 1904 brochure took
the reader on a tour: "This hotel, with all is mechanical and artistic perfec-
tions, stands in America's most fascinating region—the Rio Grande valley."
Its centerpiece was the Indian Building, a complex of half a dozen rooms.
"The Navaho Room, with its blanketed walls and decorations of pottery and
basketry, furnishes an admirable idea for a luxurious den." Elsewhere, "Indians from Acoma, Laguna [were] making pottery; skillful Pueblos plaiting
baskets." The hotel and its Indian art became major attractions promoted by
thousands of ticket agents across the Santa Fe Railway route.[18]

Also serving as prominent advertisements for New Mexico were the cre-
ative works tourists took home. For example, when Las Vegas held its music
competition in 1895, the organizers gave the judge from Chicago a "unique
souvenir of New Mexico in the form of a genuine Navajo blanket made
by the Indians of the Territory." Similarly President Theodore Roosevelt

received a Navajo blanket during his May 1903 visit, made especially for him by Elle of Ganado, who also presented it to him. Her work fascinated the "many correspondents of Eastern newspapers, and the photographs and stories of the Navajo blanket were spread across the Nation, giving Albuquerque and New Mexico's bid for Statehood considerable publicity." Elle, then about fifty years old, wove at the Alvarado Hotel's Indian Building in the artist-demonstrator room until the early 1920s. According to publicity material, "Undisturbed by the eager gaze of the tourist, the stoic works on as unconcernedly as though in [her] reservation home." On his brief visit, Roosevelt toured the recently opened Indian Building which fused Indian art with Euro-American mercantile capitalism to attract tourists.[19]

The commercialization of southwestern American Indian art also proved a boon to statehood advocates. Prominent Santa Fe businessman (and future governor) Arthur Seligman arranged with the Harvey Company to create a display promoting New Mexico at the St. Louis World's Fair in 1904. Indian art was prominently featured, and the result proved highly popular. The exhibit garnered the grand prize for the best ethnological exhibit, two gold medals, and the grand prize for the Navajo blanket exhibit. These honors especially pleased the Harvey Company because it attracted national prestige to its collection at the Alvarado, and the company lost no time in publicizing the fact that it had received more awards at the World's Fair than had the exhibit of the Smithsonian Institution.[20]

Governor Miguel Otero and an entourage from the Territory likewise left St. Louis highly satisfied with the favorable publicity the event had generated. Whereas the Santa Fe Railway and the Harvey Company wanted to bring tourists to the Territory, the governor had a more ambitious goal. As he explained, "The exhibit was designed to attract the attention of home-seekers and capitalists. In addition to Navajo blankets, Indian baskets, and pueblo pottery, there were samples of apples, cotton, and wool raised in the territory. The collection of minerals was very comprehensive," and included a special book of nearly four hundred pages promoting the potential for striking it rich through mining. The fair designated Friday, 18 November as "New Mexico Day," and Otero took the opportunity to press the case for statehood. Cognizant that "nothing is quite so good for a territory as advertising," Otero pitched the territory's prospects because "New Mexico needed both capital and immigration to develop." He concluded with an appeal to his listeners "to assist the territory to attain the dignity of a state."

New Mexico's St. Louis exhibit featured Indian art less for its creativity than for its utility in selling railroad tickets, filling hotel rooms, and promoting statehood.[21]

A week after New Mexico Day, President Theodore Roosevelt toured the fair to inspect official U.S. sponsored pavilions, one of which, the Indian Building, housed New Mexico's exhibit. Fresh from his election victory and barely able to contain his insatiable appetite for information about American Indians, an exuberant Roosevelt likely encountered a young, recently married Pueblo Indian couple—Julian and Maria Martinez of San Ildefonso Pueblo. They were among the American Indians participating as dancers and in live demonstrations of their art. For the young couple the fair was an opportunity to earn a salary of fifty dollars a month for six months. Julian danced, and "all Maria had to do was to sit and make pottery, and sometimes dance. She made little bowls and ollas, not anything big and fancy, and she left the pieces plain, without designs on them, because the white people seemed to like plain polished red bowls."[22]

St. Louis changed Maria's understanding of herself and her work. She spoke English well, but at the fair she conversed almost solely in Tewa to keep apart from the Euro-American world and remain grounded in her own culture. She quickly realized that most of the tourists were superficial and ill-mannered, and yet they were also eager to buy her pots. Thus while she was still a teenager, her pottery-making skills afforded her a way to earn an income, but more importantly, sales validated her artistry and the traditions she carried forward. The St. Louis Fair not only altered the Martinezes' lives but helped reinvigorate traditional Pueblo Indian pottery making. Within fifteen years of her return, Maria Martinez had become a key figure in the revitalization of Pueblo Indian arts. A triumphal centennial celebration of America's expansion launched the career of a young Pueblo woman whose pottery went into museums worldwide.[23]

In the realm of art, American Indians acted as agents of their own destiny even when Euro-Americans treated their work as commodities. In the political realm, and especially in protecting themselves, the Indians' capacity for self-assertion had far greater constraints. But they did enlist helpful allies among some Euro-Americans. Undoubtedly the most important aid to Pueblo Indians occurred in drafting the statehood legislation, known as the Enabling Act of 1910. Interior Department officials played a decisive role in settling a decade-long dispute precipitated in 1899 when the territorial legislature passed a law permitting counties to collect taxes on lands held by the pueblos. When the act was contested by a special attorney to the Pueblo Indians, the Territorial Supreme Court upheld it in 1904, and soon tax assessors began visiting the pueblos. The intent was purely confiscatory since creating tax delinquency was the real purpose, which would then permit the auctioning off of Pueblo lands. No actual confiscation of land occurred, but the anxiety led eighteen pueblo leaders to revive a tradition of speaking and acting collectively. They petitioned President Roosevelt and the Congress in April 1904: "Hear us in our protest against the taxation of our lands and other property which we possess," they beseeched. Later in the year their special attorney warned the secretary of the interior of pending injustice: "I feel that some action should be taken while we are yet a territory and these matters are under the control of Congress. If these people should be left to the tender mercies of the native population, their condition would be pitiable indeed." A 1905 letter from the governor of Acoma Pueblo to the special attorney expresses the consternation created by the tax issue. "We have had meeting for two days and two nights discus[s]ing against the burden of taxation of the individual of Pueblo Indians. My people they could not understand and it is difficult for them."[24]

The pleas of the governor of Acoma and the special attorney failed to budge the Congress over the next five years, until the Enabling Act of 1910. This bill mandated that the state's constitution acknowledge the federal government as the guardian of the Pueblo Indians. Immediately upon securing statehood, though, New Mexicans mounted a legal challenge to the new status of the Pueblo Indians. The U.S. Supreme Court quashed the attempt to nullify the Congress's mandate. In 1913 the court affirmed in *United States v. [Felipe] Sandoval* that "the power and duty of the U.S. . . . includes the duty to care for and protect all dependent Indian communities." The court affirmed that the Pueblo Indians were entitled to the same status as all other American Indians—wards of the federal government. This decision reversed a U.S. Supreme Court ruling in *United States v. Joseph* in 1876, which said that "the Pueblo Indians were not Indian tribes" and thus not entitled to full federal protection. The Joseph decision opened the door to legal threats separate from taxation. In a land grant case in 1892–93, for example, attorney Thomas B. Catron in his argument before the Court of Private Land Claims "denied there is such a body or person known as the Pueblo of Zia, Santa Ana, or Jemez." The three pueblos lost this suit. Statehood settled the Pueblo Indians' hitherto confusing legal status. But for the next ten years many in the new state refused to accept the Supreme Court's ruling, which led to a major confrontation over the Bursum Bill in 1922–23, which sought to grant rights to non-Indians residing on pueblo lands. Although statehood clarified the Pueblo Indians' legal status, they and all other American Indians in New Mexico had to wait until 1948 to secure the right to vote.[25]

In the years immediately preceding statehood, government policy sought to change Indian culture and represented an assault on tribal landholdings, but New Mexico's Indians proved adept at preserving their identity and their communal lands. Americanization, or the forced assimilation of American Indians, produced a skein of contradictory results. Sometimes this involved open resistance to change, but increasingly it meant adapting Euro-American practices that helped them survive. The Indians also continued practices employed for several centuries with Spanish officials and other Indian groups—diplomacy and negotiation—all the more important in the territorial period since warfare was not an option. The Americanization project launched among Native Americans in the late 1880s had one lasting unintended consequence. It prepared many American Indian leaders in New Mexico to use law and politics to defend against assaults such as the Bursum Bill beginning in the 1920s.[26]

"Making His Way, If Indeed It Be Slow and Laboriously"

Cows and plows—these were dream makers and heartbreakers for most rural African Americans in the Territory. Too often while chasing their future African Americans faced disappointment brought on by stinginess—too little rainfall and too few bank loans. Two lives are emblematic of rural African American experiences in the decade preceding statehood: George McJunkin, cowboy, and Francis M. Boyer, founder of Blackdom. Their experiences resemble those of Henry O. Flipper in the Court of Private Land Claims and of some black people in Albuquerque but differ from them in other ways. Wherever African Americans settled in the Territory, however, their skin color circumscribed their lives.

When the Supreme Court upheld the right of the state of Louisiana to segregate African Americans from Euro-Americans in *Plessy v. Ferguson* (1896), it sanctioned the spread of Jim Crow laws across the United States. Jim

Crow began with separate seating areas in passenger trains, but soon barriers divided the races into so-called separate but equal facilities throughout the South and in contiguous areas, including the Territory of New Mexico. Jim Crow practices first penetrated the eastern portion of the territory, home to more than two-thirds of all blacks in New Mexico at the turn of the century. Today the most famous of these eastside residents was George McJunkin, who very belatedly after his death in 1922 became world renowned for discovering the Folsom site in 1908, where distinctive stone tools provided evidence that pushed back the date for human settlement in the New World from 4,000 to 12,000 years before the Christian era. While credit for his discovery eluded him in his lifetime, his reputation as a ranch foreman in the Clayton area brought him local respect. McJunkin's competence earned him acceptance among cowhands, but within the larger community he was always aware of how others saw him. One Fourth of July around 1900 he joined some cowboys at a Clayton café. Two men newly arrived from the East walked in and loudly protested that a black man should not be sitting with whites. They wanted him out of their sight. McJunkin's friends picked up the easterners, carried them outside, and dropped them in a mud puddle—putting them out of his sight. McJunkin's life in Clayton confirms the universal truth that one-on-one contact can temper discrimination and even mitigate segregation. McJunkin's ranching skills afforded him steady work, but not without obstacles. He homesteaded near Folsom, gaining title to 160 acres of prime grassland, but a few years later he sold out to the rancher who employed him. He traded his small acreage for the capital needed to start his own herd and the right to run it on his boss's ranch. He became a tenant livestock raiser, an accommodation necessitated not by race but by severely limited access to capital, a universal problem in that era.[27]

Dexter, New Mexico, was more than 1,400 miles west of Pelham, Georgia, but in 1896 Francis M. Boyer and Daniel Keyes left their community in the far southwest corner of Georgia's Black Belt and, unable to afford train tickets, walked to Dexter. They went in search of a special place they had heard of from Francis's father, Henry. He had served as a wagoner with the U.S. Army when General Stephen W. Kearny invaded New Mexico, and more than half a century later, his reminiscences about a place of tall grass and opportunity inspired his son, the first in his family not born into slavery. Francis Marion Boyer did his namesake proud. Like Francis

Marion, the legendary Swamp Fox of the Revolutionary War, he took risks in defense of his beliefs and inspired others to join him. Boyer staked out property on New Mexico's eastern plains and created a self-sustaining community called Blackdom. The dream was not unique to Boyer; similar settlements were undertaken elsewhere after the Civil War, notably in Kansas and Oklahoma.[28]

Boyer and Keyes shook the dust of Georgia from their feet and headed to a new land, expecting to leave behind the political and social turbulence that had affected the Deep South as far west as Texas for the last ten years. One wrenching change after another had made life extraordinarily difficult for farmers, especially African Americans. In 1886 a drought ravaged southern farms, leading to a downward spiral of falling prices, mounting debt, foreclosures, loss of their farms, and more and more farmers slipping into tenancy and sharecropping. When even these arrangements failed, they had no choice but to become transient farm laborers at inadequate wages. This dispossession precipitated a political movement, the National Farmers' Alliance and Industrial Union, or Southern Alliance, which had 1.2 million members in twenty-seven states and territories by 1890. Soon these disaffected farmers became a key part of the populist political movement. In 1890 Georgia elected Thomas E. Watson to Congress, the first Farmers' Alliance/Populist candidate seated in the U.S. House of Representatives.

Tracing Watson's career between 1890 and 1904 illustrates the conflicted and profoundly racist atmosphere in which Francis Boyer came to adulthood in Georgia. Watson's descent into bigotry was hastened by the depression of 1893–97, whose onset coincided with his failure to gain reelection to Congress in the fall of 1893. Slowly over the next ten years he became more opportunistic and turned to strident race-baiting that played on the anxieties of voters. Watson's rhetoric especially appealed to poor white farmers and sharecroppers because it tapped into deep-seated animosities among those already hard hit by the lingering depression. In Georgia and elsewhere—both in the South and in the North—hatred spilled over into vigilante lynching. Between 1889 and 1899 these averaged 187.5 annually with 80 percent occurring in the South, where two-thirds of the victims were black. Tom Watson recognized the value of merging race-baiting and political discontent, and so "ten years removed from the equalitarianism of his Populist days, Tom Watson was preaching 'the superiority of the Aryan' and the 'hideous, ominous, national menace' of Negro domination."[29]

The charge of "Negro domination" was used to stir resentment and hatred and crush economic self-determination. It proved particularly pernicious because it occurred in tandem with racist restrictions enacted throughout the South after 1890. Within two decades, as one observer noted in 1909, the South had gone "from an undiscriminating attack upon the Negro's ballot to a like attack upon his schools, his labor, his life." In this atmosphere, an educated black such as Boyer—he and his wife, Ella, had attended black colleges—understood that pursuit of a better life, where they "could own land and live in peace," meant a long trek west. Once in New Mexico, he worked on ranches until about 1900 when he could afford to send for Ella and their family, which eventually grew to ten children. Boyer and Keyes initially settled just outside Dexter, but as more African Americans arrived, "some of the Dexter citizens did not want a colony there, so they were encouraged to go farther west [about eight miles] and file on land, which they did," thus creating Blackdom. Assessing the locals' "encouragement" to move on, one historian called it "quite firm and specific." Boyer founded Blackdom in 1901 on land he both purchased and homesteaded. Soon he recruited settlers among disaffected blacks in Texas, Oklahoma, and Mississippi. Eventually more than three hundred people lived at Blackdom, which covered nearly fifteen thousand acres. As one writer noted, "the lure of one-quarter sections of unappropriated public lands appealed to Negro citizens, accustomed to hard work, excessive heat and undesirable living conditions." Out of such inhospitable beginnings a community emerged, with its own post office from 1912 to 1919 and a school staffed by parents because they did not want "a white teacher beating on [our] kids."[30]

But as the decade of the 1920s opened, dryland farming in southeast New Mexico had not proved viable, and the windmills at Blackdom could no longer draw water sufficient for irrigation. Boyer's struggles were daunting: he had mortgaged his property for capital to buy seed and livestock, and to drill for water, but depressed agricultural prices reduced earnings, and the local bank foreclosed on him. Similar problems took a collective toll on the community, and slowly Blackdoms' residents exited, resettling in various New Mexico communities. By the end of the decade Blackdom was abandoned. Many former residents, including the Boyers and Keyes, moved to the Las Cruces area and soon settled in Vado, which had been founded by blacks mustering out of the U.S. Army in the late 1860s. After Blackdom's demise, Vado became the only predominantly Afro-American community in New Mexico for decades. By the time Vado secured a post office in 1927, its residents were raising good crops of cotton in the Mesilla Valley.[31]

But farming was not the only option for those who left Blackdom. At least one former resident, W. T. Malone from Mississippi, successfully carved out a professional career. He was the first black lawyer to pass the state bar exam in New Mexico in 1914, and about a decade later he relocated to Albuquerque. He was one of the tiny elite (8 percent) of African Americans in the city with a profession or office job. More than 70 percent of the black men had menial jobs in the city's railroad hub, with porters at the top of the work ladder. A number of African American women were domestics for the town's well-to-do families. The presence of an African American community in turn created business opportunities. For example, segregation meant public accommodations were denied to blacks, and to fill the need for lodging, "tourist houses" for African Americans existed. About the time statehood arrived, Mrs. Madora B. Bailey opened hers in Albuquerque; with six bedrooms it was the largest black-owned house in town. Another black-oriented enterprise was the newspaper *American*, published in Albuquerque from 1900 to the fall of 1901.[32]

Railroads profoundly shaped race relations in a host of ways at the turn of the century. They advertised "greatly reduced" fares to African Americans as part of special promotions known as "one-way colonists' rates" to many destinations in the Southwest, including New Mexico, and on to the Far West. They also were the major employer of African Americans in countless small and medium-sized towns, and in New Mexico these included Raton, Tucumcari, Las Vegas, and Albuquerque. Although the railroad limited blacks to menial jobs, this bias did not break their spirit. Black ministers and citizens in Albuquerque—as well as their counterparts in Santa Fe, Las Vegas, and Silver City—actively worked to better their lives. Such local collective efforts reflected a national stirring of black consciousness through organizations asserting their presence, protecting their interests, and seeking greater opportunity. In particular African Americans embraced education as a way to improve their lives. A dozen African Americans from throughout New Mexico attended the second national gathering of black educators in Denver in 1911 after receiving financial assistance from Territorial Governor William J. Mills.[33]

Other organizations found a ready following as well. After the National Association for the Advancement of Colored People (NAACP) emerged in 1909, a chapter formed in Albuquerque in 1912 under the leadership of Abraham Lincoln Mitchell, and it became a formally chartered branch of the NAACP in 1915. The National Association of Colored Women's Clubs (NACWC), founded in 1896 to advocate for improved working conditions and respect for black women, soon spread westward. "The impact of women's clubs organized to uplift colored women reached New Mexico long before statehood," and these organizations allowed their members their own social and economic space when denied full opportunity by the dominant culture. For example, Albuquerque's Home Circle Social and Industrial Club, the first to operate a day nursery, opened in 1914.[34]

Ninety-two African Americans lived in Santa Fe in 1900, including the territory's most famous black man—Henry O. Flipper. Born into slavery in Georgia in 1856, he became the first black graduate of West Point (1877) and the regular army's first black commissioned officer. Posted first to Oklahoma and then west Texas, he was court-martialed at San Angelo and dismissed on charges of conduct unbecoming an officer in 1881. He immediately turned to business interests in engineering and mining, and within a decade "by thrift and shrewd investment amassed a comfortable fortune." In 1893 U.S. Attorney General Richard Olney tapped him as a special agent of the Department of Justice and assigned him to the Court of Private Land Claims. For more than seven years Flipper served as the court's investigator: "Titles of the claimants are placed in his hands, and he makes a thorough investigation of all features of the claim, corrects translations filed by claimants, goes to Mexico and examines the archives and records, hunts up and translates all laws having any possible bearing on the case."[35]

Flipper's accomplishments shaped his outlook on race relations. "I am not an advocate of equal rights," he wrote from Santa Fe in 1900. "I believe in steady, persistent, unrelaxing determination to obtain identical rights." But fatalism pervaded his views, and he told a national publication that if any African American was "fit and competent, he is making his way, if indeed it be slow and laboriously." His own rise through hard work, education, and persistence disposed him to a conservative stance. As one scholar recently noted, "Throughout his long life [he lived to be eighty-four], Flipper's position on the virtues of self-help and gradualism in racial matters resembled those of Booker T. Washington who, like Flipper, was also born in 1856 as a slave in the Deep South." Washington and Flipper believed education to be the best means to uplift African Americans, and in Albuquerque this message inspired many young black people to participate in an organization that encouraged blacks to graduate from high school, which reportedly 50 percent did as statehood arrived.[36]

By 1900 African Americans increasingly understood how to survive under Jim Crow laws. Doing so led to situational tolerance by Euro-Americans without necessarily diminishing their prejudice. Sports provided ample opportunity for such interactions. In the decade leading up to statehood, blacks played alongside whites on semipro baseball teams fielded in Albuquerque and Santa Fe, with blacks being one-third of the latter's team in 1911. But sharing the same field did not challenge institutionalized racism. Another form of false acceptance occurred when whites encouraged former slaves to perpetuate myths that erased the brutality of slavery by replacing memories of oppression with nostalgic anecdotes. Upon Hannah Patterson's death at age eighty-eight in late June 1911, the *Albuquerque Morning Journal* called her "one of the best known colored women in this part of the country" with "distinct remembrance" of "many of the pleasant features of her slavery days," which were the first forty-two years of her life.[37]

Albuquerque had about 250 African American residents at statehood, and their urban experiences had various commonalities with the lives of rural blacks. Chief among these were community building, solidarity, and an awareness of their potential. Whether it was parents running their own schools in Blackdom or men and women in Albuquerque joining local affiliates of national reform movements, rural and urban African Americans had arrived at a similar point in their evolving social and political consciousness. In initiating self-transformation, the experiences of New Mexico's African Americans resonated with that of emerging black communities throughout the West. They were beginning to heed a call made at the sixth annual meeting of the Colorado Association of Colored Women's Clubs, to lift "a downtrodden race above the rockies [sic] of prejudice."[38]

"The Illegal Traffic of Chinese"

American immigration officials spelled his name phonetically—Jew Ki. An American consular officer in Hong Kong transliterated it as Chiu Kai. The young deportee might well have felt he had two different identities after his experiences in New Mexico. He was one of 2,492 Chinese arrested along the Mexican border between 1907 and 1909. Like most of those caught, Chiu Kai was a common laborer whose boat ride across the Pacific Ocean ended at Guaymas, a port in northwest Mexico. Intent on entering the United States to earn in five years an amount of money greater than could be made in China in decades, he made his way to Juárez. There he and fifteen other Chinese paid two Americans—Carl Adamson and W. Sullivan—to transport them to either Roswell or Carlsbad, where a train would take them to jobs arranged by the smugglers.[39]

The first three and a half days went as planned. They began by fording the Rio Grande after dark on 19 June 1908. Once across, they piled into a large freight wagon. Adamson and Sullivan threw a large white tarp over them, pulled themselves into the driver's bench, and headed toward New Mexico. The two Americans were well-known to El Paso immigration officials, who described them as having "been engaged in the illegal traffic of Chinese at El Paso for a number of years." But this time they made a mistake—we do not know exactly what happened, but twenty miles north of El Paso a rancher and his son became suspicious and sent word to the Immigration Bureau in El Paso. Twenty-one hours after Chiu Kai and fifteen others illegally entered the United States, three immigration officers—Oscar Miller, Mr. Gonzales, and Mr. Bernard—mounted their horses and set out to investigate.[40]

By entering the United States, Chiu Kai had violated the Chinese Exclusion Act of 1882, which barred laborers but did allow Chinese merchants, students, teachers, and diplomats to enter the United States. China long protested such restrictions, but it eventually signed a treaty with the United States in 1894 that included a ten-year prohibition on Chinese laborers. China's reluctant acceptance of the treaty with the United States came midway through the thirty-five-year reign of Porfirio Díaz as Mexico's president, and his policy of encouraging Chinese immigrant labor had become a mainstay of his country's railroad and agricultural expansion. An 1899 treaty between Díaz and Emperor Kuang Hsu of the Ch'ing dynasty increased immigration but led to greater discord between Mexico and the United States. As illegal U.S. entry accelerated, in 1904 President Roosevelt and the Congress unilaterally extended the 1894 treaty.[41]

Anti-Chinese sentiment existed in Mexico, but it never approached levels found in California and elsewhere in the United States. When Theodore Roosevelt began his second term in 1905, anti-Chinese vitriol was every bit as pervasive as anti-black sentiments. Many Euro-Americans considered both races to be inferior, untrustworthy, and a threat to the nation's social fabric. Concurrent with President Roosevelt's inauguration in early March 1905, his administration announced a nationwide special census of Chinese. The first report received came from the Territories of New Mexico and Arizona at the end of March. They had a total of 1,475 Chinese, the overwhelming majority of whom lived in Arizona, particularly in Tucson's large Chinatown. New Mexico's Chinese held certificates confirming their entry status, and illegal immigrants used the Territory as a transit point in moving on to jobs, especially as field hands in California, where produce growers complained about "the impossibility of inducing reliable white labor" to pick vegetables and fruits and so turned to Chinese and Japanese workers.[42]

New Mexico's several hundred legal Chinese residents worked in restaurants (Albuquerque had two Chinese restaurants, Roswell had one) and laundries as well as serving as tailors and field hands. They lived mainly in two counties bordering Mexico—Luna (37) and Grant (108), but were represented in small numbers in all but five counties—Mora, Rio Arriba, San Juan, Taos, and Torrance. There were 31 percent fewer Chinese in 1910 than in 1890, and contributing to their population decrease was the prohibition on entry of Chinese women. Although at least one Chinese man in Roswell married an African American from Blackdom, many expected to return home to take a wife. An opposite trend occurred with the Japanese, first subjected to laws barring them from the continental U.S. in 1907. Their numbers increased as mining grew, from 8 in 1900 to 258 in 1910, with the largest concentrations in the Territory's mining centers—Colfax and McKinley counties—but smaller numbers in ten other counties.[43]

The major attention to the Chinese and Japanese, though, involved whether they entered the country legally. Roosevelt's second term witnessed intensified border enforcement to curb illegal entry coupled with deportation of those lacking proper paperwork. Early in 1906 the U.S. Government redoubled its campaign against illegal entry in a crackdown on "the first illegal immigrants"—the Chinese. In New Mexico and elsewhere, the federal government appointed "Chinese inspectors" to find and arrest violators of the exclusion act. Agent Charles V. Mallatt of San Marcial covered the central region of the Territory while Agent Gregorio Garcia of Anthony patrolled along the border. U.S. Marshal Creighton B. Foraker also acted as an inspector, especially between Las Cruces and Deming. Railroad hubs particularly interested all three men, and railroad agents became vigilant partners in enforcing the exclusion act. For example, in December 1906 twenty-eight Chinese were discovered inside a sealed container labeled "Furniture" being shipped from El Paso to California. Railroad workers in Las Cruces uncovered the ruse, and all twenty-eight were arrested and deported. In 1907 the commissioner of immigration consolidated activities in New Mexico, Arizona, and much of Texas into the Mexican Border District, which involved both a modest addition of manpower and heightened expectations for surveillance, policing, and deportations.[44]

Those New Mexicans who regularly read English- or Spanish-language newspapers knew about the government's efforts to find, arrest, and deport Chinese violating the exclusion act. But they also had access to much additional information about the Chinese. If they read the *Albuquerque Morning Journal*, for instance, they regularly came across wire service articles reporting on three general topics about China and its people: international events involving diplomatic, military, and anti-U.S. activities; U.S.-based accounts giving social, economic, and human-interest perspectives (including deportations); and summaries of exclusion-related legislation. Between 1 January and 30 April 1906 the Albuquerque paper printed ninety-nine articles in these three areas, fifty-two about international relations; twenty-eight containing human interest material; and nineteen on exclusion legislation. Ongoing turmoil in China accounted for more than half of the international articles, but analysis and commentary appeared, too. One of the longest articles, entitled "The Chinese and the 'Foreign Devils,'" tackled a sensitive issue and discussed it from the Chinese perspective. In assessing "the foreign promoter," the article pointed out, "hatred of the foreigner springs from two causes—the exploitation of China's resources by foreign

promoters, and the campaign of Christian missionaries." What might
Euro-Americans have thought about such statements when they lived
amidst Nuevomexicanos and American Indians who, respectively, held
similar grievances against outsiders? The two Spanish-language newspapers of Las Cruces included only eleven articles on Chinese topics in the
first four months of 1906—two reporting international events and nine
covering human interest, of which six were on the San Francisco earth-
quake. Despite the vast quantitative difference in coverage, little qualitative
difference existed.[45]

Nuevomexicano readers, like their Euro-American counterparts, would
have had to make up their own minds about the Chinese abroad and those
entering the United States illegally. The tone of articles ranged from negative to positive, but what is noticeably absent in all the stories is rabid anti-
Chinese rhetoric. Those four months witnessed attacks on missionaries
and anti-U.S. riots in China, but the coverage never degenerated into hate-
mongering. A running account of international events and a continuously
updated view of the larger world were comparatively recent phenomena in
the Territory in 1906. How worldwide information wrought change in New
Mexicans' lives is ultimately unknowable, but what is clear is that in the
territory a nuanced and thought-provoking view of the Chinese could easily have emerged from the available newspapers. Interestingly, the *Tucson
Daily Citizen* ran 21 percent more coverage during the same four months,
but it also had a more consistently negative tone. For example, during the
week of Chinese New Year the paper had articles on "Slavery in China, Savage Cruelty" and "Rival Chinese Gangs Kill in New York Streets." They
also referred to the Chinatown celebrations as "Chink New Year," noted
the "queer manner in which the Chinese celebrate," and disliked the "weird
Chinese music."[46]

Just what M. H. Reeves, the rancher at Newman, New Mexico, and his
son Victor knew about Chinese immigrants or smugglers or why they
were motivated to report suspicious behavior is unknown. But their action
set in motion a seventy-five-hour chase, which ended successfully only
because the driver of an automobile came across the three agents and their
exhausted horses and gave two of the agents a ride into Alamogordo, where
a long-distance phone call to a deputy sheriff in Tularosa led to captur-

ing the two Americans and their cargo of sixteen Chinese and returning them to Alamogordo. There Adamson and Sullivan were jailed, indicted, and bound over for trial. Deportation followed for fifteen of the Chinese, but Chiu Kai agreed to testify against the two Americans. In doing so he postponed his deportation but was placed in the territorial prison. On his way to Santa Fe, Chiu Kai was told the government paid witnesses three dollars a day per diem as well as an additional dollar a day as a witness fee. About seven months later, with guilty verdicts rendered and appeals denied, the two Americans got eighteen months in prison and Chiu Kai was deported. He collected the dollar-a-day payment but not the per diem. Across the thousand miles from Santa Fe to San Francisco, his deportation port, and then across more than 5,600 miles of ocean to China he continued to believe he was owed just over $500 for per diem from "the middle of the twelfth moon" [14 January 1909] to the "second day of the fifth moon" [18 June]. In August 1910 the American consulate in Hong Kong forwarded Kai's claim to Washington, D.C. The State Department reviewed the matter and ruled that deportees were ineligible for per diem.[47]

So ended the transoceanic diplomatic exchange, which closed the case; however, other details in the Kai file help situate early U.S. immigration policy in New Mexico's pursuit of statehood. Following the trial in Alamogordo in December 1908, the head of El Paso's immigration office believed "this prosecution was the most important of any which have originated in this District. . . . The parties involved . . . are connected with one of the strongest groups of smugglers in the El Paso jurisdiction." That city's reputation for cozy relations between officials and smugglers gave rise to a federal investigation. In April 1909 criminal prosecutions revealed an extensive smuggling network stretching from El Paso through Albuquerque and on to Chicago. Indicted in Las Cruces were New Mexico–based W. B. Green, an immigration inspector, and two railroad employees, including a black porter. Indicted in Roswell were three men from El Paso: a former police chief, Edward M. Fink, a restaurant owner, and a railroad brakeman. Fink promptly posted bond of $5,000, ten times the usual amount in Chinese smuggling cases, and fled to Mexico.[48]

These criminal cases in the spring of 1909 piled on further evidence of New Mexico's inability to manage its affairs well. One of newly elected president William Howard Taft's first priorities was to talk with Mexican president Porfirio Díaz, and the agenda included following up on requests that his country tighten the border. A meeting in mid-October was set, and on the same trip, Taft inspected the government in New Mexico to ensure himself it was ready for statehood. By the time New Mexico entered the Union, Mexico had split apart in revolution. As two notable historians of the border region, Charles Harris and Ray Sadler, have written: "People [in El Paso] quit smuggling Chinese into the United States and began to smuggle guns into Mexico."[49]

The Llano Sheep Co. Buck

Gross Blackwell shepherds. A leading Las Vegas mercantile firm, it operated under several names from the late 1870s until statehood. It was particularly active in partidario labor contracts, a form of indentured servitude tied to sheep raising. Wool was a mainstay of New Mexico's agricultural economy throughout the territorial period and into the 1930s. (Courtesy CSWR, PC, UL, UNM, #000-096-0064)

Gallup coal mine. When mining became industrialized in the late nineteenth century, substantial capital was required to mechanize the extraction of large quantities of coal, which railroads shipped to distant markets. In 1904 the coal mines in New Mexico yielded 1.6 million tons, with McKinley and Colfax counties the most productive. (Courtesy CSWR, PC, UL, UNM, #000-119-0534)

(Facing page, top) Petition to Governor Miguel A. Otero from the citizens of Las Cruces. In schemes to publicize New Mexico and attract both settlers and investment, boosters let no opportunity pass. The governor declined to send a delegation to the 1900 World's Fair in Paris, but he did actively participate in the 1904 World's Fair in Saint Louis to promote statehood for New Mexico. (Courtesy Miguel Antonio Otero Papers, MSS 21 BC, Box 1, Folder 5, CSWR, UL, UNM)

(Facing page, bottom) Declarations and Resolutions of the 1901 Statehood Convention. Convened by Governor Otero to coincide with the Territorial Fair in Albuquerque, when people from throughout New Mexico would be in town, the forum drew several hundred delegates and as many onlookers. An example of forceful popular sovereignty in "Demanding a State Form of Government," the statement launched a decade-long campaign to enter the Union. (Library of Congress, Microform Reading Room, Reel 86, Document 7831)

To Honorable M. A. Otero.
Governor of New Mex.

The undersigned citizens of Las
Cruces respectfully urge and request that you appoint Prof. J. C.
Carrera to the position of Commissioner from the Territory of New Mexico to the Paris World's Exposition.
Prof. Carrera is highly educated in
the French language and is a graduate of the School of Mines of Paris,
and is eminently qualified for the
position in question.

W. H. H. Llewellyn
S. W. Sharpe
P. Moreno, Chairman R.C.C.
Marial Valdez, Justice of the Peace
J. D. Williams, Deputy Sheriff
Felipe Lucero, Criador de ganados
Encarnacion Garcia
Henry D. Bowman — Rev. U.S.C.O
Martin Lohman
Thos. Branigan
Eugene Van Patten
F. B. Llewellyn, Sec. R. C. C.
J. F. Lucero, Sheriff

New Mexico (Ter.) Convention, 1901.

DECLARATIONS AND RESOLUTIONS

Submitted for Adoption to the People of the Territory
of New Mexico at Their Statehood Convention,
Held at Albuquerque, October 15 and 16, 1901,
Demanding a State Form of Government From the
Congress of the United States.

187

Nestor Montoya. A key proponent
of statehood, he organized and led
Nuevomexicanos at the 1901 Statehood
Convention. As the longtime editor of
Albuquerque's *La Bandera Americana* (The
American Flag), Montoya exercised great
influence among both Euro-Americans and
Nuevomexicanos. He was speaker of the house
in the territorial legislature (1903), a delegate
to the Constitutional Convention of 1910, and
served as Republican U.S. representative in the
Congress (1921–23). (Courtesy CSWR, PC, UL,
UNM, #000-119-0274)

UNCLE SAM ADMITTING NEW-MEXICO TO THE UNION.

An odd ceremony which formed part of the welcome that Albuquerque gave to President Roosevelt the other day.

"Uncle Sam Admitting New Mexico to the Union." A crowd of 15,000 greeted President Theodore Roosevelt on his visit to Albuquerque on 5 May 1903. Directly opposite the platform from which Roosevelt spoke was a large tableau depicting a young girl seeking entry into the union of states. He told the assembled that she would surely be welcomed "when New Mexico had a little more irrigation." (Courtesy Miguel Antonio Otero Papers, MSS 21 BC, Box 1, Scrapbook, CSWR, UL, UNM)

VOL. L. No. 1294.   PUCK BUILDING, New York, December 18th, 1901.   PRICE TEN CENTS.
Copyright, 1901, by Keppler & Schwarzmann.

Puck

Entered at N. Y. P. O. as Second-class Mail Matter.

THE NEXT CANDIDATE FOR STATEHOOD.

a.   b.

Political cartoons, 1901 and 1902. National public opinion had been gradually shifting in favor of statehood since the mid-1890s. These cartoons use the common motif of maturing young girls dressed in regionally distinctive clothes seeking to be treated as grown-ups and allowed to wear the new, national garb of a state. The 1901 cartoon (a) is by Rose Cecil O'Neill, soon to become famous for creating the Kewpie doll. (a) LC, PP, LC-DIG-ppmsca-25590; (b) reproduced from the *Detroit News* in the journal *Public Opinion* 32, no. 21 (15 May 1902), 648

THE KIDS: "Say, Pop, isn't it time we were wearing pants?"
—*Detroit News*

Inside the cartoon:

VOL. LIX. No. 1524   PUCK BUILDING, New York, May 16, 1906.   PRICE TEN CENTS.

"What Fools these Mortals be!"

Puck

Copyright, 1906, by Keppler & Schwarzmann   Entered at N. Y. P. O. as Second-class Mail Matter.

ALDRICH

HOUSE BILL

STANDARD OIL

NEEDED LEGISLATION

ANTI TRUST BILL

SENATE COMMITTEE ROOM

FREE ALCOHOL BILL

TARIFF

PHILIPPINE BILL

HOUSE BILL

"KILLED IN COMMITTEE."

Senator Aldrich's power. This cartoon by John Pughe in the mid-May 1906 issue of the nation's premier political journal of satire, *Puck*, conveyed the senator's ability to entrap bills and ensure they were "killed in committee." That spring he allowed joint statehood to go forward because it cut in half the prospect of eight new senators should New Mexico, Arizona, Oklahoma, and the Indian Territory enter separately. (Courtesy LC, PP, LC-DIG-ppmsca-26059)

George Curry. A former Rough Rider officer who proved his administrative abilities as a provincial governor in the Philippines, he was brought back to New Mexico by President Theodore Roosevelt in 1907 to clean up corruption in territorial government as a precondition for statehood. He served in the U.S. House of Representatives (1912–13) but stepped down when reapportioning limited the state to one member. (Courtesy CSWR, PC, UL, UNM, #000-021-0065)

Albert B. Fall. A fiery and confrontational person, he was a Democrat until switching to the Republican Party in 1904, about the time this photograph was taken. His three-month tenure as attorney general in 1907 put him at odds with federal officials for several years, capped by publicly insulting President William Howard Taft in mid-October 1909. He always carried a revolver in New Mexico, including at the Constitutional Convention, but did not do so in Washington, D.C. as U.S. senator (1912–21) or as Secretary of the Interior (1921–23). (Courtesy LC, PP, LC-USZ62-137609)

Ormsby McHarg (in the 1940s).
Appointed as a special assistant U.S.
attorney to investigate land fraud in
New Mexico, he filed numerous lawsuits
in 1907, which infuriated Albert B. Fall.
McHarg never tempered his principles
and courted great personal danger
pursuing his federal duties. In late
February 1909 his testimony before
Senator Beveridge's committee scuttled
New Mexico's last chance for statehood
under President Theodore Roosevelt.
(Courtesy Paul A. Ryan)

A PRE

O CLEAR.

The ever-rising cost of living became an issue Democrats used to attack Republicans after 1896. This *Puck* cartoon from 1908 depicts key "stand-patters," or conservative Republicans in the Congress. President William Howard Taft, aware his political survival depended on reclaiming the initiative on economic issues, linked a bill regulating railroad rates with statehood and passed both in June 1910. (Courtesy LC, PP, LC-DIG-ppmsca-26215)

ALBUQUERQUE MORNING JOURNAL.

THIRTY-FIRST YEAR, Vol. CXXIV., No. 16. ALBUQUERQUE, NEW MEXICO, SATURDAY, OCTOBER 16, 1909. Single Copies, 5 cents. By Mail By Carrier, 60 cents

President Wins Hearts of All New Mexico

MOST POWERFUL MAN IN NATION STANDS AS CHAMPION OF STATEHOOD

FIVE THOUSAND PEOPLE HEAR CHIEF EXECUTIVE DECLARE TIME HAS COME FOR CONGRESS TO ACT

William H. Taft in Brief Visit to Albuquerque Fulfills the Hopes of Most Sanguine Believers in Near Approach of Justice for the Territory and at the Same Time Warns the People to Have a Care That the Constitution of the New State Will Win It the Place It Deserves in the Nation.

A LITTLE PATIENCE AND MUCH WISDOM IS THE BURDEN OF THE PRESIDENT'S WORD OF WARNING

THE PRESIDENT'S SPEECH

Mr. Taft said—

"Mr. Mayor, Ladies and Gentlemen of Albuquerque and New Mexico: I am very glad to be here to say what I am going to say about that thing which is uppermost in your mind, but I seem to be able to guess what it is. Every baby in this territory seems to be trained to speak the first word Statehood. Now insofar as lies in me as the chief executive recommending legislation to congress and exercising a legitimate influence in that regard—the constitutional functions being to recommend and to veto—I first will say that I will not veto a bill letting New Mexico in. (Applause.) And second, that I shall recommend that the promise of the Republican platform upon which I had the honor to be elected president should be carried out in good faith, and that the Territories of Arizona and New Mexico shall be admitted to the Union, so that we shall have nothing but states between the Atlantic and the Pacific. They have an objection to you because some of you speak Spanish. Well, I know something about the Spanish language, and they could not speak a more beautiful language than that. I know something about the Spanish descended people and I know how courteous, how chivalrous, and what high ideas they have of hospitality and kindness, generosity and courtesy, and I am glad to come here in contact with that element and certainly I am not going to use any influence to keep them out if they are citizens of the United States and entitled to be considered like other citizens that we have taken in, loyal to the flag and able to serve their country when it is necessary. I am glad to have the privilege of speaking here to veterans of the Civil War that helped to save this country, and I thank them for coming out to express what I suppose is their loyalty to the Commander in Chief of the Army and Navy in which they served so well. (Applause.) I am sorry that I am not able to say that I am a fellow-soldier with you. I have no right to wear a uniform, but the Constitution says that I am your Commander in Chief, and you have got to get along the best way...

...in the country and making it a part of the United States as a state. You have a population large enough, but, my friends, when you think of statehood it is like the aspiration of a boy to become a man and to become the head of a family, and all the independence that that gives; but it also entails some burdens; when you become a man you have got to support yourself, you have got to support your wife, your children, if you are lucky enough to have them; so it is as to statehood, you have got to select your own officials. You think that is easy, and you do not like to have them selected by somebody else, but perhaps the time will come when you will get some officials in, selected by somebody that differs with you. The majority might be such that you won't like the majority; that sometimes happens. Then you will have to stand it. You cannot then put it on to Washington. You cannot say if they only understood what the needs of New Mexico were then we would have good officials all the time; you have got to do the selecting yourself. You have got to do something else—you have to pass a Constitution that shall serve as a fundamental law, for a hundred years, it may be, because Constitutions are not easily amended. And you are going to have introduced into that convention a great many gentlemen who propose good mountain and plain notions, and if you put those into your legislature that it cannot move at all, and now you have got to meet that issue, and if you want to get in with a Constitution that barks and gags you, and ties you in every way, that is the kind of responsibility you have got to assume, but I hope you won't. I hope you won't because I mean to become as responsible as I can for your admission into the United States and I want you to come in and stand up like other states without the burden of a Constitution that is a mere statutory provision for details, but with a fundamental law that shall be like the Constitution of the United States, simple, comprehensive, with proper limitations as to vested rights, and personal liberty...

WINNING TAFT SMILE SHEDS RADIANCE FOR FIRST TIME ON NEW MEXICO AT GALLUP

EAGER THRONG AT MINING TOWN CLASPS HANDS WITH PRESIDENT

Nation's Chief Has Cordial Greeting for Members of Reception Committee Sent Out to Welcome Him at the Edge of the Territory; Tall Hats and Frock Coats of New Mexicans Marked Contrast to President's Simple and Comfortable Attire.

On his visit to New Mexico in mid-October 1909, with stops at three towns—Gallup, Albuquerque, and Las Cruces—and two pueblos—Laguna and Isleta—President William Howard Taft pledged to secure statehood. Republican newspapers, such as the *Albuquerque Morning Journal*, were enthusiastic, but the Democratic press expressed skepticism. Likewise local reaction to Albert B. Fall's verbal assault on the president split along partisan lines. (*Albuquerque Morning Journal*, 16 October 1909, p. 1)

William Howard Taft. The much underrated
twenty-seventh president, he had only one
term because after 1910 he could not escape the
shadow or the contempt of former president
Theodore Roosevelt, whom he had served as
governor general of the Philippines (1900–1904)
and as secretary of war (1904–1908), and who
had hand-picked him as his successor. He was
the first president to make extensive use of the
telephone in his political negotiations and to
have a presidential automobile, and the only
ex-president to serve as Chief Justice of the U.S.
Supreme Court (1921–30). (Courtesy LC, PP,
LC-USZ62-7757)

Postmaster General Frank H. Hitchcock. Today this pivotal figure in the congressional fight to secure statehood is all but forgotten, but besides serving in the cabinet (1909–13) he was President Taft's chief legislative liaison, which placed him in the center of all congressional negotiations over statehood from January to June 1910. During those six months he guided final passage of the Enabling Act signed by the president on 20 June 1910. (Courtesy LC, PP, LC-DIG-ggbain-05020)

Fourth of July, 1910, Las Vegas. Immediately following passage of the Enabling Act, New Mexicans began celebrating statehood, though the festive mood was premature by eighteen months. People created forty-eight-star flags (upper far left foreground) by sewing or pinning on two stars. Ceremonial stars and stripes included floral arrangements (far right foreground). The presence of children is noteworthy because they were 37 percent of New Mexico's population in 1910. (Courtesy CSWR, PC, UL, UNM, #000-742-0220)

Opening session of the Constitutional Convention of 1910. One hundred delegates working at the capitol from 3 October to 21 November 1910 wrote the state's constitution. One-third of the delegates were Nuevomexicanos and the remaining were Euro-Americans. It was approved by the voters on 21 January 1911, then submitted to the president and the Congress, both of which finally accepted it, along with Arizona's, on 21 August. (Twitchell, *Leading Facts*, facing p. 560)

President Taft signing New Mexico Statehood Proclamation on Saturday, 6 January 1912. Not until new state officials were elected on 7 November 1911 and the ballot results verified and certified to officials in Washington, D.C., on 31 December, could New Mexico's statehood ceremony be scheduled. (Courtesy LC, PP, LC-DIG-hec-20482)

Outside the White House on 6 January 1912, the old political order and the new posed on the first step. Flanking Delegate William H. Andrews (first row, center left) were newly elected Democratic Representative Harvey B. Fergusson (left) and Republican George Curry. Congressional redistricting in the fall of 1911 reduced New Mexico to one representative, but the speaker of the house postponed implementation until March 1913. Fergusson was reelected but Curry did not run. (Courtesy CSWR, PC, UL, UNM, #000-742-0256)

CHAPTER SEVEN

"Conservative and Law Loving"

The telegram brought bad news. The Justice Department informed Territorial governor William J. Mills on the night of Thursday, 4 January 1912 that statehood could not go forward. The White House canceled the 10:00 A.M. ceremony set for Friday, 5 January 1912, and the next morning's headline in the *Albuquerque Morning Journal* announced, "STATEHOOD ONCE MORE HELD UP; LITIGATION THIS TIME." The front-page article explained that the government intervened "to recover lands in New Mexico alleged to have been acquired wrongfully by the Alamogordo Lumber Company," and a five-year-old lawsuit against the company had to be transferred to a federal court as a precondition for statehood. Washington's demand poured ice water onto celebrants toasting New Mexico's final hours as a territory. The quashed jubilations also reminded New Mexicans of the most objectionable feature of their status: they were under the thumb of the federal government. Quickly, though, territorial officials acceded to the ultimatum and forwarded the required papers to the Department of Justice. After a day's delay, the president signed the statehood proclamation.[1]

The lawsuit involved land and timber rights in Otero County sold by the Territory in 1901, the first in a string of similar transactions over the following six years challenged by the Justice Department beginning in 1907. The eleventh-hour delay was not the first time a lawsuit like *U.S. v. Alamogordo Lumber Company*, related to land fraud in New Mexico, delayed statehood. Coming in the wake of the defeat of joint statehood in 1906, these cases and the federal investigations linked to them proved highly prejudicial to prospects for joining the Union. The allegations of corruption by territorial officials brought scandal into the quest for statehood, derailing its momentum and occasioning inquiries by the Justice Department, the White House, and the Congress between 1907 and 1911.

For decades the territorial government had been suspected of corruption involving land transfers, first regarding land-grant claims and then, after June 1898, in managing the 4.2 million acres ceded to support educational and charitable institutions. Within two years of taking title to these lands, territorial officials began to sell them and their resources in a manner that, when brought to public attention, fueled new charges of fraud and corruption. Consequently, just when chicanery over land grants began fading as an issue in Washington, the territory seeded a new crop of charges and provided congressional opponents of statehood further evidence that New Mexico's long-standing reputation for scandal was well deserved.

President Theodore Roosevelt had dismissed Governor Miguel A. Otero in late 1905 and, in an attempt to bring reform to the territory and honesty to its governance, appointed Herbert J. Hagerman. But within eighteen months Hagerman became entangled in allegations of land fraud. Roosevelt concluded he had become "the tool of powerful corrupt interests" and summarily removed him in April 1907. Next the president turned to George Curry, a trusted Rough Rider officer then serving as a provincial governor in the Philippines, and told him to clean up the corruption. By the time Curry took his oath of office as governor in early August, federal investigators from several departments were conducting inquiries and starting to file lawsuits. None of the suits ever came to trial, but Curry's administration got off to a very rocky start.[2]

Curry appointed as attorney general his longtime friend Albert B. Fall, who immediately ruffled feathers in the territory and in Washington, especially those of the lead federal investigator, Ormsby McHarg. Roosevelt had personally briefed McHarg on his expectations for ending the territory's land scandals and official corruption, which put McHarg on a collision course with Fall. Their clashes became personal, but they arose from a fundamental difference of opinion over sovereignty. Fall rejected the federal government's authority to prescribe the way lands deeded to the Territory were to be administered. His view was anathema to McHarg, who, like President Roosevelt, was a moral crusader who abhorred fraud and corruption and believed in holding the public domain for the benefit of future generations. Theirs was a conception of government in the Hamiltonian tradition—a collective public interest existed that had to be protected and advanced by the actions of the federal government. Territorial Attorney General Albert Fall held the opposite philosophical view, that of a Jeffersonian, enshrined in a states' rights position: the territory held sole and exclusive right to dispose of land and resources ceded to it.[3]

The pursuit of statehood became a contest of wills and principles. Not surprisingly, Fall served only four months as attorney general. But the enmity between him and McHarg over federal investigations and lawsuits, coupled with the gulf between their views of sovereignty, proved particularly damaging to statehood deliberations for more than two years. The personal and philosophical rifts came to a head in late February 1909. Roosevelt sought statehood as a final legislative triumph of his presidency, and President-elect William Howard Taft urged it, too. Then Ormsby McHarg testified before Senator Albert J. Beveridge's Committee on Territories. His public revelations set statehood back severely, but the private fifteen-minute meeting with Senate leader Nelson Aldrich that followed dealt the statehood movement a near-fatal blow. In both settings McHarg reprised accusations of misconduct by territorial officials and private citizens alleged in lawsuits he had filed in 1907. Roosevelt's planned legacy collapsed, and incoming president William Howard Taft inherited an imbroglio. Undaunted, Taft traveled to New Mexico in the seventh month of his administration. While there he pledged to deliver statehood. On his return trip he narrowly avoided an assassin in El Paso, but once safely in the White House he completed plans to place new stars onto the flag.

"Righted by You People and Not by Anybody Outside"

George Curry was appointed territorial governor in 1907, but he first arrived in New Mexico in 1879 and held law enforcement and judicial posts in both south-central and northwest New Mexico before serving several terms in the Territorial Legislature. In the late 1880s he befriended Albert B. Fall when both were active in the Democratic Party, and they served together as officers with the Rough Riders in 1898. This brief military experience helped Curry secure a commission as an army officer in the Philippines, where he distinguished himself in combat before taking on several administrative posts, including chief of police in Manila (1901–1902) and governor of Samar Province (1905–1907). The recommendation of the former governor general of the Philippines and current secretary of war, William

Howard Taft, influenced Roosevelt's decision to appoint Curry. Taft also expedited paperwork authorizing the War Department to ferry Curry from Manila to the West Coast in July. After taking a train to New York to meet with Roosevelt on 31 July, then spending a day in Washington, Curry headed to Santa Fe and took his oath of office on Thursday, 8 August.[4]

Controversy immediately engulfed him. It began when his newly appointed attorney general, Albert B. Fall, dismissed accusations of corruption in New Mexico during his welcoming address. Fall praised Nuevomexicanos and their contributions to the Territory and asked rhetorically whether "we need a dozen agents of the United States Government here to investigate these people." The audience laughed and applauded, and Albert Fall had deftly seeded the falsehood that federal investigators were focusing on Nuevomexicanos. He went on to claim "there is less graft, less corruption in the Territory of New Mexico, than in any state or territory of the United States." He concluded by saying that President Roosevelt knew the facts about New Mexico and had instructed Governor Curry as to his wishes, and "the other fellows [federal investigators] will go pretty soon." Three weeks later while in El Paso, and following a few confrontations with McHarg, he denounced the government agents as "federal spies."[5]

Fall had been asked to welcome Curry, but he used his speech to fire broadsides at critics of the territory. In downplaying malfeasance, he delivered a retort to former territorial delegate Bernard S. Rodey, who a week earlier had told the president and newspaper reporters, "There is a wonderful lot of graft going on" in New Mexico. Fall's remarks were also meant to deflect attention from ongoing grand jury investigations, one of which would deliver indictments later that same day against various prominent New Mexicans, including George W. Prichard, who had just resigned as territorial attorney general, and former governor Miguel A. Otero. While Fall's speech fooled many of those listening, his remarks ran directly counter to President Roosevelt's explicit instructions for Governor Curry. On 9 August, the president wrote Curry that "the one matter that I must insist upon in all your subordinates is that they shall live up to the standard of absolute honesty."[6]

Curry had no prior knowledge of what Fall would say, and it is unclear whether Fall, like Curry, spoke without notes. Word quickly reached the White House through the president's personal representative, Assistant

U.S. Postmaster General Frank H. Hitchcock, a key Republican Party operative. Official responses came swiftly. The governor's immediate superior, Secretary of the Interior James R. Garfield, arrived in the Territory on 9 August, a day ahead of schedule, and was met by Governor Curry. Garfield also conferred at length with Hitchcock and several of the federal investigators, and then addressed a large crowd of territorial leaders and citizens. Secretary Garfield's public speech to New Mexicans was an official rebuke of Fall's rhetorical excesses. He emphasized that the new administration would restore public confidence in government by ensuring "fair treatment for all and special favors for none." He acknowledged the ongoing federal investigations but implied that the federal government would soon step aside. Finally, he noted, "You are anxious to creep out from under the control of the Department of the Interior . . . it will not be long before you can walk alone."[7]

Garfield's words may have assuaged some in Santa Fe, but the dustup Fall had caused intensified in Washington during the following days. In mid-month the president told Curry, "his remarks at your inauguration were most unfortunate . . . [and] bound to give our enemies a handle. I suggest you get him out of office at the earliest possible moment." One of the most influential of the people who had complained to the president was the ultraconservative speaker of the house, Joseph G. Cannon (R-Ill.), who had always been lukewarm at best toward the territory. Cannon, like Roosevelt, found himself squeezed by political interests in the fallout from charges and denials of corruption in New Mexico. He was experiencing problems keeping the House under his control, and Fall's speech provided fodder for the restive progressives demanding reform and honesty in government. The issue of fraudulent land and timber sales in the territory vexed other contemporaries, too, including Ralph Emerson Twitchell, attorney, historian, and prominent Republican. When he published his history of New Mexico in 1912, Twitchell confessed to his confusion: "land fraud prosecutions in New Mexico have never been fully understood by the people."[8]

Why did Twitchell have such difficulty explaining these lawsuits? The short answer is that the chaotic factionalism that roiled the territory's political life also engulfed its legal history. Federal investigations became entangled in a web of deception and secrecy spun by many people, including Albert B. Fall and, to a lesser degree, Ormsby McHarg. Twitchell, being very close to the events, could not focus on the larger issue in the background: contested views about sovereignty. But Fall and McHarg both knew exactly what the fight was about. Both men had been preparing for this fight for much of their lives.

Born in Frankfort, Kentucky, in 1861, Fall read law under Judge William Lindsay, resided briefly in Texas, and then settled in Doña Ana County, New Mexico, in 1886. Over the next dozen years he rose in the Democratic Party, serving twice in the legislature, then as an associate justice of the territorial Supreme Court (1893–95), and as attorney general (1897). But he failed to secure the party's nomination for congressional delegate in 1900, and by 1904 he had switched to the Republican Party to position himself better for political office when statehood arrived. His intellectual mentor, William Lindsay, served as Democratic U.S. senator from Kentucky from 1893 until 1901, and he likely imbued Fall with his lifelong disdain for the regulatory power of the federal government. Lindsay had served with distinction in the army of the Confederate States of America, and after the Civil War he grudgingly reconciled himself to the new era. But he also became an ardent proponent of states' rights and of using public money to promote private economic development, ideas that became consistent themes in Fall's life, too.[9]

We remember Albert B. Fall today for the seamy side of his career, which made news fifteen years later when, as secretary of the interior he approved oil leases for drilling in the Teapot Dome reserve in Wyoming. But already visible in the summer of 1907 were his deceptiveness and his overwhelming interest in economic development at the expense of federal law and the natural environment. Curry appointed him attorney general because he wanted someone to advance the interests of the Territory, particularly its economic future, and that topic formed the major theme of the governor's acceptance speech. Fall likewise dwelled at length on economic development, arguing the need to use the Territory's resources in the pursuit of statehood. He introduced the theme with a pledge that under Curry the territory would have a "business administration" rather than a partisan political administration. Over the next five years the Curry administration intended to develop New Mexico into "the Pennsylvania of the southwest. We will be making the steel, making the iron, furnishing the coal for Mexico and for the entire southwestern country."[10]

Fall's reference to Mexico, and in particular to the raw materials needed for that nation's railroad construction, stemmed from his own business dealings there. A classic developmental capitalist, he believed that government should foster all possible opportunities for entrepreneurs and corporations to gain access to markets and natural resources and also pump public money into such large-scale projects as irrigation, reclamation, and railroads. Fall knew firsthand the benefits derived from just such friendly governmental assistance—he had accrued these in his ranching and mining operations in Mexico. Moreover, he believed Mexico represented a lucrative potential market for New Mexico agriculture.[11]

Fall regarded Mexico as an example of enlightened government support for economic advancement. President Porfirio Díaz (1876–1911) welcomed corporations willing to invest in and develop his nation's land and its resources and offered favorable concessions to investors, particularly to build railroads and open mines. This was the way Fall thought the state ought to foster investment and exploitation of its resources. In contrast, of course, the U.S. government imposed regulations and investigations that Fall saw as injurious to the Territory's future and punitive toward corporations and individuals pursuing New Mexico's best interests.[12]

One lawsuit in particular provoked Fall's ire—the indictment on inaugural day of key territorial officials, including his predecessor as attorney general, George W. Pritchard, for selling the American Lumber Company rights to timber on territorial lands. The judge in Albuquerque's Second Judicial District Court granted injunctions in three related lawsuits filed by Special Assistant United States Attorney General Ormsby McHarg. The federal government claimed in its thirty-plus pages of complaints that the territory had acted improperly in awarding rights to cut timber on lands ceded by the federal government in 1898. The court's action suspended all further logging on nearly fifty thousand acres in west-central New Mexico, which resulted in layoffs for over two hundred employees of the lumber company, many of them Nuevomexicanos.[13]

Ormsby McHarg served as a lightning rod for the federal government's legal cases in New Mexico. He was well suited to the task. A law professor in Washington, D.C., he led a team of at least fifteen federal agents sent to New Mexico at the end of June 1907 by Attorney General Charles J. Bonaparte, who provided him detailed instructions on ten specific matters the attorney general wanted investigated. McHarg also had the confidence of President Roosevelt, who urged him to pursue the investigations

vigorously. McHarg's stated his federalist legal philosophy in a straightforward manner to territorial officials: "You don't own anything down here at
all. The [federal] government owns all this [land] and my job is to recover
[it] from the people that you have undertaken to sell it to." Who was this
blunt, moralistic special attorney and how had he been drawn into New
Mexico's legal affairs?[14]

Ormsby McHarg knew frontier life. Born in 1871 in far western Wisconsin, near the Iowa border, he was raised on a homestead in the (North)
Dakota Territory. He also knew law and politics. He received his law degree
from the University of Michigan in 1896 and served in the North Dakota
House of Representatives in 1899–1900 before moving to Washington, D.C.
to teach law at George Washington University. As he later recalled, "I had
considerable leisure on my hands . . . [and] I spent a good deal of time in
the Halls of Congress, familiarizing myself with the men who were figur-
ing [prominent] there." McHarg knew he liked President Roosevelt's call for
federal officials to clean up government. At age thirty-six, McHarg wanted
to serve the president while also promoting Republican politics. His opportunity came in New Mexico.[15]

When Roosevelt and the U.S. attorney general dispatched McHarg to
New Mexico his investigations were part of the president's concerted action
during both his first and second terms to curb fraudulent land deals involving the public domain in the West. The abuses McHarg investigated were
the latest of the irregularities endemic in federal land policy under the
Homestead Act of 1862. Land grabs in New Mexico were part of a pattern
of attempts by greedy individuals and unscrupulous companies to control
vast amounts of the public domain in areas west of the Mississippi following the Civil War. President Roosevelt provided explicit instructions to
both Governor Curry and McHarg to "probe the different things [about
corruption] to the bottom" and apprise him in person of the results of their
investigations.[16]

Roosevelt was insistent that rooting out corruption would prepare the
way for statehood. The president put it bluntly to the new governor: "I
know your ambition is to have New Mexico made a state, but before you
can get statehood you must clean house in New Mexico and show to Congress that the people of New Mexico are capable of governing themselves."
Curry concurred with the president's goal; McHarg, however, never supported statehood but simply believed in attacking corruption as an end in

itself. Curry and McHarg were on a collision course over more than just statehood. McHarg's aggressive investigations led Curry to tender his resignation six days after taking office. Curry complained that the scope of the federal investigations cast a shadow over his administration and made him appear weak and of secondary importance as compared to the federal agents. Roosevelt bluntly rejected the overture: "I have no more thought of accepting your resignation than I do of flying." To placate Curry, Roosevelt pledged that the ongoing investigations would not address federal or territorial officials but would confine themselves to land and timber purchases between 1901 and 1906.[17]

In delimiting the inquiry the president reversed earlier instructions that "investigations concerning the New Mexico Federal officials should continue," but Roosevelt made a political calculation to allow Curry latitude because "you are on the ground. I shall back your judgment and do as you want." For his part, Curry realized he walked a narrow path flanked by Roosevelt and McHarg. He sought at every turn to reassure the president that he would introduce reform gradually, but he also admitted to Roosevelt that "[McHarg] does not view things from the standpoint I view them, and I shall doubtless do many things that will not meet with his approval." Curry tempered his insistence that the president back him by offering him reassuring, optimistic assessments of conditions in New Mexico. He took particular pains to show that the Republican Party in New Mexico was not as factionalized as others reported. He also stretched the truth when he said that McHarg and Fall were working "in perfect harmony" in September.[18]

In fact, a major blowup between McHarg and Fall was brewing. Their dispute involved coal leases in northwestern New Mexico on land purchased by a consortium that included Cleveland Dodge of Phelps-Dodge Corporation, a friend of President Roosevelt from their student days at Harvard University. Attorney General Fall defended the leases as fully justified and consistent with the sovereignty he believed the territory could exercise in selling land—a states' right view. McHarg rejected this argument and secured indictments from a grand jury alleging fraud in securing the valuable coal lands in San Juan County.

Fall seized upon this case to advance his and Curry's view of how capital ought to be treated if the territory were to increase its population and develop its resources. They believed indictments arising from the coal leases were uncalled for since neither malice nor fraud motivated Dodge and his associates. Moreover, they convinced President Roosevelt of their view—an easy job since he refused to believe his friend Dodge would engage in any improprieties. Roosevelt advised that the case be settled by having Dodge return the land to the Territory. Curry and Fall quickly accepted the president's remedy to end the suit and ordered McHarg to carry it out. It distressed McHarg to see that Albert Fall as well as other of the "territorial officers down there were treating territorial property as if were their own." He later recalled: "[Fall] should have been arguing on my side of the case—the government's side. He condoned the taking of the property of the territory and refused to take a hand in the prosecution of the people who took the property." McHarg, convinced of Fall's role in improper activity, overrode his own admitted lack of proof and concluded "that he [Fall] profited with them out of the profits that would be made out of these illegal practices." McHarg labeled Fall and his cronies "profound crooks." From Fall's perspective, the villains were the federal agents, particularly McHarg. The consensus among Euro-Americans, who were tired of being treated like a colony and chafed under the yoke of outside control, was that New Mexico should be able to do whatever it wanted with the land and resources deeded the territory by the federal government.[19]

But federal officials regarded unfettered states' rights as a license to misuse the lands and their associated resources. The ensuing lawsuits represented more than legal battles pitting McHarg against Fall. President Roosevelt was pushing the federal government into proactive management of western lands. In the late nineteenth century all over the West numerous confrontations between ranchers and homesteaders occurred over access, ownership, and fencing the open range of the public domain. By the early twentieth century direct violence had largely faded away, but new conflicts arose in jurisdictional disputes between states or territories and the federal government over the public's land. After 1890, federal actions to set aside large forest reserves and create national parks elicited strong adverse local reactions throughout the West. The emerging conservation ethic brought protectionist, restrictive policies to bear on western states and territories, actions that threatened local interests seeking unbridled use of public lands. In New Mexico Fall and McHarg, each convinced of the correctness of his position, became, respectively, challenger and defender of the federal government's unilateral authority to regulate western lands and impose national policies on the states and territories.

Today we can look back on this conflict as part of the decolonization process and specifically as an attempt to defend and protect against what Curry and Fall deemed heavy-handed federal encroachment upon New Mexico's limited sovereignty, but at the time New Mexicans understood it in very personal terms. For them the issues were quite concrete. The injunction against the American Lumber Company suspended logging and resulted in immediate unemployment for several hundred workers. The suit against the Alamogordo Lumber Company struck close to home for Fall. The lawsuit shut down a major employer in his community, which he called to the attention of U.S. Attorney General George W. Wickersham in May 1910: "So soon as this suit was filed by the United States, the Phelps-Dodge Company, which had acquired . . . the Alamogordo Lumber Company, closed the mills and stopped cutting timber, and the consequences of such action has been that the little towns built up through these companies and the industries operated by them, have been and are suffering exceedingly."[20]

Fall wrote to the U.S. attorney general after his fellow citizens in Alamogordo requested his help to end the lawsuit. While McHarg's investigations had generated numerous indictments, between November 1907 and the summer of 1908 most of the lawsuits had been resolved without going to trial. Presidential intervention disposed of coal lease suits, and in March 1908 the U.S. Supreme Court ruled that the American Lumber Company had violated no laws in securing rights to cut timber. In fact, the lumber company claimed the high court "found [the company] to own in fee simple three hundred thousand acres" of white pine timber. The crucial difference in this case from most of the others was that the company did not file homestead claims. It had access to alternating sections granted the railroad, and it sought to consolidate the checkerboard holdings by buying contiguous sections from the Territory.[21]

The most numerous suits were against the Pennsylvania Development Company, which obtained more than 40,000 acres of land and its timber and minerals through purchases negotiated by or on behalf of William H. Andrews. He launched his efforts in 1901 with a proposal for acquiring through the Homestead Act over 7,000 acres of land in the Manzano Mountains. The timber was needed by the railroad to build crossties, trestles, water towers, and buildings, and he also hoped to find coal and iron ore

on the land. He circumvented the 160-acre limit on homesteads by having
scores of people file on adjoining lots—each seeking the maximum allow-
able acreage. When he presented his offer to the Territory's three-member
Board of Public Lands, it turned him down. Instead, the board's members—the governor, the surveyor general, and the secretary of the territory—made a counterproposal. They rejected his terms because they could
not accept such a request from an "individual," but they then asserted their
right to initiate an offer to him for the same acreage. The board, in effect,
enforced the letter of the Homestead Act, but acting on their conception of
sovereignty became local agents of development capitalism by selling the
Pennsylvania Development Company what it sought.[22]

McHarg saw legerdemain in the Board's actions, an attempt under the
color of official business to alienate large amounts of the Territory's land.
But after closer scrutiny, the government reversed his findings. By the
late summer of 1908 the Justice Department sought dismissal of lawsuits
against the Pennsylvania Development Company, concluding that the sales
were procedurally correct as undertaken by the duly authorized Territorial
Board of Public Lands. As the Justice Department noted in reviewing the
Board of Public Lands' actions, "There was no attempt at concealment by
the company, as all the powers of attorney from the applicants, authorizing
the transfer of their interests to the company, were placed on record before
the deeds of the Territory were issued. Having adopted this method of pro-
cedure, the Land Board adhered to the practice, and intending purchasers
accepted it as a matter of course." The Justice Department concluded fault
lay with the Board of Public Lands' expanded sense of sovereignty, but since
the board had been disbanded in 1906 no further legal action followed. For
its part, the government never objected to these transfers during the board's
tenure.[23]

The negotiations for dismissal extended over nine months and involved
the U.S. attorney general, the secretary of the interior, the territorial governor, and the U.S. attorney for the Territory of New Mexico, David J. Leahy,
another of the Rough Riders to whom President Roosevelt turned to for
help in reforming New Mexico. During this time, the Justice Department
undoubtedly took into account the president's intervention in the coal case
and the U.S. Supreme Court's ruling in favor of American Lumber Company; however, the extant correspondence contains no reference to these
settlements. Instead, what emerges as the line of reasoning is that no over-

whelmingly strong case could be built against defendants, and settlement negotiations along the lines followed in the coal cases satisfied almost all the parties.[24]

But the Alamogordo Lumber Company refused to negotiate. It probably believed that pending congressional action would be more favorable than the terms offered by the Justice Department. In early February 1908, a year after the suit was filed by a predecessor of McHarg's, Secretary of the Interior James R. Garfield wrote to Representative F. W. Mondell, chair of the Public Lands Committee in the House of Representatives, to endorse a bill (H.R. 16277) "to permit the Territory of New Mexico to sell the large growth and matured timber on any of the lands granted to the Territory" and specifically "in tracts exceeding 160 acres." Garfield noted that this legislation would do much to help clarify issues now pending in lawsuits, and it would also provide guidelines for logging an estimated 100,000 acres of forest.[25]

Governor Curry testified on behalf of the bill, as did a Justice Department attorney and one of the defendants in the lawsuits. Curry began by offering a succinct summary of why the Territory and the Justice Department found themselves at cross purposes. The Territory believed it "had a right to timber of this kind that had been conveyed in trust" whereas the Justice Department "decided that it was illegal, that the Territorial officials had exceeded their authority, and they had instituted several suits to recover the title to land." The bill resulted from an agreement that the Justice Department would drop its lawsuits "if we get some legislation through Congress." H.R. 16277 prescribed paying three dollars per acre for all timber cut and reverting deeds for the land to the Territory. All future concessions were to be leases.[26]

While there was broad agreement that this bill ought to go forward, it rattled around the halls of the Congress for over two years. Meanwhile most of the defendants settled, accepting the terms proposed in the legislation. Only the Alamogordo Lumber Company balked. In early June 1910 the U.S. attorney general concluded, "There seems to be no present disposition to renew [the] request for congressional relief." He pledged to review the matter carefully in the coming months and "bring about speedy results." The Department of Justice eventually elected to pursue the case, which brought about an adverse ruling in a territorial district court late in 1911. The Justice Department insisted the law had been broken, and it intended to pursue the suit following statehood. To do so, it had the case transferred to federal court, and the Territory complied by forwarding all records to the federal appeals court in St. Louis. No further court action of consequence occurred in the final full year of the Taft administration. Shortly before Woodrow Wilson took office in 1913, the Justice Department decided to turn the matter over to the state of New Mexico and allow it to litigate, which it opted not to do. The Alamogordo Lumber Company finally emerged from under the 1907 injunction, which had hamstrung but had not ruined the business.[27]

A second and separate set of allegations concerned whether the money paid for territorial lands and their resources went to designated territorial entities, primarily educational institutions. A high-ranking Justice Department official, E. P. Holcombe, contended in October 1907 when inspecting McHarg's work, "All of the trust funds from the sale of lands have, more or less, been misused." The following May, Holcombe turned over his detailed report on the money received by the Territory from sales of its land and resources and its disbursement. Two Interior Department auditors combed through Holcombe's report and compared it to the report of the Territory's treasurer. After months of analysis, they concluded nothing untoward could be found largely because each report relied on data that could not be readily verified.[28]

By the autumn of 1908, all but one of the lawsuits filed a year earlier had been quietly resolved out of court, and the audits proved inconclusive and were not pursued further. Secretary of the Interior James R. Garfield had fulfilled the pledge he had made to New Mexicans in a speech on 9 August 1907. He had promised that any wrongs "will be righted by you people and not by anybody outside." What few in the audience could have known was just how quickly McHarg would exit the Territory and be replaced by New Mexicans. By late in 1907 territorial officials took over for McHarg when he accepted a new federal assignment to investigate irregularities in Oklahoma; before he could get started, he accepted the president's offer to join Frank H. Hitchcock, chair of the Republican Party's 1908 presidential campaign, as his chief legal counsel. McHarg's departure cleared the way for direct and active involvement of New Mexicans to resolve the federal investigations and their lawsuits. Key participants were Governor Curry and his new U.S. attorney general for the territory, David Leahy, and together, by negotiating behind the scenes, they successfully resolved allegations of corruption in land deals.[29]

"A Fine Bunch of Hoodlums"

While Secretary Garfield and Governor Curry worked behind the scenes in 1907 and 1908 to wind down the federal investigations, President Roosevelt stepped up his efforts to bring about congressional approval of statehood. He faced stiff opposition from a handful of senators led by Albert J. Beveridge and members of his committee. Between October 1907 and the end of Roosevelt's presidency on 4 March 1909, congressional opposition to statehood moved in tandem with the land fraud investigations—accelerating in 1907, subsiding in 1908, and speeding up again in late February and early March 1909.

By the summer of 1907, President Roosevelt was over his pique at the rejection of joint statehood, but it proved almost impossible to resurrect congressional support for the territories. On 24 October Roosevelt told Curry about his recent discussion with leaders of the House and Senate: "[I]t is evident that it will be worse than useless to hope to secure action for the admission of New Mexico and Arizona this year [1907]. . . . [T]he fight is too recent to give any hope of the admission . . . they could not without stultification so soon vote for such a proposition. . . . Some of them . . . declined to consider the question of separate statehood under any conditions." The president also added a short handwritten note informing Curry that other matters "of immediate and pressing importance" took precedence over the fight for statehood. Two days earlier the so-called Panic of 1907 had erupted with a run on a New York bank, and immediately stock prices plunged on Wall Street and credit collapsed. Fear of an economic catastrophe gripped the nation. Roosevelt's priority became rescuing the economy by working with the Congress to reform the country's banking and currency system. In 1908 Congress enacted stopgap legislation that offered a six-year respite from credit and currency contractions. A full year after the crisis, Roosevelt returned in earnest to advocating statehood, telling Curry, "I shall do all I can to secure Statehood for both New Mexico and Arizona this winter."[30]

The president entered the Christmas season of 1908 fully committed to bringing New Mexico and Arizona their long requested gift—entry into

the Union. Momentum had been building throughout the year, beginning in mid-June when the Republican National Convention approved a
plank favoring the immediate admission of the territories of New Mexico
and Arizona as separate states, their first such endorsement since the 1900
convention. The Democratic Party platform also endorsed statehood. In
September Governor Curry hosted a highly successful sixteenth National
Irrigation Congress in Albuquerque that brought in over 4,000 visitors.
Although the secretary of the interior had to cancel his planned trip to the
Territory, Governor Curry used the conference to promote statehood by
showcasing New Mexico's economic progress, agricultural potential, and
the forward-looking spirit of its citizens. This organization had long been
on record as favoring statehood for New Mexico, and it passed another such
resolution at the Albuquerque meeting.[31]

As January's wintry cold settled onto the nation's capitol, a chill fell on
the president's assessment of statehood. Roosevelt's cautiously told Curry
he was "trying my best to get action on statehood by Congress." While the
House overwhelming approved a statehood bill, opposition remained in the
Senate's Committee on Territories. But pressure was being applied to the
committee's chair, Senator Beveridge. Throughout January and February
New Mexicans waged a letter writing campaign to convince Beveridge (and
other senators) to honor their request. New Mexicans even enlisted people
from Indiana to write on their behalf. More than seventy-five letters are
preserved, and the tone of Beveridge's replies alternated between dismissive and deceitful. He dispatched an inquiry from an Indianapolis constituent by telling him, "Everybody who has a friend or relative in New Mexico
is having any personal friend that they know write me just as you have."
Individuals with some influence got various opaque replies. Beveridge
assured a businessman recently arrived in New Mexico from Indiana, "I
shall be pleased to give it [statehood] very careful attention." But Beveridge
did embrace the few letters from New Mexicans opposing statehood. He
told one such writer, who urged him to keep New Mexico a Territory until
"Anglo-Saxons" predominated, "I will take the opportunity to bring it to
the attention of the Committee on Territories." A number of letters simply
went unanswered. Ignored, for instance, was a four-page petition from "The
People of New Mexico" with a plaintive plea to "Let us be mature and get
out from under the federal guardian." A very few letters, though, required
a considered reply. One went to Thomas B. Catron, a two-page response to

Catron's five-page inquiry in which Beveridge offered his usual argument: show a significant increase in population in the 1910 census and matters might go better thereafter. But the most pressing concern for Beveridge and the Republican members of the committee was to keep president-elect William Howard Taft from backing the territories. They wrote to beseech him not to commit himself. In reply, Taft affirmed he had not "expressed myself upon the statehood question publicly," but the worst-kept secret of the past year was that Taft was pro-statehood. He did agree to meet with Beveridge and committee members on Saturday, 27 February to discuss their request.[32]

In the final two weeks of February Beveridge displayed both his mastery of the tactics of obstruction and his political vulnerability. In mid-February he left Washington for Indianapolis on unspecified business (he may have consulted his personal physician about a hernia that, less than a month later, necessitated a delicate, but successful surgery). While he was out of town, on 15 February 1909, the House of Representatives passed a statehood bill by an almost unanimous vote. In Beveridge's absence, fellow Indiana Republican and member of the House James Watson tacked onto the bill the stipulation that the Senate Committee on Territories must vote on the House's bill before the Congress adjourned on 4 March. Watson, a conservative or "Old Guard" Republican and a bitter foe of the progressive or "insurgent Republican" Beveridge, had seized on his absence to challenge and embarrass Beveridge by threatening to have the Senate as a whole take up statehood if Beveridge's Committee on Territories did not act immediately.[33]

Beveridge's personal secretary, John F. Hayes, sent an urgent message to the senator informing him that he must return immediately to head off the challenge. He explained that Watson had collaborated with Delegate William H. Andrews (R-N.Mex.) and Montana's Republican Senator Thomas H. Carter (who owned property in New Mexico) in this parliamentary maneuver, but it was "Watson who is more active than any other man in this fight and . . . his activity is due to his bitter feeling toward you personally." Promptly Beveridge launched a counterattack, again employing reports critical of New Mexico, as he had in the fall of 1902. He used the most damaging documents he could get his hands on: indictments handed down in 1907. He demanded the U.S. attorney general deliver all files on William H. Andrews and his involvement in the Pennsylvania

Development Company as well as everything they had from all investigations conducted by Ormsby McHarg. So voluminous were the items sought that, according to the Justice Department, not even a cadre of secretaries could complete the transcription in the few days allowed them. Similarly the secretary of the interior was instructed to provide all that agency's records relating to land fraud and its investigations as well as any reports on Albert B. Fall's activities in these matters. The Interior Department provided some materials, but the Justice Department sent only a detailed summary of the 1907 investigations. Unsatisfied, Beveridge soon contacted another source and secured 334 pages of court records from two land-fraud lawsuits.[34]

Beveridge, as he had done between November 1902 and March 1903, pursued his obstructionism both publicly and privately. He convened the committee for a partial day of hearings on Saturday, 27 February 1909 and called Ormsby McHarg to testify. The hearing dredged up all the sordid allegations set forth in lawsuits in 1907. McHarg read a long statement recounting how Governor Curry and Territorial Attorney General Fall obstructed his prosecution of land-fraud cases. The *New York Times* trumpeted the impact of the hearings with the headline "SCANDAL HALTS STATEHOOD BILL / CHARGES OF CORRUPTION AND OTHER OFFENSES MADE AGAINST NEW MEXICO'S OFFICIALS." Committee member Knute Nelson (R-Minn.) continued his longtime opposition to statehood and echoed Beveridge in attacking "the gang that is in control of political affairs in New Mexico." Other members of the committee repeated damning material gleaned from indictments McHarg had filed and Interior and Justice had dutifully provided. The last witness was Kathleen F. Lawler, the stenographer accompanying the investigators. Her testimony completed the character assassination of New Mexicans, who she said were "uncouth, illiterate, [and] unclean, [as well as] morally, mentally, and physically the very lowest type of humanity I have ever come in contact with." When Beveridge gaveled the meeting to a close, statehood had again been delayed for New Mexico—and for Arizona, for which the committee decided statehood would not go forward until more was known about the status of its public lands.[35]

To ensure that no possible parliamentary move could revive debate on statehood in the final days of the Sixtieth Congress, Beveridge maneuvered behind the scenes between Thursday, 18 February, and Friday, 26 February, to head off any attempt by the full Senate to usurp his authority. He arranged for Ormsby McHarg to meet privately with the leader of the Senate, Nelson Aldrich. During their short conversation, McHarg emphasized New Mexico's record of corruption, claiming that should it be admitted as a state "you'll have a fine bunch of hoodlums on your hands." He predicted that if New Mexico was granted statehood, Albert B. Fall would become a senator and Aldrich would have an "unmitigated scoundrel" as a new colleague. After their meeting, Aldrich reversed his recently announced support for statehood. He agreed that nothing further would be done to revive it during the final week of the current congress, but he also made it clear to New Mexicans that in the Sixty-First Congress he would support incoming President William Howard Taft's call for statehood. Aldrich knew the tide had turned, a fact confirmed in a confidential assessment offered by Delegate William H. Andrews, who claimed that "there were not a half dozen votes against it [statehood] in the Senate."[36]

Ormsby McHarg testified before the Committee on Territories on 27 February. Fourteen months after he left the Territory, he was still bitter. His investigations, dismissed quietly through deal-making, resulted in no trials. But McHarg remained convinced of the merits of his accusations and used his testimony before the committee—like his private conversation with Senator Aldrich—to exact revenge. In the waning days of Roosevelt's presidency each of the principals in the fight over statehood took the matter very personally—Representative Watson hated Senator Beveridge; Beveridge despised New Mexicans; and Ormsby McHarg loathed Governor Curry and former Territorial Attorney General Albert B. Fall. Spite and personal animosity poisoned President Roosevelt's—and New Mexico's—chances of securing the prize. But at a more fundamental level that setback had been building for two years, in the making for over a decade, and inevitable since the founding of the Republic in the competing Hamiltonian/federalist and Jeffersonian/states' rights conceptions of government. McHarg and the federalists prevailed, circumscribed sovereignty, and dictated new terms for future grants of public land. The Congress became so alarmed by McHarg's revelations that thereafter it insisted that land ceded to territories upon entering the Union had to be managed according to the newly emerging principles of the conservation movement. These were articulated by the head of the U.S. Forest Service, Gifford Pinchot, who called for the wise management of public lands to provide the greatest good for the greatest number. Henceforth territories would not be permitted to sell these lands or their resources. They could only be leased with the income managed as an endowment.

"Esteem . . . No Other President of the United States Has Ever Expressed"

Two headlines presented quite different stories about President William Howard Taft's mid-October visit. The *New York Times* announced "TAFT REBUKES NEW MEXICANS / SHARPLY ANSWERS SPEAKERS WHO UTTER DOUBTS ON STATEHOOD PROMISES" whereas the *Albuquerque Morning Journal* proclaimed "PRESIDENT WINS HEARTS OF ALL NEW MEXICANS / MOST POWERFUL MAN IN NATION STANDS AS CHAMPION OF STATEHOOD." Both headlines were accurate. The president did offer a rebuke, but he also won over his listeners—all in a half-day visit to central New Mexico on Friday, 15 October 1909. The *New York Times* correspondent accompanying President Taft went for the dramatic moment in Albuquerque and let local reporters cover the details of the president's five stops in New Mexico during his twenty-two hours in the territory. But what Taft said and did in Gallup, Laguna, Isleta, and Albuquerque on Friday—and in Las Cruces on Saturday, 16 October—proved decisive in securing entry into the Union.[37]

The president's train crossed from Arizona into New Mexico on a radiant autumn morning amid "a burst of brilliant sunshine that presented mountain and plain in a dissolving mass of fire." The president soaked in the weather and scenery and pronounced it "glorious, intoxicating . . . as stimulating as champagne." As his train pulled into Gallup at 10:00 A.M., he smiled broadly and waved to the crowd eagerly awaiting his arrival. Turning to his companion, Postmaster General Frank H. Hitchcock, he said, "I am beginning to think a great deal of New Mexico." The two men would have many more discussions about New Mexico over the following eight months. Hitchcock served as the president's closest political advisor and shepherded the legislation granting statehood. The swing through New Mexico followed a day spent in and around the Grand Canyon, which came at the end of a long train trip through the upper Midwest, to the West Coast, and across the Southwest and South before arriving in Washington. The return trip's itinerary was driven by a diplomatic engagement: meetings in both El Paso and Juárez with Mexico's President Porfirio Díaz on the weekend of 16–17 October 1909.[38]

About the time Taft arrived in New Mexico, a confidant of the president noted how much he had improved as a public speaker since his initial painfully awkward addresses in the Midwest, pronouncing him both "felicitous" and "so certain of himself that he would often speak when no speech was expected from him." Taft's forte on the trip was "to speak for five or ten minutes" and "to adapt his remarks to the locality and give to each address some local color." The half-hour stop in Gallup proved typical of this formula. It included a short speech in which Taft explicitly addressed the question uppermost in people's mind. He pledged himself to support statehood and urged New Mexicans to write a conservative constitution.[39]

Shortly after pulling out of Gallup, Taft retreated to his private car but invited Delegate William H. Andrews, Governor George Curry, and National Republican Party committeeman Solomon A. Luna to join him for lunch. They remained with the president, mostly discussing statehood for more than three hours. The private conversations allowed the president ample time to develop in detail the two points he had made in Gallup: he intended to fulfill his election platform promise to secure statehood and he counseled care and due deliberation in writing a constitution. Delegate Andrews assured the president that New Mexicans would write one "as conservative" as that of his native state of Ohio because "the people of New Mexico are as conservative and law loving as the people of Ohio."

The president's advice about a safe, conservative constitution stemmed from his legal training in constitutional law, his political instincts as a social conservative, and his disappointment over Oklahoma's adopting what he considered a radical constitution in 1907. He wanted New Mexico to push aside the reform movement ascendant in Oklahoma and some other western states and avoid incorporating into its constitution clauses calling for initiative, referendum, or recall. He especially did not want voters to be able to recall judges.[40]

The train stopped twice before it reached Albuquerque a little after 5:00 P.M.: an hour at Laguna Pueblo and three minutes at Isleta Pueblo. At the former Taft met elders and residents of both Acoma and Laguna pueblos, watched nearly forty-five minutes of ceremonial dancing, including a peace dance and a war dance, and then spoke for a few minutes. Describing himself as the "Great White Father," Taft urged his listeners to be industrious in their agriculture and sheep raising and to educate their children to become "good citizens of the United States." He also expressed the hope "that they may continue to live in comfort under the auspices of the government that is pledged to look after their welfare." At Isleta, children from the Indian school serenaded him, and he so enjoyed their music that he joined in the singing.

Finally just after 5:00 P.M., the president's train rolled into Albuquerque at the Alvarado Hotel, much to the relief of the city's organizing committee, who were anxious that repeated delays in arriving would cut short their planned motorcade west on Central Avenue toward Old Town. Between 5,000 and 6,000 cheering citizens greeted the president. He beamed at the reception and stepped forth onto a special platform to deliver in the next fifteen minutes what he said was not a "set speech." He gained the crowd's immediate and rapt attention when, several sentences into his remarks, he observed, "Every baby in this territory seems to be trained to speak [as] the first word Statehood." He reprised themes developed in Gallup and on the train. He would deliver on his pledge to secure statehood, and New Mexicans must write "a Constitution that shall serve as a fundamental law for a hundred years." It must be "like the Constitution of the United States, simple, comprehensive, with proper limitations as to vested rights, and personal liberty, but not going into all the details that a present condition presents."

President Taft also directly refuted those critics who "have an objection to you because some of you speak Spanish." He went on to offer what amount to a public rebuttal of the infamous Beveridge Report. Drawing on his experience as governor of the Philippines, he mentioned his own facility in what he deemed a "beautiful language" and then at some length praised the "Spanish descended people" for their "hospitality and kindness, generosity and courtesy," calling them a high-minded group "loyal to the flag and able to serve their country when it is necessary." President Taft's remarks sprang from a genuine respect and admiration for the culture and people of Spain. Indeed, his hispanophilic tendencies had gained public attention earlier in the year when the Spanish impressionist Joaquín Sorolla traveled from Madrid to the White House to paint a commissioned work— the president's first official portrait in office.[41]

Having forcefully dispatched racist objections to statehood, the president briefly outlined the process ahead. He hoped to secure passage in the upcoming congress of an enabling act, reassuring the audience that such legislation had already been introduced but neglecting to remind them that

it had been derailed at the end of the Sixtieth Congress. He also only casu-
ally mentioned that the first step required the bill "to go to a committee and
be considered with reference to its provisions." The president concluded his
speech by saying, "I hope I have told you what you wanted to know about
statehood." He had forthrightly addressed the issue uppermost in people's
mind, but at least one prominent person remained unconvinced—Albert
B. Fall. At a men-only dinner to honor the president that evening at the
Alvarado Hotel, sixty-five locals joined the president's traveling party. Governor Curry served as the toastmaster. The toasts followed each of four
tributes—to Statehood, the New Era in New Mexico, the Spanish American People, and Our Guest. Local dignitaries were to offer brief remarks for
each of these, and the first two responded to their topic's toast with summaries of past events and highlights of current experiences and aspirations.
The last two speakers—Thomas B. Catron and Albert B. Fall—increasingly veered away from civility. When Fall took the podium, his remarks
departed completely from decorum. As he had at the inauguration of Governor Curry twenty-one months earlier, Fall lashed out against the government. This time, though, the federal official he insulted was President Taft.
Fall questioned the sincerity of Taft's pledge to work on behalf of statehood
and complained bitterly of the long wait endured by New Mexicans. Silence
greeted Fall when he finally sat down.

The president rose quickly to rebut Fall's accusations, which he did by
telling a disarming anecdote. He recounted how a judge patiently endured
over an hour's oration by a trial lawyer and then replied, "I have heard
your argument and I am still in favor of your cause in spite of it." Then
the president delivered an impromptu endorsement of New Mexico, going
out of his way to embrace Nuevomexicanos by "expressing an esteem for
them which no other president of the United States has ever expressed."
Sustained cheers and applause greeted the president's reassurances of his
friendship and his continuing support for statehood. The *New York Times*
called Catron's and Fall's remarks "testy," and reported that Fall actually
interrupted the president to protest some of his impromptu comments.
When the president and his party exited the banquet room, they encountered a committee of women who invited the president to join them at
their ball. No doubt eager to escape recent unpleasantness, Taft accepted,
led them in their grand march, and then "greeted nearly all of the ladies
present."

Taft's hearty embrace of New Mexicans and statehood resonated well with most citizens, but newspaper coverage took a predictable political slant in Republican and Democratic-leaning papers. This political filter is evident in the coverage by the Spanish-language newspapers in New Mexico: the Republican-aligned *La Bandera Americana* approvingly noted Taft's support for Nuevomexicanos, but the Democratic *La Voz del Pueblo* found little merit in his position and reprinted a petition from residents of Alamogordo in support of former Democrat Albert J. Fall in standing up to the president. The citizens supporting Fall pointed out, as had *La Voz del Pueblo* in an editorial, that it was not disrespectful to ask the president to explain how his promises of statehood differed from those made by Republican presidents McKinley and Roosevelt. While the editorial began by saying, "We are not going to criticize President Taft's speech," it ended with a blistering rebuke: "Upon reading the address, it appeared to us more like the speech of a schoolchild than one by a great statesman." They said it was beneath the president to speak to New Mexicans as he had "unless he believed that New Mexico deserved nothing better." They objected to the very two points the president reiterated at every stop in the Territory: "that he could constitutionally only *recommend* the admission of New Mexico to the Congress and that admission would depend on the merits of the state constitution to be written [emphasis added]."[42]

At midnight Taft's train pulled out of the Albuquerque station heading south. At 8:00 A.M. Saturday he stopped in Las Cruces and addressed a large crowd. Though brief, his remarks pleased the audience that had gathered hours earlier. The president pledged that "New Mexico is to be admitted during my administration." Perhaps recalling the antics of Catron and Fall from the previous night, he also admonished those present to "elect competent men to draw up a sturdy constitution" akin to those in other states. Then his train departed "leaving the people entirely pleased." Later that day in El Paso, their joy very nearly turned to sorrow.[43]

The armed escort that accompanied Taft throughout his trip had been reinforced substantially in New Mexico by sheriffs, marshals, and their respective deputies, whose aggressiveness in protecting the president resulted in several incidents decried as "brutality" by one newspaper. In El Paso the security entourage grew substantially with the addition of military troops charged with protecting the presidents of both the United States and Mexico. The unexpected verbal assaults of Catron and Fall had created an imbroglio in Albuquerque, but in El Paso a full-blown conspiracy to assassinate Taft was afoot. His security detail apprehended a gunman within seconds of his being in Taft's immediate presence, thus averting both grave consequences for the president and for New Mexico's prospect for statehood. In hindsight, it is clear that New Mexican officials had been instructed to take extra precautions while the president was in their Territory to ensure no harm came to him—or their campaign for statehood.[44]

The two unpleasant confrontations—one verbal in Albuquerque and the other nearly violent in El Paso—surely weighed on the president's mind. Indeed, Taft may well have brooded about Fall's insolence for the rest of his presidency. Taft found disbelief in his sincerity exceedingly irksome. "The trouble is that they don't believe me when I say a thing once," Taft is said to have retorted when told upon his return that rumors abounded that he would renege on pledges he made to President Roosevelt, including the one to push for statehood. "I think the next Congress will show my sincerity. I can't reiterate and reiterate, for when I have said a thing once I see no reason to repeat it." True to his word, Taft proved all his critics wrong during the upcoming session of the Congress.[45]

President Taft's visit came exactly eight years after the statehood convention of mid-October 1901. That gathering, in turn, occurred six months after President William McKinley's quick trip through the Territory. His assessment that "more water and people" were needed before New Mexico could shed its territorial status become a constant refrain in the White House for more than five years, until a new priority emerged in 1906—restore clean government. Over the next several years allegations and grand jury indictments created perceptions of corruption by territorial officials that raised questions in Washington, D.C., about the Territory's capacity for home rule. All this changed when President Taft repeatedly pledged to secure New Mexico's place in the Union. His commitment set a new tone and launched new efforts. As a constitutional scholar, he well understood that while many serious allegations had been made, no trials had occurred, no convictions secured, and therefore no black mark existed against New Mexico's reputation. Moreover, when confronted by Albert B. Fall, he employed restraint and conciliation while also exhibiting personal resolve. It was this mix of diplomacy and determination that *La Voz del Pueblo*'s editorial misjudged. When Taft repeatedly emphasized the all-important role the Congress would have in passing a bill enabling New Mexico to move forward toward statehood, the paper confused his public explanation of the separation of powers with a lack of grit to impose his will on Capitol Hill. But the president was about to put the full power of his office behind his word.

CHAPTER EIGHT

"Injurious to the Cause of Free Government"

Senator Stephen B. Elkins (R-W.Va.) helped New Mexico gain statehood thirty-five years after he ruined its chances while serving as the Territory's delegate. In June 1910 he voted in favor of the Enabling Act approved by the Senate, which authorized the Territory to draft a constitution and prepare to enter the Union. President William Howard Taft signed the legislation on Monday, 20 June, bringing to a close fifteen months of concerted leadership in pursuit of statehood, capped by some deft political horse-trading on Capitol Hill. The centerpiece of his negotiation was a bill Elkins sponsored in the Senate and Representative James R. Mann (R-Ill.) carried in the House, and each chaired his chamber's Committee on Commerce and Foreign Trade. Moving the bill forward required President Taft to work with the leading Republican in the Senate, Nelson Aldrich of Rhode Island, to strike a "deal with the Democrats in 1910—to trade conservative Republican support for a bill to grant statehood to Arizona and New Mexico, in return for Democratic support for the Mann-Elkins railroad regulation."[1]

In March 1910 President Taft had shifted his top legislative priority from statehood to railroad rate relief. The change reflected the public's resentment over the high cost of living, an issue the Democrats campaigned hard on in 1908 and were pushing in the run-up to the 1910 midterm elections. Railroads were the linchpin of the nation's commerce and transportation, and citizen anger coalesced around excessively high rates charged for freight and passengers. Demands mounted for the federal government to curb the railroads' power by regulating their pricing practices, and in 1909 work on the legislation began. For more than six months Taft labored independently of efforts led by Mann and Elkins.

By the end of the year, though, the president decided to adopt the congressional legislation as his administration's bill. The deal Taft brokered through Senator Aldrich coupling the Enabling Act with the Mann-Elkins Act was actually the second of the president's initiatives to secure statehood. Preceding the railroad agreement was an equally decisive step to align Senator Albert J. Beveridge and his Senate Committee on Territories behind statehood. But Taft's two-part maneuvering almost unraveled during the first eight months of 1911. On four occasions prospects for adding New Mexico's star to the flag were nearly scuttled: prohibitionists pressed the Congress to reject the new constitution; the Congress reconsidered the Territory's fitness for statehood; senators filibustered against New Mexico's constitution; and President Taft vetoed Arizona's constitution in mid-August, which derailed New Mexico's push for statehood.

Surveying these delays, an editorial in the *Albuquerque Morning Journal* in early June 1911 noted that statehood "has been befogged and complicated in a thousand various ways." Two months earlier Thomas B. Catron used more picturesque language to object to the stranglehold placed on New Mexico by a few contrarians: "[W]hen things get to the point where one louzy [sic] whelp can make trouble and do harm [,] you will always find the individual who is equal to the occasion." But confusion and personal animus were not alone in besieging statehood in 1911. Causing greater damage was a shift in American politics. The old order was breaking apart. Three trends that gained strength in 1910–11 complicated the process of creating new states: the Democrats were making inroads on the Republicans' fifty-year domination of national politics; the Republican Party fractured into two rival camps of so-called Insurgents, or Progressives, and the Old Guard/Stand-Patters, or Administration Republicans; and prohibitionists targeted New Mexico and its proposed constitution in their ongoing fight to outlaw the sale and consumption of alcohol.[2]

State making necessitated both presidential leadership and deal making. Passage of the Enabling Act of 1910 transpired because President Taft employed both principled action and political expediency. But the contradictions inherent in that approach led to conflict that mobilized people dedicated to using New Mexico as a pawn in their schemes. Meanwhile the Territory's citizens never relinquished their eagerness to chart their own future, although the approach of home rule initiated a tug-of-war between Euro-Americans and Nuevomexicanos over who would rule at home. In the jockeying for advantage as statehood came into view, the most contested terrain—both locally and nationally—was the state constitution.

"In Touch with Public Opinion"

President Taft knew the depth of Senator Beveridge's opposition to statehood, but he intended to overcome the senator's resistance. Before and after his visit to New Mexico the president worked to recruit the senator's support, but doing so tried his patience. The more Beveridge balked, the more insistent Taft became that he make an up-or-down decision. Matters came to a head during their respective late summer vacations in 1909. Taft spent the first weeks of September north of Boston near the coast in Beverly, Massachusetts, while Beveridge vacationed about eighty-five miles northwest, in Dublin, New Hampshire. Statehood remained on the mind of each, and Beveridge wrote a thirteen-page letter detailing in five sections his objections to allowing New Mexico into the Union. He left no accusation, argument, or fear unstated in his last ditch effort to derail admission. In his opening section of six pages, entitled "History of the Statehood Bill," he recounted the 1902–1903 battle to delay statehood, the joint statehood bill, and the testimony about land fraud in New Mexico from late February 1909. He buttressed his points by enclosing a copy of the 1902 Beveridge Report as well as his personal copies of the confidential transcripts of the testimony of Ormsby McHarg and his secretary Kathleen Lawler.[3]

In the remaining four sections he continued familiar arguments: that Republican members of the Committee on Territories unanimously opposed statehood and wanted it postponed until after the 1910 census report; that should New Mexico became a state, "control of the public lands would be given over to the same set of men against whom Mr. McHarg secured indictments or began prosecutions"; that Democrats would dominate in the new states and therefore, to minimize their political gain, Arizona and New Mexico should be merged into a single state; and that statehood was never debated in the 1908 campaign by either presidential candidate, which was evidence it was a low priority to each political party. Beveridge also pointed out to Taft that opposition to statehood "has become a matter of deep conviction to the Committee on Territories. In this we are supported by the conservative sentiment of the country. This is because the country has become pretty generally educated upon this matter, beginning with the widespread circulation of our report eight or nine years ago."[4]

President Taft doubtless knew that Beveridge exaggerated in citing his committee's unified opposition as well as the public's support for that stance. Pro-statehood views of Beveridge's colleagues began coming to light in the summer of 1909, and in August Las Cruces's *El Labrador* reported on conversations among Republican members of his committee that claimed only Beveridge remained an implacable opponent. The article reported that longtime foe of statehood Senator Knute Nelson was "much more favorably disposed in his attitude and gave more hope for the admission of the territory in the coming session of the congress." President Taft's visit to New Mexico confirmed his decision on the Territory's future, and in early December 1909 he delivered a terse rebuke to Senator Beveridge and all others opposing statehood. He called for the immediate admission of the territories in his annual address to the Congress. This message came a few weeks after Beveridge appealed to him to wait until the next census confirmed that "the Territories are now fitted for membership in the Union."[5]

As 1909 drew to a close, the *New York Times* predicted a "do-nothing session" in advance of fall elections in 1910. They noted that Senator Nelson Aldrich, the Senate's "general manager" whose maxim in political life was "Deny nothing; explain nothing," would work tirelessly to defeat the administration's agenda. The *Times* reported Aldrich moved quietly among his colleagues to outline his legislative plans and predicted that he would ensure that most bills sought by Taft in the Sixty-First Congress would "go quickly and peacefully to the pigeonholes of the Senate committees." Indulging in a bit of doggerel, the newspaper summed up the expected fate of most of Taft's proposed legislation, including the statehood bill:

> Locked in the pigeon holes for keeps
> Full many a bill lies down and sleeps,
> And calmly, peacefully it sleeps,
> Locked in the pigeon holes for keeps.[6]

The actual events of 1910 did not play out as the *Times* had predicted. In mid-January Senator Aldrich and his wife, Abby, boarded a train and departed cold, wintry Washington for a month in southern Florida. This break from politics foreshadowed a changing set of priorities for the sixty-nine-year-old senator. He had chronic and increasingly acute insomnia that brought on physical and mental exhaustion, which required him to take total breaks from time to time. The toll on his health contributed mightily to the decision he announced on 17 April 1910 that he would not be a candidate for reelection. Aldrich became a lame duck, but he did not relinquish his power. In fact he sided with Taft on some key issues and showed himself capable of thwarting an uprising among reform-minded Republican senators, including Albert J. Beveridge.[7]

About the time Aldrich left for Florida, Beveridge began charting a new course for the statehood bill. He belonged to a faction of progressive Republicans known as Insurgents, who increasingly challenged their party's Old Guard. The Enabling Act sought by the president would not be pigeonholed, nor would it be derailed, even though just a year earlier Beveridge and Aldrich had united to do so. Instead, Beveridge would guide the statehood bill forward—but on his own terms. The actual conversations leading to his decision are lost forever since they occurred in face-to-face meetings. But we do know that a key intermediary was Frank H. Hitchcock, President Taft's political alter ego on statehood. He had been head of the 1908 Republican campaign and served as the postmaster general and Taft's trusted confidant between 1909 and 1913. Hitchcock spent a great deal of time in the West after joint statehood was defeated and had been ever present at the president's side during the October 1909 trip to Arizona and New Mexico. He also reportedly had his eye on a Senate seat from Arizona.[8]

Beveridge and the Republican members of his committee met with President Taft at the White House in January 1910 and emerged "unanimously in favor" of the statehood bill. The House of Representatives had already introduced three separate enabling bills in December 1909. Following their vetting by the Interior Department, the House took a voice vote, and "in the opinion of the Chair two-thirds having voted in favor," approving H.R. 18166 on Tuesday, 18 January 1909. Opposed to the bill was Massachusetts Republican Frederick H. Gillett, who condemned allowing "waste land with no irrigation" to become states. He reminded his colleagues of the adverse findings in the 1902 Beveridge report as well as of Daniel Webster's opposition in 1848.[9]

When Beveridge received the House's bill he immediately began rewriting it to fix what he considered its deep flaws. He cited ten areas needing revision. The first four of his priorities set a demanding tone. He insisted the constitutions be approved by the Congress and the president, that Arizona's recently passed election law be revised, that debts incurred by counties and the territories be repaid, and that the Congress safeguard lands transferred to the new states. This latter he considered "as quite the most important item in the Senate bill," and in cooperation with Senator Knute Nelson, who chaired the Senate's Committee on Public Lands, sought to "protect the government's interests in the matter of any existing land grants." Their goal was to prevent "certain corporations" from unduly benefiting from government concessions of land at statehood. The day after he began his work Beveridge told a constituent, "We will have the administration statehood bill in shape by the end of the week," but it actually took almost two weeks. Throughout the rewriting he worked with senior officials in the departments of Justice and Interior as well as staff from the Reclamation Service. They proposed solutions to such vexing problems as the legal status of the Pueblo Indians in New Mexico, taxation issues, and pending lawsuits.[10]

On Saturday, 29 January, Beveridge met with President Taft and Frank Hitchcock at the White House. After going over his changes, they gave their consent. The following Tuesday the White House announced an agreement with leaders of the Senate and House regarding five of the president's legislative priorities for the next five months. Statehood for New Mexico and Arizona headed the list of bills to be shepherded through the Congress by the end of June. Action on statehood began barely two weeks later, when Beveridge opened his committee's hearings on Senate Bill 5916, the Enabling Act, which authorized New Mexico and Arizona "to form a constitution and state government and be admitted into the Union on an equal footing with the original states." Committee debate began on Friday, 18 February, with that first day as well as Saturday and Monday allotted to New Mexico, while Arizona got its turn the following two Fridays.[11]

The tone and substance of the proceedings differed markedly from the hearings of a year earlier. The close consultations with the White House and executive department officials produced a positive atmosphere. From the outset Beveridge struck a conciliatory tone without changing his agenda. He acknowledged that "the majority of committee gladly take both the blame and praise [for their role vis-à-vis the Territories]. What we want to hear about now is these bonds." Specifically he probed ways to reduce the House's plan to give each Territory public lands valued at three million dollars to pay off their debts.[12]

In its final deliberations the Senate committee agreed to provide public lands to New Mexico sufficient to cover one million dollars of its indebtedness, with most of this amount owed railroads for construction the Congress had approved in the 1880s. They also gave the new state lands that would produce recurring revenue earned either from sale of the land's bounty or leasing rights to its mineral resources. In early March, Beveridge moved his statehood bill into the Senate's queue, which was staggeringly long—over 9,000 bills had been introduced since December 1909. Undaunted by this backlog, Beveridge sent a telegram to friends in Arizona promising that "the bill will surely pass this session. The kickers cannot stop it. The opposition is small and dissolving. Arizona and New Mexico will become states."[13]

Senator Aldrich returned to work in mid-February in response to President Taft's plea for help in fighting off Insurgent senators opposed to one of the administration's fiscal priorities—the Postal Savings Bank Bill, an idea that had first surfaced in the Populist Movement of the early 1890s. Aldrich soon delivered Senate approval of this legislation. By early March, Taft and Aldrich were discussing the prospects for the Republican Party in the fall 1910 elections. Meeting surreptitiously during drives in the president's open-air automobile, with Aldrich wrapped snugly in one of the bounteous sweaters loaned him by the three-hundred-pound president, they agreed that Beveridge did not deserve a third term. Soon Taft held discussions with several Indiana Republicans about challenging Beveridge in the upcoming party caucus.[14]

By the end of March, Beveridge knew about the president's and Aldrich's scheme to replace him. He headed the Republican Party in Indiana and believed his support was sufficiently durable to defeat moves to oust him. Confirmation of his assessment came on the first Tuesday in April, when Beveridge secured his party's nomination for the fall elections. But he neglected to factor in growing Democratic Party strength in his state, a fatal oversight. He also failed to calculate the cost of Taft's retaliating against him for criticizing his tariff policies. Throughout the late spring of 1910 and into June, Taft pursued a dual track in his dealing with Beveridge. On one level he expected Beveridge to support the statehood bill, but he also barred him from access to the White House for two full months, cut him out of key backroom negotiations, and had proxies attack his tariff reforms.[15]

The statehood bill emerged from the Committee on Territories on 10 March with a full head of steam. It immediately hit three speed bumps: the Senate's legislative queue; partisan political maneuvering; and the president's reshuffled priorities. Statehood remained high on Taft's list, but a railway bill now emerged as his top priority. The rates railroads charged passengers and shippers had been a point of contention for more than three decades. After 1900, and especially following the 1901 publication of Frank Norris's anti-railroad novel *The Octopus*, the Democrats began to hammer away at Republicans for cozying up to railroad interests. In the 1908 elections Democrats charged that Republicans supported railroads—and high protectionist tariffs, too—and disregarded the impact their policies had on most Americans' pocketbooks. Taft's first address to the Congress in early December 1909 refuted Democratic claims that Republican policies brought about high prices for consumers. He argued that the inexorable law of supply and demand was at work. He said that the growth in population led to more demand for goods but that productivity, especially of consumables, had not kept pace, thus driving up costs. But Taft knew his explanation would not tamp down Democratic criticism of him as indifferent to the common citizens' needs. The high cost of living had become politicized, and so he embraced congressional attempts to constrain rising prices. Railroad rate reform took on added political importance for the upcoming fall elections when, as the Mann-Elkins Act moved toward passage, the railroads announced a new, higher set of fees to take effect on 1 June—before the Congress passed its regulatory bill. Taft responded by securing an injunction against the rate increase on 31 May, a move that gained him—and many Republicans—much popular support.[16]

By imposing reform on the railroads Taft hoped to hold down fares Americans paid to travel as well as to trim shipping expenses so that retailers could pass the savings along to their customers. But making the railroad bill his top legislative priority did not diminished Taft's commitment to statehood. In fact, New Mexico and Arizona's fate was linked to the push to regulate the railroads. Statehood became the crucial bargaining chip in passage of the Mann-Elkins Act. Taft pressed hard for regulatory reform, but he lacked the votes from his own party because of the split with Insurgents. Beveridge and other Republicans loyal to former president Roosevelt refused to vote for what they considered the ill-advised railway bill, forcing the president to turn to the Democrats for support. He cobbled together an alliance between Democrats and Administration Republicans, an arrangement that Democrats saw as advancing one of their longtime legislative priorities—adding new states in the belief they would send Democrats to the Congress. The agreement that emerged between 20 May and early June 1910 traded Democratic votes for the railroad bill in exchange for a pledge that statehood would be the next item of business on the crowded calendar prior to adjournment at the end of June.[17]

Texas senator Joseph W. Bailey served as the Democrats' chief negotiator for the Mann-Elkins Act. Eight years earlier Bailey had grabbed and choked Beveridge during a heated exchange on the Senate floor, and his ill will never completely faded. Now Senator Bailey sought to strangle the Republican Party of New Mexico by imposing on it a restrictive election law recently approved by the Arizona legislature. In 1909 that solidly Democratic Territory had enacted a literacy requirement for voting, which was incorporated into the House version of the statehood bill. Bailey intended to include in the Senate version the same requirement for New Mexico. He believed doing so would further the ascendancy of the Democratic Party by eliminating many registered Nuevomexicano Republican voters, whom he presumed to be illiterate.[18]

In early June the Mann-Elkins Act passed the Senate, and on 6 June work began to reconcile the House and Senate versions. With that process under way, the statehood bill began moving toward a final vote in the Senate, and President Taft needed assurances of Senator Beveridge's cooperation. He ended his isolation policy and brought him to the White House for private discussions. Beveridge dutifully pushed through the statehood bill, beating back Senate Democrats seeking to add provisions such as the literacy requirement. On 16 June the Senate gave final, unanimous consent to statehood on a vote of 65–0 with 27 absences. Immediately upon its approval Senator Elkins rose and initiated Senate consideration of the House and Senate joint committee's railroad bill. Beveridge had no intention of negotiating with the House to reconcile versions of the Enabling Act. His feet were planted, but through extensive behind-the-scenes discussions Taft and Delegate Andrews were able to calm the House leadership's anger over his intransigence. Two days later the House yielded to Beveridge and accepted the Senate bill. After spending nearly a decade blocking statehood, Beveridge ended up largely defining the terms by which New Mexico and Arizona entered the Union. In a late evening session on Saturday, 18 June 1910, both the Mann-Elkins Act and the statehood Enabling Act secured final passage in both chambers. President Taft immediately signed the Mann-Elkins Act at 10:15 P.M., but he waited until Monday, 20 June to sign the Enabling Act and fulfill his promise to secure statehood.[19]

Both the Enabling Act and the Mann-Elkins Act sent important messages about presidential power. Each signaled that the president intended to secure his legislative priorities in the face of intraparty rivalries. But these laws revealed more than an activist presidency. The Mann-Elkins Act in particular marked a new relationship between government oversight and business practices. One western railroad executive immediately recognized the beginning of a new era that would require careful management of relations with the federal government and the public: "The railroads are not strictly private property, but subject to regulation by the Public through its regularly constituted authorities. . . . To meet this situation, we must endeavor to get in touch with Public opinion." As a consequence, big business redoubled its lobbying and public relations campaigns, processes the citizens of New Mexico had engaged in for years, but without the clout or access corporations enjoyed.[20]

The Mann-Elkins Act also regulated telegraph and telephone companies, and concurrent with its passage, a district court in Silver City, New Mexico, granted a preliminary injunction against Western Union and Bell Telephone companies on allegations that "a conspiracy exists between Western Union and Bell Telephone Companies to suppress telegraphic competition by other companies." This lawsuit represented, as the *New York Times* reported, "the first legal assault on the big telephone and telegraph merger completed last November [1909]." The plaintiff in New Mexico cited prevailing territorial (and state) regulatory authority and sought to force American Telephone and Telegraph Company (AT&T) to divest itself of Bell Telephone and its other local subsidiaries and allow for competition in service. But the Mann-Elkins Act placed all antitrust regulatory authority with the federal government. Not until 1982 would AT&T have to accede to the judicial remedy sought in New Mexico in 1910.[21]

"A Nineteenth-Century Product"

When the president signed the Enabling Act, everything seemed to be going smoothly: the Congress promptly adjourned; the president prepared to leave town; New Mexicans displayed "wild enthusiasm" in street celebrations; the local business community felt jubilant; and "the real estate dealers say the property in this city [Santa Fe] has already risen 10 per cent." On 29 June Territorial Governor William J. Mills set Tuesday, 6 September 1910 for the election of 100 delegates, one-third of whom were Nuevomexicanos. At noon on Monday, 3 October 1910, 71 Republicans, 28 Democrats, and one Socialist—all elected in proportion to each county's voter turnout in the 1908 election—settled in at the legislature's chamber in Santa Fe to write a constitution, a process completed on Monday, 21 November. A nonpartisan effort evaporated almost immediately as delegates—and public opinion—split over the constitution's provisions.[22]

During his visit in October 1909 President Taft had admonished New Mexicans to write a constitution that was "simple, comprehensive . . . but not going into all the details that a present condition presents." This advice proved futile. The nationwide progressive fervor for governmental reform led many New Mexicans to advocate "initiative, referendum and other Socialist doctrines," as one newspaper described the ideas gaining currency. In 1910 many elected officials took a dim view of such reforms as women's suffrage, prohibition, and the right of voters to exercise a direct influence in political life through the initiative, referendum, and recall of public officials, including judges. At New Mexico's constitutional convention, reportedly only nineteen of the delegates believed "in statewide prohibition and thirty-nine in the initiative and referendum." Among the latter were virtually all the Democrats, but Republicans split on these issues, with delegates identified as the Old Guard dominating—nearly sixty delegates—versus just twelve Insurgents or Progressive Republicans.[23]

Each of the twenty-seven committees wrote a draft for its section, forwarded it to the convention's leadership for approval, then submitted it to debate and an eventual vote. Deep philosophical differences quickly emerged, and much wrangling ensued over some committee recommendations. Democrats sought a greater voice for citizens and embraced reforms that promised them more control over officials and their actions. Republicans, who were in the majority on all the committees, generally opposed such efforts and heeded President Taft's advice to eschew citizen-driven reforms. A few matters in these debates yielded to compromise. For example, while women were not allowed full voting rights, the constitution did enfranchise them in school board elections. In practice, though, this clause applied only to sparsely populated areas since most school elections were combined with other issues on municipal election ballots in New Mexico, and thus open only to men. Other issues, including prohibition, generated much heat by women's groups such as the Anti-Saloon League and the eight New Mexico branches of the Woman's Christian Temperance Union. Also pressing for outlawing saloons and prohibiting the sale of alcohol were about two hundred Santa Clara Pueblo residents. The convention delegates refused to hear any of the prohibition groups. This dismissive attitude incurred the wrath of the anti-saloon lobby, which vowed to fight on.[24]

When the convention opened, the constitution of Oregon was a widely known model for governmental reform, including the initiative and recall. It was regarded as the most progressive document adopted in a Republican-controlled state, but New Mexico Republican delegates rejected the Democrats' request to include Oregon's constitution among the documents studied. Events in New Mexico would, in fact, run counter to general trends throughout the West, where many states had recently amended their constitutions to allow more participatory democracy.[25]

Postmaster General Frank Hitchcock met in Albuquerque with key delegates shortly before the convention opened to discuss "the adoption of the Initiative and Referendum by the New Mexico Constitutional Convention and its probable effect with reference to its rejection or otherwise by the President." Mindful that both President Taft and the Congress had to approve their constitution, the New Mexicans informed Hitchcock that almost all the proposed reforms could be held off, but "the Referendum at least, in some form, will be adopted." Exactly that happened: New Mexico's Constitution included only the referendum, but imposed greater restrictions on its use than found in any of the twenty states that had adopted it.[26]

The day after the convention opened, William H. Andrews reported to President Taft, "They are shouting for the initiative, the referendum and the recall and the Oregon constitution and some of our timid people are more or less for it." He beseeched the president to send a letter to Holm O. Bursum, chairman of the Territory's Republican Central Committee and a member of the convention, telling him the delegates must "frame a constitution that would be patterned after the Federal Constitution . . . leaving out all the new fangled notions that some of the states are crazed over."[27]

When completed, the 21,227 word constitution was almost five times the length of the U.S. Constitution. While it largely eschewed "all the new fangled notions" and became, as one scholar noted, "a nineteenth-century product," it did depart slightly from a few old political formulas. For example, counties gained a share of property taxes and citizens secured a new voice through the election of judges as well as release from the fee system whereby local officials such as sheriffs, justices of the peace, and coroners charged for their services. But in general the constitution imposed a strong measure of restraint in two fundamental ways: it curbed the power of the executive and it tightened the purse strings by "lowering the costs of government in general," particularly by reducing the rate of tax levies.[28]

The constitution also ensured the civil rights of Nuevomexicanos in politics and education, which made it unique among such documents and an early promoter of equality. Indeed, as the *Washington Post* noted the day after the convention adjourned, "Some 135,000 inhabitants of Spanish-American descent demanded protection of their equality before the law and retention of their ancient rights and privileges." The thirty-five Nuevomexicano delegates had been vigilant in turning back efforts to make them second-class citizens. An editorial from a Spanish-language newspaper in Las Cruces expressed the expectations and wariness Nuevomexicanos felt: "These are solemn times in the political life of the people and each and every citizen must diligently exercise his electoral duties." The editorial urged all New Mexicans to watch the delegates to be sure "they preserve the rights and privileges that we have today," noting that "it is in all our best interests to be represented by individuals who will look after the welfare of the people in general."[29]

Then the editorial shifted focus and explicitly addressed Nuevomexicanos, invoking a powerful blend of patriotism, self-interest, and familial obligations: "We are citizens of the country of Washington and Abraham Lincoln, and we have a right to seek what is best for our personal welfare and for a bright future for our children and descendents." To fulfill these expectations, the editorial both echoed and greatly expanded President Taft's admonitions: "We must rise up and ensure the adoption of a sane, safe, secure, and basically straightforward constitution, one that guarantees and preserves for all the people of the proposed new state their full civil, political, and religious rights." In fact, the constitution afforded strong protections for Nuevomexicanos in the use of their language, including in public affairs, in voting, and in schools.[30]

Reportedly the powerful Solomon Luna needed "only to lift a finger or his eyebrows" to beat back any perceived attack on Nuevomexicanos. But in the convention's final weeks, tension marked the discussion of segregation of blacks in schools. Albert B. Fall joined with the president of the convention, Charles A. Spiess, to champion segregated schools because eastside counties drew a large proportion of their residents from Texas and other southern states. They claimed these residents expected white-only schools as defined by the "separate but equal" doctrine affirmed by the U.S. Supreme Court in *Plessy v. Ferguson* (1896). When the Committee on Education, headed by former territorial attorney general George Pritchard, recommended segregated schools, *La Voz del Pueblo* launched a blunt counterattack. "Knowing that in the counties of the South and East of New Mexico the majority of the Americans have a mortal fear of the African race, the said Fall and Spiess in order to gain the sympathy of the counties of the South and East propose that it be written into the Constitution that there be separate schools for negro children. If this occurs in New Mexico, it seems to us very dangerous and very harmful to the future prosperity and well-being of the state[,] . . . we beg to suggest to our Hispano-Americano delegates that they have to be very careful not to do anything against others that they would not want done against themselves." The measure failed, and school segregation did not become a decisive issue when voters approved the Constitution in January 1911. It passed in twenty-two of the Territory's twenty-six counties. On the eastside, only Roosevelt County rejected it.[31]

New Mexico created its constitution at the same time that Columbia University history professor Charles A. Beard researched and wrote *An Economic Interpretation of the Constitution of the United States* (1913). Beard argued that the delegates to the Constitutional Convention in 1787 drafted a document that preserved and protected their economic status at the expense of ordinary citizens' interests. While Beard's analysis was challenged and largely rejected beginning in the 1950s, his contention remains useful in understanding the writing of New Mexico's constitution, for there is a parallel between what Beard argued and what actually occurred in New Mexico. Delegates to New Mexico's constitutional convention protected their own interests. For example, the chair of the convention, Charles Spiess, had already convinced Congress to include in the Enabling Act land worth a million dollars to be used to repay a decades-old debt owed one of his railroad clients. In the convention he allegedly worked principally on behalf of corporate clients ready to pay him "an enormous fee contingent upon the adoption of the constitution."[32]

When the constitutional convention began its deliberations, a newspaper reporter summarized the occupations of the hundred delegates. Thirty-two were lawyers, and Nuevomexicanos probably realized that many of these attorneys had pressed suits challenging land grants. The three lawyers most active in these suits were also among the most powerful delegates: Thomas B. Catron (Santa Fe County), Charles A. Spiess (San Miguel County), and Charles Springer (Colfax County). The newspaper also noted that twenty delegates represented sheep and cattle growers, signaling that large-scale agricultural interests drowned out the voices of the seven farmers selected as delegates.[33]

Scholars writing on the constitutional convention have long pointed out what was well known in 1910: "Party leaders who never before, and never again, held elective office made sure they would be on hand to shape the framework of the new state. It was not merely coincidental that the dominant economic interests of the state were represented in that close-knit group." The economic elites, in other words, mirrored the political elites, which meant they included both Nuevomexicanos and Euro-Americans. But what has not drawn attention is an incipient economic, and therefore political, shift in power. The most numerous occupational group were the emerging urban business and professional classes comprising thirty-three middle- and upper-middle-class delegates: fourteen merchants; six general retailers; four saloonkeepers; and three bankers, three newspaper editors, and three physicians. These individuals represented a service and mercantile capitalist sector whose numbers and influence would soon burgeon.[34]

A fuller understanding of the socio-economic interests of the delegates emerges in an examination of their biographical data. Many prominent businessmen were also large-scale sheep and cattle growers. No less than one-quarter of the delegates had dual economic interests anchored in the traditional livestock economy but also holding major investments in the emerging economy of retail and wholesale merchandising, banking, or service occupations. Their diversification positioned them to transition successfully over the next several decades as the farming and ranching economy contracted while urban-centered mercantile capitalism and service-sector businesses expanded.

Holm O. Bursum is a pivotal figure in understanding how Euro-American delegates invested in both the rural and urban economies, in his case ranching and banking. He chaired the committee that wrote the rules for railroads and business corporations, and more than any other individual was responsible for ensuring that the constitution consolidated their economic power. A key concern was how capital could be raised, and one of his chief economic goals was to preserve existing rules for chartering corporations. The new constitution provided favorable terms for investment through loose regulatory oversight of corporations, which boosted the new state's competitiveness in the investment arena.

The constitution continued the laissez-faire approach set forth in the *Territorial Compilation of Laws* from 1897. The 4,196 sections in this comprehensive codification included twenty-seven pages of rules governing the formation of corporations. But the major attractions for companies were the omissions, or what was not required in order to be incorporated: no stock subscriptions were needed; tax assessments were limited; and no public statement or annual reports of income and expenses were required. Business charters amounted to little more than hunting licenses to track down and entice potential investors—and all without regulatory safeguards. Bursum shared with other Territorial elites an abiding faith in their inherent right to write a constitution that protected their interests, which resulted in a document that represented "a model of fiscal and political conservatism, protected and nurtured laissez-faire, individualism, and capitalism, and . . . minimized the role of government."[35]

In 1910 the economic interests of an old, agrarian order were compatible with the expectations of the emerging leaders of mercantile capitalism; however, a fundamental divergence in their interests lay just beneath the surface. The old land-based economy was being undermined and would give way in the next twenty-five years to a new urban-based commercial and business-dominated economy that spawned a new set of elites mixing the fields of law, banking, journalism, and retail and wholesale enterprise. At the constitutional convention of 1910 the most visible signs of this impending transition were in delegates' ages and races. The new order was remarkably uniform in its characteristics—Euro-Americans recently arrived in New Mexico. In fact, these men can be labeled the Generation of 1910 because the majority of them arrived in the Territory between 1900 and 1910. They made up one-fifth of the one hundred delegates, and another ten came to the Territory in the 1890s. Thus thirty percent of the delegates were from a new generation of Euro-Americans. The quintessential figure in the Generation of 1910 was Bronson Cutting, who arrived at a tuberculosis sanatorium in June 1910 and therefore played no role in the constitutional convention; however, he would soon lead a new era in Republican politics. At the convention, a Republican delegate typifying the Generation of 1910 was Herbert F. Raynolds, who had graduated from Harvard University and Columbia Law School and returned to Albuquerque at twenty-eight years of age in 1902. He practiced law and served as an officer for the Occidental Life Insurance Company in the Territory. It was one of twenty-two insurance firms writing policies in New Mexico in 1902, and handling its work were 335 agents backed by 223 lawyers—not all of whom resided in the Territory. The insurance industry was spawned by an emerging commercial economy that drew to it such talented individuals as Raynolds from the Generation of 1910.[36]

The Generation of 1910, of course, followed an earlier Euro-American surge into New Mexico identified with the Santa Fe Ring, which can be called the Generation of 1890. By that year Fall, Bursum, Catron, Spiess, and Springer—the five Euro-Americans who dominated the Ring—had settled in New Mexico. While the Generation of 1890 was formidable, the future under statehood belonged to the Generation of 1910. Their comparative youth and numbers ensured they would supplant their predecessors. But at the constitutional convention the Generation of 1910's economic and political clout had not yet coalesced, so they yielded leadership to the Generation of 1890, "most of whom climaxed their spectacular political and business careers during the frontier's golden age, some twenty years before this time [1910]. Their final act was designing the state's master plan for the twentieth century."[37]

"To Keep Us Out Longer Would Work Irreparable Injury"

On Saturday, 21 January 1911, New Mexico's registered voters overwhelmingly approved the constitution—31,742 voting in favor and 13,399 opposing it. Governor Mills telegrammed President Taft informing him that an 18,000-vote majority approved the document. His message also rebutted rumors that had reached the White House: "The cry of fraud and intimidation was, I think, largely raised by some leaders of the prohibition party because state-wide prohibition was not inserted in the constitution." The governor's explanation came on the heels of an election-eve report Taft received from Delegate Andrews debunking prohibitionists' rumors that the election would be corrupt and fraudulent. He assured the president, "These reports are base falsehoods, without a shadow of foundation, and are circulated for the purpose of prejudicing your mind against New Mexico coming into the Union." The bluntness of these denials matched the fervor mustered by opponents of the constitution, resistance that continued for six months.[38]

Two weeks after the voters ratified the constitution, *La Revista de Taos* noted the pending departure for Washington, D.C., of "a hundred or more officials from New Mexico . . . going on the trip to counter and undo the plots and conspiracies of the prohibitionist fanatics." Their angst proved well founded. Prohibitionists wanted to stoke public and congressional anger during the upcoming hearings on the constitution to press their decades-old campaign to prohibit all sales of alcohol. In the weeks prior to 21 January Anti-Saloon League advocates and prohibitionists had coordinated a letter-writing campaign to pressure the White House and the Congress to investigate their allegations of ruses used to keep them from being heard at the convention and to lodge allegations of voter fraud plotted by supporters of the constitution. While Taft personally favored prohibition, he did not expect it to be addressed in the constitution, but his stance did not deter the prohibitionists from trying to defeat New Mexico's bid to become a state.[39]

Following ratification, opposition to the constitution intensified in Washington. Henry W. Blair, a lawyer and prohibition lobbyist, carried the fight into congressional hearings. Blair, a former Republican U.S. representative and senator from New Hampshire had, during his decade in the Congress, written a 583-page book entitled *The Temperance Movement; or, The Conflict Between Man and Alcohol* (1888). In early February 1911 Blair wrote President Taft on behalf of New Mexicans protesting the recent election. Taft in turn instructed Attorney General G. W. Wickersham to investigate charges "against the validity of the election." A flurry of accusations, petitions, and replies ensued throughout February, prompting a White House official to prepare a two-page inventory of correspondence sent by Blair and other prohibitionists to the president and the departments of interior and justice—as well as a list of the government's replies. Attorney General Wickersham responded to President Taft on 17 February and told him Blair's complaints "do not warrant Executive action by the President." Nothing in the enabling bill created an expectation that prohibition would be incorporated into the constitution. But no quarter was given by prohibitionists, who deemed their agenda morally superior to New Mexicans' desire for statehood.[40]

The same day the attorney general rebuffed Blair, the House of Representatives opened four days of hearings into his charges. Blair, the principal witness, represented the Woman's Christian Temperance Union [WCTU] and the Anti-Saloon League. He hammered away in hours of testimony on the fraudulent election and a conspiracy of liquor interests active in the writing of the constitution. In his seventy-one pages of testimony, he unleashed hyperbole that surely undermined his cause. He alleged the constitution "was written in the rest room of a liquor saloon" and that as the product of a corrupt process the "constitution assures the most accursed government on earth."[41]

Delegate Andrews retorted by introducing several hundred petitions and statements from among the more than 750 he had received from citizens and officials throughout New Mexico attesting to the integrity of the election. The verbal dueling in Washington between Blair and Andrews prompted an editorial in the *Albuquerque Morning Journal* that dripped with sarcasm: "Once more New Mexico has been grasped in the nick of time and dragged back from the verge of the pit. This time the salvation of a corrupt commonwealth has been accomplished through the heaven-sent instrumentality of an ex-senator from New Hampshire, the Hon. Henry Blair. . . . Anyway, Henry, as New Mexico's weeping prophet, went to the President and the Committee on Territories and broke the news to Taft and Congress . . . that 18,000 votes were purchased for the constitution. . . . The W.C.T.U. has determined that no more States shall be admitted to the Union unless they have constitutional prohibition."[42]

Despite Blair's allegations, the committee ended its hearings without taking any formal action. Likely the overwhelming evidence of a fair election introduced by Delegate Andrews carried much weight, but so, too, did the straightforward testimony of New Mexico's territorial governor, William J. Mills. He offered a candid perspective when he testified that Santa Fe County provided the single largest majority in favor of statehood "not only because the people agreed with the constitution but because they wished to have their [$800,000 railroad bond] debt paid . . . and this [enabling] bill provided for that debt being paid." While Blair railed against saloon interests and made prohibition the crux of his opposition, the testimony by Mills and especially the letters and petitions Andrews introduced permitted the committee to hear the voices of New Mexicans, who endeavored "to carry out everything that was set forth in the enabling act and to make this election perfectly fair in every way."[43]

Reason and patience carried the day against Blair's exaggerated accusations, and an early, representative voice from the Nuevomexicano community exhibited both qualities. Benjamin M. Read, born in Las Cruces to a Euro-American father and a Nuevomexicana mother in 1853, sent *La Revista de Taos* an open letter of more than eleven hundred words in early December 1910 arguing eloquently and passionately for approval of the constitution. Calling it "our Magna Carta," he declared, "No true patriot ought to oppose the constitution, which is now our only salvation." Read was revered by Nuevomexicanos, and part of this respect stemmed from his candor. "I, personally, am not in agreement with all that is in the constitution," he wrote, singling out omission of the "total or partial prohibition of alcohol," which he believed "at the least ought to have been left to the electors of each county, precinct, town, or village to vote for or against." But after considering the merits and limitations of the constitution, he concluded, "The good that our admission to the Union will produce for us is absolutely superior to the unpleasantness that is caused us by the omissions mentioned."[44]

As the House Committee on Territories wrapped up its hearings, President Taft signed off on New Mexico's constitution on 24 February 1911. He did so, though, after imposing his own change. When he sat down in the White House in early December 1910 with various members of the Texas congressional delegation and New Mexico's Delegate Andrews, they were joined by a Yale classmate of the president, John W. Farwell, a wealthy land investor with substantial holdings in West Texas. The topic was the legal description of New Mexico's boundary with Texas. The new constitution set the 103rd meridian running from the 32nd to the 38th parallel north of the equator to divide the two states, which followed the specifications the Congress used in creating the Territory on 9 September 1850. Asserting such a legal description in 1910, though, reclaimed 603,485 acres occupied by Texans in a narrow strip, 2.23 miles wide and 172 miles long, extending south from the bottom corner of the Oklahoma–New Mexico border.

A surveying error in 1859–60 had moved the boundary slightly west of the 103rd meridian. Discovery of this discrepancy in 1882 came after both the U.S. Congress and local residents had accepted the 1859–60 boundary line as legally binding. Congress and the White House specifically addressed the contested land in legislation in March 1891, in which the federal government—acting on behalf of the Territory of New Mexico—again recognized the legality of the flawed 1859–60 survey. President Taft concurred that the 1891 legislation settled the matter, and he informed his guests that New Mexico's constitution had to be modified to accept the 1859–60 boundary line. He sent such a message to Capitol Hill, and on 21 December 1910 the full Senate accepted the report of the senate's Judiciary Committee endorsing the president's recommendation that boundaries once set could not be changed even if the survey was later found in error. The House concurred with the Senate in a vote on 11 February 1911. But this was not the last time Taft's views prevailed on the boundary line. In 1927 and 1928, while he presided as chief justice of the U.S. Supreme Court, the high court rejected legal challenges initiated by New Mexico in 1913 to rescind the actions of the president and the Congress in accepting the erroneous 1859–60 boundary.[45]

Once Taft backed the constitution, the House committee quickly voted its approval as did the full House on 1 March. Only the Senate needed to concur to move statehood to final approval, but time was running out. Senator Beveridge had three days left in office. For several months he had privately expressed reservations over statehood based on Blair's allegations about voting irregularities, and now he once again held the Territory's fate in his hands. And so he dithered until midnight on Friday, 3 March, when, under intense pressure from Postmaster General Hitchcock and Senate colleagues, he allowed a vote by his committee. With less than twelve hours remaining in the session, the full Senate received New Mexico's constitution. But for reasons that remain unclear, a member of the Senate Committee on Territories, Oklahoma Democrat Robert Owen, demanded that

Arizona's constitution also be approved, which doomed New Mexico's prospects. Taft had not approved Arizona's constitution because it contained clauses he found highly objectionable. With only hours to go before the Sixty-First Congress adjourned, Owen launched a filibuster that halted action on the statehood bill as well as tying up important legislation including a post office bill, a postal roads bill, and a civil appropriation that reportedly included $50,000 to investigate Owen for allegedly defrauding Oklahoma Indians in a land sale.[46]

In the several hours prior to the noontime adjournment, and with the president and his cabinet cloistered just off the Senate's floor, conferences with Senate leaders hammered out a compromise that ended Owen's filibuster in exchange for a vote on the constitution for New Mexico. But it went down to defeat, 45 to 39, because Texas Democratic Senator Joseph W. Bailey and other southern Democrats defected and joined a number of Republicans in opposing it. Senator Bailey had been a key person in negotiations to pass the enabling bill nine months earlier, but he reversed himself. This switch had nothing to do with the merits of statehood. Following Bailey's assault on Senator Beveridge in June 1902, Democratic leaders ostracized him for years, but finally in 1910 and 1911 he had built a coalition among southern Democrats. He expected to join his party's Senate leadership, but suddenly he had been ignored in decisive negotiations among Democrats and Taft, his cabinet, and Senate leaders. A livid Bailey, acting out of spite, sabotaged approval of the constitution. He then promptly—and very publicly—denounced Democratic leadership and submitted his resignation as U.S. senator to the governor of Texas, who rejected it and counseled a cooling off period. Bailey reconsidered but resigned again in September 1911 and began a lucrative law practice in Washington, D.C.[47]

Thus just nine months after unanimous Senate approval for the enabling bill, that body blocked implementation. One ray of hope existed, though: President Taft wanted to convene a special session to address key legislation that did not secure passage, principally a trade and tariff bill involving Canada. The special session began on 4 April, and the statehood issue was included on the agenda. More hearings were scheduled, beginning in the House, where Democrats had secured a majority in the elections of fall 1910. The new chair of the Committee on Territories, Virginia Representative Henry D. Flood, introduced a joint resolution calling for the admission of New Mexico and Arizona (HJR 14), and his committee held hearings on it for seven days between 13 and 29 April 1911. At the outset, Flood asked whether opposition to statehood existed, and the consensus among the members was that none would be expressed. Delegate Andrews sat on the committee and in particular made the point that the opposition by prohibitionists had lapsed. Andrews obviously had not counted on Henry Blair testifying for three days, during which he discussed at considerable length the pattern of voter fraud beginning with the exhaustive investigation of the 1906 election between Andrews and Larrazolo. While he also made glancing references to prohibition, Blair focused his objections on the constitution and, in particular, the absence of initiative and recall as well as the highly restrictive amendment process in Article 19. The House Committee revised HJR 14 and added the chair's eponymous Flood Amendment to simplify amending the constitution.[48]

As approved by New Mexicans in January 1911, the constitution prescribed a complicated amendment process, including requiring a two-thirds vote of the legislature to propose amendments followed by an election in which ratification required approval by at least 40 percent of those voting in at least half of the counties. Democrats and Progressive Republicans labeled the restrictions anti-populist and an affront to the common sense of voters. Accordingly, the House Committee and then the newly ascendant Democratic majority in the House approved the Flood Amendment, which required New Mexicans to vote in the fall of 1911 to modify the original process. The Flood Amendment prescribed that a simple majority vote by the legislature and the electorate would suffice to amend New Mexico's constitution. Two exceptions were made that retained the original, restrictive process for amendments, and these applied to attempts to change voting requirements and to alter the educational rights of Spanish speakers or those of Spanish descent. Several weeks after the hearings ended, the Committee approved the joint resolution with the Flood Amendment and sent it to the full House, where it passed by an overwhelming majority on 23 May.[49]

The new chairman of the Senate Committee on Territories, Republican William A. Smith of Michigan, returned to Capitol Hill in mid-June and opened three days of hearings on Friday, 16 June. Senator Smith not only did not pursue prohibition, he excluded Blair from testifying, ending Blair's crusade against New Mexico. But his cause marched on, and Blair lived just long enough to see prohibition enacted as the eighteenth amendment of the U.S. Constitution before dying in March 1920. As expected, the Territory's political leaders from both parties testified, but the most noteworthy set of witnesses were, as Smith noted, the "many telegrams from various boards of trade and other business organizations." He opened the hearings by reading these into the record, and in doing so helped ensure that the voices of recently arrived urban, Euro-American businessmen were prominently featured. These uniformly pro-business messages came from towns small and large across all parts of New Mexico. The voices of the Generation of 1910 rang out in such telegrams as these: "Delay and suspense in passing statehood resolution admitting New Mexico and Arizona is detrimental to business interests and causing stagnation in trade" (from the Farmington Board of Trade). "The delay is stagnating business and paralyzing development. To keep us out [of the Union] longer would work irreparable injury" (Tucumcari Chamber of Commerce).[50]

As if to flesh out the generalities in these telegrams, Charles A. Spiess apprised the committee of a telegram he had received from businessmen in his hometown of Las Vegas. They reported that "a vast irrigation proposition dependent on statehood in New Mexico and right at the very doors of Las Vegas" hung in the balance. He told the committee that existing federal mandates severely limited the terms under which the city of Las Vegas could raise its share of the capital. Statehood would resolve matters by allowing enactment of a new set of laws that would remove the current, restrictive cap on debt a municipality could incur when funding infrastructure through the sale of bonds.

Democratic Senator Robert L. Owen of Oklahoma, whose obstructionist tactics in early March had necessitated the special session, became a full-fledged advocate of New Mexico's statehood during the June hearings. About halfway through the proceedings, he heartily concurred in the statement of Republican Senator Joseph L. Bristow of Kansas that the committee had heard enough to convince them "to vote to admit." But the committee continued into a third and final day before ending on Friday, 23 June. Then they, too, approved both the House Joint Resolution 14 and the Flood Amendment.[51]

On Monday, 10 July the full Senate took up the committee's recommendation, but by Thursday of that week deliberations stopped. A new roadblock appeared—an amendment by a longtime member of the Committee on Territories, Minnesota Republican Senator Knute Nelson. President Taft had never approved Arizona's constitution, and in particular objected to the provision allowing for the recall of judges. Perhaps mindful of Taft's concerns, Senator Nelson offered an amendment on 13 July that required Arizona's voters to put recall on the fall ballot and reject it. He also proposed that New Mexicans not be compelled to vote to revise their amendment process.

The Senate had before it two contradictory prescriptions on statehood, but they faced other complications as well. They had to contend with a Supreme Court decision handed down at the end of May that directly challenged the Congress's authority to prescribe special conditions for joining the Union. In *Coyle v. Smith*, which arose from a dispute over terms the Congress set for Oklahoma to become a state, the high court ruled on 29 May 1911, "The constitutional duty of Congress of guaranteeing to each State a republican form of government does not import a power to impose upon a new State, as a condition to its admission to the Union, restrictions which render it unequal to the other States." Senator Owen took considerable exception to this Supreme Court ruling, which he blasted as "usurping" the Congress's authority, charging that the court had "invade[d] the legislative function of Congress by judicial legislation."[52]

While some in the Senate fumed over the Supreme Court's ruling, most simply ignored it, and on 8 August they approved the Flood Amendment (53 to 18) and rejected the Nelson Amendment (43 to 26). Two days later the House accepted the final changes to the Flood Amendment and sent it to President Taft. Statehood for New Mexico now depended on President Taft's reaction to Arizona's provision for a recall of the judiciary. A showdown over Arizona's recall provision had been inevitable for almost a year, and a Phoenix newspaper had voiced its concern in September 1910. The newspaper worried that Arizona's Democratic delegates would write a radical constitution unacceptable to President Taft. The newspaper implored its delegates to adopt the stance of New Mexico's Old Guard Republicans and keep in mind the president's preferences.[53]

The newspaper's prophecy came to pass, and on Tuesday, 15 August President Taft informed Congress: "I return herewith, without my approval, House joint resolution No. 14. . . . If I sign this joint resolution, I do not see how I can escape responsibility for [accepting] the judicial recall of the Arizona constitution." Taft wrote his veto message as a legal brief, and as the *New York Times* reported, "The president did not spare words in condemning the recall feature of the Arizona Constitution, which he said, would compel Judges to make their decisions 'under legalized terrorism' . . . and would be 'injurious to the cause of free government.'"[54]

As chair of the Senate Committee on Territories, Senator Smith faced a deadline for adjournment of the special session the following Tuesday. The president's veto, coupled with the prospect of further delay, elicited outrage in New Mexico and elsewhere, but Senator Smith had no time for the many recriminations he heard. He immediately conferred with President Taft and then met with Representative Flood and members of both congressional committees on territories. By Thursday he had the president's assurance that he would sign new legislation Smith had drafted, known as Senate Joint Resolution 57. Smith brought it to the Senate floor on Thursday, 17 August. It stipulated that Arizona voters had to rescind the recall clause in their constitution and New Mexico had to vote on—but not approve—a less restrictive process to amend their constitution. The Senate overwhelmingly accepted the resolution on Saturday, 19 August (53 to 8), and the House passed it on a voice vote that afternoon. Just after 3:00 P.M. on Monday, 21 August President Taft signed it. The Democratic voters in Arizona proved incorrigible: that fall they repealed recall, but a year later they voted to reinstate it.[55]

The election held in New Mexico on Tuesday, 7 November settled two issues. First, the new amendment process passed—34,897 votes in favor and 22,831 opposed. Second, local and state officials were elected. Two separate ballots were used: blue for the constitutional amendment revision and white for office holders. But the election itself divided New Mexico in more ways than can be readily recapped. Suffice it to say that a veritable free-for-all erupted among Republican and Democratic party leaders. During September and October 1911, infighting and fractious meetings produced intraparty splits in which groups aligned for and against the blue ballot and to create new combinations of office seekers on the white ballot. A clean-government coalition merged reform-minded Republicans with Democrats, delivering the governorship to Democrat William C. McDonald over Republican Holm O. Bursum, both representatives of the Generation of

1890. While men from that era continued to dominate federal elected positions until well into the 1920s, at the state level the Generation of 1910 soon claimed political power, beginning with Governor Washington E. Lindsay during World War I and continuing throughout the 1920s and 1930s.[56]

"That Bright Star Added to the Flag"

Early in the afternoon of Saturday, 6 January 1912 thirteen guests from New Mexico joined President William Howard Taft in his private office. The twelve men and one woman, along with four cabinet secretaries, arrived at the White House under an overcast sky. The temperature outside was a chilly thirteen degrees, but everyone undoubtedly felt much warmer at 1:35, when the president signed the proclamation approving New Mexico's entry into the Union. Taft spoke but two sentences: "Well, it is all over[;] I am glad to give you life." Pausing to smile, he added, "I hope you will be healthy." Taft was the last of fifteen presidents to preside over New Mexico as a United States territory, and his eighteen words acknowledged the government's paternity and marked the end of six decades of hard political labor to attain self-rule. Several photographers captured the occasion, and soon the picture would hang in New Mexico's twenty-six county courthouses. Following the signing ceremony, the guests went outside for a second photograph on the White House steps.[1]

President Taft's allusions to a birth and a new creation may have been the obvious metaphor for the event, but today his words seem unduly paternalistic. What went unsaid is noteworthy. He ignored New Mexico's three-hundred-year history under three different national flags as well as its three millennia of continuous occupation by indigenous peoples. With five words—"Well, it is all over"—Taft brushed aside six decades of delays and disappointments that stemmed largely from inaction or obstruction in Washington. His words also glossed over decades of carping and misrepresentations by opponents of statehood—as if these, too, had never occurred or were insignificant. Perhaps the most surprising omission is that President Taft made no reference to his decisive role in securing statehood for both New Mexico and Arizona, which entered the Union on 14 February, culminating a fight that Taft had waged continuously since his election in November 1908. The decisive moment came a year after his election when the president told Senator Albert J. Beveridge, chair of the Senate Committee on Territories, to end his eight-year obstruction of New Mexico and Arizona statehood. Taft expected him to be a good Administration Republican and follow his lead. Beveridge and the Congress passed the enabling bill, which the president signed on 20 June 1910.[2]

The two photographs recording the arrival of New Mexico statehood are visual documents as important to "read" as the proclamation itself. Each photograph presents a separate narrative. Presidential power is the dominant theme of the ceremony in Taft's office, and the point is reinforced in the composition of the photograph, with the witnesses positioned on the periphery and their faces indistinct. But a definite shift in political authority is occurring, and by signing the proclamation Taft both cedes unchecked federal authority and ushers in the era of popularly elected state officials. The photo on the White House steps shows a new hierarchy of power: state officials in the first row, citizens behind them, and senior federal officials in the last row, their respective tiers corresponding to new responsibilities in a three-way partnership.

The photographs are celebratory and self-congratulatory, and they deliberately exclude key people, most obviously former President Roosevelt and Senator Beveridge, two politicians who will always loom large in any account of how New Mexico became a state. Also missing are representatives of four groups tallied in the 1910 census: Nuevomexicanos (155,155), American Indians (20,575), African Americans (1,628), and Asians (504). The Euro-American population was 149,439, or 45.6 percent of the Territory's 327,301 residents. The photographs also present a greater gender imbalance than existed in the Territory: in 1910 the population age fifteen and over comprised 114,295 men and 92,257 women, or 12.5 men to every 10 women. No children appear in the photographs, but youngsters under the age of fifteen were 37 percent of the total population in 1910, a proportion consistent across the West where they "made up a substantial part, in some places a majority, of western settlers."[3]

The photographs skew the narrative toward the Euro-American experience, provoking two questions whose answers will provide a different perspective: What was the significance of statehood? How does the past change our understanding of developments now and in the future? At the outset we can give one brief answer to each question. First and foremost, entering the Union conferred political independence—an end to federal control and the beginning of home rule. Statehood, according to the Las Vegas newspaper *La Voz del Pueblo*, meant "No longer will [we] be governed from afar like a foreign colony." Entering the Union completed political decolonization, and the people's liberation came in being citizens and not subjects. As New Mexicans rejoiced, Felipe Maximiliano Chacón, poet and journalist, penned verses "To New Mexico, On Being Admitted as a State." Acknowledging the struggle endured by those "who have suffered . . . numerous disappointments" and "the unjust insults of many years," he proclaimed, "a glorious and shining star" has been placed "forever on the American Flag." He urged the people to "see that honor writes your story," and he greeted the new era with "an enthusiastic chorus of hurrahs" and the cry, "Long live New Mexico, the State." [4]

"Sounding Brass and Tinkling Cymbal"

The sixteen individuals gathered on the White House steps appeared subdued as they shed the old order of territorial status and embraced the bright future of home rule and popular sovereignty. Statehood heralded a new political era not just in New Mexico but also in the nation's capital. In these two photographs the White House is not just a backdrop but a quintessential symbol of federal power, and it has a commanding presence in both photographs. The final push for statehood coincided with an unprecedented expansion of government programs after 1900 that remade the landscape of New Mexico during the height of the progressive era. Millions of acres were set aside as federal forest reserves, and government irrigation and reclamation projects brought both water and tens of thousands of new settlers—mostly homesteaders—between 1900 and 1910. Government dam building also pumped more than fifteen million dollars into New Mexico in a dozen years or so, an infusion of federal money that prepared people to seek even more government projects to enhance both their quality of life and their economic fortunes. [5]

The photographs silently assert New Mexico's political separation from Arizona, which the Congress had never acknowledged. For decades Congress had linked New Mexico and Arizona whenever statehood was addressed, and the enabling bill of 20 June 1910 still yoked the two territories together. Congress stipulated one political process to be followed by both territories, and once Taft signed the enabling bill, Democratic-controlled Arizona and Republican-dominated New Mexico wrote, approved, and forwarded their respective constitutions to the Congress and the president. But almost immediately it became clear that the two territories would not complete the required steps in a similar fashion or on the same schedule. Stark partisan differences emerged on the issue of granting direct citizen influence on state government. The most divisive issues concerned voter-created checks on government—initiatives and referenda as well as the recall of elected officials, particularly judges. All three stood at the heart of political reform in the Progressive era.

Three individuals not present at the signing ceremony played decisive roles in the statehood struggles of New Mexico and Arizona. The first was Albert J. Beveridge, the Republican senator from Indiana who used his position as chair of the Senate Committee on Territories between 1901 and 1911 to delay statehood for partisan political reasons. In his campaign of obstruction, Beveridge did the bidding of the most powerful man in the Senate, Republican Nelson W. Aldrich of Rhode Island, who is also not present in the photographs. Aldrich's decisive role has been explained by distinguished political historian Lewis W. Gould. Beginning in 1901, "an attempt to obtain the admission of the territories of Arizona and New Mexico ran into the determined opposition of Senator Aldrich and the Republican leadership." Aldrich's opposition to statehood was entangled in his bitter memory of losing power under Democratic president Grover Cleveland's second administration (1893–97). The six new states admitted to the Union in 1889 and 1890 had voted overwhelmingly for Cleveland. Aldrich's biographer, Nathaniel Wright Stephenson, noted, "He had burnt his fingers once admitting States that proved a danger to his party, and he did not propose to do it again." Accordingly, Aldrich appointed the ambitious Beveridge to chair the Senate Committee on Territories in December 1901 with the understanding he was to stall all plans for New Mexico, Arizona, and Oklahoma statehood. Beveridge jealously guarded the power and prerogatives of Aldrich and like-minded senators from the Midwest and New England for eight years.[6]

Neither Aldrich nor Beveridge ever publicly acknowledged their political motives, although newspapers openly discussed them. Instead the two senators dredged up accusations such as "lack of fitness" to justify denying statehood to southwestern territories, especially New Mexico. Beveridge railed endlessly about how Nuevomexicanos retained their language and culture and had not assimilated into Euro-American society. In 1903 he declared that New Mexico's "enormous 'Mexican' preponderance in population, whose solidity [after] fifty years of American influence has not changed[,] is the chief reason against the admission of that Territory." He repeatedly rationalized his actions to himself and others: "It wasn't material whether the people appreciate enough what I did for them or even knew of it—the chief thing was the doing of the work. . . . [W]hether I drop dead tomorrow or thirty years from now, I want to know in my heart and to have the record show that I have been of some use to the cause of righteousness and justice."[7]

For all Beveridge's railing against New Mexico and its unfit population, a countercurrent had been washing across the country since the turn of the century. The Atchison, Topeka and Santa Fe Railway (AT&SF) promoted New Mexico as a novelty to attract tourists at a time when the rest of the nation was beginning to tire of the dehumanizing effects of industrialization. New Mexico was touted in postcards, brochures, and pamphlets as a land of escape, the antidote for oppressive modern life. Thus were the objects of Beveridge's ethnocentric ridicule transformed by advertising into alluring cultural symbols with national appeal. By 1912 it was not merely the Native Americans who were tourist attractions. On 5 July "the biggest moving picture concern in the United States" filmed the De Vargas Day procession in Santa Fe. The AT&SF promoted the event "from one end of [the] Santa Fe system to the other" and expected "to bring several thousand people to Santa Fe." Over the next thirty years tourism took hold in the state's economy, and the cultural heritages of both Native Americans and Nuevomexicanos became commodities.[8]

President Theodore Roosevelt is the third absent figure in the photographs. In the months leading up to the election of 1908, President Roosevelt wrote thirteen private letters to Taft, his hand-picked successor. In these communications he offered candid—and cordial—advice on how to win the election and succeed as president. Roosevelt's implicit assumption was that Taft would continue all his policies and, in effect, be his political proxy. Within fifteen months of Taft's inauguration, though, a public rift opened between them, with differences over wilderness conservation one visible sign of the growing split. In fact, Taft had not sought a fight with Roosevelt and actually applied much of what he suggested in the letters from 1908, including recognizing the importance of the West in the upcoming election. While he did not explicitly mention statehood for New Mexico and Arizona in his letters to Taft, Roosevelt urged his successor to attend to the western states to check a drift toward Democratic voting. In the 1908 presidential election, the newest state, Oklahoma, went for the Democrat, William Jennings Bryan, and undoubtedly it occurred to Taft that creating some safe Republican states in the West would be wise for the election of 1912. New Mexico represented such a prospect, while Arizona leaned toward the Democratic Party.[9]

The 1912 election results disappointed Taft. Roosevelt created the Bull Moose Party and ran for president against Taft. New Mexico and Arizona voted overwhelmingly for Woodrow Wilson, the Democratic presidential candidate. New Mexico's popular vote was as follows: Wilson, 41.4 percent; Taft, 35.9 percent; Roosevelt, 16.1 percent; and the Socialist Eugene Debs, 5.8 percent. Despite losing in New Mexico, Taft actually fared better among its voters than he did nationwide, where he received just 23 percent to Roosevelt's 27 percent. During the election of 1912, Albert J. Beveridge, the enfant terrible of statehood, reprised his spoiler's role and served as a key advisor to Roosevelt.

History's treatment of the actions taken by Roosevelt and Taft in pursuit of statehood is cruelly ironic. Taft provided decisive leadership and imposed his will on a recalcitrant Congress, especially the Senate. He secured statehood; Roosevelt failed. Taft succeeded because he exerted the very strength of conviction that Roosevelt talked about so much but never brought to bear on New Mexico statehood. Yet today historians remember Roosevelt's critique of Taft's presidency and his claim that his successor was ineffective and weak, a theme Roosevelt hammered home in speeches during the 1912 presidential campaign when his Bull Moose Party drained votes away from Taft's reelection bid and consigned him to a one-term presidency.[10]

Today Taft receives no credit for his political adroitness in securing statehood for New Mexico and Arizona, and Roosevelt is forgiven for his inability to deliver on his promises and for pushing joint statehood for nearly five years. The different approaches taken by these two presidents reflected the divisions in the Republican Party. Until 1912, the Republicans' party platform endorsed statehood for the two territories in 1896, 1900, and 1908. In 1904, amid much turmoil over uniting Arizona and New Mexico as one state, the Republicans dropped all mention of expanding the Union. With three Republican presidents successively occupying the White House beginning in 1897—William McKinley, Theodore Roosevelt, and William Howard Taft—and with Republican majorities in both the U.S. House of Representatives and the Senate up to March 1911, why did it take Republicans so long to deliver on their promise of statehood? A large part of the answer is Senator Beveridge's obstructionist tactics, but that is an incomplete and unsatisfactory answer.

"Not Particularly Wise or Efficient as a Leader"

The differences between the presidential leadership styles of Roosevelt and Taft begin with the difference between the ways they used advisors. Roosevelt addressed himself to this matter immediately after winning reelection in November 1904. He wrote letters to two close friends—George H. Putnam, his publisher, and Owen Wister, novelist and author of the recently published *The Virginian*—chiding them for questioning his deference to certain powerful Republican senators who were not aligned with his administration's policies. In brusque and defensive language, Roosevelt lectured Putnam about the necessity of respecting the power and authority of all U.S. senators because "The Senators, under the first article of the Constitution, are the official advisors whom I must consult." Roosevelt deferred to the Senate and even allowed Republican senators to oppose him on statehood year after year. From the start of Roosevelt's presidency in 1901, the Senate's internal divisions over statehood trumped the president's desire to enlarge the Union. In contrast, President Taft cajoled and coerced the Senate to follow his lead on statehood. He always respected the Senate in public, but in private he applied pressure on its members. During 1909 and 1910 he repeatedly pledged in public to honor his party's statehood plank, and in private he leaned hard on Senator Beveridge and others to follow his lead.[11]

Taft acted as legislator-in-chief when he sparred with Congress over a bill enabling statehood, and in this effort his indispensable whip was Postmaster General Frank H. Hitchcock, the all-but-forgotten pivotal figure in navigating the choppy political waters of statehood in the years 1909 through 1911. Entirely consistent with his quiet role, he is unidentifiable in the official photograph of President Taft signing the proclamation. Just as the dim light on an overcast day conspired against a clear photograph, shadows likewise shroud much of Hitchcock's political work, particularly at crucial moments in the process. But he had the ear and the confidence of President Taft. He also allied himself with Delegate Andrews, who helped write the enabling bill and enlisted his own powerful allies in its support. Today if Hitchcock is remembered it is for being the first postmaster general to recognize the potential of airplanes to move mail faster. He also secured a spot in history when he became the first government official to pledge to the children of America that all their letters to Santa Claus would be delivered.

How did he work to promote New Mexico's statehood? Hitchcock held the various parties together and moved them forward in the middle of a very public political feud in which the fate of statehood hung in the balance. He simultaneously guided the enabling bill through the full Senate and worked the corridors of the Congress during the next two and half months to ensure passage of the Mann-Elkins Act, using statehood as the crucial bargaining chip. In exchange for their support, Democrats received assurances that statehood would also come to a final vote, affirming the longtime Democratic legislative priority of adding new states in the belief they would send Democrats to the Congress.

The extent to which Hitchcock navigated final passage of the enabling bill in such roiled waters is suggested in a letter Beveridge wrote on the day the president signed the statehood bill: "The people of the two new states ought to know how much Frank Hitchcock did to secure the passage of this bill. During the present session no man has been so powerful and effective a friend of statehood as Mr. Hitchcock." The senator also noted that Hitchcock's name had "not gotten into the public prints." Hitchcock left public service after Taft's defeat in 1912, and he had a long and highly successful career as a corporate attorney in New York City. He remained interested in New Mexico and reportedly "owned the controlling interest" in a newspaper, the *Las Vegas Optic*, in 1929. In the November election of 1910, Indiana's voters began turning toward the Democratic Party when they elected John W. Kern and denied a third term to Senator Beveridge. Woodrow Wilson carried Indiana in the election of 1912, and Senator Kern became a key ally of the new president.[12]

When Taft assumed the presidency, the Democratic Party was on the rise. In the elections of 1908 voters sent 171 Democrats to the House and 32 to the Senate. Two years later the Democrats captured the House with 230 seats and made a strong showing in the Senate with 43 members. As Taft began his third year in office on 4 March 1911, the political landscape had changed. For the first time ten states elected both a Republican and a Democratic senator, and five of the states were west of the Mississippi River. This split resulted when states enacted reforms that would eventually coalesce into federal law as the Seventeenth Amendment to the Constitution, mandating the popular election of U.S. senators. The Democratic Party's ascendancy culminated in taking over the White House and both houses of Congress in the November 1912 elections. But in 1909 and 1910 Taft saw the parties' shifting numbers and understood he needed to work with Democrats. Statehood and the Mann-Elkins Act were the fruits of that collaboration. Each side traded support for a key piece of legislation, and Taft's quid pro quo brought what had long eluded New Mexicans.

Taft was one of three presidents between 1901 and 1920 who augmented presidential power. This shift began with Roosevelt's conservation policies and the subsequent expansion of executive departments to advance that agenda. The process continued under Taft and is evident in his maneuvering to secure passage of the Enabling Act and especially in his veto of August 1911, when he forced both the Congress and the territories to accept his terms for the admission of new states. Neither Roosevelt nor Taft, though, increased presidential power as much as Woodrow Wilson did during and after World War I. But a thirteen-year rollback of presidential power began when the Senate rejected the Treaty of Versailles in 1919 and Warren G. Harding became president in 1920.

Viewed in this context, New Mexico's entry into the Union occurred at about the midpoint on the rise of presidential power early in the twentieth century. But a wide gulf separated Roosevelt and Taft in their exercise of presidential authority, and these differences had implications for their approaches to statehood. Roosevelt acted independently whenever possible, using executive orders to create national forests and national monuments. He had a tendency to play fast and loose with public lands when he thought the ends justified the means. Taft, a constitutional lawyer, never behaved this way. He worked with Congress on conservation policies and public land issues in general. These different styles of government—legal and constitutional requirements versus free-wheeling administrative man-dates—led to a public and heated dispute between Secretary of the Interior Richard A. Ballinger, a Taft appointee, and Gifford Pinchot, chief of the Forest Service, a Roosevelt-era holdover. The controversy led to Taft's dismissal of Pinchot in 1910, an act that contributed to a rupture of the Republican Party in 1912.[13]

Did Roosevelt's Bull Moose candidacy in 1912 have any connection to Taft's success in securing New Mexico and Arizona statehood? The short answer is "yes." From the time Roosevelt returned from his fifteen-month trip to Europe and Africa, disembarking in New York on the day Congress approved statehood (18 June 1910), he began finding fault with Taft's actions. Slowly he moved from private expressions of disappointment to public criticism and then an outright break in late March 1912. The antecedents of the rift were fully evident in a letter Roosevelt wrote to an old friend in late August 1911. "I have been much disappointed in Taft," he said. "But like many another man, though a most admirable lieutenant, he is not particularly wise or efficient as a leader. As was probably inevitable, he . . . [became] very anxious to emphasize the contrast between our administrations by sundering himself from my especial friends and followers, and appearing therefore as the great, wise conservative."[14]

Roosevelt packed into those sentences three grievances that intersect with statehood—the first two stem from Taft's political tactics and legal principles, while the third simply suggests a bruised ego. Almost immediately upon taking office, Roosevelt complained, Taft "sundered himself from my especial friends," and most particularly from one of Roosevelt's oldest and most trusted political allies, Senator Beveridge. The charge that Taft sought to "appear as the great, wise conservative" was a twofold criticism. Roosevelt recoiled at what he regarded as Taft's coziness with "such national Republican leaders as Nelson Aldrich and Boies Penrose" who were beholden to eastern "railroads and industrialists." These two senators, and their mutual friend Delegate William H. Andrews, had played important roles in the final push to secure statehood in 1910, perhaps none more decisive than Aldrich's aboutface in throwing his support behind Taft. Moreover, Taft's hostility toward the referendum, initiative, and recall flew in the face of Roosevelt's well-known support for these progressive-backed extensions of popular sovereignty. Finally the charge that Taft was "not particularly wise or efficient as a leader" shows more than a hint of sour grapes.

A good friend who spent an evening with Roosevelt in the early spring of 1912 noted his "egotism, faith in his own doctrines, fondness for power and present hostility to Taft." The contrast between Taft's success in attaining statehood and Roosevelt's failure to do so heightened the latter's desire to complete unfinished business as president. When his dinner companion asked him why he wanted a third term, Roosevelt replied, "It is complex. I like power; but I care nothing to be President as President. I am interested in these ideas of mine and I want to carry them through."[15]

Roosevelt, as one distinguished historian has noted, tended toward "a self-centeredness" that often blurred his understanding of people and events. As a consequence, he misread the country's support for him in 1911–12 and was oblivious to what tactics worked in getting legislation through Congress. Roosevelt wanted another chance to push his legislative agenda, but he had not adapted his approach. For example, with final approval of statehood awaiting Senate action in late May 1911, Roosevelt wrote his longtime friend Senator Henry Cabot Lodge to urge him to "take a special interest" in the matter and to expect a visit from former Territorial Governor George Curry seeking his support. But such entreaties would have no more influence in 1911 than had any of the pressure Roosevelt applied to legislators during his presidency. The times required the hardball interparty maneuvering that Taft used.[16]

A few influential New Mexicans took note of Frank Hitchcock's prominent role in securing statehood. Among them were Albert B. Fall, lawyer, Otero County legislator, and recent convert to the Republican Party. He viewed with considerable suspicion the growing influence Hitchcock exerted, especially his friendship with Delegate Andrews. In correspondence with writer Eugene Manlove Rhodes just after the White House meeting of Taft, Hitchcock, and Beveridge at the end of January 1910, Fall wrote: "I stated clearly that New Mexico would not be admitted until Mr. Hitchcock was convinced that he had control of the political situation; that I was correct in this statement I think events as reported by the associated press have conclusively established." Thirteen months later Rhodes asked, "Is he [Hitchcock] still political dictator of N.M?"[17]

Hitchcock, Taft, and Andrews are all but forgotten today for their work in securing statehood. In fact, none of the three is commemorated on a New Mexico map. Geographer Robert Julyan has noted, "Place names are the language in which the nation's autobiography is written." Curry and Catron have counties named for them (in 1909 and 1921, respectively). Amasa and Mabel McGaffey, present at the White House on 12 January 1912, are memorialized in two place names near Gallup. The cartographic amnesia toward Hitchcock and Taft is all the more puzzling when their decisive contributions are stacked against six less successful advocates of statehood commemorated in county names: McKinley (1898); Otero (1899); Luna (1901; for Solomon Luna); and Quay, Roosevelt, and Torrance (1903). The latter was named for a Pennsylvania financier and key backer of William H. Andrews. A seventh, Leonard Wood County, created by renaming Guadalupe County, existed briefly from 1903 to 1905 to honor the commanding officer of the First New Mexico Volunteer Cavalry, the Rough Riders. But in 1905 Nuevomexicano residents of Guadalupe Country (created in 1891), "being unaccustomed to this [new] name and almost unable to pronounce it," insisted the legislature restore the original name honoring Our Lady of Guadalupe.[18]

"A Chamber of Commerce and a 'Boosters' Society"

The new state's motto, *Crescit eundo*, "It grows as it goes," signaled an abiding faith in the future—one in step with a national optimism during the statehood era. The legislature had added the Latin phrase to the territorial seal in 1887, a decision reaffirmed in the 1912 session. Even movies in 1912 abetted local boosters who wanted the rest of the nation to see their community's economic potential. Albuquerque in particular excelled in advertising itself in America's theaters. In late January a movie featuring the city appeared nationwide. Several others opened in the next few months, including a release in late April that followed a log from pond to finished product at the American Lumber Company. The publicity prompted a headline: "ALBUQUERQUE GETS FINE ADVERTISING FROM FILMS."[19]

New Mexico's spirit of progress impressed the Congress when businesses and commercial associations sent petitions in the spring of 1911. President Taft received letters making similar arguments. For example, the Commercial Club of Roswell told him that further delay in statehood "means a loss of more than One Million Dollars to us" in investments. Despite expectations that statehood would unleash a torrent of investment capital, in fact entering the Union released only droplets. One reason new investment was slow was that the pace of technological innovation and its incorporation into the nation's daily life, especially in cities, had been so rapid and widespread since the early 1890s that it had largely exhausted the supply of private capital. Among recent advances that had arrived in New Mexico by 1900 were electricity (mid-1890s), telephones (1897), movies (1898), and automobiles (1900). Each in turn had a powerful transformative effect. When former president Theodore Roosevelt came face-to-face with the changing times he told his good friend Owen Wister, "In the west the old country that I knew so well has absolutely vanished." He went on, "I realized this more fully than at any other time" when he "found a thriving little prairie town with a Chamber of Commerce and a 'boosters' society" where "a quarter of a century ago" an open, desolate land stretched to the horizon.[20]

Roosevelt ended up exactly where many New Mexicans found themselves when confronting modernity: conflicted about its impact on their lives but impressed by how rapidly and enthusiastically people incorporated it. Mining in New Mexico became a case study of modernization on the eve of statehood. Technology mechanized production, drawing to it greater amounts of capital, and concentrating ownership into corporations. Gone were the miners of the 1870s and 1880s with their wheelbarrows and pick-axes. Mechanization had pushed them aside. When the federal coal-mining inspector reported on New Mexico's mines in 1904, he noted that thirty-seven mines in seven counties had collectively removed more than 1.6 million tons of coal. Also listed were the sources of power used to operate twenty-nine of the mines: steam (thirteen), horses (nine), electricity (two), electricity and steam (two), steam and compressed air (two), compressed air (one), and gasoline (one). The type of power used at a mine correlated with the size of the mine: horses worked at the smallest mines and the two largest coal mines used electricity—the Dawson mines and the W. A. Clark Mine, located, respectively, in the two largest coal-producing counties, Colfax and McKinley. For almost fifty years the Dawson mines were an economic mainstay in northeast New Mexico. When they closed in 1950 the company town became an instant ghost town.[21]

The W. A. Clark Mine belonged to William A. Clark, a Democratic U.S. Senator from Montana from 1899 to 1907. He amassed a fortune in mining, banking, and railroads that made him one of the fifty richest men in the nation when he died in 1925. The W. A. Clark Mine, five miles west of Gallup, created its own community, Clarkville, when it began operations in late 1897. The mine was founded to supply coal to Clark's copper mines in

Jerome, Arizona, but it soon found markets elsewhere, too. Ten years after it opened, Clark sold the mine to the John D. Rockefeller–owned consortium Colorado Fuel and Iron Company (CFI), which had been operating in New Mexico's Colfax and McKinley counties since the late 1890s and quickly dominated mining in McKinley County.[22]

In late 1907 the mine changed hands again when a former manager with CFI bought it and created Victor-American Fuel Company, which operated eight mines in McKinley County. On 15 February 1908 "a big seventy-horse-power boiler at the Clarkville coal mine electric haulage plant exploded without warning, wrecking the boiler room, instantly killing Electrician R. A. Bell." The new owners dismantled the mine and abandoned it. The damage from the explosion was the fatal blow to a mine in decline since 1904, when demand for oil began to rise and made coal less desirable. "California oil replaced coal from this mine for railroad purposes in the Pacific States and Territories, and . . . Texas oil replaced the coal in Old Mexico, New Mexico, and Texas for railroad, manufacturing, and domestic uses." Each year demand dropped and Victor-American Fuel Company shut mines. It operated only three in 1909.[23]

What lessons did the W. A. Clark Mine hold for statehood? Five merit brief mention. The mine's rise and fall foreshadows the boom-bust cycle of many extractive industries in the state's history. The competition coal faced from oil also serves as an object lesson about the life-cycle of extractive industries. Demand fluctuates depending on advances in technology, cheaper alternative sources, shifts by major customers, or changes in patterns of consumption. The financial interest of an out-of-state owner teaches a third lesson, since it results in the entrance and exit of capital without regard for—and often without any sustained connection to—local communities.

A detail from the electric motor explosion embodies a fourth object lesson—this one about employment. The electrician Bell came from Philadelphia and was returned there for burial. His fireman, José Montoya, "had a miraculous escape from death," but the division between high-wage jobs and lesser paying ancillary positions for minorities persisted within the state's labor pool. The fifth lesson is the environmental bill that is coming due in the twenty-first century for the underground mining that occurred from the 1880s to the 1950s. A mapping of abandoned and inactive coal mines in McKinley County in 2010 found that "many of these old underground mines are within the Gallup city limits and underlie areas where there has been surface development of housing tracts, schools, and shopping centers. Subsidence [sinking] has been a problem in this area since the 1980s." The report continues by cautioning that "numerous environmental and public safety issues are now facing the city." All these lessons are the by-products of modernity. Change cannot be avoided, of course, but neither can questions about consequences be ignored or dismissed.[24]

That statehood had a downside began to draw comment the second week of January 1912. An editorial in the *Santa Fe New Mexican* offered a warning: "The advertising that statehood has given New Mexico and the capital has brought many people to Santa Fe who are seeking work and cannot find it." Reportedly in Santa Fe there were "a thousand families living on less than six dollars a week, and a thousand men who have no steady employment." Albuquerque experienced a similar influx, which prompted an appeal that "in the publicity work of the future" care be taken to warn newcomers that unless they had "money to tide them over the first year," they should not plan to stay.[25]

While New Mexico's motto expressed the boosterism common to the era, the fragility of local development soon became apparent. Barely three months into statehood the *Titanic* went down on 15 April 1912, and the world—and New Mexicans—saw how quickly expectations could be dashed. A passenger who died, Lord Pierson, headed a syndicate pledged to purchase a railroad being built to connect El Paso to Artesia. The project was heralded as prefiguring prosperity for several communities along the route, most particularly the town of Hope, twenty-one miles west of Artesia. But the railroad—and Hope's plans—sank along with the *Titanic*.[26]

Las Vegas, New Mexico, also believed fortune was smiling on it in the spring of 1912. Three months later its dreams, too, were dashed. Among the federal restrictions that ended with statehood was the ban on boxing engineered by Delegate Thomas B. Catron in 1896. Within two weeks of statehood, businessmen in Las Vegas planned to revive boxing with a premier contest. The heavyweight champion of the world since December 1908, Jack Johnson, the first black man to hold the title, had fought a series of opponents all dubbed "white hopes" in the expectation each would prove the physical superiority of their race. But none had, and a January 1912 announcement of the next opponent, Jim Flynn of Pueblo, Colorado, prompted several in Las Vegas to pledge $100,000 to secure the fight, scheduled for Thursday, 4 July 1912. News that Las Vegas was the venue came on 17 April.

The local promoters believed a heavyweight title fight would simultaneously bring national attention to the new state and their town, drum up
interest in the area's potential for investment, and turn a tidy profit for the
local backers. The date also marked the official release of the new flag of
the United States with its forty-seventh and forty-eighth stars. But just as
agitation by religious zealots had contributed to the 1896 ban on boxing,
so, too, did the planned fight in Las Vegas draw widespread criticism. Even
Governor William McDonald repeatedly voiced disapproval of a black man
fighting a white man. Many in the boxing world thought Flynn a weak
opponent who had no chance of winning and would likely resort to illegal
tactics like head-butting. Nevertheless the fight, scheduled to last forty-five
rounds, began shortly before 3:00 P.M. Neither the quality of the contest
nor its financial return pleased anyone. It lasted nine rounds before being
stopped by a state official sent by Governor McDonald to monitor the event.
Flynn was badly outclassed and had, as predicted, flagrantly tried to injure
Johnson. Most of Johnson's previous defenses of his title drew audiences
of over 20,000. Fewer than 5,000 watched the contest in Las Vegas. The
amount of the promoters' loss was never disclosed, but the town's debt from
building a 17,000-seat arena drained its finances for years.[27]

These economic setbacks in 1912 were a microcosm of New Mexico's
stalled development. In 1910 nine New Mexico lumber companies sought
to lure investors with stock offerings totaling $10.1 million dollars, but the
industry's luster was rapidly fading and the offerings withered. The American Lumber Company, the crown jewel of Albuquerque manufacturing
and a centerpiece of two presidential visits, fell on hard times shortly after
statehood. Too much lumber was being harvested north and east of New
Mexico and supplied to buyers in Dallas and elsewhere at costs lower than
what the Albuquerque Lumber Company could offer. The firm shut down
in 1913, displacing hundreds of workers.[28]

Other sectors of the economy struggled, too, in the early decades of
statehood. Drought visited hardship on farmers and ranchers with crushing regularity for nearly thirty years after 1906, especially across the east
side. One woman recalled, "The droughts were as impressed on our souls as
the rains. When we spoke of the Armistice of World War I, we always said,
'The drought of 1918 when the Armistice was signed.'" Between 1906 and
World War I, tens of thousands of homesteaders arrived full of hope, but
disillusion soon set in. After attempting dryland farming for "three or four

years, all but a handful moved to other states or went back to their home-land." Unable to coax seed to grow during drought, they "realized that their Utopia was a cruel land ready to suck the last trace of hope from them." Small-scale investors attempted to launch irrigation projects, but increas-ingly these initiatives required a level of capitalization and access to tech-nology that only large companies could command. For example, a report on irrigation in the Portales area in 1915 found that "the Westinghouse [Machine Company] interests are now in control of the irrigation system here."[29]

While World War I significantly boosted demand for farm and ranch products, prices were artificially constrained. Owners of agricultural land were encouraged to increase their output, and new federal loan policies gave them the capital to do so. After the war ended in November 1918 a triple dose of bad times hit. Prices collapsed, drought settled in again, and the loans came due. Many of the new state's small-town banks failed, which compounded economic problems. The community of Hope, exactly ten years after its setback in April 1912, sought to enlist U.S. Senator Holm O. Bursum to introduce legislation appropriating $3,500 to the Reclamation Service to survey the Peñasco River to "determine whether or not they will construct a reservoir for irrigation purposes."[30]

During the year of back-and-forth discussions that followed, the town's bank failed. That loss was triggered by uncollectable loans to local farmers, who, as the Hope Chamber of Commerce told Bursum in 1923, suffered under "drought conditions in this section." Bursum got the appropria-tion through the Senate, and in the spring of 1923 it cleared the House. Expectations ran high, and the editor of the *Hope Booster* told Bursum the money "will help us more than anyone can guess, coming at a time when the drought and financial condition were working hardship on the people." But late that summer the Department of Interior halted new activity by the Reclamation Service.[31]

An inquiry launched in 1923 at President Warren G. Harding's request resulted in the secretary of the interior, Hubert Work, appointing "a Fact Finding Commission to make an intensive study of the policy, application, and operation of Government methods of reclaiming arid lands by irriga-tion, which has become a matter of national concern." Organized twenty-one years after passage of the National Reclamation Act of 1902, the inquiry scrutinized the high default rate on loans. Only about 11 percent of the tens of millions of dollars spent on irrigation projects had been repaid through water rights income and sale of reclaimed lands. The section of the report on New Mexico found that the state's southeastern communities' irrigation projects were not repaying their original outlays. The Hondo Project, so highly touted in the late territorial period, had "proven a failure and its operation . . . discontinued." The report recommended it be "sold and the losses incurred charged to the Reclamation Fund." The Carlsbad project, which had soaked up several million dollars of taxpayers' money, was in jeopardy. "The ultimate failure of the project is certain unless additional storage [reservoir] be provided as an early date." The Reclamation Service poured funding into Carlsbad and bypassed the irrigation project Hope requested.[32]

Three significant exceptions to prevailing economic reversals are worthy of note. The first two involved agriculture, where communities tied to the acequia culture in the Rio Arriba, which had not been drawn into the wartime expansion, continued subsistence farming throughout the 1920s. Additionally, a pocket of prosperity was found below the recently opened Elephant Butte Dam. There new crops of vegetables and especially cotton brought in much needed cash, in excess of nine million dollars in 1923 alone. Immediately after statehood one of the few enterprises attracting new investment was the railroad. The AT&SF embarked on a massive construction project in 1912 that laid a second set of tracks across Arizona and New Mexico, an expansion propelled by the competition expected from ships hauling freight through the Panama Canal beginning in 1915. This building boom was short-lived, though. World War I paused it for nearly a decade, and by the 1940s the railroad faced vigorous competition from the trucking industry.[33]

One of the most consequential events in the early years of statehood occurred between 1910 and 1917 when New Mexico found itself on a collision course with the Mexican Revolution. When *La Voz del Pueblo* explained to its readers the details of the Enabling Act in its issue of 25 June 1910, a short, adjacent notice carried the headline México Tendrá Eleciones, "Mexico Will Have Elections." The story reported that the next day, Sunday, Mexico would reelect eighty-year-old Porfirio Díaz, who had ruled the country since 1876. Almost as an aside the article explained that his opponent, Francisco Madero, the thirty-seven-year-old son of a wealthy landowner from the province of Coahuila along the Texas border, had been

jailed since 6 June "accused of insulting the nation and defaming Díaz."
La Voz del Pueblo reported growing speculation that the "discontented in
Mexico were gathering in the northern provinces of that Republic to ignite
a revolution against the government." The uprising's first spark coincided
with the writing of New Mexico's constitution. On 19 November Madero,
who had fled to Texas during the summer, led insurrectionists across the
Rio Grande and unleashed decades of pent-up hostilities toward the regime.
Within six months he toppled Díaz and twenty-one months later he was
murdered on the orders of one of his generals, Victoriano Huerta, who took
over as president. Two other generals would overthrow a president during a
civil war that moved quickly beyond tepid reforms to radical demands for
land redistribution and social justice for the masses of peasants. Finally a
new group of elites imposed themselves on the nation and crushed a genuine social uprising between 1917 and 1920, ending the Mexican Revolution.[34]

For ten months in 1914 more than thirty-seven hundred Mexican men,
women, and children found refuge at Fort Wingate, New Mexico—the largest number of detained refugees held in the United States during the Mexican Revolution. Their ordeal began when they fled a ten-day battle in the
Mexican border town of Ojinaga, Chihuahua (across from Presidio, Texas)
on 10 January 1914. All of Ojinaga's defenders, forces under General Pascual Orozco loyal to President Victoriano Huerta, faced certain death if
captured by insurgent leader Francisco "Pancho" Villa and his army. After
spending a month at Fort Bliss, the detainees were relocated farther from
the border to Fort Wingate, twelve miles east of Gallup.[35]

The census of the interned listed 3,755 Mexicans held at what was officially called "The Mexican Detention Camp." During their stay several federal agencies, and even the White House, had a voice in decisions affecting
their status, but the Army directed their day-to-day lives, an unwelcome
assignment and a drain on army finances. At Fort Sam Houston, Texas,
headquarters of the Army's Southern Department, shuttering the Mexican
Detention Camp became a priority.[36]

While the Army was reluctantly footing the bill, decisions on the internees' status resided with two other federal departments: Labor (immigration office) and State (foreign relations). An Immigration Service officer
eventually headed "a board of special inquiry . . . to investigate their status under the Immigration laws." Among detainees seeking to remain in

the United States, the majority could be admitted "contingent upon their ability to promptly secure employment." In late August the El Paso office of the Immigration Service noted that "the Santa Fe Railway Company (main lines) requires a large number of track laborers, and it is probable this class can in the main secure immediate employment." Significantly, Pancho Villa also recognized the internees as a potential labor pool and sought their return to northern Mexico.[37]

Several events complicated negotiations. In mid-July President Huerta resigned and went into exile. Some of his supporters fled as well, but most aligned with other factions in the civil war. In this period of shifting alliances, the Mexican officers detained at Fort Wingate sent letters to the presidential palace and to the secretary of Mexico's army and navy pledging their loyalty to the new regime and disassociating themselves from Huerta. On August 31, 1914, Mexico's consul in El Paso responded for the new government of President Venustiano Carranza. The noncommissioned soldiers could return "to any part of the country," but "the officers will not be desirable in Mexico." In late May the State Department had agreed "to take the matter [of Mexican detainees] under further consideration." It took until November to close the Mexican Detention Camp, which is quite prompt considering neither government trusted the other. The last detainee released from Fort Wingate, General José Inés Salazar, left for the Bernalillo County jail in the custody of the U.S. marshal.[38]

Salazar faced perjury charges related to court statements made in a May 1914 trial and an August affidavit about his military role at Ojinaga. A new trial awaited him in El Paso on 30 November. But on the evening of 16 November, two masked men overpowered a guard and freed him from the Albuquerque jail. He surfaced publicly in El Paso on 5 December, when he joined with other exiles backing a return by President Huerta and his military chief, Pascual Orozco. For six months in 1915 he sought to mobilize support and troops in Chihuahua, but the arrest of Huerta and Orozco in late June 1915 extinguished his dimming hopes of any part in their counterrevolution. General Salazar returned to New Mexico in July 1915, surrendered to law enforcement, and spent nearly five months incommunicado at the penitentiary in Santa Fe.

A federal jury acquitted him of perjury charges on 9 December 1915. Just nine days later, a jury acquitted six defendants named as conspirators in Salazar's jailbreak. A seventh alleged conspirator, Celestino Otero, the only one lacking an alibi, never made it to trial. He was shot and killed by another alleged accomplice on 31 January 1915. A year later, on 25 January 1916, after deliberating all of twelve minutes, a jury announced that the accused murderer, Socorro lawyer Elfego Baca, had acted in self-defense in shooting and killing Otero. The link between Elfego Baca and these events is straightforward. Baca served as President Huerta's well-paid legal representative in the Southwest in the first half of 1914, earning a reported $25,000 for acting as General Salazar's attorney. Baca's rumored roles as organizer of the jailbreak and Otero's executioner are only speculation, but the incidents did add to the folklore associated with Elfego Baca.[39]

Freed in December 1915, Salazar returned to northern Mexico and switched allegiances. He now backed his former archenemy, Pancho Villa, who on 9 March 1916 led a predawn raid on Columbus, New Mexico, that killed eighteen Americans, women as well as men, including ten soldiers. The next day President Wilson ordered General John J. Pershing to lead an expeditionary force of about 5,000 soldiers to pursue Villa and disperse his revolutionary band. In mid-June 1916 war between Mexico and the United States seemed imminent, and in anticipation of such hostilities a federally mandated mobilization ordered 125,000 National Guardsmen from all states to the border. In September 1916 Salazar became Villa's chief of staff, largely responsible for holding his army together during the final six months of General Pershing's unsuccessful punitive expedition, which pulled out of Mexico in early February. Ten weeks later the United States entered World War I. By 26 July 1917, only three soldiers remained with General José Inés Salazar, and all four perished in a shootout that day.[40]

Events in Columbus, New Mexico, attracted international attention, particularly among the German high command. Early in the punitive expedition, the German armed forces claimed "the military incompetence of the United States has been clearly revealed by the campaign against Villa. . . . The United States not only has no army, it has no artillery, no means of transportation, no airplanes, and lacks all other instruments of modern warfare." Moreover, after 1916 German military strategists consistently disparaged American preparedness, an attitude some scholars believe emboldened them to resume submarine warfare early in 1917 and to make their war plans in the summer of 1918 assuming ineptness among American troops.[41]

"That Future Will Be What We Make It"

January was a most appropriate month for granting statehood. Its name-sake, Janus, the Roman god of beginnings and endings, simultaneously faced the future and the past, as did New Mexicans in 1912. The citizens looked ahead to more than a new year, of course. They were stepping into a new era, but they also carried baggage from the preceding decades, and both realism and optimism are reflected in personal experiences and news-paper commentary from January 1912. Statehood marked a momentous political shift, but people's daily activities changed little.

William Gallacher got up before dawn on 6 January, just as he had every day for most of his young working life. He had grown up in White Oaks, graduated from New Mexico State University in 1908, and soon had his own ranch twenty miles from Carrizozo. The day statehood arrived he worked from first light to after dark doing such wintertime chores as breaking ice on the watering troughs, feeding his livestock, and tending to sick ani-mals. Then he went to bed, got up Sunday before sunrise, and did it all over again—and continued living on his ranch for more than seventy years. On the sixty-fifth anniversary of statehood in 1977, Gallacher spoke about the life of "working people back then" and how they "were too busy just trying to stay alive, to feed ourselves and to carve out a place that would become our home" to celebrate or even take note of statehood—even though the first governor was nearby rancher William C. McDonald.[42]

In Las Cruces federal employee Fabian Garcia would have worked the obligatory six hours on Saturday, 6 January and was also probably too busy to celebrate. He was assembling materials for a six-train-car exposition and series of demonstrations to tour southern New Mexico beginning the fol-lowing Thursday, a traveling display he had organized annually for more than eight years. Garcia's purpose aligned with Gallacher's need: ensuring farmers and ranchers succeeded by sharing scientific information in Eng-lish and Spanish about soils, crops, plant diseases, and irrigation. Garcia graduated from the local land-grant college in 1894, and two years later he began a distinguished fifty-year career in agricultural sciences with the U.S. Department of Agriculture's Experiment Station in Las Cruces, where he served as director from 1913 to 1945.[43]

Throughout New Mexico on Saturday, 6 January, little formal celebra-tion occurred. First to receive news of Taft signing the statehood proclamation was the *Santa Fe New Mexican*, whose Washington correspondent, Ira Bond, attended the signing and telephoned just before noon. The paper's editor immediately called Governor Mills and a few other officials. Staff readied a large unofficial flag of forty-seven stars, the first to be hoisted from the paper's new building. Back inside "the telephones kept ringing to inquire the truth of the report, showing the general interest in Statehood and gradually the Star [sic] and Stripes were thrown to the breezes at various points." A bitterly cold day with temperatures just above zero made it impossible for steam whistles to blow, so "the noise was lacking in the patriotic demonstration." But attention immediately shifted to the inauguration of William McDonald, which came just a week and a day later. The offices of the *Santa Fe New Mexican* became headquarters for planning his swearing in, and the parties that followed were the people's celebration of statehood.[44]

To the north, a 12 January editorial in the weekly *La Revista de Taos* offered admonitions about the future in both prose and poetry. It called upon "the neo-mexicano people to put themselves in the best position, to act wisely and sensibly, and to show that they are worthy of possessing the rights that have been achieved after so many years of effort and so many dashed hopes." The editorial ended with a rousing verse: "So, now you are a state / you possess sovereignty / and your soul is full of pride." In the south, the *Rio Grande Republican* of Las Cruces ran brief wire service announcements in the Tuesday edition, but the centerpiece of the paper's statehood coverage was the official announcement of the upcoming inauguration, which was enthusiastically predicted to "be the finest thing of its kind ever seen in New Mexico." Later in the month one of the city's Spanish-language newspapers offered a wholly different perspective. Gone was the exuberant flag waving of the *Santa Fe New Mexican*, the pontificating of *La Revista de Taos*, and the breathless endorsement of inaugural celebrations by the *Rio Grande Republican*. In their place was a fact-laden checklist of "Government Statistics Concerning the State of New Mexico." If the past is prologue, then these data collected by federal agencies were a blueprint for the state's future, revealing a very mixed set of assets and liabilities. New Mexico entered the Union with a substantial lag in education, weak investor interest, an undiversified economy heavily dependent upon mineral extractions, and agriculture tied to water-thirsty crops.[45]

Democratic Governor William C. McDonald's inauguration on Monday,

15 January became the authentic celebration of statehood. Between six and seven thousand citizens thronged the main entrance of the Capitol, where under a cloudless sky the "warm New Mexico sunshine made wraps unnecessary." McDonald was sworn in at 12:29 P.M. Three minutes of applause greeted the new governor, and clapping interrupted and extended his address to twenty-five minutes. McDonald set both a celebratory and solemn tone by telling those assembled, "You are here not simply to inaugurate a governor, but also to celebrate the inauguration of a state." He then deftly separated the territorial era from the dawn of statehood, reminding the audience that in "struggling for the boon . . . that we were entitled long ago," they had prevailed against "prejudice and mis-information at Washington." He spoke bluntly of "our emancipation from federal interference, except as the power of such is granted in the Constitution," and embraced the people's "full rights as citizens."[46]

With pride he pointed to "the glory and dignity of that bright star added to the flag" and discussed how to honor it. He spoke earnestly about ultimate authority vesting in the people through popular sovereignty. "The will and voice of a just and intelligent people," he told them, must hold government accountable and "the force of public condemnation should render it powerless for evil." In a veiled reference to recent scandal-riddled Republican administrations, he said that public officials "cannot afford to use questionable methods to obtain desired results." He also signaled his intent to end "personal power, based upon control of money and upheld by government for a long time," as well as his intention to "guard the voter in every possible way . . . [from] those who would tamper with the sacred right of a free and uncontrolled ballot." When he turned to public education, he called it "our first concern" and pledged that "the public lands now held by the state" would be wisely stewarded "in such a manner that the proceeds and revenues coming therefrom may go to our children as a vast heritage." In looking ahead he urged recognition that narrow-minded self-interests did not trump "the general advancement of our great commonwealth," that "partisanship cannot bring success," and that "upon the proper and wise use of our water rights depends much of the real development of our great areas of land."[47]

McDonald's address has a contemporary ring with its references to governmental exercise of power and citizens' responsibilities. He spoke truth to future generations in words worth repeating and passing forward. "As we look into the future bright hopes of promise appear to some and dark forebodings may dim the horizon of others. The past is history, the present is the dawn of the future. It is to the future we look—and that future will be what we make it."[48]

Notes

Preface

1. Moore, *Cricket in the Web;* Hillerman, *Seldom Disappointed*, 208–11.
2. Contemporary national newspaper support is described in two May 1902 articles: "The Admission" and "Passage of the Bill," in *Public Opinion*, 648, 666.
3. *Atlanta Constitution*, 21 February 1903, 6.
4. *Albuquerque Morning Journal*, 20 & 21 June 1910, 1; 21 August 1911, 1. *Santa Fe New Mexican*, 6 January 1912, 1.
5. The history of popular sovereignty is in Morgan, *Inventing the People*.
6. Holtby, "Introduction," in Roberts, *Our New Mexico*, 2–4; Simmons, *People of the Sun*, 11–21, 51–64. On agency by subalterns, or the capacity of a conquered people to hold onto their identity and core beliefs, early studies are De León, *Tejano Community,* and Utley, *Indian Frontier*. Recent discussions are Emmons, *Beyond the American Pale*, 332–35; Scharff and Brucken, *Home Lands*, 1–45; De León, "Foreword" in Weber, *Foreigners*, vii–xvi; Rivera, *Acequia Culture*; and Rodríguez, *Acequia*.

Introduction

1. Burns, *Workshop of Democracy*, 152–242, 297–306, 531–38; West, "Reconstructing," 6–26; Whitman, "Preface to the 1855 Edition," 411.
2. Larson, *New Mexico's Quest*, 18–22, 50–58; Remini, *At the Edge*, 63–89, 131–55; Stegmaier, *Texas, New Mexico;* Foner, *Fiery Trial*, 148–54; Stegmaier, "New Mexico's Delegate, Part I," 385–92.
3. West, "Reconstructing," 9. Webster, *Writings and Speeches*, 10: 21, 29–30, 27–28, 31. Ruxton, *Adventures*, 192. See Remini, *Daniel Webster*, 647–49, on Webster's March speech and its place in his presidential ambitions. Powell, *Tree of Hate*, on the Black Legend, or hostility to all things connected to Spain in the Old World and New.
4. Twitchell, *Leading Facts,* 2: 403–406, n. 329.

5. Lamar, *American Southwest,* 75–176; Etulain, *Beyond the Missouri,* 232–37, 250–52, 299–315.

6. Parish, *Charles Ilfeld Company,* 35–97; Kelly, *Buffalo Head,* 35–63; White, *Railroaded,* 1–38, 371–409; Heilbroner, *Worldly Philosophers,* 143–213. West, "Reconstructing," 8 n. 2, estimates the expansion added about 1.23 million square miles to the U.S. land base.

7. Twitchell, *Leading Facts,* 2: 482–83. Jacobson, *Barbarian Virtues,* 73.

8. *Chicago Daily Tribune,* 14 January 1894, 36.

9. *El Nuevo Mundo,* 29 May 1897, 1; *El Hispano Americano,* 30 January 1905, 3; McMurry, *George Washington Carver,* 32–51. Unless otherwise noted, all translations are by the author.

10. Smith et al., eds., *Autobiography of Mark Twain,* 207–208.

11. Dargan, "New Mexico's Fight, Part I," 3–4. West, "Reconstructing," 12.

12. Hillerman's endorsement appeared on the dust jacket of the book's second printing.

Chapter 1

1. Catron to Otero, 14 December 1896, MAOP, MSS 21 BC, box 1, fld. 2, CSWR, UL, UNM; *Atlanta Constitution,* 11 December 1896, 2; Westphall, *Thomas Benton Catron.* A detailed obituary by a longtime foe is in the *Santa Fe New Mexican,* 17 May 1921, 2. Larson, *New Mexico's Quest,* 183–88. An incisive appraisal by someone acquainted with Catron is in Keleher, *Fabulous Frontier,* 117–40. Two boxes contain Catron's official correspondence during his tenure as a delegate; see TBCP, MSS 29 BC, Series 106, CSWR, UL, UNM.

2. Westphall, *Thomas Benton Catron,* 19.

3. For Catron's land holdings, see Westphall, *Thomas Benton Catron,* 70–72, quoted 72. For the Santa Fe Ring, see Lamar, *Far Southwest,* 121–49, quoted 129. A benign view of the Ring and Catron's role is in Westphall, *Thomas Benton Catron,* 98–99. On his extensive mining and ranching interests, ibid., 66–69.

4. Lamar, *Far Southwest,* 151–76.

5. Ibid., 161. On Las Gorras Blancas, see Arellano, "The People's Movement," in Gonzales-Berry and Maciel, eds., *Contested Homeland.*

6. "Address Advocating Statehood," n.d. [1895/96], TBCP, MSS 29 BC, series 404, fld. 4, CSWR, UL, UNM; Westphall, *Thomas Benton Catron,* 312; precarious financial status, ibid., 73; tax delinquency and artful arguments against the assessed valuation, *Albuquerque Morning Democrat,* 29 March 1896, 2. The substantial burden of his debt, "borrowed to finance his land grant speculations," is in Keleher, *Fabulous Frontier,* 131.

7. Four representative preelection attacks on Catron are in *Santa Fe New Mexican,* 5 October 1894, 2, 6 October 1894, 4, 1 November 1894, 1, 3 November 1894, 4. Paying the requisite poll tax, due sixty days in advance of the election, and his principled opposition to the tax as a Democratic scheme to limit voting by Nuevo-

mexicanos, ibid, 13 September 1892, 2, 21 September 1892, 2. Democrat Antonio Joseph, born in Santa Fe but long the proprietor of the hot springs at Ojo Caliente, served five consecutive terms as delegate in the Forty-ninth through the Fifty-third U.S. Congress. He defeated Catron by just under twenty-five hundred votes in November 1892 but lost to him in the 1894 election by fewer than two thousand votes. On Catron's electoral success, see *Santa Fe New Mexican*, 22 October 1894, 2.

8. Two contrasting assessments are, Durán, "Francisco Chavez, Thomas B. Catron," 291–310, and Westphall, *Thomas Benton Catron*, 217–68. For the libel charge, see Keleher, *Fabulous Frontier*, 128–30.

During the fall of 1896 and into the winter Catron lost an appeal to the Territorial Supreme Court and two appeals to the U.S. Supreme Court to overturn the convictions. The second of these Supreme Court appeals was *Gonzales v. Cunningham*, 164 U.S. 612, decided on 21 December 1896. In February and March 1897, while finishing his term as delegate, Catron waged a very public campaign, including appeals by prominent Catholic bishops, to convince Presidents Cleveland and McKinley to commute the sentences to life imprisonment. Each president reviewed the case but decided not to reverse the sentences, which were carried out in Santa Fe on 2 April 1897.

Newspapers outside New Mexico lost no opportunity to impugn Catron. Keleher, *Fabulous Frontier*, 124, quoted a particularly offensive racist accusation made by a Durango newspaper in registering disapproval of Catron as a delegate. I am indebted to Dr. Calvin A. Roberts for reminding me of this graphic epithet. Contemporary accounts linking Catron to politically motivated murders produced these headlines in *Los Angeles Times*, 4 April 1897, 9: "POLITICAL HISTORY OF THE TERRITORY IS A SERIAL STORY OF MIDNIGHT ASSASSINATION," and "MURDERS COMMITTED BY A SECRET SOCIETY ORGANIZED TO PROMOTE THE INTERESTS OF THOMAS B. CATRON."

9. Catron to Otero, 14 December 1896, MAOP, MSS 21 BC, box 1, fld. 2, CSWR, UL, UNM.

10. *El Independiente*'s article was reproduced by other Spanish-language Republican-leaning newspapers, a common practice in that period. See *El Tiempo*, 12 December 1895, 1. No copies of *El Independiente* exist, so citations are to *El Tiempo*.

11. *Los Angeles Times*, 7 January 1897, 5. On pension requests, TBCP, MSS 29BC, series 106, box 1, flds. 1–4, CSWR, UL, UNM.

12. *El Tiempo*, 12 December 1895, 1. For the prizefight legislation and the social and political milieu, see Jessup, "Force of Public Opinion." On Culberson's water-grab legislation, see Clark, *Water in New Mexico*, 95.

13. *El Tiempo*, 12 December 1895, 1. For Elkins, *Los Angeles Times*, 1 December 1895, 25.

14. *New York Times*, 28 March 1896, 1. On Senator Clark, *Las Vegas Optic*, [1903], clipping, BSRP, MSS 175 BC, Scrapbook, CSWR, UL, UNM.

15. *St. Louis Globe-Democrat*, 5 December 1895, 4.

16. *Albuquerque Morning Democrat*, 5 January 1896, 2.

17. *Los Angeles Times*, 11 January 1896, 2; *New York Times*, 14 February 1896, 2, and *Los Angeles Times*, 20 February 1896, 1, 3 April 1896, 2; *Santa Fe New Mexican*, 16 April 1896, 2; *Washington Post*, 29 April 1896, 6; *El Tiempo*, 12 December 1895, 1; *Santa Fe New Mexican*, 16 April 1896, 2.

18. *Albuquerque Morning Democrat*, 18 March 1896, 2. Larson, *Populism*.

19. Neither Quay nor others involved revealed any details of the arrangement; see *New York Times*, 12 April 1896, 4. Quay's political maneuverings in 1896 are in his biography by Kehl, *Boss Rule*, 195–205. A political biography of Reed and first-hand details on the Fifty-fourth Congress and the 1896 election are in Robinson, *Thomas B. Reed*, 321–50.

20. Congress, House. Committee on the Territories, *Admission of New Mexico* 6 June 1896, 19.

21. *Santa Fe New Mexican*, 10 June 1896, 1–2.

22. *Santa Fe New Mexican*, 22 June 1896, 1.

23. Ibid.

24. *El Labrador*, 8 September 1896, 1, 31 October 1896, 1. The paper used the word "bulldozer."

25. *Atlanta Constitution*, 11 December 1895, 2. Catron's set-piece critique of the Anti-Alien Act is in "Address Advocating Statehood," n.d. [1895–96], TBCP, MSS 29 BC, series 404, fld. 4, CSWR, UL, UNM.

26. *Chicago Daily Tribune*, 11 December 1896, 4.

27. Fergusson land bill, see Twitchell, *Leading Facts*, 521–22 n. 439, 522 n. 440; *Santa Fe New Mexican*, 17 November 1898, 2. *Los Angeles Times*, 1 January 1899, D9, quoted Catron: "The recent election has had much to do with causing a change in sentiment of the eastern Senators and Representatives, but the rush of business and the shortness of time precludes any action at the present term."

28. *Socorro Advertiser* quoted in the *Santa Fe New Mexican*, 5 June 1896, 2. For Catron's caustic comments on the position of a delegate, see Catron to Beveridge, 9 February 1909, Box 169, AJBP, LC, MD.

29. Beck and Haase, *Historical Atlas*, 21, for acreage lost. Additional studies on land grants in the nineteenth and early twentieth century that I drew on are these, listed in rough order of priority in my account: Ebright, *Land Grants and Lawsuits*; Montoya, *Translating Property*; Westphall, *Mercedes Reales*; Bowden, "Private Land Claims"; Gonzales, "Struggle for Survival"; Nostrand, *El Cerrito*; Schiller, "San Miguel del Vado Grant," newmexicohistory.org; Hall, "San Miguel del Bado"; Schiller, "History and Adjudication"; Sánchez, *Between Two Rivers*; Matthews-Lamb, "'Designing and Mischievous'"; Bradfute, *Court of Private Land Claims*; Dunbar-Ortiz, *Roots of Resistance*; GAO, Report, "Treaty of Guadalupe Hidalgo."

30. *United States v. Santa Fe*, 165 U.S. 675. Catron argued his cases in what is today known as the old Supreme Court chamber, located directly under the Senate in the Capitol.

31. On Article 10, see Gómez, *Manifest Destinies*, 125.

32. *Hutchings v. Low*, 82 U.S. 77; Duncan, *National Parks*, 8–22. On expropriation throughout the nineteenth century, see Scheiber, "Property Law, Expropriation," 243.

33. Quoted in Schiller, "History and Adjudication," 1058; Reynolds, *Spanish and Mexican Land Laws*.

34. Bogue and Bogue, eds., *Jeffersonian Dream*, especially chapters 1–3. The respective percentages of land held by the federal government as public domain at statehood: Nevada, 85.5; Utah, 57.4; Oregon, 53.1; Idaho, 50.2, California, 45.3; New Mexico, 41.8. Data extracted from GSA, *Federal Real Property*.

35. On the legal flaws in the U.S. Supreme Court's understanding of Spanish law, see Schiller, "San Miguel del Vado Grant," www.newmexicohistory.org; *El Labrador*, 24 June 1897, 2; *El Nuevo Mundo* 11 September 1897, 2. The 1895 view of the Supreme Court is in Jackson, "Chavez Land Grant," 361.

36. *United States v. [Julian] Sandoval*, 295, 296.

37. The Morton appeal is in *United States v. [Julian] Sandoval* 167 U.S 278 290–98, quoted 298.

The Supreme Court's exasperation with the *Recopilación* led it to declare in *United States v. Santa Fe* at 683: "The veneration of the compilers for laws which had received the royal sanction seems to have been so great that they did not consider themselves at liberty to omit them. This mode of proceeding has swelled this code to its present dimensions when, if a more rational method had been adopted, it could readily have been compressed into one-third of the space it actually occupies." This is a complete misrepresentation of both the process behind the compilation and the spirit of the effort, which reduced more than 400,000 laws to 6,385; see Manzano Manzano, *Historia de las Recopilaciones de Indias*, 2:303. The *Recopilación* resulted not from a "veneration" of royal dictates but a desire to trace the evolution of arguments about matters large and small so that colonial officials knew the relevant precedents. The Supreme Court completely missed this point. Moreover, even a cursory reading of the nine books that make up the *Recopilación* brings an appreciation of the attempt by distant authorities to deal with peoples and lands unknown to them, which is why the sovereigns applied a guiding principle of Spanish law—protecting the rights of all, including the people as a collective body as well as its individual citizens.

38. *Hayes v. United States*, 170 U.S. 637 quoted 645.

39. For an assessment of the Court's impact, see Griswold del Castillo, *Treaty*, 89. For Rodey's testimony, see Congress, Senate, "New Statehood Bill," 335.

40. Lane to Davis, 23 June 1892, TBCP, MSS 29 BC, series 404, fld. 3, CSWR, UL, UNM, and Lane to Davis, 18 June 1892, ibid. For the reply, see Davis to Lane, 21 June 1892, ibid.

41. Otero, *My Nine Years*, 161–98, 372–85, quoted 381.

42. *Albuquerque Morning Democrat*, n.d. [1901], clipping BSRP, MSS 175 BC, box 1, Scrapbook, CSWR, UL, UNM.

43. Library of Congress, "Declaration and Resolutions," 1. On Childers's comments, see Congress, Senate. Committee on Territories, *Statehood for the Territories* [1903], 4.

44. Library of Congress, "Declaration and Resolutions," 2,4. The convention appointed twelve men, Republicans and Democrats, to serve on the Resolutions Committee chaired by Bernard S. Rodey; see *Santa Fe New Mexican*, 16 October 1901,1. They produced two versions, one introduced at the convention and a second, cited above, submitted to the Congress and the president. I believe Delegate Rodey wrote this second document's preamble and much of the text.

45. *Deming Herald*, 8 October 1901, 1

46. Otero, *My Nine Years*, 203.

Chapter 2

1. Gould, *Presidency of Theodore Roosevelt* [1991], 109.

2. Stephenson, *Nelson W. Aldrich*, 210. Ibid., 76–103 for his loss of power to Democrats after the 1892 election. *Atlanta Constitution*, 22 January 1903, 5, reporting on a key test vote in the Senate, tallied pro-statehood votes at 37 votes and anti-statehood at 27. Delegate Bernard S. Rodey in an interview had a similar count; see *Pittsburg[h] Gazette*, 7 December 1903 in BSRP, MSS 175 BC, Scrapbook, CSWR, UL, UNM.

3. *New York Times*, 1 July 1902, 1; Braeman, *Albert J. Beveridge*, 58; Congress, Senate, *New Statehood Bill*, 32779.

4. *New York Times*, 3 July 1902, 8.

5. An on-line version of Beveridge's "March of the Flag" speech is my source for quotations, at www.historytools.org.

6. Ibid.

7. Ibid.

8. *Chicago Daily Tribune*, 17 September 1898, 2. (Throughout the book this newspaper is cited by its modern title, the *Chicago Tribune*, although in the footnotes the historical title is retained.), 12 January 1899, 7; *Washington Post*, 26 September 1898, 4. Quotation is from *Los Angeles Times*, 29 January 1899, A14.

9. *New York Times*, 10 January 1900, 5; "March," www.historytools.org; *Congressional Record*, 9 January 1900, 56th Congress, 1st Session, 704–12, quote at 711.

10. Hofstadter, *Social Darwinism*, 179–80; Horseman, *Race and Manifest Destiny*, 208–303; Lamar, *Far Southwest*, Introduction and ch. 19.

11. Speeches [1905], AJBP, box 298, LC, MD. For Aldrich's imperialist views, see Stephenson, *Nelson W. Aldrich*, 209–11. Braeman, *Beveridge*, 85; Speeches [1902], box 298, AJBP, LC, MD; "March," www.historytools.org; Newspapers [1900], box 325, LC, MD. My emphasis on Beveridge's speeches in 1898 and 1900, and the continuous thread of his thought that extends from the Philippines to New Mexico, differs from the view of Love, *Race Over Empire*, 6. He maintains Beveridge was irrelevant to the colonial debates because he did not enter the Senate until after the

votes on the peace treaty and annexation. Essential to an understanding of Beveridge's intellectual formation and beliefs is Levine, "Social Philosophy."

12. Braeman, *Beveridge*, chaps. 4, 5, 7 on his presidential ambition. Assessment of his abilities, see *Chicago Daily Tribune*, 22 January 1904, p. 6: "He came to be recognized as one of the best debaters in the senate. . . . He became one of the mainstays of his party in debate." Stephenson, *Nelson W. Aldrich*, 266, 463 n. 8, in which Stephenson interviewed him about his relationship with Aldrich shortly before the senator's death in 1927.

13. Shaw to Beveridge, 8 January 1902, box 282, AJBP, LC, MD.

14. Ibid. The seven new western states were North Dakota (1889), South Dakota (1889), Montana (1889), Washington (1889), Idaho (1890), Wyoming (1890), and Utah (1896). An early study is Paxson, *Admission,* and a fine collection of essays marked Washington's centennial, Stratton, *Washington Comes of Age.*

15. Beveridge to Shaw, 10 January 1902, box 282, AJBP, LC, MD. *Washington Post*, 18 January 1899, 11. Senators joining Beveridge on the tour of the Territories were Republicans Henry E. Burnham of New Hampshire and William P. Dillingham of Vermont and Idaho's Populist Henry Heitfield.

16. Otero, *My Nine Years*, 142–86.

17. Catron is quoted ibid., 373. The full list of his accusations against Otero is reproduced ibid., 373–85, and his rebuttal ibid., 393.

18. Congress, HR, Bill 12543. *Report No. 1309, 57th Congress, 1st Session,* quotations 4–5, 15.

19. Clipping, *St. Louis Globe-Democrat*, 8 June 1902, BSRP, MSS 175 BC, Scrapbook, CSWR, UL, UNM.

20. The infamous Beveridge Report comprises two transcripts, and the portions on New Mexico in the 394-page report are pp. 1–120 (November) and 327–79 (June); see Congress, Senate, *New Statehood Bill.* For the exchange over "carpetbaggers," see 336.

21. Kehl, *Boss Rule*, 245. Quay also sat on the Senate's Committee on Territories in the Fifty-seventh Congress.

22. Congress, Senate, *New Statehood Bill*, 338–41. Braeman, *Albert J. Beveridge*, 85–86 and quoted 85. For Beveridge's outrage over public officials profiting from their position, especially with railroad investments, see Beveridge to Shaw, 2 May 1901, box 282, AJBP, LC, BP; Kehl, *Boss Rule*, 247. Beveridge had a double standard since his patron Nelson Aldrich had amassed a fortune through railroad investments; for representative examples of these deals, see Aldrich to United Traction & Electric Co., 18 June 1898 and Aldrich to Law Offices of Burdett and Snow, 16 December 1898, microfilm reel 22, NWAP, LC, MD.

23. Quotations Congress, Senate, *New Statehood Bill*, 329, 331–32; Rodey's full testimony 327–38.

24. *Los Angeles Times*, 6 June 1901, 1.

25. Nelson to Beveridge, 20 August 1902, box 105, AJBP LC, MD. Between 16 and 19 November they toured Arizona, and they spent 22 November in

Oklahoma, departing from Guthrie for Chicago.

26. On the 1900 census data for Indiana and New Mexico, see Bureau of the Census, *Twelfth Census, Population*, 1: cciii–ccv, cxcvii–cxcix; 2: xx–xxi, lxvii, cxii. On the figures for non-English-speaking Nuevomexicanos and those with parent(s) born in Mexico, 2: cxxv–cxxvi.

27. *New Statehood Bill*, 9–11, 54–55. Christopher Columbus, see Otero, *My Nine Years*, 214. The judiciary: Congress, Senate, *New Statehood Bill*, 40. Andrews, ibid., 64, 72, 74. Examples of testimony from census enumerators, see from Mora County, ibid., 15–21. *Santa Fe New Mexican*, 14 November 1902, 1.

28. Congress, Senate, *New Statehood Bill*, 105, for Amador's testimony. Queries about Christopher Columbus, see Hening, ed. *George Curry*, 192; and *New York Times*, 20 August 1905, SM3.

29. Beveridge to Shaw, 27 October 1902, box 282, AJBP, LC, MD. On Remington's various trips to the territory, see the dissertation by White, "Artists of Territorial New Mexico," 127–41.

30. Butler, *Meaning of Education*, quoted 364, 352, 355, 356. Beveridge to Shaw, 29 November 1902, box 282, AJBP, LC, MD. Shaw to Beveridge, 26 November 1902, ibid. *Albuquerque Morning Journal*, 24 December 1903, 1.

31. Beveridge to Shaw, 3 November 1902, box 282, AJBP, LC, MD. *Review of Reviews*, December 1902, 649.

32. Beveridge to Aldrich, 5 November 1902, microfilm reel 23, NWAP, LC, MD. Beveridge to Shaw, 3 November 1902, box 282, AJBP, LC, MD. Beveridge to Shaw, 29 November 1902, ibid. The financing scheme had been hinted at in testimony by Delegate Bernard Rodey in June 1902; see Congress, Senate, *New Statehood Bill*, 338–39. The newspapers' position on statehood is in Bowers, *Albert J. Beveridge*, 198. The *Santa Fe New Mexican*, 14 November 1902, 1, commented on the grueling work schedule of "the stenographers and reporters who write out in full each day's proceedings before retiring."

33. *Chicago Daily Tribune*, 4 December 1902, 1.

34. Pennsylvania Development Company and its subsidiaries, see box 1, flds. 1, 2,3,7,8, WSHP, MSS 56 BC, CSWR, UL, UNM. Investment opportunities are discussed in Torrance to Hopewell, 22 April 1904, box 1, fld. 1, ibid.

35. Theodore Roosevelt singled out Beveridge and Henry Cabot Lodge as the senators he most consulted on any matter domestic or foreign; see Roosevelt, *Autobiography*, 367–68. Shaw, Butler, and Roosevelt are discussed in Graybar, *Albert Shaw*, 66–68; Shaw and Butler were members of the president's famous Tennis Cabinet. For Beveridge on the subcommittee's assessment of New Mexico, see Congress, Senate, *New Statehood Bill*, 9.

36. Quay to McKinley, 21 May 1900, box 9, MSQP, LC, MD. Quay's decisive role at the convention is in Morris, *Rise of Theodore Roosevelt*, 726–28. Roosevelt to Quay, 4 December 1902, box 10, MSQP, LC, MD.

37. Beveridge to Aldrich, 3 November 1902, microfilm reel 23, NWAP, LC, MD. *Chicago Daily Tribune*, 4 December 1902, 1.

38. The ties of Senators Foraker and Elkins to New Mexico are well known, and representative actions are reported in Otero, *My Nine Years*, 5–7. On Senators Foster and Mitchell, see *Chicago Daily Tribune*, 9 December 1902, 3.

39. For Beveridge's later account, see Speeches [c. 1911], box 303, AJBP, LC, MD.

40. *Congressional Record*, 7 January 1903, 57th Congress, 2nd Sess., quoted 566, 568.

41. Ibid., pp. 571, 574. On Nelson, see Gieske and Keillor, *Norwegian Yankee*, quoted 256.

42. *Congressional Record*, 7 January 1903, 57th Congress, 2nd Session, quoted 572, 574.

43. *Las Cruces Progress*, 14 March 1903, 4.

44. *Atlanta Constitution*, 22 January 1903, 5; *New York Times*, 27 January 1903, 2. Many details about the Beveridge-Quay standoff are drawn from the in-depth coverage of their Senate debates reported by Jos[eph] Ohl of the *Atlanta Constitution* between 4 December 1902 and 25 February 1903. He also likely wrote other unsigned shorter pieces in this period in addition to the following ten under his byline: 4 December 1902, 1; 5 December 1902, 4; 21 January 1903, 1; 22 January 1903, 5; 23 January 1903, 5; 30 January 1903, 2; Ibid., 9; 15 February 1903, B7; 24 February 1903, 5; 25 February 1903, 1.

45. Speeches [c.1911], box 303, AJBP, LC, MD. Depew, *My Memoirs*, 180,190. He made only one brief mention of Beveridge (183) and nothing about his own role in talking for two days to prevent a vote on statehood.

46. Bowers, *Albert J. Beveridge*, 200–201. On the appropriation, see *New York Times*, 19 February 1903, 7.

47. *Las Cruces Progress*, 29 November 1902, 4; *El Tiempo*, 6 December 1902, 3; *El Labrador*, 19 December 1902, 3; *El Tiempo*, 17 January 1903, 1.

48. *El Tiempo*, 7 February 1903, 2; *El Labrador*, 6 February 1903, 3; *El Tiempo*, 14 February 1903, 2; *El Labrador*, 6 March 1903, 3.

49. *Las Cruces Progress*, 29 November 1902, 4. For the recent critical assessment of Beveridge, see Martin, *Indiana*, 270. After leaving the Senate in 1911, Beveridge had a distinguished writing career, receiving a Pulitzer Prize in 1920 for his four-volume biography of Chief Justice John Marshall while his two-volume biography of Abraham Lincoln appeared posthumously (1928).

50. *El Labrador*, 13 March 1903, 1. Otero, *My Nine Years*, 63, 217. On the fail-safe position that the president would veto statehood, see Bowers, *Albert J. Beveridge*, 200. *Albuquerque Morning Journal*, 24 December 1903, 1.

Chapter 3

1. "Manhood and Statehood" 2 August 1901, reprinted in Roosevelt, *Strenuous Life*, 245–59. The New Mexico officers of the Rough Riders Association were from, respectively, Santa Fe (president), Raton (vice-president), and Cerrillos (sec-

retary/treasurer). Roosevelt's 4 July 1886 speech is discussed in Hawley, *Theodore Roosevelt*, 74.

2. Roosevelt, *Strenuous Life*, 252. Roosevelt's 4 July 1886 speech, "Doing as Our Forefathers Did," is online at www.theodorerooseveltcenter.org/TR_Dakota_ july4.asp.

3. Roosevelt, *Strenuous Life*, 252.

4. Roosevelt to Twitchell, quoted in *New York Times*, 16 September 1900, 2.

5. Arguing that righteousness was the central tenet in Roosevelt's political life, Hawley, *Theodore Roosevelt*, 52–57 and *passim*; quoted is Gifford Pinchot, ibid., v.

6. Transcript of Roosevelt's Sorbonne speech, "The Man in the Arena: Citizenship in a Republic," is at www.theodore-roosevelt.com/trspeechescomplete.html and click on document file 630 for 23 April 1910.

7. On late-nineteenth-century attitudes on manhood in New Mexico, see Ball, "Cool to the End," in Matthew Basso et al., eds., *Across the Great Divide*, quoted 102.

8. As quoted in Hawley, *Theodore Roosevelt*, 71. Roosevelt, *Strenuous Life*, 246.

9. Ibid., 257, 256. Roosevelt, "The Man in the Arena," www.theodore-roosevelt.com.

10. Graybar, *Albert Shaw*, 130.

11. *Santa Fe New Mexican*, 14, 15 September 1901, 1; *La Bandera Americana*, 14 September 1901, 2, 25 September 1901, 1.

12. *Las Vegas Optic*, 9 May 1901, 2. Nieto-Phillips, *Language of Blood*, 118–43 on the Bureau.

13. *La Bandera Americana*, 17 August 1901, 2, 25 September 1901, 3. On McKinley's civility, see Gould, *Presidency of William McKinley*, 159. Presidential protection initially irritated Theodore Roosevelt because uniformed D.C. police accompanied him in public. The unrestricted access Dr. Jacobs reported in Canton was a pattern with McKinley, who enjoyed unaccompanied walks in D.C. where he could smoke a cigar and see and be seen by the public. A fascinating account of how both presidents "trusted the people" and sought to be among them is in "Special dispatch from Washington, D.C.," *The Deming Herald*, 10 December 1901, 2.

14. *La Bandera Americana*, 14 September 1901, 1, 18 October 1901, 2.

15. *Las Vegas Optic*, 9 May 1901, 2.

16. Second inaugural address, *New York Times*, 5 March 1901, 1. On his appointment as governor, see Otero, *My Nine Years*, 2–7. Late in the fall of 1896, Otero had requested Thomas B. Catron's assistance in securing the position of U.S. Marshal. Catron demurred, citing the complexities of the current political situation. He went on to state, "I am not certain how much influence or power I may have, but I think I have some." In fact the White House was cutting off Catron's national influence and shifting its support to Otero. See Catron to Otero, 14 December 1896, MAOP, MSS 21 BC, box 1, fld. 2, CSWR, UL, UNM.

17. *New York Times*, 9 August 1900, 8. On McKinley's December 1900 address to Congress, much of which dealt with China and the Philippines, see *New York*

Times, 4 December 1900, 6. His second inaugural address is in *New York Times,* 5 March 1901, 1. A judicious history of the McKinley presidency and especially his domestic policy is Gould, *Presidency of William McKinley,* 153–77.

18. *New York Times,* 5 March 1901, 1.

19. Roosevelt, *Autobiography,* 209–78. Otero on his support for the Rough Riders is in Otero, *My Nine Years,* 36–61. On 25 April 1898 Otero put out the initial call for volunteers, which drew 340 enlisted men and 13 commissioned officers—all sworn in on 6 May 1898. The next day two more enlisted men and one officer were accepted, for a total of 356. This initial contingent so impressed Colonel Leonard Wood that on 24 June 1898 he requested an additional 250 soldiers. According to Otero, New Mexico "furnished 600 men and officers" as Rough Riders; see *My Nine Years,* 39–45, quoted 45. An overview essay is Melzer and Mingus, "Wild to Fight."

20. *Los Angeles Times,* 15 June 1899, 5, and *La Voz del Pueblo,* 3 June 1899, 2. The latter included a notice of Wood and Lodge as invitees. Roosevelt's speech is quoted in Otero, *My Nine Years,* 63.

21. Roosevelt to Lodge, 1 July 1899, in Roosevelt, *Selections from the Correspondence,* 2: 403–404. Governor Roosevelt's problems in New York are in Morris, *Rise of Theodore Roosevelt,* 711–28. Kehl, *Boss Rule,* 225–29 discusses Quay's key role in Roosevelt's nomination in 1900.

22. *Santa Fe New Mexican,* 17 October 1901, 1, 18 October 1901, 4. The unidentified journalist is quoted by Hawley, *Theodore Roosevelt,* 51.

23. Roosevelt to Quay, 14 and 17 October 1902, MSQP, box 9, fld. 11, LC, MD.

24. Otero, *My Nine Years,* 328. On McMillan's removal, *New York Times,* 23 June 1903, 1.

25. Otero's recollection of the president's remark (including the strategic use of a dash) is found in Otero, *My Nine Years,* 328; also see ibid., 326–28 on McMillan's conduct as a public official.

26. The late nineteenth century had seen several strong advocates of joint statehood, particularly in debates between 1885 and 1890 over admitting North and South Dakota, with proposals by Senator Benjamin Harrison (R-Ind.) and particularly congressman and chair of the House Committee on Territories William McKendree Springer (D-Ill.). For a succinct account of Roosevelt, Quay, and Hanna's "political dances" during 1901–1903, see Kehl, *Boss Rule,* 236–37. On Hanna and his opposition to Roosevelt, which produced "swearing and thumping dramatically on his desk" at the mention of his name in the months prior to the convention, see Morris, *Rise of Theodore Roosevelt,* 719–20, quoted 719.

27. *Washington Post,* 9 May 1902, 4; Beveridge to Shaw, 29 November 1902, AJBP, box 282, LC, MD.

28. Beveridge to Shaw, 16 November 1906, ibid. Beveridge to Shaw, 19 December 1902, ibid.

29. *Washington Post,* 9 December 1902, 4; Spiess to Otero, 18 December 1902, MAOP, MSS 21 BC, box 1, fld. 1, CSWR, UL, UNM; Otero, *My Nine*

Years, 216–17, 325.

30. Gould, *Presidency of Theodore Roosevelt*, 123–29. Great Loop is in Brinkley, *Wilderness Warrior*, 507–509, 524–25.

31. *Atlanta Constitution*, 22 January 1903, 5. Discussion of expanding presidential power is in Roosevelt, *Autobiography*, 371–72.

32. *Los Angeles Times*, 26 February 1903, 6.

33. *New York Times*, 5 February 1903, 3.

34. Roosevelt to Quay, 7 October 1903, 12 November 1903, MSQP, box 10, fld. 1, LC, MD; Beveridge to Aldrich, 2 July 1903, NWAP, microfilm reel 24, LC, MD; Beveridge to Aldrich, 7 September 1903, ibid.

35. Pancoast, "Presidential Visit," 45.

36. The only complete text of President Theodore Roosevelt's speech is reproduced in Otero, *My Nine Years*, 322–24. Quotations, ibid., 323; *New York Times*, 6 May 1903, 3; *Las Cruces Progress*, 25 April 1903, 4 (train tickets); *Santa Fe New Mexican*, 5 May 1903, 1 (audience response).

37. *El Combate*, 16 May 1903, 2.

38. *Washington Post*, 6 May 1903, 3; clipping, *New York Tribune*, 7 June 1903, BSRP, MSS 175 BC, box 1, Scrapbook, CSWR, UL, UNM. An eyewitness's recollection is Pancoast, "Presidential Visit," 45.

39. *Las Cruces Progress*, 25 April 1903, 4. See Morison, *Cowboys and Kings*, 14 for Roosevelt's comment.

40. Need for a translator in 1912, see *New York Times*, 9 March 1919, 35. The impact Edmond Demoulins' book had on Roosevelt is in Brinkley, *Wilderness Warrior*, 317–18.

41. *Washington Post*, 2 July 1899, 13.

42. *La Voz del Pueblo*, 9 May 1903, 1.

43. On the Las Vegas Board of Trade, see *Las Vegas Optic*, 4 May 1901, 1.

44. *Las Cruces Progress*, 21 March 1903, 4; *La Bandera Americana*, 29 January 1904, 2.

45. For 1900 census data on New Mexico's towns, see Williams, ed., *New Mexico in Maps*, 132. The largest communities, in order, were Albuquerque including Old Town at 8,848; Las Vegas City with Old Town; Santa Fe; Raton; Gallup; Las Cruces; and finally Silver City with 2,735. The second tier of towns with more than 1,000 but fewer than 2,500 were, in order: Roswell with 2,049; the mining town of Santa Rita; Alamogordo; Socorro; Deming; and Taos at 1,125. The communities of fewer than 1,000 inhabitants were, in order: Carlsbad, 963; Wagon Mound; Lordsburg; Tularosa; Belen; Kelly (three miles south of Magdalena and now a ghost town); Magdalena; and Dawson at 100 (also a ghost town).

46. Comparative data on New Mexico and New York, Bureau of the Census, *Twelfth Census*, 1:2, 6. While only two territories (Ala., Ariz.) and two states (Nev., Wyo.) had fewer people per square mile than New Mexico, New York trailed only four states (R.I., N.J., Mass., Conn.) and the District of Columbia in population density. On Sagamore Hill, see Roosevelt, *Autobiography*, 328–30, quoted at

330. Brinkley, *Wilderness Warrior*, especially chaps. 1–4, on Roosevelt as amateur naturalist. Just a month prior to his trip to the West, on 14 March 1903, President Roosevelt decreed creation of the first of the fifty-one bird reservations established during his tenure in seventeen states and territories—with two in New Mexico. Following his departure from New Mexico, his stop at the Grand Canyon on 6 May is hailed as "one of greatest days in environmental history" because it sparked his resolve to preserve forever this natural treasure; see ibid., chap. 19, quoted 526.

47. García, ed., *Abuelitos*, 242. On birds' rights activities, see Brinkley, *Wilderness Warrior*, 354–69.

48. *El Hispano Americano*, February 1905, 2, reproduced this news item from the *Santa Fe New Mexican*.

49. Rivera, Acequia Culture, especially chaps. 1 and 2. This account of economic and agricultural patterns in the Rio Puerco Valley is drawn from two collections of their traditions, see: Garcia, ed., *Abuelitos*, and Garcia, ed., *Recuerdos de los Viejitos*. A different chronology of the Rio Puerco Valley's settlement and the overuse of its land is in Nostrand, *Hispano Homeland*, 88–90.

50. My narrative of this excursion is drawn from various published sources: Proctor, *William Randolph Hearst*, 182–83; Nasaw, *Chief*, 171–72; *Washington Post*, 23 October 1903, 6; *Atlanta Constitution*, 18 October 1903, B4.

51. Clipping, *Chicago Examiner*, 13 October 1903, BSRP, MSS 175 BC, Scrapbook, CSWR, UL, UNM.

52. Quoted in *Washington Post*, 25 October 1903, 5. For a poignant last communication, see Roosevelt to Quay, 28 May 1904, MSQP, box 10, fld. 2, LC, MD.

53. Sarasohn, "Election of 1916," 287, 289, 296–97.

Chapter 4

1. Otero, *My Nine Years*, 99–101. A later tribute to Chaves is Walter, et al., *Colonel José Francisco Chaves*. A hearsay confession is "Interview of Prisoner George W. Mosher in the Matter of Charles Bell's Confession," 29 January 1906, GovHJHP, TANM, reel 162, NMSL. Chaves owned at least ten thousand acres in Valencia County, and following the creation of Torrance County in 1903 he began to acquire land there through the Homestead Act; see Chaves to Sedillo, 5 January 1904, Misc. L&D, box 2, fld. 40, ser. # 15818, SRCA.

2. *New York Times*, 28 November 1904, 1; *Washington Post*, 28 November 1904, 1. *Los Angeles Times*, 25 August 1904, 2, is an early report, but the kidnapping received more sensational attention in accounts printed several months later: *Washington Post*, 4 December 1904, E3; *Atlanta Constitution*, 4 December 1904, 3. Duran, "Francisco Chavez, Thomas B. Catron," 291–94, surveys violence.

3. *El Nuevo Mundo*, 29 May 1897, 1. An article from the *Des Moines Register and Leader* reprinted in *Washington Post*, 4 January 1905, 6, discussed homicide and the 1900 census. A collection of essays on violence in the territory is Torrez, *Myth of the Hanging Tree*.

4. *New York Times*, 3 November 1905, 6, called into question statehood because of violence. The Mounted Police are discussed in Ball, *Desert Lawmen*, 296–98. On the shifting public mood and expectations for territories, see Lamar, "Statehood," 115–17.

5. "Chaotic factionalism" is described in Owens, "Pattern and Structure," 377. For Otero's political capital garnered by supporting the Rough Rider regiment, see Twitchell, *Leading Facts*, 525–26.

6. Roosevelt's management principles and practices are discussed in Gould, *Presidency of Theodore Roosevelt*, 189–214. Roosevelt's clean government bias is in Blum, *Republican Roosevelt*, 12–21.

7. *La Bandera Americana*, 12 February 1904, 3.

8. *Washington Post*, 24 June 1904, 6. For examples of interviews Otero had with national reporters, see *Washington Post*, 4 August 1904, 6; *Chicago Daily Tribune*, 27 December 1904, 3.

9. Otero, *My Nine Years as Governor*, 139, is Otero's version of the revolt against Rodey.

10. On Hubbell, ibid., 240–45. Circular, 20 October 1903, ELBP, MSS 153 BC, box 1, fld. 5, CSWR, UL, UNM is an attack on Hubbell. Quotations on the ouster, in order, are *La Voz del Pueblo*, 15 October 1904, 1, 3, 1. On Chaves's political activities in Torrance County, see ibid., 15 October 1904, 2.

11. Andrews to Los Votantes del Nuevo Mexico, 17 September 1904, LBPP, Col. #1959-174, box 1, fld. 22, SRCA. Rodey to Dear Friend, 22 October 1904, ibid. On intimidation and vote buying, see *La Voz del Pueblo*, 19 November 1904, 2.

12. An unflattering but no doubt accurate description of Andrews's relationship with Senator Quay is in Kehl, *Boss Rule*, 113 ("henchmen"), 190 (a political "Machiavelli"), and 210 ("machine politician"). The symbiotic relationship between Quay and Andrews in New Mexico between 1900 and 1904 is ibid, 244–48.

13. One of the properties Andrews controlled along the route of his railroad was a salt bed in Torrance County, which he immediately commercialized by demanding payment from "the thousands of people who until then were used to getting salt there without paying anyone for it." see *La Voz del Pueblo*, 29 October 1904, 2.

14. *Washington Post*, 5 December 1905, 2, 5 November 1905, 6.

15. On the investment climate, see *Atlanta Constitution*, 15 February 1903, B7; Braeman, *Albert J. Beveridge*, 85–86; Kehl, *Boss Rule*, 247–48.

16. *Philadelphia Inquirer*, 18 and 22 April 1899, 1. On the bank's failure, *New York Times*, 19 October 1905, 1; *Philadelphia Inquirer*, 19 October 1905, 1. On Clark's final hours, *Wilkes-Barre Times*, 19 October 1905, 1.

17. *New York Times*, 3 November 1905, 6; on the arrest warrants, ibid., 27 March 1906, 3. Nichols's acquittal, *Philadelphia Inquirer*, 8 November 1907, 2. The government did find Andrews liable for $450,000 owed by the Pennsylvania Development Company; see ibid., 6 June 1907, 4. *Wilkes-Barre Times*, 13 November 1907, 7, reported an indictment charged Andrews with fraud and collusion

with the Pennsylvania treasurer in depositing state money in the bank, but the case fell apart before trial.

18. *La Voz del Pueblo*, 19 November 1904, 2. Otero's nepotism, ibid., 15 October 1904, 2.

19. Ibid., 2 June 1906, 1.

20. *Washington Post*, 11 March 1905, 1. On the plots and the overall loss of administrative control, see *Los Angeles Times*, 24 September 1905, IV 12. The divorce papers are found in his attorney's records, *Caroline Emmett Otero v. Miguel A. Otero*, 7 October 1909, GWPFP, MSS 187 BC, box 1, fld. 6, CSWR, UL, UNM. Otero subsequently remarried, to Maud Frost, his second Euro-American wife. Federal legislation on marriage and divorce, *Washington* Post, 8 December 1906, 13.

21. Eblen, *First and Second*, 271–86. Public announcement of his removal, *Washington Post*, 25 November 1905, 4. On longevity, Eblen, *First and* Second, 271, 285 n. 13.

22. Roosevelt to Hagerman, 13 March 1906, in Morrison, *Letters*, 5:177.

23. Kanegsberg, *Addresses*, 119.

24. *Washington Post*, 6 December 1905, 2; Foraker, *Notes*, 2:184–89. On challenging Roosevelt, see *New York Times*,13 December 1905, 4.

25. *Washington Post*, 10 March 1906, 4.

26. *Washington Post*, 9 April 1906, 4; *New York Times*, 3 June 1906, 7. On the compromise as it unfolded, see *Atlanta Constitution*, 18 April 1906, 8; *Washington Post*, 2 June 1906, 4. For coverage of the "political pyrotechnics," ibid., 14 June 1906, 1.

27. *El Tiempo*, 17 January 1903, 1; *Carlsbad Argus*, 18 September 1903, 1,8; *El Combate*, 5 December 1903, 1.

28. Nuevomexicanos would support whatever Congress approved; see *El Labrador*, 13 February de 1903, 1.

29. For the Spanish and English text of President Roosevelt's letter, dated 27 June, see *El Labrador*, 13 July 1906, 2; *New York Times*, 4 July 1906, 2.

30. Martin's letter, *New Mexican Review*, 12 July 1906, 7. Rodey's letter, *La Voz del Pueblo*, 18 August 1906, 1. Bipartisan support, *Albuquerque Morning Journal*, 25 September 1906, 7. Highlights of the fight over joint statehood are in Leonard, "Joint Statehood"; Andrews's strategy, ibid., 244.

31. Foraker, *Notes*, 2:189. Arizonans reportedly believed it imperative to defeat jointure decisively. A narrow rejection would, they feared, mean that "Congress will pass a joint Statehood act, forcing the Territory into union with New Mexico"; see *Los Angeles Times*, 21 October 1906, V 18. Congress required each Territory to approve it separately, but the measure also fell short by 1,664 votes when the total combined vote of 60,336 is considered: 29,336 in favor and 31,000 opposed.

32. *New York Times*, 3 February 1905, 6.

33. On the election returns, see *Albuquerque Morning Journal*, 9 & 10 November 1906, p. 1.

34. *La Voz del Pueblo,* 10 November 1906, 1. Mining companies had long and routinely manipulated voting; see Zinn, "Colorado Coal Strike," 11. On Republican papers alleging fraud in the election, *La Voz del Pueblo,* 17 November 1906, 1.

35. *La Voz del Pueblo,* 13 October 1906, 1, anti-Andrews articles and Republican pro-Larrrazolo papers.

36. All quotations in this dispute are from the newspaper *La Voz del Pueblo,* 2 June 1906, 1.

37. Ibid.

38. Ibid.

39. *Washington Post,* 13 June 1905, 6; *New York Times,* 20 August 1905, SM3; Larson, *New Mexico's Quest,* 303.

40. Congress, HR,. *Contested Election Case,* 3–30 for summary of Larrazolo's charges; 31–57 for summary of Andrews's replies; and 58–67 for Andrews's countercharges against Larrazolo. On Larrazolo's accusation of illegal activities by mining companies; see ibid., 276–79.

41. Ibid., 31.

42. Bogue and Bogue, eds., *Jeffersonian Dream,* 43–45. The most complete account of a single investigation (from Oregon) is Messing, "Public Lands." For western land fraud cases, including ones in New Mexico, giving rise to a special investigative unit within the Justice Department, see Special Agent Findlay to Director Hoover, 19 November 1943, at Historical Documents from the Bureau's Founding, www.fbi.gov.

43. Twitchell, *Leading Facts,* 2: 522; Congress, HR, *Sale of Certain Lands,* 2–4; correspondence summarizing findings by the Justice Department and Congress, Roosevelt to Hagerman, 1 May 1907, in Twitchell, *Leading Facts,* 2:555–57 n. 467.

44. Congress, HR, *Sale of Certain Lands,* 2–4.

45. On Hagerman's mandate, Twitchell, *Leading Facts,* 2:554. Hitchcock's criticism, *Washington Post,* 15 July 1906, 13. For ongoing land fraud investigations, *Washington Post,* 8 July 1906, 5. On meeting between Roosevelt and Garfield, see PJRG, JRG Diary 1907, box 8, LC, MD.

46. For the extensive confidential files of the secretary of the interior regarding the investigations into land fraud in New Mexico during Governors Otero and Hagerman's tenures, see NARA II, RG 126, OS, Terr., boxes 731, 732. Early calls for a formal investigation, Llewellyn to Roosevelt, 1 December 1906, ibid., box 732, and Moody to Roosevelt, 16 October 1906, ibid., box 731. A defense of the benefits of the Territory's land sales is Kelly, *Buffalo Head,* 72–78.

47. On the forwarded reports, see Roosevelt to Garfield, 27 March 1907, NARA II, RG 126, OS, Terr., box 732. *Santa Fe New Mexican,* 18 March 1907, 1; *Las Vegas Optic,* 18 March 1907, 1.

Shortly after being dismissed from office, Governor Hagerman published at his own expense a booklet in his defense (Hagerman, *Statement*). Hagerman never convincingly explained his actions in the land sales, and it was this transgression that most concerned the president. But in Hagerman's defense, it needs to be remembered that he alienated the powerful Republican leader Holm O. Bursum and thereby precipitated a rift that fueled more "chaotic factionalism" within the Territory. For Hagerman's version of the origin of the conflict with Bursum, see ibid., 7–9. For a revealing eyewitness account by a member of the prison's oversight board, highly critical of Hagerman's judgment and management practices, see Twitchell, *Leading Facts*, 2: 553–54 n. 466. Clearly Hagerman overreached in a situation he knew to be highly charged and created an enemy by dismissing Bursum amid allegations of theft of public money. A court eventually found no basis for the malfeasance alleged, but by then the enmity of these two led to bitterness and retaliation that divided Republicans in the Territory.

A double standard existed in making accusations. As seen in fraudulent land sales involving Holt and Andrews, a number of prominent Republicans in the Territory had benefited from improper land transactions and no Territorial Republican politician said anything; however, when it surfaced that Hagerman's father had made such transactions, the governor's opponents proclaimed shock and dismay at the revelation. For the explanation from father to son about this "suspect" land acquisition, see J. J. Hagerman to H. J. Hagerman, 21 May 1906, GovHJHP, TANM, reel 162, NMSL.

48. Roosevelt to Garfield, 11 February 1907, NARA II, RG 126, OS, Terr., box 731.Exchange of correspondence, Roosevelt to Hagerman, 1 May 1907, in Twitchell, *Leading Facts*, 2:555–57 n. 467 and Hagerman to Roosevelt, 15 May 1907, ibid., 2:558–59 n. 468. For national newspaper coverage of the tiff, see *New York Times*, 31 May 1907, 2.

49. *New York Times*, 3 December 1902, 2. On the origins of this bill, see Pisani, *To Reclaim*.

50. For the impact of federal actions on water policy and practices in New Mexico in the wake of the Reclamation Act, see Clark, *Water in New Mexico*, 67–99; Hall, *High and Dry*, 24–47; Baxter, *Dividing New Mexico's Waters*, 79–106.

51. Gould, *Presidency of Theodore Roosevelt*, 189–90.

52. *New York Times*, 3 December 1902. 2 For the convoluted early history of this federal-private dispute, see Clark, "The Elephant Butte Controversy."

53. Boyd to Otero, 8 March 1901, GovMAOP, TANM, reel 130, NMSL, 31 August 1901, ibid., reel 131. For early federal activity at Elephant Butte, Sullivan, *Report of the Territorial Engineer*, 16.

54. Teller, "The State's Control Over Its Water," 3–8 quoted 4, 3; Boyd sent copies to everyone he knew; see LBPP, serial # 14019, fld. 54, SRCA.

55. On the Culberson-Stephens Bill, Clark, *Water in New Mexico*, 95–97, 714 n. 47; and Boyd, *New Mexico and Statehood*. Nuevomexicanos as laborers on the new dam, see Interview, Frank and Frieda Montoya by David Holtby, July 2008, in the author's possession.

56. Bogener, *Ditches Across the Desert*, 143–81, quoted 156, 167. On the monopolizing effects of requests for federal dollars to aid Carlsbad's irrigation schemes,

Hervey to Bursum, 14 August 1922, HOBP, MS 305, box 56, fld. 22, RGHC, ASC, NMSU.

57. Andrews to Los Votantes del Nuevo Mexico, 17 September 1904, LBPP, col. #1959-174, box 1, fld. 22. Twitchell, *Leading Facts*, 2:558 n. 468.

Chapter 5

1. "The Recent," *Musical Visitor*, 327.

2. Opera houses, see box 10, flds. 1–3, box 11, fld. 3, RCHC, AC 110, FACHL, NMHM.

3. Frank, *From Settler to Citizen*, 47–48. The censuses of 1850 and 1900 are summarized in comparative statistics included in the 1910 census, see Bureau of the Census, *Thirteenth Census*, 3:158, 169, 171–72, 176–81. Mitchell, *Coyote Nation*, 11, places the Nuevomexicano population much lower, at 93,356, in 1900. His figure is based on secondary source data cited by Gutmann et al., "Los efectos demográficos," 150, 153. To reconcile these very low estimates with the actual census data from 1900 requires including children under fifteen years of age, who accounted for 39 percent of the total population in 1900. Assuming equal distribution among Nuevomexicanos, adding 36,408 (39 percent) brings the total to 129,764, or 3.9 percent below my figure. The clearest statement in census reports on the number of Nuevomexicanos in 1900, and the basis of my calculations, is found in Bureau of the Census, *Twelfth Annual Census*, v. 1, *Population*, Part I (Washington, D.C.: U.S. Census Office, 1901), p. cxvii.

4. Limerick, *Legacy of Conquest*, 82–87, on expanding federal presences.

5. Horn, *New Mexico's Troubled Years*, 21–35, covers Calhoun's governorship. On "peace structure," Montejano, *Anglos and Mexicans*, 34, 310. My analysis of Nuevomexicano political culture is a reformulation of a large body of data found in Ramirez's dissertation, "The Hispanic Political Elite," part II, 401–588. Declining numbers of Nuevomexicano legislators are noted in *El Nuevo Mexicano*, 3 November 1906, 1. Two non-elite Nuevomexicano families who produced politicians as part of the post-1879 generation are discussed in Peña, *Memories of Cíbola*, 5–30.

6. Baxter, *Dividing New Mexico's Waters*, 83.

7. Mitchell, *Coyote Nation*, 149–73; Deutsch, *No Separate Refuge*, 55–56; Kelly, *Buffalo Head*, 21–29, 103–20; Brown et al., *Hispano Folklife*, 93–95; Jaramillo, *Romance*, 83–90, 120–26, all discuss aspects of consumerism leading up to statehood. Also useful as sources on consumerism are the nearly fifty debtor petitions in bankruptcy filings beginning in 1898, see boxes 1–6, Bankruptcy, NMDC, 4th, RG 21, NARA-D. Spanish-language newspapers between 1900 and 1912, particularly *La Bandera Americana*, had many advertisements on pages 1 and 2 of each issue for products and services aimed at Nuevomexicanos. Parish, *Charles Ilfeld Company*, 35–97, analyzes mercantile capitalism 1870–1900.

8. Flint and Flint, "Fort Union and the Economy," 27–55, for early wage labor. On Nuevomexicanos and the sheep trade as an indicator of modernization, see

Baxter, *Las Carneradas*. On Nuevomexicanos and the Santa Fe Trail trade, Boyle, *Los Capitalistas*. See Deutsch, *No Separate Refuge*, 13–40 on labor migration, and 33–34 on sugar beet workers. On the migration tracked by the 1900 census, see *Twelfth Census of the United States*, 1: cxxx. Other socioeconomic data from the 1900 census are in Nostrand, *Hispano Homeland*, 131–49. Institutionalized migration is from deBuys, *Enchantment and Exploitation*, 206.

Another source on Nuevomexicano migrations is petitions as part of adjudication by the U.S. Land Office, with the issue of occupancy compromised by extended absences. See, for example, a Nuevomexicano claimant who had worked his homestead continuously since April 1903 and in March 1910 noted he always "would go away for two months or so, to work for the support of his family who always remained on the land," file 0761-0808, 8 March 1910, box 2, NM, Comm. Re: Entries, SF, RG 49, NARA-D. A multigeneration account on labor migration is in file 02157-02179, 16 June 1915, box 5, ibid.

9. Hoffmann, *Depression of the Nineties*. Remley, *Bell Ranch*, 152–60, for seventy-plus Nuevomexicano families dispossessed in eastern New Mexico in the 1890s but also aided in securing homesteads on the public domain.

10. On Tejano loss of land after 1885 and especially in the 1890s, see Alonzo, *Tejano Legacy*, 227–70. Watrous to Andrews, 26 December 1910, serial no. 14019, fld. 41, LBPP, SRCA for quotation, also Watrous to Andrews, 29 April 1911, fld. 33, ibid. On tax collecting, Ball, *Desert Lawmen*, 246–64. Nuevomexicano tax delinquency and foreclosures 1899–1904, *Santa Fe New Mexican*, 16 January 1904, 1. For a recollection of that era's problematic tax policies by a leading politician, see clipping Thornton to *Santa Fe New Mexican*, 8 February 1913, serial no. 14019, fld. 62, LBPP, col. #1959-174, SRCA. In her dissertation, Moussalli, "Accounting for Government," 30–31, found taxes were undercollected and underassessed in the territorial period. On criticism of the lack of official land surveys, see *Santa Fe New Mexican*, 4 September 1901, 1.

11. Otero, *Report of the Governor of New Mexico, 1904*, 13. County populations in 1910, Bureau of the Census, *Thirteenth Census*, 3: 163–67.

12. The data are from land office records for Nuevomexicano and Euro-American surnamed individuals and retrieved through searches on land entries available at the database www.glorecords.blm.gov. I am indebted to Dr. Kari Schleher who, as my research assistant while completing her Ph.D., brought to the task of compiling this data the same painstaking care she exhibits in her fieldwork in southwest archaeology.

13. Smith, "Single Women Homesteaders," 161–82; Harris, "Homesteading in Northeastern Colorado," 165–78. Data about Nuevomexicanas in 1900 are in Jensen, *Promise to the Land*, 83–84.

14. Montoya, "Wedding Chest," 43–45. The complexities of race, class, gender, identity, and social norms in New Mexico between 1880 and 1930 have given rise two recent books, Mitchell, *Coyote Nation* and Nieto-Phillips, *Language of Blood*. Their sources are outstanding entry points for pursuing these issues.

15. Nostrand, *El Cerrito*, 66–90. Remley, *Bell Ranch*, 158–60, offers a nuanced discussion of Nuevomexicano adaptation to the loss of their land by taking up homesteads. Some Nuevomexicano families went south into the Stanley area to homestead after 1901, personal communication Yolanda Pacheco to author, July 2008.

16. Roosevelt and Gifford Pinchot worked against reelection of those opposing the administration's conservation policies; see for example, McHarg to Nagel, 31 August 1909, reel 6, RABP, MS Coll. 0015-001, UWLSC. Ringland's background and his account of the National Forest Homestead Act are in "[Arthur C. Ringland] Oral History Transcript," 1–32, Ringland Oral History Interview, Bancroft Library, University of California at Berkeley, available online at Internet Archive Texts.

17. C. de Baca to Fergusson, 22 September 1913, box 2, fld. 13, GovECdeBP, col. # 1959-095, SRCA. Supreme Court's ruling on the San Miguel del Vado land grant, *United States v. [Julian] Sandoval* (1897), 167 U.S. 278.

18. Secretary of the Interior, *Reports for the Fiscal Year 1914*, 113. Nationwide for the same period 1,405,000 acres were restored as homesteads, ibid., 145. In New Mexico, accounts of restoration of homesteading are in *La Revista de Taos*, 9 December 1910, 3; *La Voz del Pueblo*, 11 March 1911, 4; Nostrand, *El Cerrito*, 66–90; Hall, "San Miguel del Bado," 415–23. For a Nuevomexicano making a "speculative claim," file 0304-0379, 13 September 1910, box 1, NM, Comm. Re: Entries, SF, RG 49, NARA-D.

19. DeBuys, *Enchantment and Exploitation*, 177, 197, and 223–25 for examples of the effects in villages of land subdivision and ceaseless cultivation and/or grazing throughout the Territorial Period. *Las Cruces Progress*, 21 March 1903, 4, and *La Bandera Americana*, 29 January 1904, 2, on new industries in Albuquerque. On Barelas and San José, see Simmons, *Albuquerque*, 298, 338. On the railroad, Nostrand, *Hispano Homeland*, 143. Mitchell, "You Just Don't Know," 437–58 on Albuquerque's social milieu and its impact on Nuevomexicanos. Four private communications readily elicited family stories about pull factors associated with improved opportunity: Juan Mora (Albuquerque); Ernesto and Richard Chavez (Tucumcari); Felix Trujillo (San Marcial); Frank and Frieda Montoya (Elephant Butte Dam). More migration stories are in Griego, *Voices*, 8–9, 18–19, 24, 35, 64–66, 71–74, 75–76, 84–85, 105–106.

20. *Garcia de Garcia v. Sandoval*, box 1, DCUS, NMTR, 1st, Misc., RG 21, NARA-D. On the Guadalupe Country post offices, see reel 382, 60A/01, NMPO, RG 28, NARA I. Dike, "Territorial Post Offices," 324.

21. Tobias, *History of the Jews*, 65–79, for a succinct account of how early territorial merchants created a kind of vertical integration in their control over financial transactions. On mercantile capitalism as a source of economic stimulus, see Kelly, *Buffalo Head*, 65–78. See Parish, *Charles Ilfeld Company*, 150–73, on the *partido* system, and 169, on a generally favorable assessment of its impact. Another, harsher view of Ilfeld's activities involving an Anglo partidario is found in a bank-

ruptcy suit filed almost immediately after the Congress enacted bankruptcy legislation in 1898; see Gerhardt, Box 2, NMDC, 4th, Bankruptcy, RG 21, NARA-D. Rothman, *On Rims and Ridges*, 20–38 for the negative results of Nuevomexicanos entering the wage labor economy. In one of the great ironies of economic valuation, rare coin collectors now pay premium prices for scrip. For example, an uncirculated scrip issued by Spiegelberg Hermanos in their Santa Fe store from January 1863, printed in Spanish for a value of *cincuenta centavos* [fifty cents], sells for over $9,000. I am indebted to Jesse Roberge for information on prices in the collector market.

22. Boyle, *Los Capitalistas*, 10–12, on the socioeconomic divide between Nuevomexicanos of the río abajo and the río arriba. A Nuevomexicano in the río abajo expanding enterprises and continuing to be financially successful after 1848 is discussed in Simmons, *The Little Lion*, 147–49, 189–219. In Las Cruces, Martin Amador's considerable business acumen is noteworthy and discussed in Stephens, "Women of the Amador Family," 258–62. On tariff policy, see Congress, Senate, *Memorial of the National Woolgrowers'*, quoted at 110. One of the wealthiest Nuevomexicanos of the era, Solomon Luna from the río abajo, was assessed taxes of $28,837.31 by Valencia County in 1897, see serial no. 14019, fld. 39, LBPP, col. #1959-174, SRCA.

23. DeBuys, *Enchantment and Exploitation*, 257, on post-1900 federal control of land grants. Intragrant rivalries, see Sánchez, *Between Two Rivers*, 154–74. On Las Gorras Blancas, Arellano, "The People's Movement," 59–82. Criticism of the land-grant board is in Undated [1913] typescript, box 2, fld. 13, GovECdeBP, Col. #1959-095, SRCA.

24. Norris and Ingelhart, *Sacred and Secular*, 53; on "The Secularization Debate," see ibid, 3–32.

25. Salas, "Ethnicity, Gender, and Divorce," 369–70; Mitchell, "'You Just Don't Know,'" 440–42.

26. Griego, *Voices of the Territory*, 35–36.

27. Jaramillo, *Romance*, 71, 69–72, 91–108, and quoted 107.

28. Stephens, "Women of the Amador Family," 257–77, quoted 270.

29. For the records of cases from the First Judicial District, see cases # 1233-1343, CD, DCUS, NM, 1st, RG 21, NARA-D. On the Fifth Judicial District, see boxes 1, 2, USCommCF, DCUS, NM, 5th, RG 21, NARA-D.

30. Nuevomexicana with four lovers, *U.S. v. Gonzales*, 31 July 1896, box 1, ibid. *Washington Post*, 13 January 1902, 4.

31. Mitchell, *Coyote Nation*, 55 on racializing sex crimes. Simmons, *Witchcraft*, 36. On divorce in the West, see Riley, *Building and Breaking Families*, 116–17.

32. Nieto-Phillips, *Language of Blood*, 200–204, and Jaramillo, *Romance*, xvi–xviii, 173–83; Steele, *Bishop Lamy*, 43; Horgan, *Lamy of Santa Fe*, is the standard biography and received the Pulitzer Prize for history in 1976.

33. *Revista Católica*, V. 15 (14 April 1889), 3–5, quoted 4.

34. The article from *La Demócrata de Mora* is reproduced in *Revista Católica*,

V. 15 (28 April 1889), 4. The Jesuits disapproved of the Mora newspaper meddling in Church matters with its endorsement of the political influence of the Penitentes, but Mora—like Taos—had long been an epicenter of dissent. A little more than a year later, *Revista Católica* vehemently denied an accusation in a letter sent from Tucson that Jesuits had ever established or supported a *penitente morada*; see *Revista Católica*, V. 16 (29 June 1890), 5. In 1881, a year after Lamy's denunciation, Army Lieutenant John G. Bourke reconnoitered much of New Mexico and testified to the overwhelming influence of *los hermanos penitentes*; see Kessell, *Missions*, 102; Lummis, *Land*, 78–79. The scholar quoted is Weigle, *Brothers of Light*, 96. The Catholic official quoted is Monsignor Jerome J. Martínez y Alire, rector of the Cathedral Church of Saint Francis of Assisi in Santa Fe (2011), see "Foreword" in Steele, ed. and trans., *The Alabados*, xiv.

35. Marta Weigle, *Brothers of Light* remains an authoritative account. Her attention to social welfare activities remains an essential insight into their pivotal role in communities. On their political role, especially in the decades between 1910 and 1940, see Holmes, *Politics*, 33–49. Holmes argues that voting by the Penitentes occurred after much discussion and that group cohesion stemmed from moral suasion rather than overt pressure. Anti-Catholic bias in Whig/Republican party politics is in Emmons, *Beyond the Pale*, 51–69. For allegiance to the Democratic Party, especially in cities, see ibid., 271–75.

36. Espinosa, "New Mexico," 11:4. Spain's church-state relations in general and resistance to secularizing education are discussed, respectively, in Callahan, "Catholicism," and Holtby, "Education, Primary and Secondary."

37. On the Marian tradition in New Mexico, see *Revista Católica*, V. 14 (5 August 1888), 8–9; ibid., 14:9–10 (26 August 1888), 9–10, quoted 10; and ibid., V. 20 (25 November 1894), 4–5. On the "feminization" of the faith in the nineteenth century, see Heilbronner, "The Age of Catholic Revival," 241–42.

38. Rivera, *La Sociedad*, 21. On the importance of acequia associations, see Rivera, *Acequia Culture*, chaps. 5, 6.

39. Rivera, *La Sociedad*, 51–55, quoted 53–54. Early calls for ethnic pride and labor organizing among Nuevomexicanos were made in editorials from Las Cruces' *El Labrador* in 1904; see Weber, *Foreigners*, 251–53.

40. Foner, "Class, Ethnicity, and Radicalism," 179, for the contention that anti-Catholicism in America had less impact after the 1890s. Religious affiliations in Indiana in 1900, see *Statesman's Yearbook*, 459.

41. The complete sermon is in Steele, ed., *New Mexico Spanish*, 212–15, quoted 215.

42. Stovall, ed., *Prose Works*, 2:552–54. An abridgment is in Wilson, *Myth of Santa Fe*, 188–89.

43. Miller, ed., *Walt Whitman*, "By Blue Ontario's Shore," 241; ibid., "Spain, 1873–74," 334.

44. Mack, *The Pragmatic Whitman*, chap. 7 and Conclusion, quoted 135–36.

45. Las Gorras Blancas is an important example of how popular will emerged

and evolved. My account is drawn largely from Arellano, "The People's Movement," 59–82, and Larson, "The Knights of Labor," 31–52.

46. *La Voz del Pueblo,* 14 November 1891, 1, quoted in Meyer, *Speaking for Themselves,* 12. For the quotation about *La Voz del Pueblo,* see Meléndez, *So All Is Not Lost,* 83.

47. On La Prensa Asociada Hispano-Americana, see ibid., chap. 3; quote in ibid., 63.

48. Ibid., 225 n. 10. My translation differs slightly from that found in Meléndez, 69–70. On the association's political partisanship and factionalism, ibid., 65. Democrat Ezéquiel C. de Baca served as the state's first lieutenant governor and its second governor before dying of tuberculosis in his second month in office in February 1916. Republican Nestor Montoya served as a U.S. Representative in the Sixty-seventh Congress (1921–23).

49. *La Bandera Americana,* 4 October 1901, 1. These six counties among the twenty in 1900 had the highest proportion of Nuevomexicano voters: Rio Arriba, Taos, Mora, San Miguel, Valencia, and Socorro. *El Labrador,* 4 October 1901, 3, on popular will at the convention.

50. For Walt Whitman's earliest and uncompromising declaration in favor of "the common man" as the essence of American government, see Whitman, "Preface," 411–12. His reworking of the same words and phrases is found in "By Blue Ontario's Shore," ibid., 244.

51. Morgan, *Inventing the People,* part 3, 235–306. A succinct, provocative piece on tensions within the concept of popular sovereignty is his 1983 essay reprinted in Morgan, *American Heroes,* 222–40. For another interpretation of early popular sovereignty, see Wood, *American Revolution,* 143–44. On the power of President Lincoln's Gettysburg Address to revive and redefine America's political formula, see Wills, *Lincoln at Gettysburg,* 121–47.

52. "Third International Seminar on Decolonization," 60–61.

53. *Albuquerque Morning Democrat,* 29 September 1901, clipping in BSRP, Scrapbook, MSS 175 BC, box 1, CSWR, UL, UNM. Eblen, *First and Second* on U.S. territories as internal colonies of the United States.

54. *La Revista de Taos,* 20 February 1904, 1.

55. Frank, *From Settler to Citizen,* 228–33.

Chapter 6

1. *Albuquerque Morning Journal,* 9 August 1907, 4.

2. Census data for 1900 and 1910 are from *Thirteenth Census,* 3:169–81.

3. Ibid., 171.

4. Gómez, *Manifest Destinies,* 117–71. Nullification is discussed in the dissertation by Moussalli, "Accounting for Government," 129–30.

5. Secretary of the Interior, *Report of the Governor* [1903], 495–98.

6. Ibid., 497.

7. Ibid.

8. Deloria, *Indians in Unexpected*, 231. Lyons, *X-Marks*.

9. Serna and Steely, "Mescalero Apache," at www.newmexicohistory.org,

10. Secretary of the Interior, *Report of the Governor* [1903], 498.

11. Secretary of the Interior, *Report of the Governor* [1902], 439.

12. Ibid., 505.

13. Allen, *Sacred Hoop,* 31. Her three essays in part 1, "The Ways of Our Grandmothers," discuss examples of woman-centered cultures among American Indians. On sacredness as a lifeway, see Swentzell, "Pueblo Space," 45–48. On homemaking and the role of teachers, Secretary of the Interior, *Report of the Governor* [1903], 505. Jacobs, *Engendered Encounters*, especially chaps. 1 and 2 for agency at the turn of the twentieth century. The colonial era assault on Indian culture is argued in Gutiérrez, *When Jesus Came.* A succinct discussion of Indian education in the territorial era is Connell-Szasz, "Cultural Encounters," 204–205. These sources reveal a continuum of responses by Native peoples to domination. Collective resistance, community assertiveness, and cultural continuity provided some models in guiding people's survival. But increasingly evident since the 1950s is the loss of cultural habits and traditions vital to maintaining balanced lives. The late twentieth century gave rise to research that confronted historical trauma and its negative impact on human behavior. First steps in effecting emotional recovery are under way in programs and processes that restore resilience and reclaim wholeness in people's lives. For American Indians in New Mexico, significant developments include two projects at the University of New Mexico: the work of Dr. Maria Yellow Horse Brave Heart at the UNM Department of Psychiatry Outreach Office in assisting healing through resolving historical grief and the numerous discussions of healing strategies offered on *Native America Calling,* a daily radio broadcast that originates at KUNM (89.9 FM).

14. For the classic statement on imperialism fracturing and the corresponding empowerment of the colonized, see Orwell, "Shooting an Elephant," 91–99. A summary of the Jicarilla Apache exploiting divisions and weaknesses within U.S. policy in the decades preceding statehood is Tiller, *Jicarilla Apache Tribe,* 97–98.

15. For the Dawes Act and the Jicarilla Apache, see Tiller, *Jicarilla Apache Tribe,* 99–117, and Emily Greenwald, *Reconfiguring the Reservation,* 1–34, 93–107. The difficulties an Indian agent had in implementing the allotment is in Secretary of the Interior, *Report of the Governor* [1903], 492.

16. Vlasich, *Pueblo Indian Agriculture,* 98–106. On Jicarilla Apache agriculture and returning students, see Secretary of the Interior, *Report of the Governor* [1903], 440–41. For extensive correspondence on Navajo and Pueblo Indians adapting to BIA agricultural, especially irrigation initiatives, see boxes 209, 210 (Navajo), 212 (Pueblo Indians), SC, I, RG 75, NARA I.

17. Russell, "Apache Medicine Dance," 367–72. Pueblo students' wintertime absences are noted in Secretary of the Interior, *Report of the Governor* [1903], 504. On the general theme of the persistence of traditional religious practices among

the Pueblos, particularly the adaptive and redemptive capacity of resistance and agency, see Ortiz, "Ritual Drama," 135–61. The Jemez confrontation was reported in *Albuquerque Morning Journal*, 23 March 1906, 7. On the U.S. government versus Pueblo religion in the early 1920s, see Wenger, *We Have A Religion*.

18. Weigle and Babcock, eds., *The Great Southwest*, 102 (founding), 168–71, (Elle of Ganado), 90 (artist's room).

19. "Recent Territorial Music," 327. On Roosevelt's Navajo blanket, see Pancoast, "Presidential Visit," 45. Elle of Ganado also made a blanket for President William Howard Taft in 1909.

20. Weigle and Babcock, eds. *Great Southwest*, 94.

21. Otero, *My Nine Years*, quoted 305, 304, 310.

22. "Daily Official Program, World's Fair, St. Louis, No. 181, Saturday, November 26, 1904—The Louisiana Purchase Exposition" (St. Louis: n.p., 1904), HCL, TRC. Marriott, *María*, 120.

23. Dilworth, *Imagining Indians*, is a cultural discourse analysis of the construction and production of Indian life.

24. Petition to "The President of the United States, The Department of the Interior, and Congress," 6 April 1904, RG 75, Letters Received, Land Division, 1880-1908, MEJNAM, NMSL. On the tax assessments, Abbott to Commissioner of Indian Affairs, 12 December 1904, ibid. and Governor of Pueblo of Acoma to Commissioner of Indian Affairs, 6 January 1905, ibid. On the Territorial Supreme Court's ruling upholding taxation of the Pueblo Indians, see Commissioner of Indian Affairs to Secretary of the Interior, 15 December 1904, RG 48, Records of the Office of the Secretary of the Interior, Letters Received, Indian Division, 1873-1905, MEJNAM, NMSL. On the repeated unsuccessful attempts to secure resolution in Congress of the Territory's taxation policy, U.S. Attorney General to Secretary of the Interior, 11 January 1907, Office of the Secretary of the Interior, BIA, RG 48, MEJNAM, NMSL. Beveridge discussed his work with several department officials in Beveridge to Whitman, 19 January 1910, box 96, AJBP, LC, MD; Bowers, *Beveridge*, 378–79.

25. *United States v. [Felipe] Sandoval*, 231 U.S. 28 [1913], 46. Ibid., 41 for the court's ruling on the exemption from taxation. In *United States v. Joseph*, 94 U.S. 614 [1876] the Supreme Court said the Pueblos were not Indians and not entitled to special status as wards of the government. Catron's use of the ruling is discussed in Sando, *Nee Hemish*, 35–36. On attitudes among some New Mexicans between 1913 and 1923 that contributed to the ill-fated Bursum Pueblo Lands Bill, see Crane, *Desert Drums*, 170–71.

26. Connell-Szasz, *Education and the American Indian*.

27. Three sources offer useful information: Folsom, *Black Cowboy*, 111 (café incident), 108–109 (homestead); Wagner, *Black Cowboys*, 140–55; and Gibson, "Blackdom," 225–31.

28. On African-American community initiatives in Kansas and Oklahoma, see Taylor, *In Search*, 138–52. Blackdom in the context of African-American colo-

nization is discussed in Baton and Walt, *A History of Blackdom.*

29. Woodward, *Origins,* quoted 352, on lynchings, 351–52. His biography is Woodward, *Tom Watson.*

30. Woodward, *Origins,* quoted 353. The General Land Office patents for Boyer and other Blackdom homesteads are in the on-line archive for New Mexico entries at www.glorecords.blm.gov. Family names of Blackdom residents and history of the community are at www.soulofnewmexico.com, years 1901 and 1914. Homesteading urged to the west of Dexter, see [Dexter Historical Society], *As We Remember It,* 67. On the appeal of homesteads to African Americans, see Mock, *Bridges,* viii. On Blackdom in general, its school, and local reaction, ibid., 8–9.

In Justice Henry Brown's ruling for the majority in the Plessy decision, he separated political rights guaranteed in the Thirteenth and Fourteenth amendments from social and civil rights under the purview of the states. He wrote: "We consider the underlying fallacy of the plaintiff's argument [Homer Adolph Plessy] to consist in the assumption that the enforced separation of the two races stamps the colored race with a badge of inferiority. It this be so, it is not by reason of anything found in the act, but solely because the colored race chooses to put that construction upon it. . . . The argument also assumes that social prejudice may be overcome by legislation, and that equal rights cannot be secured except by an enforced commingling of the two races [163 U.S. 537 at 551]."

The sole dissent came from Justice John Marshall Harlan, who presciently voiced a legal argument decades ahead of the prevailing political and social milieu sustained by an oppressive state rights' position. He argued, "I am of the opinion that the statute of Louisiana is inconsistent with the personal liberties of citizens, white and black, in that State, and hostile to both the spirit and letter of the Constitution of the United States. . . . Slavery as an institution tolerated by law would, it is true, have disappeared from our country, but there would remain a power in the States, by sinister legislation, to interfere with the blessings of freedom; to regulate civil rights common to all citizens, upon the basis of race; and to place in a condition of legal inferiority a large body of American citizens, now constituting a part of the political community, called the people of the United States [163 U.S. 537 at 563]."

31. Mock, *Bridges,* 9. On Vado, Baton, *Do Remember Me,* 7–9.

32. On Malone, see www.soulofnewmexico.com, year 1901. Black business elite and unskilled laborers, see Mitchell, *Coyote Nation,* 15. On Madora B. Bailey, Mock, *Bridges,* 32. The short-lived newspaper *America* is referenced in *Colored American,* 12 October 1901, 3.

33. Railroad rates for colonists, *Washington [D.C.] Bee,* 21 March 1903, 1. On early community organizing by blacks in Albuquerque and three other cities, see Proclamation by Governor William J. Mills, Second National Negro Educational Congress [in Denver], 5 July 1911, box 731, SO, Terr., RG 126, NARA II.

34. On the NAACP, www.soulofnewmexico.com, year 1912. For quotation on the presence of black women's clubs in New Mexico, see Mock, *Bridges,* p. viii. On NACWC, see Wesley, *History of the National Association,* 501–6, on the day

nursery, 501.

35. Robinson, *The Fall.* On Flipper's background and court appointment, see *Colored American,* 19 March 1898, 1. His service to the court is described in Twitchell, *Leading Facts,* 2:472 n. 395.

36. *Colored American,* 8 September 1900, 6. The assessment is in Harris, comp. and ed., *Black Frontiersman,* 126.

37. Sutter, *New Mexico Baseball,* 128–29. Obituary is in *Albuquerque Morning Journal,* 23 June 1911, 6. On racism, see Baton, *Do Remember Me,* 13.

38. Quoted in Taylor, *In Search,* 219.

39. Jew Ki [Chiu Kai] file, box 408, INS, Chinese, RG 85, NARA I. One of seventy-two detention and deportation files in this box, it yielded many—but not all—of the details in this account. Economic gain sought by Chinese working in the U.S. is discussed in a Boston newspaper article reprinted in *Deming Headlight,* 26 November 1906, 4.

40. Jew Ki [Chiu Kai] file, box 408, INS, Chinese, RG 85, NARA I. For Agent Miller's four-page field report, see Miller to Commissioner-General, 8 August 1908, ibid. On the smugglers, see Berkshire to Commissioner-General, 12 December 1908, ibid.

41. The historical context draws on Lee, "Enforcing the Border," 54–86, 59; Hansen, "Chinese Six Companies," 37–61.

42. *Washington Post,* 31 March 1905, 4. California produce-growers' opposition is in *Albuquerque Morning Journal,* 5 December 1907, 1.

43. Bureau of the Census, *Thirteenth Census,* 3: 174. Chinese population decline was as follows: 361 (1890); 342 (1900); and 248 (1910). On the marriage, see [Dexter Historical Society], *As We Remembered It,* 67. On economic motives of Chinese immigrants, see Cash to U.S. Attorney General, 5 March 1909, box 408, INS, Chinese, RG 85, NARA I. On 1906 U.S. ban on entry of Chinese women married in Mexico, see *Albuquerque Morning Journal,* 6 April 1906, 5. Japanese immigration is from *Albuquerque Morning Journal,* 4 April 1907, 1, and 2 July 1907, 1. For a Spanish-language article endorsing U.S. legislation restricting Japanese immigration, see *El Labrador,* 8 November 1907, 2.

44. On "first illegal immigrants," see Lee, "Enforcing the Borders," 55. On Mallat, Garcia, and Foraker, respectively, see *Albuquerque Morning Journal,* 28 March 1906, 1; *El Labrador,* 11 January 1907, 1; and *Albuquerque Morning Journal,* 6 August 1907, 5. Also on Foraker in broader terms, see Ball, *United States Marshals,* 189–213. Chinese caught in Las Cruces was reported in *El Eco del Valle,* 15 December 1906, 1. On the new immigration enforcement district, see Lee, "Enforcing the Border," 83. For the context of immigration issues in 1906–1907 as reported by the Commissioner General of Immigration, Frank Sargeant, in his annual report, see *Albuquerque Morning Journal,* 7 January 1907,1, in which he said, "on the Mexican border Chinese coolies are constantly being smuggled into this country from Mexico."

45. Foreigners in China, see *Albuquerque Morning Journal,* 27 February

1906, 4.

46. A detailed account in a Spanish-language weekly is *El Labrador*, 27 April 1906, 1. On anti-Chinese rhetoric in Arizona, see *Tucson Daily Citizen*, 19 January 1906, 3 (slavery); 24 January 1906, 1 (gangs in New York); 4 (Chinese New Year); 25 January 1906, 4 (celebrating and music). An influential African-American publication, *Colored American*, 28 December 1901, 8 used similar derogatory terms and sought tighter Chinese exclusion laws to fend off unwanted competition for jobs. The attitudinal difference between Arizona and New Mexico in the late statehood era has been researched by Noel, "'I Am an American,'" 430–67.

47. On the Reeves, see Jew Ki [Chiu Kai] file, Berkshire to Commissioner-General of Immigration, 9 July 1908, box 408, Chinese Detention, RG 85, NARA I. On staying deportation for Kai, ibid., 2 January 1909. On Kai's complaint, Jew Ki [Chiu Kai] file, Vice Consul General, Hong Kong, to Secretary of State, 10 August 1910, ibid. The translation of dates from a lunar to Gregorian calendar was done by the consulate officer. For Washington's reply, see Jew Ki [Chiu Kai] file, Acting Secretary of Department of Commerce and Labor to Secretary of State, 19 October 1910, ibid.

48. Jew Ki [Chiu Kai] file, Berkshire to Commissioner-General of Immigration, 12 December 1908, ibid. On 1909 indictments, see *Albuquerque Morning Journal*, 12 April 1909, 3, on Fink skipping out, 30 April 1909, 2.

49. Harris and Sadler, *Secret War*, 34.

Chapter 7

1. *Albuquerque Morning Journal*, 6 January 1912, 1. The early legal history of the suit is explained in Holcombe to Secretary of the Interior, 19 August 1908, box 731, OS, Terr., RG 126, NARA II. E. P. Holcombe had filed the government's first lawsuit in February 1907. Telegram, Poldervaart, *Black-Robed Justice*, 210.

2. President Roosevelt's reaction is in Morison et al., eds., *Letters of Theodore Roosevelt*, 5: 733–34.

3. Staloff, *Hamilton, Adams, Jefferson*, chaps. 1 and 3.

4. Hening, ed., *George Curry*, 1–192, for his experiences prior to becoming territorial governor.

5. Fall's speech was about 3,000 words and is reproduced in *Albuquerque Morning Journal*, 9 August 1907, 1, 4. In contrast, Curry's address (ibid., 4) was about 1,800 words. The most caustic sections in Fall's comments related to federal investigations, and these were excerpted and reproduced in Hagerman, *Statement in Regard*, 73. *Los Angeles Times*, 31 August 1907, I12, for Fall's comments in El Paso.

6. Roosevelt to Curry, 9 August 1907, reel 346, PPTR, PPS, LC.

7. See entry in Garfield's diary, 9 August 1907, box 8, PJRG, JRG Diary 1907, MD, LC. *Albuquerque Morning Journal*, 10 August 1907, 1; *Los Angeles Times*, 10 August 1907, 13.

8. Roosevelt to Curry,15 August 1907, reel 346, PPTR, PPS, LC. Speaker Cannon's complaints were relayed in Roosevelt to Curry, 17 August 1907, ibid. Also Twitchell, *Leading Facts*, 2:560.

9. On William Lindsay and Democratic politics in Kentucky post-1865, Matthews, *Basil William Duke*, 266–74. For Fall's career, see Stratton, *Tempest over Teapot Dome*. Fall formally and publicly allied with the Republicans in 1904; see Fall to Cortelyou, 19 September 1904, box 8, fld. 29, ABFFP, MS 8, RGHC, ASC, NMSU. Fall to Roosevelt, 29 April 1907, ibid., confirms he voted "the Republican ticket" in 1904.

10. *Albuquerque Morning Journal*, 9 August 1907, 4.

11. On Fall's investments in Mexico, see "Necrology, Albert Bacon Fall," 78–80, which dates his initial investments in Mexico to the 1880s but says that "in 1907, Fall had sold his Mexico interests" (p. 79). He actually maintained considerable investment there, but the disruptions from the Revolution cost him dearly, and by 1913 he was telling confidants that he had "a great deal of money invested in mines in Mexico, and for the last two years I have been compelled to pay out quite large sums for protecting my interests there, with no income whatsoever"; see Fall to Hilton, 8 July 1913, box 8, fld. 4, ABFFP, MS 8, RGHC, ASC, NMSU. U.S. government fostering railroads and the negative consequences attendant to unchecked developmental capitalism, see White, *Railroaded*.

12. On nineteenth-century Porfirian liberalism as both philosophy and practice in promoting economic development, three books are indispensable: Coatsworth, *Growth Against Development*; Knight, *The Mexican Revolution*, vol. 1; and Hart, *Empire and Revolution*. The economic and political conditions in Mexico's northern states are crucial to an understanding of early twentieth-century Mexico and New Mexico; see Benjamin and Wasserman, eds., *Provinces of the Revolution*. A prime example of the influence U.S. laws had on Porfiriato officials is found in Mexico's mining law prior to the new Constitution of 1917. It duplicated the terms of the U.S. mining law of 1872, which gave all rights and benefits to claimants and yielded no tax revenue to the government.

13. These three lawsuits and various others filed over the next two months are found in box 733, OS, Terr., RG 126, NARA II. On indictments, see *Albuquerque Morning Journal*, 9 August 1907, 1.

14. Four-page letter from Attorney General Bonaparte to McHarg, 29 June 1907, reel 75, PPTR, PPS, LC. The instructions from the president to McHarg, sent in a confidential letter, are in Morison et al., eds., *Letters of Theodore Roosevelt*, 5: 739–41. For McHarg's recollection of New Mexico, see Oral History of Ormsby McHarg (1951) pp. 37–57, CUCOHO. A mid-August 1907 meeting lasting several hours between McHarg, President Roosevelt, and former Territorial Delegate, see *Los Angeles Times*, 15 August 1907, 14.

Accompanying McHarg to New Mexico were E. Peyton Gordon, pardon attorney for the Department of Justice; Francis C. Wilson, a recent law school graduate working in the Department of Commerce and Labor, who elected to stay in

New Mexico and had a prominent legal career; McHarg's stenographer Kathleen F. Lawler, a well-respected professional with Capitol Hill experience; and a number of investigators provided by the Department of Interior. The U.S. Marshal as well as local law enforcement officials were pressed into service, too. In total, McHarg's contingent likely numbered at least fifteen individuals. He also requested permission to hire "a number of Mexicans" to conduct investigations against the Spanish-speaking "lawless element of their own nationality," but nothing resulted from this phase of his work. See McHarg to Bonaparte, reel 76, 3 August 1907, PPTR, LC. McHarg also brought his wife along, and in her later years she told her grandson stories about living in the only safe place in Santa Fe—with nuns at a sanitarium they served; Paul A. Ryan personal communication, May 2009. In 1912 McHarg became a key figure in Roosevelt's Bull Moose Party.

15. Oral History of Ormsby McHarg (1951), p. 27, CUCOHO.

16. Between 1901 and 1908, corrupt practices in land sales had been exposed in Oregon, Washington, California, Arizona, and New Mexico; see Messing, "Public Lands, Politics," 35–66. On the problems plaguing management of the public domain in this period, see Bogue and Bogue, eds., *Jeffersonian Dream*, 43–45. Instructions are in Morison et al., eds., *Letters of Theodore Roosevelt*, 5:740.

17. Quoted in Hening, ed., *George Curry*, 208. On refusal to accept his resignation, see Roosevelt to Curry, 23 August 1907, reel 346, PPTR, PPS, LC.

18. First quotation, Woodruff to Bonaparte, 8 July 1907, box 732, OS, Terr., RG 126, NARA II. Second quotation, Roosevelt to Curry, 21 August 1907, reel 346, PPTR, PPS, LC. Third and fourth quotations, Curry to Roosevelt, 30 August 1907, ibid., and 5 September 1907, ibid.

19. Hening, *George Curry*, 209–10. McHarg's first quotation, Oral History of Ormsby McHarg (1951), p. 39, CUCOHO. McHarg's second quotation, ibid., 51.

20. Fall to Wickersham, 26 May 1910, box 7, fld. 1, ABFFP, MS 8, RGHC, ASC, NMSU.

21. American Lumber Company circular, 10 March 1910, box 732, OS, Terr., RG 126, NARA II. The legal maneuvering that brought this suit to the U.S. Supreme Court is discussed in the *Los Angeles Times*, 31 August 1907, I12. On logging in the Zuni Mountains and the activities of American Lumber Company, see Glover and Hereford, Jr., *Zuni Mountain Railroads*.

22. Holcombe to Secretary of the Interior, 19 August 1908, box 731, OS, Terr., RG 126, NARA II.

23. Ibid.

24. On the facts and law leading to the settlement, see Bonaparte to Secretary of the Interior, 20 January 1908, box 732, OS, Terr., NARA II. Full explanation of the settlement negotiations is in two key documents: Garfield to [Representative] Gaines, 24 March 1908, box 169, AJBP, MD, LC, and Holcombe to Secretary of the Interior, 19 August 1908, box 732, OS, Terr., RG 126, NARA II.

25. Garfield to Mondell, 6 February 1908, box 736, ibid.

26. Congress, HR,"Hearings Held, 1908," 4.

27. Acting U.S. Attorney General to Fall, 3 June 1910, box 7, fld. 1, MS 8, ABFFP, RGHC, ASC, NMSU. The Territory of New Mexico's file on the Alamogordo Lumber Company case is found in box 182, fld. 1458, USTerrSCR, col. # 1983-041, SRCA. On the decision to turn loose of this lawsuit late in the Taft administration, see Secretary of the Interior to the U.S. Attorney General, 17 January 1913, box 731, OS, Terr., RG 126, NARA II. The company's attorney was Herbert B. Holt, and other of the company's legal records throughout these years are in PHBH, box 3, fld. 7, MS 61, RGHC, ASC, NMSU.

28. Holcombe to Secretary of the Interior, 6 October 1907, box 732, OS, Terr., RG 126, NARA II. For Holcombe's audit report, see ibid., 5 May 1908. For the final, unsigned assessment of the reports, see Memorandum for the Secretary, 3 October 1908, box 730, ibid.

29. Curry's account of McHarg's removal, Hening, *George Curry,* 209. McHarg's version is found in Oral History of Ormsby McHarg (1951), p. 52, CUCOHO. Both these accounts are deliberately vague on key details. A contemporary, though partisan, version is much more revealing: Hagerman, *Statement in Regard,* 74–83, and especially the newspaper articles he reproduces in full from the *New York Sun,* 24 November 1907, 76–79, and *Los Angeles Times,* 16 December 1907, 79–80.

30. Roosevelt to Curry, 24 October 1907, reel 347, PPTR, PPS, LC. On the Panic of 1907, see Silber, *When Washington Shut Down,* chap. 2 on 1907. On his 1908 pledge to Curry, see Roosevelt to Curry, 11 November 1908, reel 352, PPTR, PPS, LC.

31. For the behind-the-scenes maneuvering needed to secure this platform plank, especially the key role played by Holm O. Bursum, see Hening, *George Curry,* 220–22. On the irrigation congress, see Simmons, "When the Irrigation Congress," 4. In April 1908 the Albuquerque Commercial Club assisted the city's government in publishing a forty-two-page booklet with multiple photographs reproduced on each page. This booklet contributed to the boosterism associated with the upcoming irrigation congress; see Hening and Johnson, *Albuquerque, New Mexico.* The failure of Secretary Garfield to show up as promised occasioned a dustup with Curry; see Curry to Garfield, 10 and 15 August 1908, box 733, OS, Terr., RG 126, NARA II. Also, see entries for July and August in PJRG, JRG Diary 1908, box 8, MD, LC. Curry stepped down from office on 28 February 1910.

32. Roosevelt to Curry, 22 January 1909, reel 353, PPTR, PPS, LC. Beveridge to Denny, 18 January 1909, box 169, AJBP, MD, LC. Beveridge to Lee, 28 January 1909, ibid. For an example of an anti-statehood letter, see Blair to Beveridge, 8 January 1909, ibid., and Beveridge to Blair, 16 January 1909, ibid. The undated and unsigned petition is also from ibid. Beveridge to Catron, 11 February 1909, ibid. The inside address was typed "Cortner" and then crossed out and "Catron" handwritten. In many thousands of pieces of Beveridge's correspondence, this was the only surname strikeover I saw. Certainly Beveridge was not above the politi-

cal gamesmanship implicit in misspelling Catron's name and correcting it, but his actual motive is unknowable. Beveridge to Taft, 9 February 1909, ibid. Taft's reply is Taft to Beveridge, 18 February 1909, reel 122, PPWHT, PPS, LOC.

33. Beveridge discussed his operation in Beveridge to Durre, 12 April 1909, box 169, AJBP, MD, LC. Short biographies of Beveridge and Watson and their contrasting political philosophies are in *CR*, V. 142, No. 58, 1 May 1996, S4453–54. Watson entered the Senate in 1916, served as its majority leader during the presidency of Herbert Hoover, and lost his seat in the 1932 Democratic landslide.

34. Hayes's three-page letter is [unsigned] to Beveridge, 17 February 1909, box 169, AJBP, MD, LC. For the request to the Justice Department, see Beveridge to U.S. Attorney General, 16 February 1909, ibid. Their reply is Assistant Attorney General to Beveridge, 22 February 1909, box 732, OS, Terr., RG 126, NARA II. For the Department of Interior request, see Beveridge to Garfield, 16 February 1909, box 169, AJBP, MD, LC. Providing Beveridge transcripts of two lawsuits and all related motions and filings, see Venable to Beveridge, 24 February 1909, ibid.

35. *New York Times*, 28 February 1909, 2, 1 March 1909, 3. None of McHarg's testimony and only one page of Lawler's testimony has survived. For her one retyped page of testimony, see [undated/unsigned], box 169, AJBP, MD, LC., to which someone appended a typed note of identification.

36. McHarg's account of his meeting with Senator Aldrich is in Oral History of Ormsby McHarg (1951), pp. 53–54, CUCOHO. For Curry's account of Senator Aldrich's actions the final week in February 1909, see Henning, *George Curry*, 227–29, 239–41. For a glimpse into Beveridge's backstage strategy during the final week of February 1909, see Hays to Beveridge, 17 February 1909, box 169, AJBP, MD, LC. Andrews's confidential appraisal is Andrews to Prince, 12 February 1909, serial # 14019, fld. 13, LBPP, col. # 1959-174, SRCA.

37. *New York Times*, 17 October 1909, 2, and the *Albuquerque Morning Journal*, 16 October 1909, 1.

38. Ibid., 1, 2, 6, is the main source for this and the following seven paragraphs. Unless otherwise cited, all quotations are from the *Albuquerque Morning Journal's* extensive coverage of the president's visit.

39. Butt, *Taft and Roosevelt*, 1:200.

40. Oklahoma constitution, see *New York Times*, 25 August 1907, 3.

41. *New York Times*, 3 June 1909, 1. Sorolla worked on the 59-inch-by-31.5-inch oil-on-canvas portrait during April 1909, and today it is part of the Ohio Historical Society's collection. In the mid-1970s personnel at the Joaquín Sorolla Museum in Madrid spoke fondly of how this commission further elevated Sorolla's international reputation.

42. Petition in support of Fall is in *La Voz del Pueblo*, 30 October 1909, 1. Editorial is ibid., 23 October 1909, 2, along with criticism of the speech. The summary of Taft's "preconditions" is found in ibid., 16 October 1909, 1. Although no copies of *La Bandera Americana* survive for October 1909, a rebuff of the paper's support for Taft does appear in *La Voz del Pueblo*, 23 October 1909, 1.

43. *El Labrador*, 22 October 1909, 2.

44. For a full account of this plot, see Harris and Sadler, *The Secret War*, 1–16. Harris and Sadler note that the president's security detail knew in advance of a possible plot to kill the president, and all along his route in New Mexico uncommonly tight security measures were in place and drew comment from journalists. See *Albuquerque Morning Journal*,16 October 1909, 1, on the large number of military and civilian forces guarding Taft as he spoke to the crowd assembled at the train station adjacent to the Alvarado Hotel; *La Voz del Pueblo*, 23 October 1909, 1, on the military guards clearing streets during the president's automobile drive west on Central Avenue to Old Town, resulting in one man having his hand crushed when a mounted patrol's horse knocked him down and stepped on it and when some "Mexicans," not understanding commands given them in English, had their wagon confiscated and were hustled away.

45. Butt, *Taft and Roosevelt*, 1: 208.

Chapter 8

1. Cooper, *Pivotal Decades*, 168.

2. Quotations from clippings, *Albuquerque Morning Journal*, 6 June 1911, and Carrizozo *Outlook*, 21 April 1911, in Scrapbook, WHAP, MSS 19 BC, CSWR, UL, UNM. For a detailed political history of 1910–1912, see Gould, *Four Hats in the Ring*.

3. Beveridge to Taft, 2 September 1909, box 169, AJBP, MD, LC.

4. Ibid.

5. *El Labrador*, 6 August 1909, 1. *New York Times*, 8 December 1909, 6, for President Taft's first message to congress, which at about 14,000 words was half the length of President Roosevelt's final message. Taft's call for statehood, though brief and near the end of the text, marked a legislative priority he intended to secure. Delay until the new census, see Beveridge to Taft, 18 November 1909, box 169, AJBP, MD, LC.

6. *New York Times*, 27 December 1909, 16. Stephenson, *Nelson W. Aldrich*, 404, for Aldrich's coda.

7. Ibid., 366–70.

8. Beveridge to Ely, 20 June 1910, box 169, AJBP, MD, LC. On Hitchcock's six summers in Arizona and New Mexico, and his special interest in the statehood bill, see *Los Angeles Times*, 30 January 1910, 17. Albert B. Fall viewed with considerable suspicion the role Frank Hitchcock played in navigating passage of the statehood bill. In an exchange of correspondence with novelist and essayist Eugene Manlove Rhodes, he reminded Rhodes in early February 1910, "I stated clearly that New Mexico would not be admitted until Mr. Hitchcock was convinced that he had control of the political situation; that I was correct in this statement I think events as reported by the associated press have conclusively established." Thirteen months later, Rhodes informed Fall, "I would

like to be posted on the present political situation in N.M.: I would like to have data on which to base a dig—not an attack—but a sly and oblique little dig, at Mr. Hitchcock. Is he still political dictator of N.M?" See Fall to Rhodes, 2 February 1910, box 8, fld. 27, ABFFP, MS 8, RGHC, ASC, NMSU, and Rhodes to Fall, 9 March 1911, ibid. Fall saw Hitchcock as a potential threat for the influence he might exercise in selecting Andrews for the senate seat Fall coveted.

9. For the mid-January White House meeting, see *Los Angeles Times*, 19 January, I4. On the Department of Interior's tracking of the bills, see H.R. 12329, H.R. 14560, and H.R. 18166 and related correspondence, 6 December 1909–17 January 1910, box 734A, OS, Terr., RG 26, NARA II. On final comments and the vote in the House, see *CR*, 17 January 1910, 62nd Congress, 1st Session, 723–24. Gillett also read portions of Daniel Webster's opposition from 1848.

10. *Los Angeles Times*, 19 January 1910, I4, called for guarding against abuses in the public lands turned over to the new states; ibid., 20 January 1910, I15; ibid., 30 January 1910, I7. Beveridge's critique of problems with the House version of the enabling bill is in *CR*, 17 June 1910, 61st Congress, 1st Session, 8523-26. On Beveridge's plans and his work with several executive departments, see Beveridge to Whitman, 19 January 1910, Box 96, AJBP, MD, LC, and Bowers, *Albert J. Beveridge*, 378–79.

11. *New York Times*, 3 February 1910, 2. The transcript is Congress, Senate, Committee on Territories, *Statehood, Hearing* [1910].

12. Ibid., 4, Beveridge's acknowledgment and agenda; ibid., 13, House bill and debt liquidation; ibid., 7–8, total indebtedness of the Territory; ibid., 18, public lands provided New Mexico.

13. *Washington Post*, 25 June 1910, 1, on backlog. Telegram to Arizona, *Los Angeles Times*, 13 March 1910, V15.

14. Butt, *Taft and Roosevelt,* 1:299-300, is an eyewitness account of the meeting between Taft and Aldrich. Butt claimed (301) that Taft "felt, I think, a little bit ashamed of himself entering into political plots with the Rhode Islander [Aldrich] as a matter of retaliation."

15. Beveridge and his hold on his state party, see *Christian Science Monitor*, 2 April 1910, 1, and Bowers, *Albert J. Beveridge*, 377–78. On the rift between Taft and Beveridge, *Chicago Daily Tribune*, 7 April 1910, 4; *New York Times*, 10 May 1910, 13; *Washington Post*, 15 June 1910, 4; and Taft to Aldrich, 12 May 1910, reel 502, PPWHT, PPS, LC. *New York Times*, 10 May 1910, 13, on Taft's proxy criticizing Beveridge.

16. Margulies, *Reconciliation and Revival*, 28–33. A contemporary analysis of the Mann-Elkins Act by an influential economist at Harvard is Ripley, *Railroads*, 557–78. *New York Times*, 8 December 1909, 6. In 1910 elections the Democrats again settled on the high cost of living, ibid., 2 August 1910, 2.

17. *New York Times*, 20 May 1910, 5, on the deal. Bailey's understanding of its terms, *Washington Post*, 15 June 1910, 3.

18. *Los Angeles Times*, 7 March 1910, I4, on voter qualification. Dropping the

House version of literacy standard, see *Los Angeles Times*, 17 June 1910, 11, and ibid., 19 June 1910, 11. Bailey and Beveridge's heated exchange over Arizona's voting restrictions, *CR*, 61st Congress, 1st Session, 17 June 1910, 8523.

19. Twitchell, *Leading Facts*, 2:580, for Taft and Andrews' role in gaining House consent.

20. Quoted in Wiebe, *Businessmen and Reform*, 88.

21. *New York Times*, 26 June 1910, 1.

22. *Los Angeles Times*, 19 June 1910, 11. A succinct interpretive account of the convention is Cline, *New Mexico's 1910 Constitution*. After just three days in Santa Fe, the lone Socialist, Green B. Patterson of Chaves County, got derailed in his plan to fight for numerous political reforms. Delegates had him quarantined sixty days on trumped up allegations he had smallpox; ibid., 29 n. 12.

23. Larson, *New Mexico's Quest*, 272, 275. Ibid., 272–86, on the political machinations in writing the Constitution. The *New Mexico Historical Review* published three invaluable articles between 1944 and 1952 offering both recollections and analysis by three Democratic participants; see Mabry, "New Mexico's Constitution," 168–84; Heflin, "New Mexico Constitutional," 60–68; and Tittman, "New Mexico's Constitutional Convention," 177–86. These eyewitness accounts contain numerous invaluable insights that have found their way into other works, not always with citations, especially about Albert J. Fall and the contentious divisions between Republicans and Democrats.

24. Cline, *New Mexico's 1910 Constitution*, 63–64, lists the twenty-seven committees and their chairs. Heflin, "New Mexico Constitutional," 61, gives the ethnic composition as "35 members of Spanish descent, and 65 members of the so-called Anglo American descent." Nine committees were headed by Nuevomexicanos, a number proportionate to their overall presence in the convention. Women's suffrage had gained a foothold in the West by 1910, and Jensen and Miller, eds., *New Mexico Women*, 304–306, discuss how the constitutional convention addressed it and the course of the suffrage movement in New Mexico from 1910 to 1920. Also see Tittman, "New Mexico Constitutional Convention," 182, who wrote, "The Spanish speaking delegates, faithfully representing the then prevailing ideas of their people, were opposed to the theory that it was a good thing to let women vote." On prohibitionists' complaints and the refusal to allow Santa Clara Pueblo, under the guidance of Indian agent Clara True, to protest, Mrs. C. D. Faunce of the Santa Fe Woman's Christian Temperance Union to Secretary of the Interior, 16 January 1911, box 734, OS, Terr., RG 126, NARA II.

25. On the Oregon constitution, Cline, *New Mexico's 1910 Constitution*, 43.

26. On Hitchcock and the delegates, Mann to Hitchcock, 7 October 1910, reel 401, PPWHT, PPS, LC. On the restrictions of the referendum, see Mabry, "New Mexico's Constitution," 180.

27. Andrews to Taft, 4 October 1910, reel 401, PPWHT, PPS, LC.

28. *New York Times*, 22 November 1910, 4. Cline, *New Mexico's 1910 Constitution,* uses the characterization of the constitution as the book's subtitle.

Bakken, *Rocky Mountain Constitution Making*, 47–49, quoted 48, on restraints imposed. One of the consistent arguments against statehood was that it would result in higher taxes because the federal government would no longer cover many expenses; see Moussalli, "The Fiscal Effects of Statehood," 119–26.

29. *Washington Post*, 22 November 1910, 11. *El Eco del Valle*, 18 August 1910, 1.

30. Ibid. The editorial used the rather uncommon expression *"los hombres de color Moreno"* in addressing Nuevomexicanos. The referent should likely be understood in terms of the presence of Mexican immigrants.

31. Larson, *New Mexico's Quest*, 275, on Luna's influence. *La Voz del Pueblo*, 5 November 1910, 1. The four counties of Lincoln, Roosevelt, San Juan, and Sierra rejected the Constitution. Every registered voter in the Territory received in the mail in early January a copy of the Constitution printed in either English or Spanish depending on his language preference.

32. On Spiess's ties to railroad and other corporate interests, see Larson, *New Mexico's Quest*, 363, n. 34. Collecting on defaulted bonds had long generated keen interest on Wall Street. While five New Mexico counties had "repudiated issues of bonds," so had fourteen states, thirteen of which were in the South, for a total in excess of $310 million dollars. Investors looked on Spiess's handiwork as a highly valuable precedent. On defaulted bonds nationwide and one early plan to collect on these if New Mexico gained statehood, see *New York Times*, 31 December 1905, 12.

33. The delegate occupation data cited in Larson (275) and Cline (30) are drawn from an unnamed, undated contemporary newspaper account found in a clipping album kept by William H. Andrews, see WHAP, MSS 19 BC, box 1, Scrapbook, CSWR, UL, UNM.

34. Holmes, *Politics in New Mexico*, 49, on self-interest motivating men to become delegates. Biographical data on the delegates are drawn from two contemporary sources: *New Mexico Constitutional Convention* and Peterson, *Representative New Mexicans*. I thank my research assistants, Natalie Heberling (2007–2008) and Dr. Kari Schleher (2008–2010), for carefully extracting data on the dozen variables I identified. Delegates with economic ties to both the traditional agrarian economy and the emerging mercantile capitalism were such powerful individuals as E. A. Miera (Sandoval Co.), Onésimo Martínez (Taos Co.), Solomon Luna (Valencia Co.), Vencesiao Jaramillo (Rio Arriba Co.), Eufracio Gallegos (Union Co.), J. J. Aragon (Lincoln Co.), Charles A. Kohn (Quay Co.), William McIntosh (Torrance Co.), James B. Gilchrist (Grant Co.), Daniel Cassidy, Sr. (Mora Co.), John I. Hinkle (Chaves Co.), Charles Springer (Colfax Co.), and Holm O. Bursum (Socorro Co.).

35. Victory et al., *Compiled Laws*. The rules imposed on corporations are at ibid, 205–31. Incorporations applied broadly to commercial activity as well as community and even civic and charitable efforts; see ibid., section 412, 206. For the constitution's economic philosophy, see Cline, *New Mexico's 1910 Constitution*, 49. The conscience of the convention was Democrat Harvey B. Fergusson,

who vehemently denounced the economic philosophy imposed; see Mabry, "New Mexico's Constitution," 178–79. Heflin, "New Mexico Constitutional Convention," 62, observed, "All the [special] interests grouped together made a combination in which the general public was almost helpless."

36. For statistics on the insurance industry in 1902, see New Mexico Office of the Auditor, *Report of the Auditor,* 49.

37. Cline, *New Mexico's 1910 Constitution,* 24. The leadership of the Santa Fe Ring is defined differently by each of five authors studying it; see ibid., 20 n. 2.

38. Mills to Taft, 23 January 1911, reel 401, PPWHT, PPS, LC. Andrews to Taft, 20 January 1911, ibid.

39. *La Revista de Taos,* 3 February 1911, 1. Various New Mexico prohibitionist groups sent letters and petitions to the White House; for samples, see Faunce, 16 January 1911, Box 734, OS, Terr., RG 126, NARA II and Cooper, 17 January 1911, ibid.

40. Blair to Taft, 7 February 1911, reel 401, PPWHT, PPS, LC. Memorandum, "New Mexico Statehood and the Constitution," undated and unsigned, ibid., Wickersham to Taft, 17 February 1911, ibid.

41. *Albuquerque Morning Journal,* 28 February 1911, 1, included Blair's quotes in its reporting.

42. Congress, HR. Committee on Territories, *Constitution for the Proposed State of New Mexico.* For two representative letters to Blair from prohibitionists in New Mexico, see ibid., 44–45. The 750-plus documents Andrews collected are in WHAP, MSS 19 BC, box 1, CSWR, UL, UNM.

43. Congress, HR. Committee on Territories, *Constitution for the Proposed State of New Mexico,* 6, 13.

44. *La Revista de Taos,* 9 December 1910, 1.

45. Brock, "Perhaps the Most Incorrect," 454–58. The Court's decisions are *New Mexico v. Texas,* 275 U.S. 279 (1927) and *New Mexico v. Texas,* 276 U.S. 557 (1928).

46. Beveridge's changing attitude on statehood is seen in letters in February 1911: Beveridge to Ketcham, 27 February 1911, box 185, AJBP, MD, LC; Pope to Beveridge, 23 February 1911, ibid; and Beveridge to Heard, 2 February 1911, ibid. For some details about the final day of the Sixty-first Congress, see *Washington Post,* 5 March 1911, 1, and Larson, *Quest for Statehood,* 290–91.

47. *Christian Science Monitor,* 4 March 1911, 1–2, had extensive coverage. Texas State Historical Association, *Handbook of Texas Online,* entry "*Bailey, Joseph Weldon*" by Holcomb.

48. Congress, HR, Committee on Territories. *Hearings . . . on House Joint Resolution No. 14,* 3-4. Larson, *New Mexico's Quest,* 292–93.

49. Ibid., 295–97.

50. Congress, Senate, Committee on Territories, *Hearings before the Committee . . . House Joint Resolution 14,* 3, on telegrams; 6, telegrams quote. Among the communities forwarding messages were Deming, Springer, Willard, Carlsbad,

Mountain Air [*sic*], Farmington, Roswell, Clovis, Tucumcari, Columbus, Vaughn, Belen, Portales, Artesia, and Santa Fe.

51. Ibid. 58, Spiess's testimony and Owen's support for statehood.

52. *Coyle v. Smith*, 221 U.S. 559. Democrat Senator Owen soon found an ally in Republican senator from Oregon Jonathan Bourne, the Senate's most vocal advocate of recall and other direct participation measures. These two senators quickly drafted bills submitted to the Senate Judiciary Committee. Owen sought to impose the recall onto the Supreme Court as well as the entire federal judiciary. Senator Bourne proposed that a "unanimous vote of the Supreme Court" would be necessary to overturn a congressional statute. As the *New York Times*, 1 August 1911, 2 wryly noted, such bills would be "buried" in committee. See also *Washington Post*, 17 August 1911, 4.

53. Representative of debate on statehood in July and August, see *CR*, 12 July 1911, Senate, 62nd Congress, Special Session, 2917; ibid., 14 July 1911, 3010; and ibid., 3 August 1911, 3660. *Albuquerque Morning Journal*, 12 September 1910, 4, for the Arizona newspaper's premonition,

54. William Howard Taft, "Special Message of the President," 15 August 1911, box 734, OS, Terr., RG 126, NARA II, is an original copy of the veto message. On the veto, see *New York Times*, 16 August 1911, 3. Hubbard, "The Arizona Enabling Act," 307–22 is an early, insightful discussion.

55. *Washington Post*, 17 August 1911, 4; 19 August 1911, 4.

56. Larson, *New Mexico's Quest*, 298.

Conclusion

1. The original photograph is held by the Library of Congress, Prints and Photographs Digital Collection, image no. hec2009007180. A low-quality reproduction is in Twitchell, *Leading Facts*, 2: recto facing 596, and 603–605 n. 513. *Santa Fe New Mexican*, 6 January 1912, 1. *Albuquerque Morning Journal*, 7 January 1912, 1. *New York Times*, 7 January 1912, 11. Keleher Collection, digital image #000-742-0256, CSWR, UL, UNM. Hening, ed., *George Curry*, verso 257. First row—from left, Harvey B. Fergusson, Democratic Congressman; William H. Andrews, Republican Delegate; and George Curry, Republican Congressman; Albuquerque attorney and Democratic state legislator John Baron Burg. From the left in the second row are Amasa B. McGaffey, prominent in the lumber industry in western New Mexico; Edith (Talbot) Barnes, daughter of a politically prominent Phoenix businessman and wife of Will C. Barnes; Mabel (Fox) McGaffey, daughter of an Albuquerque jeweler and wife of A. B. McGaffey; Will C. Barnes, in charge of the Forest Service grazing division; John Roberts, aide to George Curry; Curry's son, Charles; and Ira M. Bond, Washington correspondent for various New Mexico newspapers throughout the past eleven years. At the top row left is James G. Darden, a lobbyist representing New Mexico businesses; the next two men are most likely Secretary of Interior Walter L. Fisher and Postmaster General Frank

H. Hitchcock; next is Arthur C. Ringland, the district forester for New Mexico and Arizona; an unidentified man is on the end.

2. Beveridge to Taft, 2 September 1909, box 169, AJBP, MD, LC. Beveridge to Taft, 18 November 1909, ibid. Taft to Beveridge, 20 November 1909, ibid. *New York Times*, 8 December 1909, 6. Taft's set piece on Administration Republicans is in Butt, *Taft and Roosevelt*, 1:297. Larson, *New Mexico's Quest*, 272–304.

3. Bureau of the Census, *Thirteenth Census*, 3: 169-81. West, *Growing Up*, xviii.

4. *La Voz del Pueblo*, 18 November 1911, 1. Chacón, "A Nuevo México," 309.

5. *La Estrella*, 28 August 1915, 1–2.

6. Gould, *Presidency of Theodore Roosevelt* (1991), 109. Stephenson, *Nelson W. Aldrich*, 210. Ibid., 76–103 on his loss of power 1893–97. Stephenson interviewed Beveridge shortly before the latter's death in 1927, and he spoke candidly about Aldrich; see ibid., 266, 463 n 8.

7. Braeman, *Albert J. Beveridge*, 85. Beveridge to Murdock, 7 September 1908, box 162, AJBP, MD, LC.

8. On the invention of tourism aiding Santa Fe's rise from "economic stagnation at the close of the nineteenth century," see Wilson, *Myth of Santa Fe*. On the 1912 filming of the De Vargas parade, see ibid., 200. On movies and Albuquerque, *Albuquerque Morning Journal*, 19 January 1912, 4; 21 February 1912, 5; 25 April 1912, 8.

9. The *Philadelphia Evening Bulletin* printed these letters between 15 and 31 October 1932. They were written between 29 June and 10 November 1908. See "Correspondence Clippings," Roosevelt to Taft, TRC, HCL, HU. On the discussion of politics in the West, ibid., 11 July 1908. The letter is also reproduced in Morison et al., eds., *Letters of Theodore Roosevelt*, 6: 1123–24 and 1124 n. 2.

10. Two recent studies of the 1912 campaign and election are Gould, *Four Hats in the Ring* and Chace, *1912*.

11. Roosevelt to Putnam, 15 November 1904, reel 336, PPTR, PPS, LC. Roosevelt to Wister, 19 November 1904, ibid.

12. Beveridge to Ely, 20 June 1910, box 169, AJBP, MD, LC. On newspaper ownership, Otero to Cutting, 4 December 1929, box 8, PBC, MD, LC.

13. A reinterpretation of presidential and national power in the early twentieth century is Novak, "The Myth of the 'Weak,'" 752–72. A standard account of the Ballinger-Pinchot conflict is Penick, *Progressive Politics and Conservation*.

14. Roosevelt to Spring Rice, 22 August 1911, in Morison, *Letters of Theodore Roosevelt*, 7:332–35, quoted 334.

15. Chandler, "Origins of Progressive Leadership," 8: 1464. Expanding citizen participation, see Roosevelt to Willard, 28 April 1911, in Morison et al., eds, *Letters of Theodore Roosevelt*, 7:250–57. On Roosevelt's ego, Grant to Rhodes, 22 March 1912, ibid., 8: 1456–61, quoted 1457, 1459.

16. Burton, *Taft, Roosevelt*," 144. My critique of the Roosevelt-Taft split cites only contemporary correspondence, but it is influenced by two recent studies, although neither makes special reference to statehood: Morris, *Colonel Roosevelt*,

116–86, with 131–32 paralleling my criticisms; and Burton, *Taft, Roosevelt*, 80–100 and especially 140–44, in which his discussion of personality, role reversal, and legal interpretations have exact counterparts in my analysis. An example of old-style, passive leadership is Roosevelt to Lodge, 23 May 1911, in Morison et al., eds, *Letters of Theodore Roosevelt*, 7:269. A counterargument on the issue of Roosevelt's political tactics can be made in terms of his legislative priorities, especially early in his second term. See Morris, *Theodore Rex*, 449–60.

17. Fall to Rhodes, 2 February 1910, box 8, fld. 27, ABFFP, MS 8, RGHC, ASC, NMSU. Rhodes to Fall, 9 March 1911, ibid.

18. Julyan, *Place Names*, vi. General Leonard Wood, although born in New Hampshire in 1860, claimed New Mexico as his home at the turn of the twentieth century. *El Tiempo*, 18 February 1905, 3, also reported, "The natives petitioned their representative, the Honorable Manuel C. de Baca, that said name be abolished, and complying with the wishes of his people, he passed the act without difficulty in the legislature."

19. *Albuquerque Morning Journal*, 19 January 1912, 4; 21 February 1912, 5; 25 April 1912, 8.

20. McClure to Taft, 11 March 1911, reel 401, PPWHT, PPS, LC. Roosevelt to Wister, 23 May 1911, in Morison et al., eds., *Letters of Theodore Roosevelt*, 7:269.

21. Secretary of the Interior, *Report of the Governor, 1904*, 19–68 and quoted 19. Ibid., 58–61, on electricity. On Dawson, see Smith, *Coal Town*.

22. Mark Twain intensely disliked Clark, and his trenchant biographical sketch is in DeVoto, ed., *Mark Twain in Eruption*, 70–77.

23. On 1907 sale, see Secretary of the Interior, *Report of the Mine Inspector* [1907], 26–27; *Albuquerque Morning Journal*, 18 February 1908, 1; Secretary of the Interior, *Report of the Secretary, 1898*, 107. On competition from fuel oil, see Secretary of the Interior, *Report of the Governor, 1904*, 40–41. On economic slump in 1909, see Secretary of the Interior, *Reports of the Department June 30, 1909*, 2: 694. For a detailed account of operations and procedures at the Clark mine, see Secretary of the Interior, *Annual Report of the United States Mine Inspector June 30, 1903*, 24–29.

24. *Albuquerque Morning Journal*, 18 February 1908, 1. For the recent survey of underground mines, see Hoffman and Wilks, "Abandoned & Inactive Coal Mines of the Gallup Coal Field," Introduction. The deterioration of the state's environment is the subject of Price, *The Orphaned Land*.

25. *Santa Fe New Mexican*, 13 January 1912, 4.

26. [WPA-NM], *New Mexico*, 393.

27. *Las Vegas Optic and Live Stock Grower*, 20 January 1912, 1. Wilson, "Another White Hope," 30–39. City's debt information is from personal communication, Toby Smith to the author, August 2011.

28. All lumber company incorporations are tabulated from the report by the Secretary of New Mexico, *Corporation Filings, 1910*. For the demise and temporary revival of the American Lumber Company, see *Albuquerque Morning Journal*,

16 August 1913, 5; 28 April 1918, 7. For a discussion of the modernization of the logging industry in New Mexico, see Holtby, "Two Photographs," 21–24. An outstanding analysis of the changing nature of corporations and stock sales from the 1890s to 1929 is in Mitchell, *Speculation Economy.*

29. Cabeza de Baca, *We Fed Them Cactus,* 12, 147, 153. *Albuquerque Morning Journal,* 15 September 1915, 3.

30. Moon to Bursum, 27 April 1922, box 56, fld. 22, HOBP, MS 305, RGHC, ASC, NMSU. Moon to Bursum, 26 May 1922, ibid.

31. Calhoun to Bursum, 16 September 1922, ibid., on bank failure. On drought, Hope Chamber of Commerce to Bursum, 2 August 1922, ibid. On the House's appropriation, see Smith [Chairman of the House Committee on Irrigation of Arid Lands] to Bursum, 7 March 1923, ibid. On *Hope Booster,* see Johnson to Bursum, 24 February 1923, ibid.

32. "Report of Special Advisory Committee on Reclamation," 10 April 1924, box 149, JRGP, MD, LC.

33. *El Defensor del Pueblo,* 18 February 1924, 2, crops irrigated by Elephant Butte. On the impact of World War I, see Bloom, ed., *New Mexico in the Great War.* On railroad expansion, see *Albuquerque Morning Journal,* 25 November 1912, 2. Railroad contraction in New Mexico after World War I brought opportunity for those willing to relocate to Colorado, including one Nuevomexicano family leaving Albuquerque and moving to La Junta, Colo., to work on the railroad in 1923; personal communication, Frieda Montoya to the author.

34. Knight, *The Mexican Revolution* at two volumes is the best comprehensive account. On the Mexican Revolution and insurgents in Texas in 1910–11, see Harris and Sadler, *Texas Rangers and the Mexican Revolution,* 51–85.

35. General Scott to HQ Ft. Bliss, 16 January 1914, box 11, Ft. Wingate, Mexican, RG 393, NARA I.

36. HQ Southern Command to Elliott, 8 July 1914, ibid.

37. El Paso Office of Immigration Service to Department of Labor, 25 August 1914, ibid. Ft. Wingate Executive Officer to Commanding Officer, 24 July 1914, ibid. Knight, *Mexican Revolution,* 2:340–41.

38. Muzquiz to Estes, 31 August 1914, box 11, Ft. Wingate, Mexican, RG 393, NARA I.

39. Vigil, "Revolution and Confusion," 145–70.

40. Katz, *Life and Times,* 546–74, is an authoritative account of the raid. Harris and Sadler, *Secret War,* 308–309, recount the death of Salazar, who changed his politico-military allegiances ten times in seven years.

41. Katz, *Life and Times,* 612. Martin, "German Strategy and Military Assessments," 160–96.

42. Michael Swickard, "Celebrating Statehood Day New Mexico Style," online newspaper interview at www.nmpolitics.net/2009/01/celebrating-state hood-day-new-mexico-style. I thank Michael Kelly, Director, Center for Southwest Research, University Libraries, University of New Mexico, for this citation.

43. *El Labrador*, 5 January 1912, 2. On Garcia's career, see College of Agriculture, *Agricultural Research*, 4–5.

44. *Santa Fe New Mexican*, 6 January 1912, 1.

45. *La Revista de Taos*, 12 January 1912, 1. *Rio Grande Republican*, 9 January 1912, 1. On the federal data, see *El Labrador*, 26 January 1911, 1. Social indices—forty-fourth of forty-seven states in school attendance and the number of teachers, forty-third in population, and forty-first in the number of volumes in bookstores, and fifth in population increase between 1900 and 1910; general economic indicators—ranked forty-fourth in use of steam power, fortieth in invested capital, thirty-fourth in wood products, thirtieth in total livestock, and sixteenth for land with potential petroleum deposits; agriculture—rankings of thirty-fifth for corn, thirty-fourth for wheat and oats, thirty-first for hay, twelfth for sugar beets, eleventh for apple production; and for extractive industries—tenth for gold, ninth for copper, eighth for silver and coal, and fifth for lead.

46. *Albuquerque Morning Journal*, 16 January 1912, 1, all quotations in this paragraph.

47. Ibid., all quotations in this paragraph.

48. Ibid. For two organizations dedicated to effective state government in the spirit of Governor McDonald's remarks, see New Mexico First (www.nmfirst.org) and Think New Mexico (www.thinknewmexico.org). Among historians' assessments of New Mexico's development since 1912, see Tórrez, "New Mexico at 90."

Bibliography

Archives

CSWR—Center for Southwest Research, University Libraries, University of New Mexico, Albuquerque

William Henry Andrews Papers, MSS 19 BC (cited as WHAP, CSWR, UL, UNM)

Edward L. Bartlett Papers, MSS 153 BC (cited as ELBP, CSWR, UL, UNM)

Thomas B. Catron Papers, MSS 29 BC (cited as TBCP, CSWR, UL, UNM)

Willard S. Hopewell Papers, MSS 56 BC (cited as WSHP, CSWR, UL, UNM)

Miguel Antonio Otero Papers, MSS 21 BC (cited as MAOP, CSWR, UL, UNM)

George W. Prichard Family Papers, MSS 187 BC (cited as GWPFP, CSWR, UL, UNM)

Bernard S. Rodey Papers, MSS 175 BC (cited as BSRP, CSWR, UL, UNM)

CUCOHO—Oral History of Ormsby McHarg (February–March 1951), on pages 1–57, in the Columbia University Center for Oral History Collection.

LC, MD—Library of Congress, Manuscripts Division, Washington, D.C.

Nelson W. Aldrich Papers, microfilm (cited as NWAP, reel, LC, MD)

Albert J. Beveridge Papers (cited as AJBP, LC, MD)

Papers of Bronson Cutting (cited as PBC, LC, MD)

Papers of James R. Garfield (cited as PJRG, LC, MD)

Matthew S. Quay Papers (cited as MSQP, LC, MD)

LC, PPS—Library of Congress, Presidential Papers Series

Presidential Papers of Theodore Roosevelt. Microfilm. Washington, D.C.: Library of Congress, 1967 (cited as reel, PPTR, PPS, LC)

Presidential Papers of William Howard Taft. Microfilm. Washington, D.C.: Library of Congress, 1969 (cited as reel, PPWHT, PPS, LC)

NARA I—National Archives and Records Administration I, Washington, D.C.

Record Group 28, microfilm, [cabinet] 60A/ [drawer] 01, New Mexico

Post Offices (cited as reel, 60A/01, NMPO, RG 28, NARA I)

Record Group 75, Special Cases, Irrigation (cited as SC, I, RG 75, NARA I])

Record Group 85, Immigration and Naturalization Service, Chinese Detention (cited as INS, Chinese, RG 85, NARA I)

Record Group 393, Fort Wingate, Mexican Detention (cited as Ft. Wingate, Mexican, RG 393, NARA I)

NARA II—National Archives and Records Administration II, College Park, Md.

Record Group 126, Office of the Secretary, Territories (cited as OS, Terr., RG 126, NARA II)

NARA-D—National Archives and Records Administration, Denver, Colo.

Record Group 21, Bankruptcy Case Files, 1899–1911, New Mexico District Court, 4th Judicial District [Las Vegas] (cited as Bankruptcy, NMDC, 4th, RG 21, NARA-D)

Record Group 21, Criminal Docket 1881–1911, Records of the District Courts of the U.S., Territory of New Mexico, 1st Judicial District, Santa Fe (cited as CD, DCUS, NM, 1st, RG 21, NARA-D)

Record Group 21, Miscellaneous Case Files, 1874–99, District Courts of the United States, New Mexico Territorial Records, 1st Judicial District [Santa Fe] (cited as Misc., DCUS, NM, 1st, RG 21, NARA-D)

Record Group 21, U.S. Commissioners' Case Files, Records of the District Courts of the United States, New Mexico Territory, Records of the 5th Judicial District, Roswell (cited as USCommCF, DCUS, NM, 5th, RG 21, NARA-D)

Record Group 49, New Mexico, Letters from the Commissioner Concerning Serial Entries, Santa Fe (cited as NM, Comm. Re: Entries, SF, RG 49, NARA-D)

NMHM— New Mexico History Museum, Fray Angélico Chávez History Library, Santa Fe

Rex C. Hopson Collection, Collection # AC 110 (cited as RCHC, AC 110, FACHL, NMHM)

NMSL—New Mexico State Library, Santa Fe

Governor Herbert J. Hagerman Papers, Territorial Archives of New Mexico, microfilm reel (cited as reel, GovHJHP, TANM, NMSL)

Papers of Governor Miguel A. Otero, Territorial Archives of New Mexico, microfilm reel (cited as reel, GovMAOP, TANM, NMSL)

Record Group 48/75, Myra Ellen Jenkins National Archives microfilm (cited as RG, MEJNAM, NMSL)

RGHC—Rio Grande Historical Collections, Archives and Special Collections Department, New Mexico State University, Las Cruces

Holm O. Bursum Papers, MS 305 (cited as HOBP, MS 305, RGHC, ASC, NMSU)

Albert B. Fall Family Papers, MS 8 (cited as ABFFP, MS 8, RGHC, ASC, NMSU)

Papers of Herbert B. Holt, MS 61 (cited as PHBH, MS 61, RGHC, ASC, NMSU)
SRCA—State Records Center and Archives, Santa Fe
    Miscellaneous Letters and Diaries, serial no. 15818 (cited as Misc.L&D, ser. #15818, SRCA)
    L. Bradford Prince Papers, collection no. 1959-174 (cited as LBPP, col. no. 1959-174, SRCA)
    Governor Ezéquiel C. de Baca Papers, collection no. 1959-095 (cited as GovECdeBP, col. no. 1959-095, SRCA)
    U.S. Territorial and Supreme Court Records, Collection No. 1983-041 (cited as USTerrSCR, col. no. 1983-041, SRCA)
TRC—Theodore Roosevelt Collection, Harvard College Library, Harvard University, Cambridge, Mass. (cited as TRC, HCL, HU)
UWLSC—University of Washington Libraries Special Collections, Seattle
    Richard A. Ballinger Papers, MS Coll. 0015-001, microfilm (cited as reel, RABP, MS Col. 0015-001, UWLSC)

Government Publications

Bureau of the Census

Twelfth Census of the United States Taken in the Year 1900, Population. Vols. 1, 2. Washington, D.C: U.S. Census Office, 1901.
Thirteenth Census of the United States Taken in the Year 1910, Reports by States. Vol. 3. Washington, D.C.: Government Printing Office, 1913.

Congress

CR—*Congressional Record*

HOUSE

Committee on Public Lands. *Hearings Held Before the Committee on Public Lands of the House of Representatives, February 8, 1908, H.R. 16277.* 60th Congress, 1st Session. Washington, D.C.: Government Printing Office, 1908.
Committee on Territories. *Admission of New Mexico into the Union.* 54th Congress, 1st Session. Report No. 2259. Washington, D.C.: Government Printing Office, 1896
———. [Omnibus Statehood] *Bill 12543.* Report No. 1309. 57th Congress, 1st Session. Washington, D.C.: Government Printing Office, 1902.
———. [Hearings on] *Constitution for the Proposed State of New Mexico: Statements of Hon.* [Governor]. *William J. Mills, Hon. Henry W. Blair* [D.C. lobbyist], *Mrs. Margaret Dye Ellis* [Woman's Christian Temperance Union], *Hon. S. E. Nicholson* [Anti-Saloon League], *Hon.* [Delegate] *W. H. Andrews. February 17, 18, 21, 27, 1911.* 61st Congress, 2nd Session. Washington, D.C.:

Bibliography

Government Printing Office, 1911

———. *Hearings Before the Committee on Territories of the House of Representatives on House Joint Resolution No. 14: Approving the Constitutions Formed by the Constitutional Conventions of Territories of New Mexico and Arizona.* 61st Congress, 3rd [Special] Session. Washington, DC: Government Printing Office, 1911.

Contested Election Case of Octaviano A. Larrazolo v. William H. Andrews: From the Territory of New Mexico [filed 20 February 1907 and closed 17 April 1907]. 60th U.S. Congress, 1st Session. Washington, D.C.: Government Printing Office, 1907.

Sale of Certain Lands in New Mexico. Document Number 780. 59th Congress, 1st Session Washington, D.C: Government Printing Office, 1906.

[Joint] *Statehood Bill, June 13, 1906.* Report No. 4925. 59th Congress, 1st Session. Washington, D.C.: Government Printing Office, 1906.

SENATE

Committee on Territories. *New Statehood Bill: Hearings Before the Subcommittee of the Committee on Territories on House Bill 12543, to Enable the People of Oklahoma, Arizona, and New Mexico to Form Constitutions and State Governments.* 57th Congress, 2nd Session. Senate Document No. 36. Washington, D.C.: Government Printing Office, 1902.

———. *Statehood for the Territories,* 57th Congress, 2nd Session. Senate Document No. 153. Washington, D.C.: Government Printing Office, 1903.

———. *Statehood. Hearing before the Committee on Territories, United States Senate, on the Bill S. 5916.* Washington, D.C.: Government Printing Office, 1910.

———. *Hearings before the Committee on Territories, United States Senate, House Joint Resolution 14,* 62nd Congress, [3rd] Special Session. Washington, D.C.: Government Printing Office, 1911.

Memorial of the National Woolgrowers' Association and Others, with Accompanying Papers, Asking Protective Legislation for Sheep Husbandry, 54th Congress, 1st Session. Document No. 17, Washington, D.C.: Government Printing Office, 1895.

Department of the Interior

Secretary of the Interior. *Annual Report of the United States Mine Inspector for the Territory of New Mexico to the Secretary of the Interior for the Fiscal Year Ended June 30, 1903.* Washington: Government Printing Office, 1903.

———. *Report of the Secretary of the Interior for the Fiscal Year 1898.* Washington, D.C: Government Printing Office, 1898.

———. *Report of the Governor of New Mexico* [Otero] *to the Secretary of the Interior* [1902]. Washington, D.C.: Government Printing Office, 1902.

———. *Report of the Governor of New Mexico* [Otero] *to the Secretary of the Interior* [1903]. Washington, D.C.: Government Printing Office, 1903.

———. *Report of the Governor of New Mexico* [Otero] *to the Secretary of the Interior, 1904.* Washington, D.C: Government Printing Office, 1904.

———. *Report of the Governor of New Mexico* [Hagerman] *to the Secretary of the Interior, 1906.* Washington, D.C.: Government Printing Office, 1906]

———. *Report of the Governor of New Mexico* [Curry] *to the Secretary of the Interior, 1908.* Washington, D.C: Government Printing Office, 1908.

———. *Report of the Mine Inspector for the Territory of New Mexico to the Secretary of the Interior* [1907]. Washington, D.C.: Government Printing Office, 1907.

———. *Reports of the Department of the Interior for the Fiscal Year Ended June 30, 1909.* 2 Vol. Washington, D.C.: Government Printing Office, 1910.

———. *Reports of the U.S. Department of the Interior for the Fiscal Year Ended 30 June 1914.* Washington, D.C.: Government Printing Office, 1915.

GAO—Government Accountability Office

Report. *Treaty of Guadalupe Hidalgo: Findings and Possible Options Regarding Longstanding Community Land Grant Claims in New Mexico.* Washington, D.C.: Government Accountability Office, 2004.

GSA—General Services Administration

Report. *Federal Real Property Profile 2004.* Washington, D.C.: Government Printing Office, 2005.

Library of Congress

"Declaration and Resolutions Submitted for Adoption to the People of the Territory of New Mexico at Their Statehood Convention, Held at Albuquerque, October 15 and 16, 1901, Demanding a State Form of Government from the Congress of the United States." Microform Reading Room, microfilm reel 86, document 7831.

New Mexico

College of Agriculture and Mechanic Arts. *Twenty-fourth Annual Report, Agricultural Experiment Station, State College, New Mexico, 1912-1913.* Las Cruces: Rio Grande Republican, 1914.

Office of the Auditor, *Report of the Auditor of the Territory of New Mexico* [1901–1902]. Santa Fe: New Mexican Printing Co., n.d. [1903].

Secretary of New Mexico. *Corporation Filings, Territory of New Mexico, 1910.* Santa Fe: New Mexico Printing Co., 1911.

[Sullivan, Vernon L.] *Report of the Territorial Engineer to the Governor of New Mexico for the Year Ending June 30, 1907.* Santa Fe: New Mexico Printing Company, 1907.

Territorial Auditor. *Report of the Auditor, Territory of New Mexico, for the Two Years Ending November 30, 1906.* Santa Fe: New Mexican Printing Co., 1907.

U.S. Supreme Court Decisions

Coyle v. Smith, 221 U.S. 559 (1911).
Gonzales v. Cunningham, 164 U.S. 612 (1896).
Hayes v. United States, 170 U.S. 637 (1898).
Hutchings v. Low, 82 U.S. 77 (1872).
New Mexico v. Texas, 275 U.S. 279 (1927).
New Mexico v. Texas, 276 U.S. 557 (1928).
Plessy v. Ferguson 163 U.S. 537 (1896).
Rio Arriba Land and Cattle Company v. United States 167 U.S. 298 (1897).
United States v. Joseph, 94 U.S. 614 (1876).
United States v. [Felipe] Sandoval, 231 U.S. 28 (1913).
United States v. [Julian] Sandoval, 167 U.S. 278 (1897).
United States v. Santa Fe, 165 U.S. 675 (1897).

Newspapers

Albuquerque Morning Democrat
Albuquerque Morning Journal
Atlanta Constitution
La Bandera Americana (Albuquerque)
Carlsbad Argus
Chicago Daily Tribune
Christian Science Monitor
Colored American (Washington, D.C.)
El Combate (Wagon Mound)
El Defensor del Pueblo (Socorro)
Deming Headlight
Deming Herald
El Eco del Valle (Las Cruces)
La Estrella (Las Cruces)
El Independiente (Las Vegas)
El Hispano Americano (Roy)
El Labrador (Las Cruces)
Las Cruces Progress
Las Vegas Optic
Las Vegas Optic and Live Stock Grower
Los Angeles Times
New Mexican Review (Santa Fe)
New York Times

New York Tribune
El Nuevo Mexicano (Santa Fe)
El Nuevo Mundo (Albuquerque)
Philadelphia Inquirer
Pittsburg[h] Gazette
Revista Católica (Las Vegas)
Rio Grande Republican (Las Cruces)
St. Louis Globe-Democrat
Santa Fe New Mexican
Socorro Advertiser
El Tiempo (Las Cruces)
La Voz del Pueblo (Las Vegas)
Washington [D.C.] *Bee*
Washington Post
Wilkes-Barre [Pa.] Times

Books

Allen, Paula Gunn. *The Sacred Hoop: Recovering the Feminine in American Indian Traditions.* Boston, Mass.: Beacon Press, 1992.
Alonzo, Armando. *Tejano Legacy: Rancheros and Settlers in South Texas, 1734–1900.* Albuquerque: University of New Mexico Press, 1998.
Anschuetz, Kurt F., and Thomas W. Merlan. *More Than a Scenic Mountain Landscape: Valles Caldera National Preserve Land Use History.* Fort Collins, Colo.: U.S. Department of Agriculture, Forest Service, Rocky Mountain Research Station, 2007.
Armitage, Susan, and Elizabeth Jameson. *The Women's West.* Norman: University of Oklahoma Press, 1987.
Bakken, Gordon Morris. *Rocky Mountain Constitution Making, 1850–1912.* Westport, Conn.: Greenwood Press, 1987.
Ball, Larry D. *Desert Lawmen: The High Sheriffs of New Mexico and Arizona, 1846–1912.* Albuquerque: University of New Mexico Press, 1996.
———. *United States Marshals of New Mexico and Arizona Territories, 1846–1912.* Albuquerque: University of New Mexico Press, 1978.
Basso, Matthew, Laura McCall, and Dee Garceau, eds. *Across the Great Divide: Cultures of Manhood in the American West.* New York: Routledge, 2001.
Baton, Maisha. *Do Remember Me: Conversations with New Mexico Black History.* Albuquerque: n.p., 2000.
———, and Henry J. Walt. *A History of Blackdom, N.M. in the Context of the African American Post-Civil War Colonization Movement.* Santa Fe: Historic Preservation Division, Office of Cultural Affairs, 1996.
Baxter, John O. *Dividing New Mexico's Waters, 1700–1912.* Albuquerque: University of New Mexico Press, 1997.

——. *Las Carneradas: Sheep Trade in New Mexico, 1700–1860.* Albuquerque: University of New Mexico Press, 1987.

Beard, Charles A. *An Economic Interpretation of the Constitution of the United States.* 1913. Reprint, New York: Macmillan, 1972.

Beck, Warren A., and Ynez D. Haase. *Historical Atlas of New Mexico.* Norman: University of Oklahoma Press, 1969.

Benjamin, Thomas, and Mark Wasserman, eds. *Provinces of the Revolution: Essays on Regional Mexican History, 1910–1929.* Albuquerque: University of New Mexico Press, 1990.

Berger, Stefan, ed. *A Companion to Nineteenth-Century Europe.* Malden, Mass.: Blackwell, 2006.

Bloom, Lansing B., ed. *New Mexico in the Great War.* Santa Fe: El Palacio Press, 1927.

Blum, John Morton. *The Republican Roosevelt.* 2nd ed. Cambridge, Mass.: Harvard University Press, 1971.

Bogener, Stephen D. *Ditches across the Desert: Irrigation in the Lower Pecos Valley.* Lubbock: Texas Tech University Press, 2003.

Bogue, Allan G., and Margaret B. Bogue, eds. *The Jeffersonian Dream: Studies in the History of American Land Policy and Development [by] Paul W. Gates.* Albuquerque: University of New Mexico Press, 1996.

Bowers, Claude G. *Beveridge and the Progressive Era.* New York: Literary Guild, 1932.

Boyd, Nathan E. *New Mexico and Statehood: Admission into the Union Essential to Territory's Material Progress. Analysis of the Culberson-Stephens Bill. Presented to the Committee on Territories, U.S. House of Representatives, 57th Congress, 1st Session.* Washington, D.C.: Judd & Detweiler Printers, 1902.

Boyle, Susan. *Los Capitalistas: Hispano Merchants on the Santa Fe Trail.* Albuquerque: University of New Mexico Press, 1997.

Bradfute, Richard W. *The Court of Private Land Claims: The Adjudication of Spanish and Mexican Land Grant Titles.* Albuquerque: University of New Mexico Press, 1975.

Braeman, John. *Albert J. Beveridge: American Nationalist.* Chicago: University of Chicago Press, 1971.

Brinkley, Douglas. *The Wilderness Warrior: Theodore Roosevelt and the Crusade for America.* New York: HarperCollins, 2009.

Brown, Lorin W. with Charles L. Briggs and Marta Weigle. *Hispano Folklife of New Mexico: The Lorin W. Brown Federal Writers' Project Manuscripts.* Albuquerque: University of New Mexico Press, 1978.

Burns, James MacGregor. *The Workshop of Democracy.* Vol. 2, *The American Experiment.* New York: Alfred A. Knopf, 1985.

Burton, David H. *Taft, Roosevelt, and the Limits of Friendship.* Madison, N.J.: Fairleigh Dickinson University Press, 2005.

Butler, Nicholas Murray. *The Meaning of Education: Contributions to a Philosophy of Education.* Revised and enlarged edition. New York: Charles Scribner's Sons, 1915.

Butt, Archibald W. *Taft and Roosevelt: The Intimate Letters of Archie Butt, Military Aide.* 2 vols. Garden City, N.Y.: Doubleday, Doran & Co., 1930.

Cabeza de Baca, Fabiola. *We Fed Them Cactus.* Introduction by Tey Diana Rebolledo. 2nd ed. Albuquerque: University of New Mexico Press, 1994.

Caffey, David L. *Frank Springer and New Mexico: From the Colfax County War to the Emergence of Modern Santa Fe.* College Station: Texas A & M University Press, 2006.

Chace, James. *1912: Wilson, Roosevelt, Taft, and Debs: The Election That Changed the Country.* New York: Simon & Schuster, 2004.

Clark, Ira B. *Water in New Mexico: A History of Its Management and Use.* Albuquerque: University of New Mexico Press, 1987.

Cline, Dorothy L. *New Mexico's 1910 Constitution: A 19th Century Product.* Santa Fe: Lightning Tree, 1985.

Coatsworth, John. *Growth against Development: The Economic Impact of Railroads in Porfirian Mexico.* DeKalb: Northern Illinois University Press, 1981.

College of Agriculture and Home Economics. *Agricultural Research at New Mexico State University since 1889.* Las Cruces: New Mexico State University, 1969.

Connell-Szasz, Margaret. *Education and the American Indian: The Road to Self-Determination.* Revised, enlarged edition. Albuquerque: University of New Mexico Press, 1999.

Cooper, John Milton, Jr. *Pivotal Decades: The United States, 1900–1920.* New York: W. W. Norton, 1990.

Crane, Leo. *Desert Drums: The Pueblo Indians of New Mexico, 1540–1928.* Boston: Little, Brown, 1928.

DeBuys, William. *Enchantment and Exploitation: The Life and Hard Times of a New Mexico Mountain Range.* Albuquerque: University of New Mexico Press, 1985.

De León, Arnoldo. *The Tejano Community, 1836–1900.* Albuquerque: University of New Mexico Press, 1982.

Deloria, Philip J. *Indians in Unexpected Places.* Lawrence: University Press of Kansas, 2004.

Depew, Chauncey M. *My Memoirs of Eighty Years.* New York: Charles Scribner's Sons, 1921.

Deutsch, Sarah. *No Separate Refuge: Culture, Class, and Gender on an Anglo-Hispanic Frontier in the American Southwest.* New York: Oxford University Press, 1987.

Deverell, William. *A Companion to the American West.* Malden, Mass.: Blackwell, 2004.

DeVoto, Bernard, ed. *Mark Twain in Eruption.* New York: Harper and Brothers, 1940.

[Dexter Historical Society], *As We Remember It by Dexter Old Timers*. Roswell: Hall-Poorbaugh Press, [1974].

Dilworth, Leah. *Imagining Indians in the Southwest: Persistent Visions of a Primitive Past*. Washington, D. C.: Smithsonian Institution Press, 1996.

Dunbar-Ortiz, Roxanne. *Roots of Resistance: A History of Land Tenure in New Mexico*. Norman: University of Oklahoma Press, 2007.

Duncan, Dayton. *The National Parks: America's Best Idea*. New York: Alfred A. Knopf, 2009.

Eblen, Jack Ericson. *The First and Second United States Empires: Governors and Territorial Government, 1784–1912*. Pittsburgh: University of Pittsburgh Press, 1968.

Ebright, Malcolm. *Land Grants and Lawsuits in Northern New Mexico*. Rev. ed. Santa Fe: Center for Land Grant Studies Press, 2008.

Emmons, David M. *Beyond the American Pale: The Irish in the West, 1845–1910*. Norman: University of *Oklahoma Press, 2010*.

Etulain, Richard W. *Beyond the Missouri: The Story of the American West*. Albuquerque: University of New Mexico Press, 2006.

Folsom, Franklin. *Black Cowboy: The Life and Legend of George McJunkin*. Niwot, Colo.: R. Rinehart Publishers, 1992.

Foner, Eric. *The Fiery Trial: Abraham Lincoln and American Slavery*. New York: W. W. Norton, 2010.

Foote, Cheryl. *Women of the New Mexico Frontier, 1846–1912*. 1991. Reprint. Albuquerque: University of New Mexico Press, 2005.

Foraker, Joseph Benson. *Notes of a Busy Life*. 2 vols. Cincinnati: Stewart & Kidd Co., 1916.

Frank, Ross. *From Settler to Citizen: New Mexican Economic Development and the Creation of Vecino Society, 1750–1820*. Berkeley: University of California Press, 2000.

García, Nasario, ed. *Abuelitos: Stories of the Río Puerco Valley*. Albuquerque: University of New Mexico Press, 1992.

———. *Recuerdos de los Viejitos: Tales of the Río Puerco*. Albuquerque: University of New Mexico Press, 1987.

Gieske, Millard L., and Steven J. Keillor. *Norwegian Yankee: Knute Nelson and the Failure of American Politics, 1860–1923*. Northfield, Minn.: Norwegian-American Historical Association, 1995.

Glover, Vernon J., and Joseph P. Hereford, Jr. *Zuni Mountain Railroads, Cibola National Forest, New Mexico*. Albuquerque: USDA Forest Service, Southwestern Region, 1986.

Gómez, Laura A. *Manifest Destinies: The Making of the Mexican American Race*. New York: New York University Press, 2007.

Gonzales-Berry, Erlinda, and David R. Maciel, eds. *The Contested Homeland: A Chicano History of New Mexico*. Albuquerque: University of New Mexico Press, 2000.

Gould, Lewis L. *Four Hats in the Ring: The 1912 Election and the Birth of Modern American Politics*. Lawrence: University Press of Kansas, 2008.

———. *The Presidency of Theodore Roosevelt*. Lawrence: University Press of Kansas, 1991.

———. *The Presidency of Theodore Roosevelt*. 2nd ed. Lawrence: University Press of Kansas, 2011.

———. *The Presidency of William McKinley*. Lawrence: Regents Press of Kansas, 1980.

Graybar, Lloyd J. *Albert Shaw of the* Review of Reviews. Lexington: University Press of Kentucky, 1974.

Greenwald, Emily. *Reconfiguring the Reservation: The Nez Perce, Jicarilla Apache, and the Dawes Act*. Albuquerque: University of New Mexico Press, 2002.

Griego, Alfonso. *Voices of the Territory of New Mexico: An Oral History of People of Spanish Descent and Early Settlers Born During the Territorial Days*. N.p.: self-published, 1985.

Griswold del Castillo, Richard. *The Treaty of Guadalupe Hidalgo: A Legacy of Conflict*. Norman: University of Oklahoma Press, 1990.

Gutiérrez, Ramón. *When Jesus Came the Corn Mothers Went Away: Marriage, Sexuality, and Power in New Mexico, 1500–1846*. Stanford: Stanford University Press, 1991.

Hagerman, Herbert J. *A Statement in Regard to Certain Matters Concerning the Governorship and Political Affairs in New Mexico, 1906–1907*. Roswell, N. Mex.: privately printed, 1908.

Hall, G. Emlen. *High and Dry: The Texas–New Mexico Struggle for the Pecos River*. Albuquerque: University of New Mexico Press, 2002.

Harris, Charles H. III, and Louis R. Sadler. *The Secret War in El Paso: Mexican Revolutionary Intrigue, 1906–1920*. Albuquerque: University of New Mexico Press, 2009.

———. *The Texas Rangers and the Mexican Revolution: The Bloodiest Decade, 1910–1920*. Albuquerque: University of New Mexico Press, 2004.

Harris, Theodore D., comp. and ed. *Black Frontiersman: The Memoirs of Henry O. Flipper*. Fort Worth: Texas Christian University Press, 1997.

Hart, John. *Empire and Revolution: The Americans in Mexico since the Civil War*. Berkeley: University of California Press, 2002.

Hawley, Joshua David. *Theodore Roosevelt: Preacher of Righteousness*. New Haven: Yale University Press, 2008.

Heilbroner, Robert L. *The Worldly Philosophers: The Lives, Times, and Ideas of the Great Economic Thinkers*. Rev. ed. New York: Simon and Schuster, 1961.

Hening, H. B., editor. *George Curry, 1861–1947: An Autobiography*. Albuquerque: University of New Mexico Press, 1958.

Hening, H. B., and E. Dana Johnson. *Albuquerque, New Mexico: Chief City of a New Empire in the Great Southwest*. Albuquerque: privately printed, 1908.

Herbermann, Charles G., et al., eds. *The Catholic Encyclopedia.* New York: Robert Appleton Co., 1911.

Hicks, John D., George E. Mowry, and Robert E. Burke. *The American Nation,* vol. 2. 4th ed.; Boston: Houghton Mifflin, 1965.

Hillerman, Tony. *Seldom Disappointed: A Memoir.* New York: HarperCollins, 2001.

Hoffmann, Charles. *The Depression of the Nineties: An Economic History.* Westport, Conn.: Greenwood Publishing, 1970.

Hofstadter, Richard. *Social Darwinism in American Thought.* Rev. ed. Boston: Beacon Press, 1955.

Holmes, Jack E. *Politics in New Mexico.* Albuquerque: University of New Mexico Press, 1967.

Horgan, Paul. *Lamy of Santa Fe.* New York: Farrar, Straus, and Giroux, 1975.

Horn, Calvin P. *New Mexico's Troubled Years: The Story of the Early Territorial Governors.* Albuquerque: Horn & Wallace, Publishers, 1963.

Horsman, Reginald. *Race and Manifest Destiny: The Origins of American Racial Anglo-Saxonism.* Cambridge, Mass.: Harvard University Press, 1981.

Jacobs, Margaret D. *Engendered Encounters: Feminism and Pueblo Cultures, 1879–1934.* Lincoln: University of Nebraska Press, 1999.

Jacobson, Matthew Frye. *Barbarian Virtues: The United States Encounters Foreign Peoples at Home and Abroad, 1876–1917.* New York: Hill and Wang, 2000.

Jaramillo, Cleofas M. Introduction by Tey Diana Rebolledo. *Romance of a Little Village Girl.* 1955. Reprint. Albuquerque: University of New Mexico Press, 2000.

Jensen, Joan M. *Promise to the Land: Essays on Rural Women.* Albuquerque: University of New Mexico Press, 1991.

———, and Darlis A. Miller, eds. *New Mexico Women: Intercultural Perspectives.* Albuquerque: University of New Mexico Press, 1986.

Julyan, Robert. *The Place Names of New Mexico.* Albuquerque: University of New Mexico Press, 1996.

Kanegsberg, Henry. *Addresses at the Republican National Convention, 1904.* New York: N.p., 1904.

Katz, Friedrich. *The Life and Times of Pancho Villa.* Stanford: Stanford University Press, 1998.

Keleher, William A. *The Fabulous Frontier, 1846–1912.* 1962. Facsimile edition. Santa Fe: Sunstone Press, 2008.

Kehl, James A. *Boss Rule in the Gilded Age: Matt Quay of Pennsylvania.* Pittsburgh: University of Pittsburgh Press, 1981.

Kelly, Daniel T., with Beatrice Chauvenet. *The Buffalo Head: A Century of Mercantile Pioneering in the Southwest.* Santa Fe: Vergara Publishing Co., 1972.

Kern, Robert W. *Labor in New Mexico: Unions, Strikes, and Social History since 1881.* Albuquerque: University of New Mexico Press, 1983.

———, and Meredith D. Dodge, eds. *Historical Dictionary of Modern Spain, 1700–1988.* New York: Greenwood Press, 1990.

Kessell, John L. *The Missions of New Mexico since 1776.* Albuquerque: University of New Mexico Press, 1980.

Knight, Alan. *The Mexican Revolution.* 2 vols. Cambridge: Cambridge University Press, 1986.

Lamar, Howard R. *The American Southwest, 1846–1912.* Rev. ed. Albuquerque: University of New Mexico Press, 2001.

Larson, Robert W. *New Mexico's Quest for Statehood, 1846–1912.* Albuquerque: University of New Mexico Press, 1968.

———. *Populism in the Mountain West.* Albuquerque: University of New Mexico Press, 1986.

Limerick, Patricia Nelson. *The Legacy of Conquest: The Unbroken Past of the American West.* New York: W. W. Norton, 1987.

———. *Something in the Soil: Legacies and Reckonings in the New West.* New York: W. W. Norton, 2000.

Love, Eric T. L. *Race over Empire: Racism and U.S. Imperialism, 1865–1900.* Chapel Hill: University of North Carolina Press, 2004.

Lummis, Charles F. *The Land of Poco Tiempo.* 1893. Reprint. Albuquerque: University of New Mexico Press, 1952.

Lyons, Scott Richards. *X-Marks: Native Signatures of Assent.* Minneapolis: University of Minnesota Press, 2010.

McMurry, Linda O. *George Washington Carver: Scientist and Symbol.* New York: Oxford University Press, 1981.

Mack, Stephen John. *The Pragmatic Whitman: Reimaging American Democracy.* Iowa City: University of Iowa Press, 2002.

Manzano Manzano, Juan. *Historia de las Recopilaciones de Indias.* 2 vols. Madrid: Ediciones Cultura Hispánica, 1950–56.

Margulies, Herbert F. *Reconciliation and Revival: James R. Mann and the House Republicans in the Wilson Era.* Westport, Conn.: Greenwood Press, 1996.

Marriott, Alice. *María: The Potter of San Ildefonso.* Norman: University of Oklahoma Press, 1948.

Martin, John Bartlow. *Indiana: An Interpretation.* 1947. Reprint. Bloomington: Indiana University Press, 1992.

Matthews, Gary Robert. *Basil William Duke, CSA: The Right Man in the Right Place.* Lexington: University Press of Kentucky, 2005.

Meléndez, A. Gabriel. *So All Is Not Lost: The Poetics of Print in Nuevomexicano Communities, 1834–1958.* Albuquerque: University of New Mexico Press, 1997.

Meyer, Doris. *Speaking for Themselves: Nuevomexicano Cultural Identity and the Spanish-Language Press, 1880–1920.* Albuquerque: University of New Mexico Press, 1996.

Mitchell, Lawrence E. *The Speculation Economy: How Finance Triumphed over Industry*. San Francisco: Berrett-Koehler Publishers, 2007.

Mitchell, Pablo. *Coyote Nation: Sexuality, Race, and Conquest in Modernizing New Mexico, 1880–1920*. Chicago: University of Chicago Press, 2005.

Mock, Charlotte K. *Bridges: New Mexico Black Women, 1900–1950*. Albuquerque: New Mexico Commission on the Status of Women, 1985.

Montaño, Mary. *Tradiciones Nuevomexicanas: Hispano Arts and Culture of New Mexico*. Albuquerque: University of New Mexico Press, 2001.

Montejano, David. *Anglos and Mexicans in the Making of Texas, 1836–1986*. Austin: University of Texas Press, 1987.

Montgomery, Charles. *The Spanish Redemption: Heritage, Power, and Loss on New Mexico's Upper Rio Grande*. Berkeley: University of California Press, 2002.

Montoya, María E. *Translating Property: The Maxwell Land Grant and the Conflict over Land in the American West, 1840–1900*. Berkeley: University of California Press, 2002.

Moore, Paula. *Cricket in the Web: The 1949 Unsolved Murder that Unraveled Politics in New Mexico* Albuquerque: University of New Mexico Press, 2009.

Morgan, Edmund S. *American Heroes: Profiles of Men and Women Who Shaped Early America*. New York: W. W. Norton, 2009.

———. *Inventing the People: The Rise of Popular Sovereignty in England and the United States*. New York: W. W. Norton, 1988.

Morison, Elting E. *Cowboys and Kings: Three Great Letters by Theodore Roosevelt*. Cambridge, Mass.: Harvard University Press, 1954.

———, et al., eds. *The Letters of Theodore Roosevelt*. 8 vols. Cambridge, Mass.: Harvard University Press, 1951–54.

Morris, Edmund. *Colonel Roosevelt*. New York: Random House, 2010.

———. *The Rise of Theodore Roosevelt*. New York: Coward, McCann & Geoghegan, 1979.

———. *Theodore Rex*. New York: Random House, 2001.

Myrick, David F. *New Mexico's Railroads: A Historical Survey*. Albuquerque: University of New Mexico Press, 1990.

Nasaw, David. *The Chief: The Life of William Randolph Hearst*. Boston: Houghton Mifflin, 2000.

Nieto-Phillips, John. *The Language of Blood: The Making of Spanish-American Identity in New Mexico, 1880s–1930s*. Albuquerque: University of New Mexico Press, 2004.

Norris, Pippa, and Ronald Ingelhart. *Sacred and Secular: Religion and Politics Worldwide*. Cambridge: Cambridge University Press, 2004.

Nostrand, Richard L. *El Cerrito, New Mexico: Eight Generations in a Spanish Village*. Norman: University of Oklahoma Press, 2003.

———. *The Hispano Homeland*. Norman: University of Oklahoma Press, 1992.

Ortiz, Alfonso, ed. *New Perspectives on the Pueblos*. Albuquerque: University of New Mexico Press, 1972.

Orwell, George. *Inside the Whale and Other Essays*. London: Penguin Books, 1962.

Otero, Miguel Antonio. *My Life on the Frontier, 1882–1897: Death Knell of a Territory and Birth of a State*. Albuquerque: University of New Mexico Press, 1939.

———. *My Nine Years as Governor of the Territory of New Mexico, 1897–1906*. Albuquerque: University of New Mexico Press, 1940.

Parish, William J. *The Charles Ilfeld Company: A Study of the Rise and Decline of Mercantile Capitalism in New Mexico*. Cambridge, Mass.: Harvard University Press, 1961.

Paxson, Frederic L. *The Admission of the "Omnibus" States, 1889–1890*. Madison: State Historical Society of Wisconsin, 1912.

Peña, Abe. *Memories of Cíbola: Stories from New Mexico Villages*. Albuquerque: University of New Mexico Press, 1997.

Penick, James Jr. *Progressive Politics and Conservation: The Ballinger-Pinchot Affair*. Chicago: University of Chicago Press, 1968.

Peterson, C. S. *New Mexico Constitutional Convention Book: Containing Photographs and Biographical Sketches of the Members*. Denver: C. S. Peterson, 1911.

———. *Representative New Mexicans: The National Newspapers Reference Book of the New State*. Denver: C. S. Peterson, 1914.

Pisani, Donald J. *To Reclaim a Divided West: Water, Law, and Public Policy, 1848–1902*. Albuquerque: University of New Mexico Press, 1992.

Poldervaart, Arie W. *Black-Robed Justice: A History of the Administration of Justice in New Mexico from the American Occupation in 1846 until Statehood in 1912*. Santa Fe: Historical Society of New Mexico, 1948.

Powell, Philip Wayne. *Tree of Hate: Propaganda and Prejudice Affecting United States Relations with the Hispanic World*. Reprint; Albuquerque: University of New Mexico Press, 2008.

Price, V. B. *The Orphaned Land: New Mexico's Environment since the Manhattan Project*. Albuquerque: University of New Mexico Press, 2011.

Prince, L. Bradford. *New Mexico's Struggle for Statehood: Sixty Years of Effort to Obtain Self Government*. Santa Fe: New Mexican Printing Co., 1910.

Proctor, Ben. *William Randolph Hearst: The Early Years, 1863–1910*. New York: Oxford University Press, 1998.

Remini, Robert V. *At the Edge of the Precipice: Henry Clay and the Compromise That Saved the Union*. New York: Basic Books, 2010.

———. *Daniel Webster: The Man and His Time*. New York: W. W. Norton, 1997.

Remley, David. *Bell Ranch: Cattle Ranching in the Southwest, 1824–1947*. Albuquerque: University of New Mexico Press, 1993.

Reynolds, Matthew. *Spanish and Mexican Land Laws: New Spain and Mexico*. St. Louis: Buxton and Skinner Stationery Co., 1895.

Riley, Glenda. *Building and Breaking Families in the American West.* Albuquerque: University of New Mexico Press, 1996.

Ripley, William Z. *Railroads: Rates and Regulation.* New York: Longmans, Green, 1913.

Rivera, José A. *Acequia Culture: Water, Land, and Community in the Southwest.* Albuquerque: University of New Mexico Press, 1998.

———. *La Sociedad: Guardians of Hispanic Culture along the Río Grande.* Albuquerque: University of New Mexico Press, 2010.

Roberts, Calvin A. *Our New Mexico: A Twentieth Century History.* Albuquerque: University of New Mexico Press, 2005.

Robinson, Charles M. III. *The Fall of a Black Army Officer: Racism and the Myth of Henry O. Flipper.* Norman: University of Oklahoma Press, 2008.

Robinson, William A. *Thomas B. Reed, Parliamentarian.* New York: Dodd, Mead, & Co., 1930.

Rodríguez, Sylvia. *Acequia: Water-Sharing, Sanctity, and Place.* Santa Fe: School of Advanced Research Press, 2006.

Roosevelt, Theodore. *An Autobiography.* 1913. Reprint. New York: Da Capo Press, 1985.

———. *Selections from the Correspondence of Theodore Roosevelt and Henry Cabot Lodge, 1884–1918.* 2 vols. New York: Charles Scribner's Sons, 1925.

———. *The Strenuous Life: Essays and Addresses.* New York: Century Co., 1902.

Rosenbaum, Robert J. *Mexicano Resistance in the Southwest: The Sacred Right of Self-Preservation.* Austin: University of Texas Press, 1981.

Rothman, Hal. *On Rims and Ridges: The Los Alamos Area Since 1880.* Lincoln: University of Nebraska Press, 1992.

Ruxton, George F. A. *Adventures in Mexico and the Rocky Mountains.* New York: Harper & Brothers, 1848.

Sánchez, Joseph P. *Between Two Rivers: The Atrisco Land Grant in Albuquerque History, 1692–1968.* Norman: University of Oklahoma Press, 2008.

Sando, Joe. *Nee Hemish: A History of Jemez Pueblo.* 1982. Reprint. Santa Fe: Clear Light Publishing, 2008.

Schackel, Sandra K. *Western Women's Lives: Continuity and Change in the Twentieth Century.* Albuquerque: University of New Mexico Press, 2003.

Scharff, Virginia, and Carolyn Brucken. *Home Lands: How Women Made the West.* Berkeley: University of California Press, 2010.

Silber, William L. *When Washington Shut Down Wall Street: The Great Financial Crisis of 1914 and the Origins of America's Monetary Supremacy.* Princeton, N.J.: Princeton University Press, 2007.

Simmons, Marc. *Albuquerque: A Narrative History.* Albuquerque: University of New Mexico Press, 1982.

———. *The Little Lion of the Southwest: A Life of Manuel Antonio Chaves.* Chicago: Swallow Press, 1973.

———. *People of the Sun: Some Out-of-Fashion Southwesterners.* Albuquerque: University of New Mexico Press, 1979.

———. *Witchcraft in the Southwest: Spanish and Indian Supernaturalism on the Rio Grande.* Lincoln: University of Nebraska Press, 1974.

Smith, Harriet Elinor, et al., eds. *Autobiography of Mark Twain.* Berkeley: University of California Press, 2010.

Smith, Toby. *Coal Town: The Life and Times of Dawson, New Mexico.* Santa Fe: Ancient City Press, 1993.

Staloff, Darren. *Hamilton, Adams, Jefferson: The Politics of Enlightenment and the American Founding.* New York: Hill and Wang, 2005.

The Statesman's Yearbook: Statistical and Historical Annual of the States of the World for the Year 1913. New York: MacMillan & Co., 1913.

Steele, Thomas J., ed. and trans. *The Alabados of New Mexico.* Albuquerque: University of New Mexico Press, 2005.

———. *Bishop Lamy: In His Own Words.* Albuquerque: LPD Press, 2000.

———, ed. *New Mexico Spanish Religious Oratory, 1800–1900.* Albuquerque: University of New Mexico Press, 1997.

Stegmaier, Mark J. *Texas, New Mexico, and the Compromise of 1850: Boundary Dispute and Sectional Crisis.* Kent, Ohio: Kent State University Press, 1996.

Stephenson, Nathaniel Wright. *Nelson W. Aldrich: A Leader in American Politics.* New York: Charles Scribner's Sons, 1930.

Stratton, David. *Tempest over Teapot Dome: The Story of Albert B. Fall.* Norman: University of Oklahoma Press, 1998.

———, ed. *Washington Comes of Age: The State in the National Experience.* Pullman: Washington State University Press, 1992.

Sutter, L. M. *New Mexico Baseball: Miners, Outlaws, Indians, and Isotopes, 1880 to the Present.* Jefferson, N.C.: McFarland, 2010.

Taylor, Quintard. *In Search of the Racial Frontier: African Americans in the American West, 1528–1990.* New York: W. W. Norton, 1998.

Tiller, Veronica E. Velarde. *The Jicarilla Apache Tribe: A History.* Rev. ed. Lincoln: University of Nebraska Press, 1992.

Tobias, Henry. *A History of the Jews in New Mexico.* Albuquerque: University of New Mexico Press, 1990.

Tórrez, Robert J. *Myth of the Hanging Tree: Stories of Crime and Punishment in Territorial New Mexico.* Albuquerque: University of New Mexico Press, 2008.

Twitchell, Ralph Emerson. *Leading Facts of New Mexican History.* 5 vols. 1912. Reprint. Albuquerque: Horn & Wallace, Publishers, 1963.

Utley, Robert M. *The Indian Frontier of the American West, 1845–1890.* Albuquerque: University of New Mexico Press, 1984.

Victory, John P., et al., eds. *Compiled Laws of New Mexico, 1897: In Accordance with an Act of the Legislature, Approved March 16th, 1897.* Santa Fe: New Mexico Printing Co., 1897.

Vlasich, James A. *Pueblo Indian Agriculture.* Albuquerque: University of New Mexico Press, 2005.

Wagner, Tricia Martineau. *Black Cowboys of the Old West.* Guilford, Conn.: Twodot, 2011.

Walter, Paul A. F., Frank W. Clancy, and Miguel A. Otero. *Colonel José Francisco Chaves, 1833–1904.* Santa Fe: Historical Society of New Mexico, 1926.

Weber, David J. *Foreigners in Their Native Land: Historical Roots of the Mexican American.* 30th anniversary edition. Albuquerque: University of New Mexico Press, 2003.

Webster, Daniel. *The Writings and Speeches of Daniel Webster.* 18 vols. Boston: Little, Brown, & Co., 1903.

West, Elliott. *Growing Up with the Country: Childhood on the Far Western Frontier.* Albuquerque: University of New Mexico Press, 1989.

Weigle, Marta. *Brothers of Light, Brothers of Blood: The Penitentes of the Southwest.* Albuquerque: University of New Mexico Press, 1976.

———, and Barbara Babcock, editors. *The Great Southwest of the Fred Harvey Company and the Santa Fe Railway.* Phoenix: Heard Museum, 1996.

———, with Frances Levine and Louise Stiver, editors, *Telling New Mexico: A New History.* Santa Fe: Museum of New Mexico Press, 2009.

Wesley, Charles H. *The History of the National Association of Colored Women's Clubs: A Legacy of Service.* Washington, D.C.: The Association, 1984.

Wenger, Tisa. *We Have A Religion: The 1920s Pueblo Indian Dance Controversy and American Religious Freedom.* Chapel Hill: University of North Carolina Press, 2009.

Westphall, Victor. *Thomas Benton Catron and His Era.* Tucson: University of Arizona Press, 1973.

———. *Mercedes Reales: Hispanic Land Grants of the Upper Rio Grande Region.* Albuquerque: University of New Mexico Press, 1983.

White, Richard. *"It's Your Misfortune and None of My Own": A History of the American West.* Norman: University of Oklahoma Press, 1991.

———. *Railroaded: The Transcontinentals and the Making of Modern America.* New York: W. W. Norton, 2011.

———. *The Roots of Dependency: Subsistence, Environment, and Social Change among the Choctaws, Pawnees, and Navajos.* Lincoln: University of Nebraska Press, 1983.

Whitman, Walt. *Complete Poetry and Selected Prose.* Edited by James E. Miller, Jr. Boston: Houghton Mifflin, 1959.

———. *Prose Works, 1892.* 2 vols. Edited by Floyd Stoval, New York: New York University Press, 1964.

Wiebe, Robert H. *Businessmen and Reform: A Study of the Progressive Movement.* Cambridge, Mass.: Harvard University Press, 1962.

Williams, Jerry L., editor, *New Mexico in Maps.* 2nd ed. Albuquerque: University of New Mexico Press, 1986.

Wills, Garry. *Lincoln at Gettysburg: The Words That Remade America.* New York: Simon & Schuster, 1992.

Wilson, Chris. *The Myth of Santa Fe: Creating a Modern Regional Tradition.* Albuquerque: University of New Mexico Press, 1997.

Wood, Gordon S. *American Revolution: A History.* New York: Random House, 2003.

Woodward, C. Vann. *Origins of the New South, 1877–1913.* Baton Rouge: Louisiana State University Press, 1971.

———. *Tom Watson: Agrarian Rebel.* 1938. Reprint, New York: Oxford University Press, 1963.

[WPA-NM] Writers' Program of the Work Projects Administration in the State of New Mexico. *New Mexico: A Guide to the Colorful State.* New York: Hastings House, 1940.

Zinn, Howard, Dana Frank, and Robin D. G. Kelley, editors. *Three Strikes: Miners, Musicians, Salesgirls, and the Fighting Spirit of Labor's Last Century.* Boston: Beacon Press, 2001.

Articles and Book Chapters

"The Admission." *Public Opinion* 32, no. 21 (15 May 1902): 648.

Arellano, Anselmo. "The People's Movement: Las Gorras Blancas." In *The Contested Homeland: A Chicano History of New Mexico,* edited by Erlinda Gonzales-Berry and David R. Maciel, 59–82. Albuquerque: University of New Mexico Press, 2000.

Ball, Durwood. "Cool to the End: Public Hangings and Western Manhood." In *Across the Great Divide: Cultures of Manhood in the American West,* edited by Matthew Basso et al., 97–108. New York: Routledge, 2001.

Brock, Ralph H. "'Perhaps the Most Incorrect of Any Land Line in the United States': Establishing the Texas–New Mexico Boundary along the 103rd Meridian." *Southwestern Historical Quarterly* 109, no. 4 (April 2006):431–62.

Callahan, William J. "Catholicism." In *Historical Dictionary of Modern Spain, 1700-1988,* edited by Robert W. Kern and Meredith D. Dodge, 129–39. New York: Greenwood Press, 1990.

Chacón, Felipe Maximiliano. "A Nuevo México, en su admisión como Estado." In *Tradiciones Nuevomexicanas: Hispano Arts and Culture of New Mexico,* edited by Mary Montaño, 309. Albuquerque: University of New Mexico Press, 2001.

Chandler, Alfred D. Jr. "The Origins of Progressive Leadership." In *The Letters of Theodore Roosevelt,* edited by Elting E. Morison et al., 8:1462–65. Cambridge, Mass.: Harvard University Press, 1954.

Clark, Ira G. "The Elephant Butte Controversy: A Chapter in the Emergence of Federal Water Law." *Journal of American History* 61, no. 4 (March 1975): 1006–33.

Connell-Szasz, Margaret. "Cultural Encounters: Native People, New Mexico, and the United States, 1848-1948." In *Telling New Mexico: A New History,* ed. Marta Weigle with Frances Levine and Louise Stiver, 195–207. Santa Fe: Museum of New Mexico Press, 2009.

Dargan, Marion. "New Mexico's Fight for Statehood, 1895–1912, Part I." *New Mexico Historical Review* 14, no. 1 (January 1939): 1–33.

De León, Arnoldo. "Foreword." In *Foreigners in Their Native Land: Historical Roots of the Mexican American,* by David J. Weber, 30th anniversary edition, vii–xvi. Albuquerque: University of New Mexico Press, 2003.

Dike, Sheldon H. "The Territorial Post Offices of New Mexico." *New Mexico Historical Review* 33, no. 4 (October 1958): 322–24.

Durán, Tobías. "Francisco Chavez, Thomas B. Catron, and Organized Political Violence in Santa Fe in the 1890s." *New Mexico Historical Review* 59, no. 3 (July 1984): 291–310.

Espinosa, Aurelio M. "New Mexico." In *The Catholic Encyclopedia,* ed. Charles G. Herbermann et al., 11: 3–4. New York: Robert Appleton Co., 1911.

Flint, Richard, and Shirley Cushing Flint. "Fort Union and the Economy of Northern New Mexico 1860–1868." *New Mexico Historical Review* 77, no. 1 (Winter 2002): 27–55.

Foner, Eric. "Class, Ethnicity, and Radicalism in the Gilded Age: The Land League and Irish-America." In *Politics and Ideology in the Age of the Civil War,* ed. Eric Foner, 150–200. New York: Oxford University Press, 1980.

Gibson, Daniel. "Blackdom, Chaves County." In *Telling New Mexico: A New History,* ed. Marta Weigle with Frances Levine and Louise Stiver, 225–31. Santa Fe: Museum of New Mexico Press, 2009.

Gonzales, Phillip B. "'La Junta de Indignación': Hispano Repertoire of Collective Protest in New Mexico, 1884–1933." *Western Historical Quarterly* 31, no. 2 (Summer 2000): 161–86.

———. "Struggle for Survival: The Hispanic Land Grants of New Mexico, 1848–2001." *Agricultural History* 77, no. 2 (Spring 2003): 293–324.

Gutmann, Myron P., et al. "Los efectos demográficos de la Revolución Mexicana en [Los] Estados Unidos." In *Historia Mexicana* 50, no. 1 (July–September 2000): 145–65.

Hall, G. Emlen. "San Miguel del Bado and the Loss of Common Lands of New Mexico Community Land Grants." *New Mexico Historical Review* 66, no. 4 (October 1991): 413–32.

Hansen, Lawrence Douglas Taylor. "The Chinese Six Companies of San Francisco and the Smuggling of Chinese Immigrants across the U.S.-Mexico Border, 1882–1930," *Journal of the Southwest* 48, no. 1 (Spring 2006): 37–61.

Harris, Katherine. "Homesteading in Northeastern Colorado, 1873–1920: Sex Roles and Women's Experiences." In *The Women's West,* ed. Susan Armitage and Elizabeth Jameson, 165–78. Norman: University of Oklahoma Press, 1987.

Heflin, Reuben W. "New Mexico Constitutional Convention." *New Mexico Historical Review* 21, no. 1 (January 1946): 60–68.

Heilbronner, Oded. "The Age of Catholic Revival." In *A Companion to Nineteenth-Century Europe*, ed. Stefan Berger, 236–47. Malden, Mass.: Blackwell, 2006.

Hoffman, Gretchen, and Maureen Wilks. "Abandoned & Inactive Coal Mines of the Gallup Coal Field McKinley County, New Mexico, Final Report for Office of Surface Mining Reclamation and Enforcement." Socorro: New Mexico Bureau of Geology and Mineral Resources, 2010.

Holtby, David V. "Education, Primary and Secondary." In *Historical Dictionary of Modern Spain, 1700–1988*, ed. Robert W. Kern and Meredith D. Dodge, 183–85. New York: Greenwood Press, 1990.

———. "Introduction." In *Our New Mexico: A Twentieth Century History*, by Calvin A. Roberts, 1–6. Albuquerque: University of New Mexico Press, 2005.

———. "Two Photographs and Their Stories of Statehood." *New Mexico Historical Review* 87, no. 1 (Winter 2012):1–32.

Hubbard, H. A. "The Arizona Enabling Act and President Taft's Veto." *Pacific Historical Review* 3, no. 3 (September 1934): 307–22.

Jackson, W. Turrentine. "The Chavez Land Grant: A Scottish Investment in New Mexico, 1881–1940." *Pacific Historical Review* 21, no. 4 (November 1952): 349–66.

Jensen, Joan M., and Darlis A. Miller, editors. "'Disfranchisement is a Disgrace:' Women and Politics in New Mexico, 1900-1940. In *New Mexico Women: Intercultural Perspectives*, ed. Joan M. Jensen and Darlis A. Miller, 301–31. Albuquerque: University of New Mexico Press, 1986.

Jessup, Robert J. "Force of Public Opinion." *The Independent* 48, no. 2468 (19 March 1896): 4.

Lamar, Howard R. "Statehood for Washington: Symbol of a New Era." In *Washington Comes of Age: The State in the National Experience*, ed. David H. Stratton, 113–33. Pullman: Washington State University Press, 1992.

Larson, Robert W. "The Knights of Labor and Native Protest in New Mexico." In *Labor in New Mexico: Unions, Strikes, and Social History Since 1881*, ed. Robert Kern, 31–52. Albuquerque: University of New Mexico Press, 1983.

Lee, Erika. "Enforcing the Border: Chinese Exclusion along the U.S. Borders with Canada and Mexico, 1882–1924." *Journal of American History* 89, no. 1 (June 2002): 54–86.

Leonard, Donald D. "Joint Statehood: 1906." *New Mexico Historical Review* 34, no. 4 (October 1959): 241–47.

Levine, Daniel. "The Social Philosophy of Albert J. Beveridge." *Indiana Magazine of History*, 58, no. 2 (June 1962):101–16.

Limerick, Patricia Nelson. "Going West and Ending Up Global." *Western Historical Quarterly* 32, no. 1 (Spring 2001): 4–23.

Mabry, Thomas J. "New Mexico's Constitution in the Making—Reminiscences of 1910." *New Mexico Historical Review* 19, no. 2 (April 1944): 168–84.

Martin, Gregory. "German Strategy and Military Assessments of the American Expeditionary Force (AEF), 1917–1918." *War in History* 1, no. 2 (1994): 160–96.

Martínez y Alire, Jerome J. "Foreword." In *The Alabados of New Mexico*, edited and translated by Thomas J. Steele, xiii–xiv. Albuquerque: University of New Mexico Press, 2005.

Mathews-Lamb, Sandra K. "'Designing and Mischievous Individuals': The Cruzate Grants and the Office of the Surveyor General. *New Mexico Historical Review* 71, no. 4 (October 1996): 341–59.

Melzer, Richard. "New Mexico in Caricature: Images of the Territory on the Eve of Statehood." *New Mexico Historical Review* 62, no. 4 (October 1987): 335–60.

———, and Phyllis Ann Mingus. "Wild to Fight: The New Mexico Rough Riders in the Spanish-American War." *New Mexico Historical Review* 59, no. 2 (April 1984): 109–36.

Messing, John. "Public Lands, Politics, and Progressives: The Oregon Land Fraud Trials, 1903–1910." *Pacific Historical Review* 35, no. 1 (February 1966): 35–66.

Mitchell, Pablo. "'You Just Don't Know Mrs. Baca'": Intermarriage, Mixed Heritage, and Identity in New Mexico." *New Mexico Historical Review* 79, no. 4 (Fall 2004): 437–58.

Montoya, María E. "The Dual World of Governor Miguel A. Otero: Myth and Reality in Turn-of-the-Century New Mexico." *New Mexico Historical Review* 67, no. 1 (January 1992):13–32.

———. "L. Bradford Prince: The Education of a Gilded Age Politician." *New Mexico Historical Review* 66, no. 2 (April 1991): 179–202.

———. "Wedding Chest." In Virginia Scharff and Carolyn Brucken, *Home Lands: How Women Made the West*, 43–45. Berkeley: University of California Press, 2010.

Moussalli, Stephanie D. "The Fiscal Effects of Statehood: New Mexico and Arizona, 1903–1919." *Public Choice* 137, nos. 1–2 (2008): 119–26.

Nash, Gerald D. "New Mexico in the Otero Era: Some Historical Perspectives." *New Mexico Historical Review* 67, no. 1 (January 1992):1–12.

"Necrology, Albert Bacon Fall." *New Mexico Historical Review* 31, no. 1 (Winter 1945): 78–80.

Noel, Linda C. "'I Am an American': Anglos, Mexicans, *Nativos*, and the National Debate over Arizona and New Mexico Statehood." *Pacific Historical Review* 80, no. 3 (August 2011): 430–67.

Novak, William J. "The Myth of the 'Weak' American State." *American Historical Review* 113, no. 3 (June 2008): 752–72.

Ortiz, Alfonso. "Ritual Drama and Pueblo World View." In *New Perspectives on the Pueblos*, ed. Alfonso Ortiz, 135–61. Albuquerque: University of New Mexico Press, 1972.

Orwell, George. "Shooting an Elephant." In *Inside the Whale and Other Essays*, 91–99. London: Penguin Books, 1962.

Owens, Kenneth N. "Pattern and Structure in Western Territorial Politics." *Western Historical Quarterly* 1, no. 4 (October 1970): 373–92.

Pancoast, Chalmers Lowell. "Presidential Visit—1903." *New Mexico Magazine*, June 1950, 25, 45.

"Passage of the Bill." *Public Opinion* 31, no. 22 (22 May 1902): 666.

Prince, L. Bradford. "The Race Issue: Opportunities for Native New Mexicans." *New Mexican*, February 28, 1912, p. 1.

"The Recent Territorial Music Contest." *The Musical Visitor, A Magazine of Musical Literature and Music* 24, no. 12 (December 1895): 327.

Russell, Frank. "An Apache Medicine Dance." *American Anthropologist* 11, no. 12 (December 1898): 367–72.

Salas, Elizabeth. "Ethnicity, Gender, and Divorce: Issues in the 1922 Campaign by Adelina Otero-Warren for the U.S. House of Representatives." *New Mexico Historical Review* 70, no. 4 (October 1995): 367–82.

Sarasohn, David. "The Election of 1916: Realigning the Rockies." *Western Historical Quarterly* 11, no. 3 (July 1980): 285–305.

Scheiber, Harry N. "Property Law, Expropriation, and Resource Allocation by Government: The United States, 1789–1910." *Journal of Economic History* 33, no. 1 (March 1973): 232–51.

Schiller, Mark. "The History and Adjudication of the Antonio Chávez Grant." *Natural Resources Journal* 48 (Fall 2008): 1057–80.

Simmons, Marc. "When the Irrigation Congress Came to Town." *Prime Time*, November 2007, 4.

Smith, Sherry L. "Single Women Homesteaders: The Perplexing Case of Elinor Pruitt Stewart." In *Western Women's Lives: Continuity and Change in the Twentieth Century*, ed. Sandra K. Schackel, 161-82. Albuquerque: University of New Mexico Press, 2003.

Stegmaier, Mark J. "New Mexico's Delegate in the Secession Winter Congress, Part 1: Two Newspaper Accounts of Miguel Otero in 1861." *New Mexico Historical Review* 86, no. 3 (Summer 2011): 385–92.

Stephens, Sandra L. "The Women of the Amador Family, 1860–1940." In *New Mexico Women: Intercultural Perspectives*, ed. Joan Jensen and Darlis Miller, 257–77. Albuquerque: University of New Mexico Press, 1986.

Swentzell, Rina. "Pueblo Space: An Understated Sacredness." In *Telling New Mexico: A New History*, ed. Marta Weigle with Frances Levine and Louise Stiver, 45–48. Santa Fe: Museum of New Mexico Press, 2009.

Teller, Henry M. "The State's Control over Its Water." Reproduced from the *Congressional Record*, 31 March and 2 April 1908, 60th Congress, 2nd Session. Washington, D.C.: privately printed, 1908.

"The Third International Seminar on Decolonization: A Report." *Perspectives in History* 46, no. 47 (October 2008): 60–61.

Tittman, Edward D. "New Mexico's Constitutional Convention: Recollections." *New Mexico Historical Review* 27, no. 3 (July 1952): 177–86.

Tórrez, Robert J. "New Mexico at 90." *La Herencia* (Spring 2002):18–19.

Twain, Mark. "Senator Clark of Montana." In *Mark Twain in Eruption*, ed. Bernard DeVoto, 70–77. New York: Harper & Bros., 1940.

Vigil, Ralph H. "Revolution and Confusion: The Peculiar Case of José Inés Salazar." *New Mexico Historical Review* 53, no. 2 (April 1978): 145–70.

West, Elliott. "Reconstructing Race." *Western Historical Quarterly* 34, no. 1 (Spring 2003): 6–26.

Westphall, Victor. "Fraud and Implications of Fraud in the Land Grants of New Mexico." *New Mexico Historical Review* 49, no. 3 (July 1974): 189–218.

Whitman, Walt. "Preface to the 1855 Edition of *Leaves of Grass*." In *Complete Poetry and Selected Prose*, ed. James E. Miller, Jr., 411-27. Boston: Houghton Mifflin, 1959.

Wilson, Raymond. "Another White Hope Bites the Dust: The Jack Johnson–Jim Flynn Heavyweight Fight in 1912." *Montana: The Magazine of Western History* 29, no. 1 (Winter, 1979): 30–39

Zinn, Howard. "The Colorado Coal Strike, 1913-14." In *Three Strikes: Miners, Musicians, Salesgirls, and the Fighting Spirit of Labor's Last Century*, ed. Howard Zinn, Dana Frank, and Robin D. G. Kelley, 5–56. Boston: Beacon Press, 2001.

Theses and Dissertations

Bowden, J. J. "Private Land Claims in the Southwest." 6 vols. Master of Laws in Oil and Gas, Southern Methodist University, 1969.

Cottrell, Beatrice. "Senate Action on the Omnibus Statehood Bill of 1902." M.A. thesis, University of New Mexico, 1938.

Key, M. David. "Progressivism and Imperialism in the American Southwest, 1880–1912." Ph.D. diss., University of New Mexico, 2005.

Maddox, Charles Edgar. "The Statehood Policy of Albert J. Beveridge, 1901–1911." M.A. thesis, University of New Mexico, 1938.

Masters, Mary J. "New Mexico's Struggle for Statehood, 1903–1907." M.A. thesis, University of New Mexico, 1939.

McDowell, Archie M. "The Opposition to Statehood within the Territory of New Mexico, 1888–1903." M.A. thesis, University of New Mexico, 1939.

Moussalli, Stephanie D. "Accounting for Government on the Frontier from the Late Nineteenth to the Early Twentieth Century: The Fiscal and Accounting Effects of Statehood in Arizona and New Mexico." Ph.D. diss., University of Mississippi, 2005.

Noel, Linda C. "'The Swinging Door': U.S. National Identity and the Making of the Mexican Guestworker, 1900–1935. Ph.D. diss., University of Maryland, 2006.

Ramirez, Carlos Brazil. "The Hispanic Political Elite in Territorial New Mexico: A Study in Classical Colonialism." 2 vols. Ph.D diss., University of California, Santa Barbara, 1979.

Thomas, Dorothy E. "The Final Years of New Mexico's Struggle for Statehood, 1907–1912." M.A. thesis, University of New Mexico, 1939.

White, Robert R. "Artists of Territorial New Mexico, 1846–1912." Ph.D. diss., University of New Mexico, 1993.

Interviews or personal communications

Ernesto and Richard Chavez, September 2010
Frank and Frieda Montoya, July–August 2008
Juan Mora, January 2011
Yolanda Pacheco, July 2008
Paul A. Ryan, May 2009
Toby Smith, August 2011
Felix Trujillo, July 2009

Websites

African Americans in New Mexico, www.soulofnewmexico.com
Almanac of Theodore Roosevelt, www.theodore-roosevelt.com/trspeechescomplete.html
    4 July 1886, speech at document file 630.
    23 April 1910, speech at document file 634.
Department of the Interior, www.glorecords.blm.gov
Historical Documents from the Bureau's Founding, www.fbi.gov
Historical Sources Online, www.historytools.org/sources
    Albert J. Beveridge, "March of the Flag"
Internet Archive Texts, www.archive.org/details/universallibrary
    Arthur C. Ringland, oral history transcript
New Mexico First, www.nmfirst.org
New Mexico Office of the State Historian, www.newmexicohistory.org
    J. J. Bowden, "Private Land Claims in the Southwest," 100 entries
    Mary M. Serna and James W. Steely, "Mescalero Apache"
    Mark Schiller, "San Miguel del Vado Grant"
Texas State Historical Association, *Handbook of Texas Online*, www.tshaonline.org
    Bob C. Holcomb, "Bailey, Joseph Weldon."
Think New Mexico, www.thinknewmexico.org

Index

Abiquiú, N.Mex., 33

Acequias, 89–90, 150, 276

Acoma Pueblo, 168, 171, 225

Adultery, 145–46

African Americans: economic adversity, 174–76; education, 175, 177, 178; Jack Johnson, 273–74; Jim Crow, 161, 173, 178; population data, 52, 160, 173, 175, 176, 178; rural life, 172–76; slavery, 174, 178; urban life, 176–78. *See also* Blackdom, N.Mex.; Boyer, Ella; Boyer, Francis Marion; Flipper, Henry O.; McJunkin, George; *Plessy v. Ferguson*

Agency: African Americans, 178; American Indians, 163–64; Asians, 180; defined, 285n6; Nuevomexicanos, 7–8, 133–35, 140, 143, 148

Alamogordo, N.Mex., 119, 182, 215, 228

Alamogordo Lumber Company, 205, 215, 217

Albuquerque: African Americans, 176–77, 178; Asians, 180, 183; economic conditions, 87–88; irrigation congress, 220; newspapers, 20, 21, 73, 88, 116, 117, 118, 178, 181, 205, 224, 228; Nuevomexicanos, 140, 143; Roosevelt visits, 84–85, 86; statehood convention of 1901, 35, 155; Taft visits, 226–27, 228, 229

Aldrich, Senator Nelson W.: background, 39–40; Beveridge and, 45, 55, 58, 82, 83, 207, 237; Enabling Act, 231; politics of statehood, 76, 79, 81–82, 223, 234–35, 262; Taft and, 237, 268

Alvarado Hotel, 87, 168–69, 226

Americanization: American Indians, 68, 161–63, 164, 165, 172; Nuevomexicanos, 7, 8, 44, 64, 68, 144. *See also* Dawes Act

American Indians: art and statehood, 168–70; population data, 52, 160, 161; Taft greets, 225–26; women's role, 164–65, 308n13. *See also names of individual tribes; names of specific pueblos*

American Lumber Company: business status, 270, 274; legal problems, 205, 215, 216

Andrews, William H. "Bull": background, 50, 53, 87; bank failure, 110–11; constitution of 1910, 242–43, 248–49; delegate to Congress, 109–10, 116–17, 225, 239, 256–57; election of 1904, 108–109; election of 1906, 117–19; investigated, 120–21, 123, 215–16, 217, 225, 249; statehood, 108, 116–17, 225, 239, 249, 254. *See also* Pennsylvania Development Company